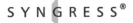

MISSION CRITICAL!
INTERNET SECURITY

SYNGRESS®

KEY	SERIAL NUMBER
001	STP692AD43
002	JY536842C4
003	C392K28FA7
004	BG57C87BC2
005	22PCA94DZF
006	55ZP2ALT73
007	DUDR527749
008	XRDYEW42T3
009	MPE28494DS
010	SM359PS25L

PUBLISHED BY
Syngress Publishing, Inc.
800 Hingham Street
Rockland, MA 02370

Mission Critical Internet Security

Printed in the United States of America

1 2 3 4 5 6 7 8 9 0

ISBN: 1-928994-20-2

Copy edit by: Adrienne Rebello
Technical edit by: Stace Cunningham
Project Editor: Kate Glennon

Index by: Robert Saigh
Page Layout and Art by: Shannon Tozier
Co-Publisher: Richard Kristof

Distributed by Publishers Group West

Acknowledgments

We would like to acknowledge the following people for their kindness and support in making this book possible.

Richard Kristof, Duncan Anderson, Jennifer Gould, Robert Woodruff, Kevin Murray, Dale Leatherwood, Rhonda Harmon, and Robert Sanregret of Global Knowledge, for their generous access to the IT industry's best courses, instructors and training facilities.

Ralph Troupe, Rhonda St. John, and the team at Callisma for their invaluable insight into the challenges of designing, deploying and supporting world-class enterprise networks.

Karen Cross, Lance Tilford, Meaghan Cunningham, Kim Wylie, Harry Kirchner, John Hays, Bill Richter, Kevin Votel, Brittin Clark, and Sarah MacLachlan of Publishers Group West for sharing their incredible marketing experience and expertise.

Mary Ging, Caroline Hird, Simon Beale, Caroline Wheeler, Victoria Fuller, Jonathan Bunkell, and Klaus Beran of Harcourt International for making certain that our vision remains worldwide in scope.

Annabel Dent, Anneka Baeten, and Laurie Giles of Harcourt Australia for all their help.

David Buckland, Wendi Wong, Daniel Loh, Marie Chieng, Lucy Chong, Leslie Lim, Audrey Gan, and Joseph Chan of Transquest Publishers for the enthusiasm with which they receive our books.

Kwon Sung June at Acorn Publishing for his support.

Ethan Atkin at Cranbury International for his help in expanding the Syngress program.

Joe Pisco, Helen Moyer, and the great folks at InterCity Press for all their help.

From Global Knowledge

At Global Knowledge we strive to support the multiplicity of learning styles required by our students to achieve success as technical professionals. As the world's largest IT training company, Global Knowledge is uniquely positioned to offer these books. The expertise gained each year from providing instructor-led training to hundreds of thousands of students worldwide has been captured in book form to enhance your learning experience. We hope that the quality of these books demonstrates our commitment to your lifelong learning success. Whether you choose to learn through the written word, computer based training, Web delivery, or instructor-led training, Global Knowledge is committed to providing you with the very best in each of these categories. For those of you who know Global Knowledge, or those of you who have just found us for the first time, our goal is to be your lifelong competency partner.

Thank your for the opportunity to serve you. We look forward to serving your needs again in the future.

Warmest regards,

Duncan Anderson
President and Chief Executive Officer, Global Knowledge

Contributors

Bradley Dunsmore (A+, Network+, i-Net+, MCDBA, MCSE+I, CCNA) is currently working for Cisco Systems in Raleigh, NC. He is a Technical Trainer in the Service Provider Division where he develops and issues training to the solution deployment engineers. He has eight years of computer experience, the last four in enterprise networking. Bradley has worked with Bell Atlantic, Adtran Telecommunications, and Electronic Systems Inc., a Virginia-based systems integrator. He specializes in TCP/IP and LAN/WAN communications in both small and large business environments.

Joli Annette Ballew (MCSE, MCP, MCT, A+) is a technology trainer and network consultant. She has worked as a technical writer, educational content consultant, PC technician, and MCSE instructor.

Joli attended the University of Texas at Arlington and graduated with a Bachelor's degree in Mathematics. The following year, she earned her teaching certificate from the state of Texas. After teaching for ten years, she earned her MCSE, MCT, and A+ certifications and entered the field of computer training and consulting. Joli lives near Dallas, TX and has a beautiful daughter, Jennifer.

Jeffrey W. Brown (CISSP) is a Vice President of Enterprise Information Security at Merrill Lynch in New York City, where he is responsible for security analysis, design, and implementation of global computing infrastructures. Jeff has over eight years of information technology experience. He is co-author of the *Web Publisher's Design Guide for Windows* (Coriolis) and is a member of the SANS Windows Security Digest editorial board. He has been a participant in several SANS efforts including "Windows

NT Security Step-by-Step," the Windows 2000 Security Improvement Project, and the Center for Internet Security. Jeff was recently a panelist for a discussion on virtual private networking (VPN) technology at Security Forum 2000, sponsored by the Technology Manager's Forum. He has a BA in Journalism and an MS in Publishing from Pace University.

Michael Cross (MCSE, MCPS, MCP+I, CNA) is the Network Administrator, Internet Specialist, and a Programmer for the Niagara Regional Police Service. In addition to administering their network and providing support to a user base of over 800 civilian and uniform users, he is Webmaster of their Web site (www.nrps.com).

Michael also owns KnightWare, a company that provides consulting, programming, networking, Web page design, and computer training. He has served as an instructor for private colleges and technical schools in London, Ontario in Canada. He is a freelance writer and and has authored over two dozen articles and chapters. He currently resides in St. Catharines, Ontario, Canada.

Jason Harper (MCSE) is a published author and technology consultant who concentrates exclusively on network and systems security, policy and network architecture technologies. Thanks go to his family, Noah, Stacey, and Laurie for all their support.

Technical Editor and Contributor

Stace Cunningham (CMISS, CCNA, MCSE, CLSE, COS/2E, CLSI, COS/2I, CLSA, MCPS, A+) is a security consultant currently located in San Antonio, TX. He has assisted several clients, including a casino, in the development and implementation of network security plans for their organizations. He held the positions of Network Security Officer and Computer Systems Security Officer while serving in the United States Air Force.

While in the Air Force, Stace was heavily involved in installing, troubleshooting, and protecting long-haul circuits, ensuring the appropriate level of cryptography necessary to protect the level of information traversing the circuit as well the circuits from TEMPEST hazards. This included American equipment as well as equipment from Britain and Germany while he was assigned to Allied Forces Southern Europe (NATO).

Stace has been an active contributor to The SANS Institute booklet "Windows NT Security Step by Step." In addition, he has co-authored or served as the Technical Editor for over 30 books published by Osborne/McGraw-Hill, Syngress Publishing, and Microsoft Press. He has also written articles for "Internet Security Advisor" magazine.

His wife Martha and daughter Marissa have been very supportive of the time he spends with the computers, routers, and firewalls in the "lab" of their house.

Contents

Chapter 1

Securing Your Internetwork

Solutions in this chapter:

- Introduction to Internetworking Security
- Differentiating Security Models and Attacks
- Designing a Site Scenario
- Network Communication in TCP/IP
- Security in TCP/IP

Introduction to Internetworking Security

Internetworking security has become a very big issue in recent months. Companies who went through corporate life thinking, "it will never happen to me" suddenly found themselves the victim of some sort of attack on their network. High profile companies are most certainly a bigger target for several reasons, including the notoriety the hacker receives for damaging their network or Web site, and the amount of financial damage that can be done by bringing down a successful e-commerce site. Recent attacks easily racked up 100 million dollars in damage.

Is this issue anything new? Some may say yes, but the fact of the matter is network security has always been a concern and hackers have always been out there ready to prove themselves on your network. Most hackers don't do it because of a specific vendetta against a company, but because of the notoriety mentioned earlier. The best thing that you can do is take charge of your network and set up security measures to ensure that your company doesn't become an accomplishment on a hacker's resume.

This book will give you the information necessary to secure your internetwork and the knowledge to identify possible problems that could arise from each option. It will not only cover technologies and security design, but also specific vendor products and tips for configuration. This book will also include types of attacks that you can expect and ways that you can safeguard your network against them. Remember, the worst thing that you can do as a Network Administrator is nothing.

Why the Change of Heart Toward Network Security?

The "2000 CSI/FBI Computer Crime and Security Survey," conducted in early 2000 by the Computer Security Institute (CSI) with participation by the San Francisco office of the Federal Bureau of Investigation (FBI), showed that 90 percent of survey participants from large U.S. corporations, financial institutions, medical institutions, universities, and government agencies detected security breaches in 1999. About 70 percent of the participants experienced breaches more serious than viruses or employee Web abuse. Forty-two percent of survey participants (273 organizations) claimed financial losses totaling over 265 million dollars from cyber attacks. These security threats were composed of an assortment of attacks and abuses that originated both internally and externally to their network borders.

The CSI survey showed financial losses were larger than in any previous year in eight out of twelve categories. The largest loss was attributed to theft of proprietary information, followed by financial fraud, virus, insider net abuse, and unauthorized insider access.

Many organizations are increasing their use of electronic commerce for business-to-business and business-to-consumer transactions. New initiatives, such as Applications Service Providers (ASPs), expose vital corporate information and services to the Internet. People have altered the way that they work, now extending the workday or working full time from home. Telecommuters and mobile workers now require remote access to information resources normally protected within the organization's network.

Businesses and individuals now depend upon information systems and data communications to perform essential functions on a daily basis. In this environment of increasingly open and interconnected communication systems and networks, information security is crucial for protecting privacy, ensuring availability of information and services, and safeguarding integrity. These new technologies and increased connectivity via public access networks and extranets have allowed businesses to improve efficiency and lower costs, but at the price of increased exposure of valuable information assets to threats.

Differentiating Security Models and Attacks

Attack techniques are constantly evolving. Over the last twenty years, tools for attacking information systems have become more powerful, but more important, they have become easier to use. Ease of use has lowered the technical knowledge required to conduct an attack, and has thus increased the pool of potential attackers exponentially. *Script kiddie* is a term used to describe a person who acquires a program to launch an attack but doesn't need to understand how it works.

Many network security failures have been widely publicized in the world press. An advantage to this unfortunate situation is the lowered resistance from upper management to support security initiatives. Getting upper management support is the first step in creating an effective network security program. Management must provide the authority to implement security processes and procedures. Management commits to security of information assets by documenting the authority and obligations of departments or employees in an information security policy, and supports it by providing the resources to build and maintain an effective security program.

An effective security program includes awareness, prevention, detection, measurement, management, and response to minimize risk. There is no such thing as perfect security. The determined and persistent attacker can find a way to defeat or bypass almost any security measure. Network security is a means of reducing vulnerabilities and managing risk.

Awareness should be tailored to the job requirements of employees. Employees must understand why they need to take information security seriously. End-users choosing weak passwords or falling for social engineering attacks can easily neutralize the best technical security solutions. Upper management must provide for training, motivation, and codes of conduct to employees to comply with security measures.

Protection of assets must be cost effective. In analyzing your security needs, you first identify what assets you want to protect, and the value of those assets. Determine the threats that may damage these assets, and the likelihood of those threats occurring. Prioritize the relationships, so you concentrate on mitigating the risks with the highest potential damage, and greatest likelihood of occurring. To determine how to protect the asset, consider the cost of your protection measured against the value of the asset that you're trying to protect. You don't want to spend more for preventing a potential adversity than the asset is worth.

Monitor your network and systems to detect attacks and probes—and know what "normal" for your network and systems looks like. If you are not used to seeing normal behavior on your network, you may not recognize or be able to isolate an attack. Many systems on the network can provide clues and status information in their logs. Be sure to log enough information so that you can recognize and record an attack, and examine these logs carefully. Use intrusion detection systems to watch the network traffic.

Recovery is as important as protection. A planned response to recover from incidents or attacks is a necessary part of network security. Have a plan in place, so you know what to do when a security crisis arises. It is a lot easier to think about what needs to be done and who needs to be notified while you're not in the middle of a crisis. A well thought-out plan can help you make the right decisions, save valuable time, and minimize damage in an emergency.

Management of security requires coordination and planning. The pervasive need for communications and the complexity of networks that support those needs has made security management a difficult task. Security will be only as good as the weakest link in the security chain. Security management tools that can create, distribute, and audit consistent security configurations and policies are critical for large and distributed organizations.

Hackers and Attack Types

You are probably reading this book because you are:

1. Interested in protecting your system against intrusions from unauthorized users.

2. Tasked with defending your system against attacks that can crash it.

3. A fledgling hacker who wishes to learn more about how to crash or break into systems.

To many, a hacker is simply a bad guy who breaks into systems or tries to crash them so that they cannot function as intended. However, many in the security industry make a distinction between *white hat* hackers, who are benign and helpful types, and *black hat* hackers, who actually cross the line into criminal behavior, such as breaking into systems unsolicited, or simply crashing them. Others define themselves as *grey hat* hackers, in that they are not criminal, but do not consider themselves tainted (as a strict white hat would) by associating with black hats. Some security professionals refer to white hat hackers as *hackers*, and to black hat hackers as *crackers*. As mentioned earlier, another hacker term, *script kiddie*, describes those who use previously written scripts from people who are more adept. As you might suspect, script kiddie is a derisive term.

Many professionals who are simply very talented users proudly refer to themselves as hackers, not because they break into systems, but because they have been able to learn a great deal of information over the years. These professionals are often offended by the negative connotation that the word hacker now has. So, when does a hacker become a cracker? When does a cracker become a benign hacker? Well, it all depends upon the perspective of the people involved. Nevertheless, this book will use the terms hacker, cracker, and malicious user interchangeably.

What Do Hackers Do?

Truly talented hackers know a great deal about the following:

1. Programming languages, such as C, C++, Java, Perl, JavaScript, and VBScript.

2. How operating systems work. A serious security professional or hacker understands not only how to click the right spot on an interface, but also understands what happens under the hood when that interface is clicked.

3. The history of local area network (LAN)- and Internet-based services, such as the Network File System (NFS), Web servers, Server Message Block (SMB, which is what allows Microsoft systems to share file and printing services), and of course e-mail servers.

4. Protocols used in networks, which many hackers attack. The Internet uses Transmission Control Protocol/Internet Protocol (TCP/IP), which is a fast, efficient, and powerful transport and addressing method. This protocol is in fact an entire suite of protocols. Some of these include Telnet, Domain Name System (DNS), the File Transfer Protocol (FTP), and all protocols associated with e-mail servers, which include the Simple Mail Transfer Protocol (SMTP), Post Office Protocol 3 (POP3), and the Internet Message Access Protocol (IMAP).

5. How applications interact with each other. Today's operating systems contain components that allow applications to "talk" to each other efficiently. For example, using Microsoft's Component Object Model (COM) and other technologies, one application, such as Word, can send commands to others on the local machine, or even on remote machines. Hackers understand these subtle relationships, and craft applications to take advantage of them.

A talented hacker can quickly create powerful scripts in order to exploit a system.

Attack Types

Don't make the mistake of thinking that hackers simply attack systems. Many different types of attacks exist. Some require more knowledge than others, and it is often necessary to conduct one type of attack before conducting another. Following is a list of the common attacks waged against all network-addressable servers:

- **Scanning** Most of the time, hackers do not know the nature of the network they wish to compromise or attack. By using TCP/IP programs such as ping, traceroute, and netstat, a hacker can learn about the physical makeup (topology) of a network. Once a hacker knows more about the machines, it is possible to attack or compromise them.

- **Denial of Service (DoS)** This type of attack usually results in a crashed server. As a result, the server is no longer capable of offering services. Thus, the attack denies these services to the public. Many of the attacks waged against e-mail servers have been Denial of Service attacks. However, do not confuse a DoS attack with other attacks that try to gather information or obtain authentication information.

- **Sniffing and/or man-in-the-middle** This attack captures information as it flows between a client and a server. Usually, a hacker attempts to capture TCP/IP transmissions, because they may contain information such as usernames, passwords, or the actual contents of an e-mail message. A sniffing attack is often classified as a man-in-the-middle attack, because in order to capture packets from a user, the machine capturing packets must lie in between the two systems that are communicating (a man-in-the-middle attack can also be waged on one of the two systems).

- **Hijacking and/or man-in-the-middle** Another form of a man-in-the-middle attack is where a malicious third party is able to actually take over a connection as it is being made between two users. Suppose that a malicious user wants to gain access to machine A, which is beginning a connection with machine B. First, the malicious user creates a Denial of Service attack against machine B; once the hacker knocks machine B off of the network, he or she can then assume that machine's identity and collect information from machine A.

- **Physical** Thus far, you have learned about attacks that are waged from one remote system to another. It is also possible to walk up to the machine and log in. For example, how many times do you or your work-mates simply walk away from a machine after having logged in? A wily hacker may be waiting just outside your cubicle to take over your system and assume your identity. Other, more sophisticated, attacks involve using specialized floppy disks and other tools meant to defeat authentication.

- **System bug/back door** No operating system, daemon, or client is perfect. Hackers usually maintain large databases of software that have problems that lead to system compromise. A system bug attack takes advantage of such attacks. A back door attack involves taking advantage of an undocumented subroutine or (if you are lucky) a password left behind by the creator of the application. Most back doors remain unknown. However, when they are discovered, they can lead to serious compromises.

- **Social engineering** The motto of a good social engineer is: Why do all the work when you can get someone else to do it for you? *Social engineering* is computer-speak for the practice of conning someone into divulging too much information. Many social engineers are good at impersonating systems administrators. Another example of social engineering is the temporary agency that is, in reality, a group of highly skilled hackers who infiltrate companies in order to conduct industrial espionage.

Types of Defenses

So now that you understand how your systems can be attacked, it's time to discuss how they can be protected. Each layer of your network—physical, network, and applications—must be addressed to ensure security. You will need to employ several different technologies and implement policies and procedures to make certain that security is enforced properly.

Education

Perhaps the most important thing that can be done to enhance network security is to promote education of network security issues by training or self-study. Network administrators are not the only ones who should be concerned about education, but users, IT managers, and executives should also have an appropriate understanding.

Users need to be adequately trained about procedures they will need to follow because they will attempt to do it "the old way" if they have problems. They also need to understand the risks that are associated with recording passwords on paper, giving passwords to social engineers, and so on. Since users are in control of the majority of systems on your network, it would be a big mistake to ignore the need to educate those users.

Network administrators obviously need to understand the technical details of network security and how to make the network as secure as is reasonable. Managers and executives, on the other hand, need to be generally aware of security issues so that security-related projects can get the proper priority for allocation of resources. Security projects are usually an easy sell to corporate executives who generally have a good understanding of the value of the organization's data. They often don't realize how vulnerable it is, though, and will go to great lengths to secure that valuable data when adequately informed.

Application Security

Various client and server applications have security settings that will help prevent unauthorized access and violation of system integrity. Web browsers, for instance, can be configured to implement certain restrictions depending on the Web site being viewed. Database servers often have user accounts separate from LAN access, and a hacker may simply try to break into a database without bothering to steal a LAN user account. Understanding the vulnerabilities and capabilities of your client and server applications is crucial to providing a secure network environment.

Physical Security

Access to wiring closets, server rooms, and even offices by unauthorized users presents a tremendous security risk. Keeping doors locked and unused network ports disabled are starting points. Many corporate buildings have security personnel and require badges for access. If the enforcement of building access is lax, intruders won't need to attack via the Internet; they will just walk in and attach a laptop computer at a vacant desk.

Firewalls, Proxy Servers, and NAT

Many organizations implement firewall software on a server or router that is configured with rules that determine what type of traffic is allowed to pass between their network and the Internet. Firewalls enable administrators to block traffic completely on specific ports, or to filter certain types of traffic on specific ports. Typically, firewalls are configured to deny all traffic except for the ports specified by the administrator, and separate rules can be defined for both inbound and outbound network traffic. Figure 1.1 shows very generally how a firewall works, with traffic being filtered by the rules configured on the firewall device.

Figure 1.1 Firewalls filter both inbound and outbound Internet traffic.

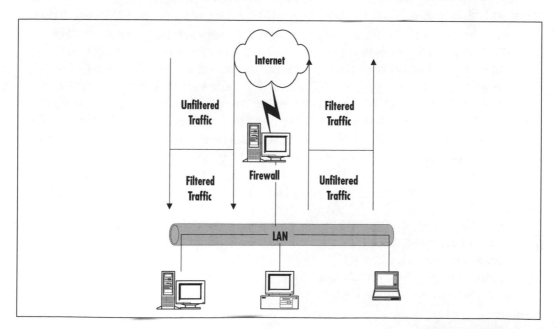

Securing Applications Using TCP/IP and Ports

TCP/IP uses ports to direct network traffic received by a computer to the appropriate application. Applications that use TCP/IP to communicate are assigned default ports so that other computers can access services easily by establishing a session on the default port. For instance, Web servers use port 80 by default, so Web browsers try to establish sessions using port 80 unless otherwise specified. Applications can be configured to use ports other than the default, however, which can be either a security strength or weakness depending on the circumstances. Firewalls and proxy servers can specify exactly which ports are allowed to exchange traffic between your network and the Internet. By keeping the number of allowed ports to a minimum, you can secure many of your applications from external attacks.

A firewall will not protect your network from every type of attack since it does not block all traffic, but it will limit your risk significantly. For example, if your organization utilizes virtual private networks (VPNs) for mobile users to access the network, the firewall must be configured to allow VPN connections. If an unauthorized user obtains a valid username and password and establishes a VPN connection, the firewall then does nothing to inhibit the intruder since the intruder is a virtual node on the network.

Proxy servers are used to process all Internet traffic, and can log information about the Internet sites your users are accessing. Proxy servers can also fill the role of a firewall by limiting the types of traffic that are allowed to pass between networks. Proxy servers can also be used to reverse host or reverse proxy WWW and FTP sites from internal servers to the Internet. Reverse hosting and reverse proxying provide a limited measure of security since users can never access your internal servers directly.

Network address translation (NAT) is a service provided by a server or router that enables networks utilizing private IP address ranges to communicate on the Internet. The NAT host has two network interfaces, one connected to the Internet with a registered IP address and one on the local network. Systems on your network are configured to use the NAT device as the gateway, and it handles the traffic by translating the source network address to that of its Internet connected interface. When the remote host replies, the NAT device forwards the traffic to the computer on your network that established the session. Since computers on the Internet cannot access your computers directly, they cannot initiate a session with them, and thus cannot attack them easily.

Designing a Site Scenario

Business needs and technology are both evolving rapidly. A revolution in the ways that people work and companies interact is being brought about by the capabilities provided by telecommunications. Networks have to provide availability, integrity, and confidentiality under diverse conditions.

Networks must provide ubiquitous connectivity to all corners of your organization, including branch offices, mobile workers, and telecommuters. It may also include connections to business partners. Services made accessible to the public to improve availability and lower costs increase the exposure of some systems to millions of people. Figure 1.2 shows a typical site scenario.

Figure 1.2 Typical site scenarios.

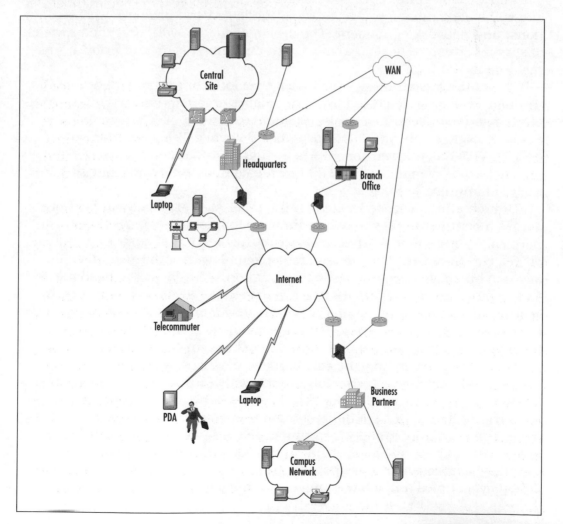

The headquarters is a source of information vital to the operation of the organization. It also needs to collect data from all parts of the organization to conduct business, manage resources, and monitor the status of its business environment. This central site must accommodate many types of connections. It may use multiple wide area network (WAN) technologies to connect to branch offices or business partners. These connections may be permanent or on-demand. It should provide dial-up for mobile users or telecommuters. Most organizations also have an Internet connection to provide public information or business services.

The central site network is usually confined to a small geographic area. It may be a single building or a campus environment, but it will form the core of the network. Small or medium organizations may only have a presence at one geographic location, and large enterprises have several core sites on various continents, interconnected by a global WAN. This central site will have a mix of private servers, public servers, printers, workstations, and network equipment. The design of the network and the provision of services must be flexible to meet with changing needs and priorities of the organization.

Before the advent of VPN technology, remote connections were usually through expensive dedicated lines, or smaller organizations may have used on-demand connection technologies such as dial-up over Integrated Services Digital Network (ISDN) or Public Switched Telephone Network (PSTN). VPN has allowed companies to shift their connections to the Internet and save money, but still provide confidentiality and integrity to their communication traffic.

Branch offices can be located on the other side of the city or scattered across a continent. They may exist to provide business services, distribution, sales, or technical services closer to the location of customers. These offices can have one, two, or hundreds of employees. A branch office usually has business needs to access information securely at the headquarters site or other branch offices, but due to its smaller size, is constrained by cost for its connectivity options. When the costs or business needs are justified, the branch office would have a permanent connection to the central headquarters. Most branch offices will also have an Internet connection.

Business partners may be collaborative partners, manufacturers, or supply chain partners. Technologies such as Electronic Data Interchange (EDI) over proprietary networks have been used by large businesses to perform transactions, but are difficult and expensive to use. Many companies have implemented extranets by using dedicated network connections to share data and operate joint business applications. Extranets and business-to-business transactions are popular because they reduce business transaction cycle times and allow companies reduce costs and inventories while increasing responsiveness and service. This trend will only continue to grow. Business-to-business interactions are now rapidly shifting to the Internet. Extranets can be built over the Internet using VPN technology.

Mobile users and telecommuters typically use dial-up services for connectivity to their headquarters or local office. Newer technologies such as Digital Subscriber Line (DSL) or cable modems offer permanent, high-speed Internet access to the home-based telecommuters.

TIP

Modems inside your campus network can create a backdoor to your network by dialing out to another network, or being left in answer mode to allow remote access directly to a workstation on your internal network. These backdoors bypass the firewall and other security measures that you may have in place.

The always-on Internet connections from home now offer the ability to create the backdoor remotely. It is possible to have an employee or contractor online with a modem to the corporate network remote access facility, while they still have an Internet connection through their DSL or cable modem. Attention to detail in the security policy, workstation configuration, and user awareness is critical in order to ensure that vulnerabilities don't creep into your system.

Ensuring Host Security

Any vendor's software is susceptible to harbouring security vulnerabilities. Almost every day, Web sites that track security vulnerabilities, such as the Computer Emergency Response Team (CERT) at Carnegie Mellon University, are reporting new vulnerability discoveries in operating systems, application software, server software, and even in security software or devices. Patches are implemented for these known bugs, but new vulnerability discoveries continue. Sometimes patches fix one bug, only to introduce another. Even open source software that has been widely used for ten years is not immune to harbouring serious vulnerabilities. In June 2000, CERT reported that MIT's Kerberos protocol had multiple buffer overflow vulnerabilities that could be used to gain root access.

Many sites do not keep up with applying patches and thus leave their systems with known vulnerabilities. It is important to keep all of your software up-to-date. Many of the most damaging attacks have been carried out through office productivity software and e-mail. Attacks can be directed at any software and can seriously affect your network.

The default configuration of hosts makes it easy to get them up and running, but many default services are unnecessary. These unnecessary services increase the vulnerabilities of the system. On each host, all unnecessary services should be shut down. Misconfigured hosts also increase the risk of an unauthorized access. All default passwords and community names must be changed.

TIP

> SANS (System Administration, Networking, and Security) Institute has created a list of the top ten Internet security threats from the consensus of a group of security experts. The list is maintained at www.sans.org/topten.htm. Use this list as a guide for the most urgent and critical vulnerabilities to repair on your systems.
>
> This effort was started because experience has shown that a small number of vulnerabilities are used repeatedly to gain unauthorized access to many systems.
>
> SANS has also published a list of the most common mistakes made by end-users, executives, and information technology personnel. It is available at www.sans.org/mistakes.htm.

The increased complexity of systems, the shortage of well-trained administrators, and the lack of enough resources all contribute to reducing security of hosts and applications. We cannot depend on hosts to protect themselves from all threats.

To protect your infrastructure, you must apply security in layers. This layered approach is also called *defence in depth*. You should create appropriate barriers inside your system so that intruders who may gain access to one part of it do not automatically get access to the rest of the system. Use firewalls to minimize the exposure of private servers from public networks. Firewalls are the first line of defense, and packet filtering on routers can supplement the protection of firewalls and provide internal access boundaries.

Access to hosts that contain confidential information needs to be carefully controlled. Inventory the hosts on your network, and use this list to categorize the protection that they will need. Some hosts will be used to provide public access, such as the corporate Web site or online storefront; others will contain confidential information that may be used only by a single department or workgroup. Plan the type of access needed and determine the boundaries of access control for these resources.

Characteristics of Network Security

The purpose of information and network security is to provide *availability*, *integrity*, and *confidentiality* (see Figure 1.3). These terms are described in the following sections. Different systems and businesses will place different importance on each of these three characteristics. For example, although Internet service providers (ISPs) may be concerned with confidentiality and integrity, they will be more concerned with protecting availability for their customers. The military places more emphasis on confidentiality with its system of classifications of information and clearances for people to access it. A financial institution must be concerned with all three elements, but they will be measured closely on the integrity of their data.

Figure 1.3 Balancing availability, integrity, and confidentiality.

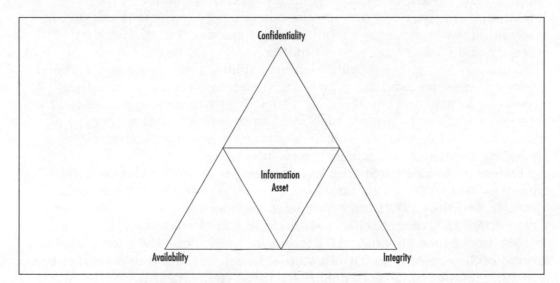

You should consider the security during the logical design of a network. Security considerations can have an effect on the physical design of the network. You need to know the specifications that will be used to purchase network equipment, software features or revision levels that need to be used, and any specialized devices used to provide encryption, quality of service, or access control.

Networks can be segmented to provide separation of responsibility. Departments such as finance, research, or engineering can be restricted so only the people that need access to particular resources can enter a network. You need to determine the resources to protect, the origin of threats against them, and where your network security perimeters should be located. Determine the level of availability, confidentiality, and integrity appropriate for controlling access to those segmented zones. Install perimeter devices and configurations that meet your security requirements. Controlling access to the network with firewalls, routers, switches, remote access servers, and authentication servers can reduce the traffic getting to critical hosts to just authorized users and services.

Keep your security configuration up-to-date and ensure that it meets the information security policy that you have set. In the course of operating a network, many changes can be made. These changes often open new vulnerabilities. You need to continuously reevaluate the status of network security and take action on any vulnerabilities that you find.

Availability

Availability ensures that information and services are accessible and functional when needed. Redundancy, fault tolerance, reliability, failover, backups, recovery, resilience, and load balancing are the network design concepts used to assure availability. If systems aren't available, then integrity and confidentiality won't matter.

Build networks that provide high availability. Your customers and end-users will perceive availability as being the entire system—application, servers, network, and workstation. If they can't run their applications, then it is not available. To provide high availability, ensure that security processes are reliable and responsive. Modular systems and software, including security systems, need to be interoperable.

Denial of Service (DoS) attacks are aimed at attacking the availability of networks and servers. DoS attacks can create severe losses for organizations. In February 2000, large Web sites such as Yahoo!, eBay, Amazon, CNN, ZDNet, E*Trade, Excite, and Buy.com were knocked off line or had availability reduced to about 10 percent for many hours by Distributed Denial of Service Attacks (DDoS). Actual losses were hard to estimate, but probably totalled millions of dollars for these companies.

TIP

Having a good inventory and documentation of your network is important for day-to-day operations, but in a disaster you can't depend on having it available. Store the configurations and software images of network devices *off-site* with your backups from servers, and keep them up-to-date. Include documentation about the architecture of your network. All of this documentation should be available in printed form because electronic versions may be unavailable or difficult to locate in an emergency. This information will save valuable time in a crisis.

Cisco is one vendor that makes many network products designed for high availability. These devices are characterized by long mean time between failure (MTBF) with redundant power supplies, and hot-swappable cards or modules. For example, devices that provide 99.999 percent availability would have about five minutes of unscheduled downtime per year.

Availability of individual devices can be enhanced by their configuration. Using features such as redundant uplinks with Hot Standby Router Protocol (HSRP), fast convergent Spanning Tree, or Fast Ether Channel provides a failover if one link should fail. Uninterruptible Power Supplies (UPS) and back-up generators are used to protect mission-critical equipment against power outages.

Although not covered in this book, Cisco Internetworking Operating System (IOS) includes reliability features such as:

- Hot Standby Router Protocol (HSRP)
- Simple Server Redundancy Protocol (SSRP)
- Deterministic Load Distribution (DLD)

Integrity

Integrity ensures that information or software is complete, accurate, and authentic. We want to keep unauthorized people or processes from making any changes to the system, and to keep authorized users from making unauthorized changes. These changes may be intentional or unintentional.

For network integrity, we need to ensure that the message received is the same message that was sent. The content of the message must be complete and unmodified, and the link is between valid source and destination nodes. Connection integrity can be provided by cryptography and routing control.

Integrity also extends to the software images for network devices that are transporting data. The images must be verified as authentic, and they have not been modified or corrupted. When copying an image into flash memory, verify that the checksum of the bundled image matches the checksum listed in the README file that comes with the upgrade.

Confidentiality

Confidentiality protects sensitive information from unauthorized disclosure or intelligible interception. Cryptography and access control are used to protect confidentiality. The effort applied to protecting confidentiality depends on the sensitivity of the information and the likelihood of it being observed or intercepted.

Network encryption can be applied at any level in the protocol stack. Applications can provide end-to-end encryption, but each application must be adapted to provide this service. Encryption at the transport layer is used frequently today, but this book focuses on encryption at the Open Systems Interconnection (OSI) network layer. Virtual private networks can be used to establish secure channels of communication between two sites or between an end-user and a site. Encryption can be used at the OSI data-link layer, but at this level, encryption is a point-to-point solution and won't scale to the Internet or even to private internetworks. Every networking device in the communication pathway would have to participate in the encryption scheme. Physical security is used to prevent unauthorized access to network ports or equipment rooms. One of the risks at these low levels is the attachment of sniffers or packet analyzers to the network.

Customizing Access Control

Access control is the process of limiting the privilege to use system resources. There are three types of controls for limiting access:

Administrative controls are based upon policies. Information security policies should state the organization's objectives regarding control over access to resources, hiring and management of personnel, and security awareness.

Physical controls include limiting access to network nodes, protecting the network wiring, and securing rooms or buildings that contain restricted assets.

Logical controls are the hardware and software means of limiting access and include access control lists (ACLs), communication protocols, and cryptography.

Access control depends upon positively verifying an identity (authentication), and then granting privilege based upon identity (authorization). The access could be granted to a person, a machine, a service, or a program. For example, network management using Simple Network Management Protocol (SNMP) has access control through the use of community names. One community name gives nonprivileged access and another gives privileged access by the management program into the network device. A person can access the same device in user mode or privileged mode using different passwords. Network access control can be provided at the edge of a security perimeter by a firewall or a router using ACLs.

Authentication

Authentication is the verification of a claimed identity of a user, process, or device. Other security measures depend upon verifying the identity of the sender and receiver of information. Authorization grants privileges based upon identity. Audit trails would not provide accountability without authentication. Confidentiality and integrity are broken if you can't reliably differentiate an authorized entity from an unauthorized entity.

The level of authentication required for a system is determined by the security needs that an organization has placed on it. Public Web servers may allow anonymous or guest access to information. Financial transactions could require strong authentication. An example of a weak form of authentication is using an IP address to determine identity. Changing or spoofing the IP address can defeat this mechanism easily. Strong authentication requires at least two factors of identity. Authentication factors are:

What a person knows. Passwords and personal identification numbers (PINs) are examples of what a person knows. Passwords may be reusable or one-time use. S/Key is an example of a one-time password system.

What a person has. Hardware or software tokens are examples of what a person has. Smart cards, SecureID, CRYPTOCard, and SafeWord are examples of tokens.

What a person is. Biometric authentication is an example of what a person is, because identification is based upon some physical attributes of a person. Biometric systems include palm scan, hand geometry, iris scan, retina pattern, fingerprint, voiceprint, facial recognition, and signature dynamics systems.

A number of systems are available for network authentication. TACACS+ (Terminal Access Controller Access System), Kerberos, and RADIUS (Remote Access Dial-In User Service) are authentication protocols supported by Cisco. These authentication systems can be configured to use many of the identification examples listed previously. The strength of the techniques used to verify an identity depends on the sensitivity of the information being accessed and the policy of the organization providing the access. It is an issue of providing cost-effective protection.

Reusable passwords, by themselves, are often a security threat because they are sent in clear text in an insecure environment. They are given easily to another person, who can then impersonate the original user. Passwords can be accessible to unauthorized people because they are written down in an obvious location or are easy to guess. The password lifetime should be defined in the security policy of the organization, and they should be changed regularly. Choose passwords that are difficult to guess, and that do not appear in a dictionary.

Although the details are beyond the scope of this book, Cisco routers can authenticate with each other. Route authentication assures that routing updates are from a known source and have not been modified or corrupted. Cisco can use the MD5 hash or simple algorithm. Several Cisco routing protocols support authentication:

- Open Shortest Path First (OSPF)
- Routing Information Protocol version 2 (RIPv2)
- Enhanced Interior Gateway Routing Protocol (Enhanced IGRP)
- Border Gateway Protocol (BGP)
- Intermediate System-to-Intermediate System (IS-IS)

Preventing Systems from Use as Intermediaries for Parasitic Attacks

Parasitic attacks take advantage of unsuspecting accomplices by using their systems to launch attacks against third parties. One type of parasitic attack is the Distributed Denial of Service (DDoS) attack, like those used to bring down Yahoo! and eBay in February 2000. An attacker will install zombies on many hosts, and then at a time of their choosing, command the zombie hosts to attack a single victim, overwhelming the resources of the victim's site.

Your responsibility is not just to protect your organization's information assets, but also to protect the Internet community as a whole. Companies who follow the recommendations of www.cert.org/tech_tips/denial_of_service.html under Prevention and Response will help to make the Internet more secure for everyone.

In the future, we may see civil legal actions that will hold intermediaries used in an attack liable for damages if they have not exercised due care in providing security for their systems.

Authorization

Authorization is a privilege granted by a designated utility to enable access to services or information for a particular identity or group of identities. For highly secure systems, the default authorization should be no access, and any additional privileges are based on least privilege and need-to-know.

For public systems, authorization may be granted to guest or anonymous users. You need to determine your security requirements to decide the appropriate authorization boundaries.

The granting of authorization is based on trust. The process granting access must trust the process that authenticated the identity. Attackers may attempt to get the password of an authorized user, hijack a Telnet session, or use social engineering to impersonate an authorized user and assume their access rights. Authentication is the key to ensuring that only authorized users are accessing controlled information.

Accounting

Accounting is the recording of network activity and resource access attempts. Though this information can be used for billing purposes, from a security perspective it is most important for detecting, analyzing, and responding to security incidents on the network. System logs, audit trails, and accounting software can all be used to hold users accountable for what happens under their logon ID.

Network Communication in TCP/IP

The Transmission Control Protocol/Internet Protocol (TCP/IP) suite has become the de facto standard for open system data communication and interoperability. The suite is made up of several protocols and applications that operate at different layers. Each layer is responsible for a different aspect of communication.

The TCP/IP Internet Protocol is organized into four layers as shown in Figure 1.4. The TCP/IP layers are compared to the equivalent layers in the seven-layer Open Systems Interconnection (OSI) reference model. The standards for TCP/IP are published as Requests for Comments (RFC) and are available at www.rfc-editor.org. RFCs are categorized as standards, draft standards, proposed standards, experimental, informational, and historical. The list of current standards RFCs can be found at www.rfc-editor.org/categories/rfc-standard.html.

Layered protocols are designed so a specific layer at the destination receives the same object sent by the equivalent source layer. Each layer communicates with its corresponding layer on the other host. It does not worry about the parameters or formats used in the layers above or below it. Physically, a layer hands its data to the interface of the layer above or below on the same system. Figure 1.5 illustrates how the layers communicate. The vertical arrows show the physical communication within a host and the horizontal arrows show the logical communication between peer layers on different hosts.

Figure 1.4 The layers of the TCP/IP protocol suite.

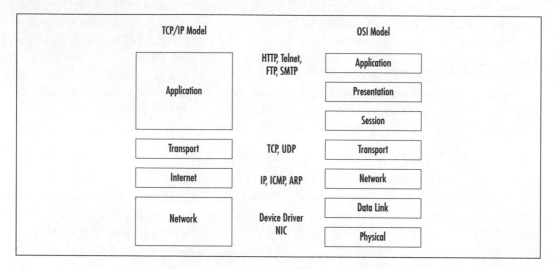

Figure 1.5 Logical and physical communication between protocol layers.

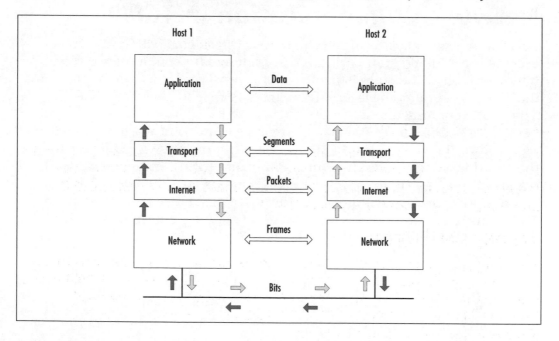

As data is handed from the application, to transport, to Internet, and to the network, each protocol does its processing and prepends a header, encapsulating the protocol above it. On the system receiving this stream of information, the headers are removed as the data is processed and passed up the stack. This approach provides flexibility because, in general, upper layers don't need to be concerned with the technology used in the layers below. For example, if the IP layer is encrypted, the TCP and applications remain unchanged. Figure 1.6 shows an example of encapsulation on the source host.

Figure 1.6 Encapsulation of protocol layers.

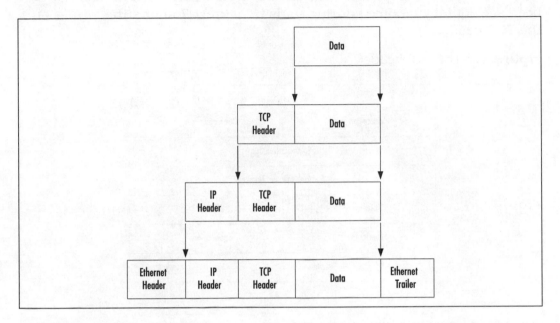

Application Layer

The application layer provides file transfer, print, message, terminal emulation, and database services. Some protocols included at this layer are Hypertext Transfer Protocol (HTTP), Telnet, File Transfer Protocol (FTP), and Simple Mail Transfer Protocol (SMTP).

Transport Layer

The transport layer provides duplex, end-to-end data transport services between applications. Data sent from the application layer is divided into segments appropriate in size for the network technology being used. Transmission Control Protocol (TCP) and User Datagram Protocol (UDP) are the protocols used at this layer.

TCP

TCP provides reliable service by being connection-oriented and including error detection and correction. The connected nature of TCP is used only for two endpoints to communicate with each other. The connection must be established before a data transfer can occur, and transfers are acknowledged throughout the process. Acknowledgements assure that data is being received properly. The acknowledgement process provides robustness in the face of network congestion or communication unreliability. TCP also determines when the transfer ends and closes the connection, thus freeing up resources on the systems. Checksums assure that the data has not been accidentally modified during transit. Figure 1.7 shows the format of the TCP header.

Figure 1.7 The TCP header.

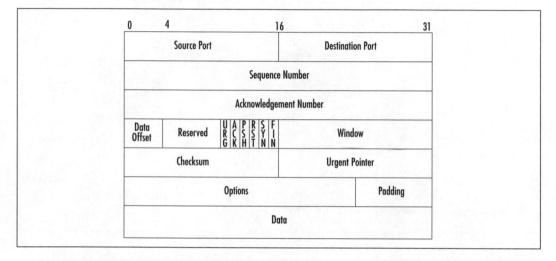

TCP ports are used to multiplex this protocol layer to the layer above with multiple applications on the same host. A source port and a destination port are associated with the sending and receiving applications, respectively. The ports from 0 to 1023 are Well Known Ports, and are assigned by Internet Assigned Numbers Authority (IANA). Ports from 1024 to 49151 are Registered Ports, and ports from 49152 through 65535 are Dynamic/Private Ports. The Well Known and Registered Port numbers are available at www.isi.edu/in-notes/iana/assignments/port-numbers.

The sequence numbers allow recovery by TCP from data that was lost, damaged, duplicated, or delivered out of order. Each host in the TCP connection selects an Initial Sequence Number (ISN), and these are synchronized during the establishment of the connection. The sequence number is incremented for each byte of data transmitted across the TCP connection, including the SYN and FIN flags. Sequence numbers are 32 bits and will wrap around to zero when it overflows. The ISN should be unpredictable for a given TCP connection. Some TCP implementations have exhibited vulnerabilities of predictable sequence numbers. Predicting the sequence number can allow an attacker to impersonate a host.

The acknowledgement number has a valid entry when the ACK flag is on. It contains the next sequence number that the receiver is expecting. Since every data segment sent over a TCP connection has a sequence number, it also has an acknowledgement number.

The following are TCP flags:

URG The urgent control bit indicates that Urgent Pointer is a valid offset to add to the Sequence Number. The sender of data can indicate to the receiver that there is urgent data pending.

ACK The acknowledgement control bit indicates that the Acknowledgement Number contains the value of the next sequence number the sender of the segment is expecting to receive. ACK is always set for an established connection.

PSH This indicates that all data received to this point has been pushed up to the receiving application. This function expedites the delivery of urgent data to the destination.

RST This TCP flag indicates that the connection is reset. This function flushes all queued segments waiting for transmission or retransmission, and puts the receiver in listen mode.

SYN This synchronizes sequence numbers. The SYN control bit indicates that the Sequence Number contains the initial sequence number.

FIN This indicates that the sender has finished sending data. The FIN control bit is set by the application closing its connection.

The ACK and RST play a role in determining whether a connection is established or being established. For example, Cisco uses the established keyword in Access Control Lists (ACL) to check whether the ACK or RST flags are set. If either flag is set, the packet meets the test as established. If neither flag is set, the device at the source TCP address is trying to establish a new connection to the device at the destination TCP address.

HTTP, SMTP, FTP, Telnet, and rlogin are examples of applications that use TCP for transport. Applications that need reliability support from the transport layer use Remote Procedure Calls (RPCs) over TCP. Applications that do not depend on the transport layer for reliability use RPC over UDP.

TCP Connection

Establishing a TCP connection requires three segments:

1. To initiate the connection, the source host sends a SYN segment (SYN flag is set) and an initial sequence number (ISN) in the sequence number field to the destination port and host address.

2. The destination host responds with a segment containing its initial sequence number, and both the SYN and ACK flags set. The acknowledgement number will be the source's sequence number, incremented by one.

3. The source host acknowledges the SYN from the destination host by replying with an ACK segment and an acknowledgement number that is the destination's sequence number incremented by one.

Once a TCP connection between the two systems exists, data can be transferred. As data is sent, the sequence number is incremented to track the number of bytes. Acknowledgement segments from the destination host increment the acknowledgement number as bytes of data are received.

The states that TCP goes through in establishing its connection allows firewalls to easily recognize new connections versus existing connections. Access lists on routers also use these flags in the TCP header to determine whether the connection is established.

A socket is the combination of IP address and TCP port. A local and remote socket pair (quadruplet) determines a connection between two hosts uniquely:

- The source IP address
- The source TCP port
- The destination IP address
- The destination TCP port

Firewalls can use this quadruplet to track the many connections on which they are making forwarding decisions at a very granular level. During the establishment of the connection, the firewall will learn the dynamic port assigned to the client for a particular connection. For the period of time that the connection exists, the dynamic port is allowed through the firewall. Once the connection is finished, the client port will be closed. By tracking the state of a particular connection in this way, security policy rules don't need to compensate for dynamic port assignments.

UDP

UDP is a simple, unreliable transport service. It is connectionless, so delivery is not assured. Since connections aren't set up and torn down, there is very little overhead. Lost, damaged, or out of order segments will not be retransmitted unless the application layer requests it. UDP is used for fast, simple messages sent from one host to another. Due to its simplicity, UDP packets are more easily spoofed than TCP packets. If reliable or ordered delivery of data is needed, applications should use TCP.

Simple Network Management Protocol (SNMP), Trivial File Transfer Protocol (TFTP), BOOTstrap Protocol (BOOTP), Network File System (NFS), and Dynamic Host Configuration Protocol (DHCP) are examples of applications that use UDP for transport. UDP is also used for multimedia applications. Unlike the connection-oriented TCP, which only can connect between two hosts, UDP can broadcast or multicast to many systems at once. The small overhead of UDP eases the network load when running time-sensitive data such as audio or video.

Internet Layer

The Internet layer is responsible for addressing, routing, error notification, and hop-by-hop fragmentation and reassembly. It manages the delivery of information from host to host. Fragmentation could occur at this layer because different network technologies have different Maximum Transmission Units (MTU). Internet Protocol (IP), Internet Control Message Protocol (ICMP), and Address Resolution Protocol (ARP) are protocols used at this layer.

IP

IP is an unreliable, routable packet delivery protocol. All upper layer protocols use IP to send and receive packets. IP receives segments from the transport layer, fragments them into packets, and passes them to the network layer.

The IP address is a logical address assigned to each node on a TCP/IP network. IP addressing is designed to allow routing of packets across internetworks. Since IP addresses are easy to change or spoof, they should not be relied upon to provide identification in untrusted environments. The source and destination addresses are included in the IP header.

The protocol parameter indicates the upper level protocol that is using IP. The decimal value for TCP is 6 and for UDP, 17. The list of assigned numbers for this field is available at www.isi.edu/in-notes/iana/assignments/protocol-numbers. The checksum is computed only on the header, so it does not check the integrity of the data payload.

ICMP

ICMP provides diagnostic functions and error reporting for IP. For example, ICMP can provide feedback to a sending host when a destination is unreachable or time is exceeded (TTL=0). A ping is an ICMP echo request message, and the response is an ICMP echo reply.

ARP

ARP is responsible for resolving the logical IP address into the hardware address for the network layer. If the destination IP address is on the same subnet as the source host, then IP will use ARP to determine the hardware address of the destination host. If the destination IP address is on a remote subnet, then ARP will be used to determine the hardware address of the default gateway. The ARP cache, a table of translations between IP address and hardware, stores its entries dynamically and flushes them after a short period of time.

WARNING

Some attacks have been based upon forging the ARP reply and redirecting IP traffic to a system that sniffs for clear text passwords or other information. This attack overcomes the benefit of a switched Ethernet environment because ARP requests are broadcast to all local network ports. The spoofing machine can respond with its hardware address and become a man-in-the-middle. Research is being conducted on a new ARP protocol that would be resistant to these types of attacks. In the meantime, avoid the use of clear text passwords or community names.

Network Layer

The network layer includes the network interface card and device driver. These provide the physical interface to the media of the network. The network layer controls the network hardware, encapsulates and transmits outgoing packets, and accepts and demultiplexes incoming packets. It accepts IP packets from the Internet layer above.

Security in TCP/IP

The Internet provides no guarantee of privacy or integrity for data. Cryptography should be considered for private, valuable, or vulnerable data. Data is encrypted as it is transmitted, and decrypted as it is received. Most layers in the OSI model can be used to provide data integrity and confidentiality. The application of security to each layer has its own particular advantages and disadvantages. The characteristics of security applied at a particular layer provide features that can be used as a decision point in determining the applicability of each technique to solve a particular problem.

Cryptography

Cryptography is the science of writing and reading in code or cipher. Information security uses cryptosystems to keep information private, and to authenticate the identity of the sender or receiver of the information. Cryptography can also provide integrity for information, because it allows only authorized people or processes to access it, and can detect corruption or modification of the original message or file. Cryptography works by making the effort required to break the encryption much more expensive than the value of the data, or by taking much longer to break than the time the data will hold its value.

There are three categories of cryptographic functions: symmetric key, asymmetric key, and hash functions. Most of the standard algorithms are public knowledge, and have been thoroughly tested by many experts. Their security depends on the strength of the algorithm and the strength of the key. A key is a sequence that is used for the mathematical process of enciphering and deciphering information. The hash functions do not use a key. The hash is performed by a specialized mathematical function.

There are many algorithms for encrypting information. To exchange encrypted messages, the parties must agree on the algorithms that will be used, and the keys for each algorithm. The protocols will be configured to negotiate a particular algorithm, and a key management system will generate, distribute, and manage the keys.

Symmetric Cryptography

Symmetric key cryptography uses the same key to encrypt and decrypt the message. Each pair of users shares a key for exchanging messages. By being able to encrypt or decrypt a message, each partner assumes that the other entity is the same entity with which they exchanged keys. It provides some degree of authentication. For this scheme to work, the key must be kept secret between the two parties involved.

Examples of symmetric key algorithms are as follows:

- Data Encryption Standard (DES) (56 bits)
- Triple DES (3DES) (168 bits)
- International Data Encryption Algorithm (IDEA) (128 bits)
- Rivest Cipher 4 (RC4) (variable length key)
- Advanced Encryption Standard (AES) (will replace DES as a federal standard)

For stored files that are encrypted, the loss or destruction of the sole copy of a symmetric key could result in the loss of access to the files. Sometimes keys are archived or backed up to protect the organization from such potential loss. For network transfers, this vulnerability is not an issue. New keys can be generated, exchanged, and the information resent.

A symmetric key, including any backup copies, has to be protected to the same extent as the information that it protects. The distribution of the keys must be accomplished by a secure means. If someone intercepted a key during the exchange or acquired a key from a user's system, they could also participate in the exchange of encrypted information. Privacy and integrity would be lost.

Symmetric key algorithms are fast and can encrypt a lot of information in a short period of time. They are strong when large keys are used. Symmetric key algorithms are used for the bulk of communication link encryption.

Asymmetric Cryptography

Asymmetric key cryptography is also known as public key cryptography. It uses a pair of keys that are mathematically related, but given one key, the other is very unlikely to be calculated. One key is for encrypting or signing, and the other is used for decrypting or verifying. One of the keys is kept private or secret, and the other is distributed publicly.

Here are some examples of asymmetric key algorithms:

- Diffie-Hellman
- Rivest, Shamir, Adleman (RSA)
- Digital Signature Algorithm (DSA) / ElGamal
- Elliptic Curve Cryptosystem (ECC)

The asymmetric algorithms are trapdoor one-way functions. They are easy to compute in one direction, but extremely difficult to calculate in the reverse direction unless you have the other key to the trapdoor. Even with the keys, asymmetric key functions are very compute-intensive. They are about 100 times slower than symmetric key algorithms. They are not practical for encrypting and decrypting large amounts of data.

When used to provide confidentiality, the sender encrypts the message using the public key of the receiver. Only the intended receiver's private key can decrypt the message. Messages going to multiple receivers must be encrypted for each one of the receivers. When used for authentication in digital signatures, the message is encrypted with the sender's private key. Only the sender's public key can decrypt it, verifying that it came from the sender. Confidentiality is the most common use for public key cryptography. It is used to exchange the session keys for symmetric key algorithms.

Hash Function

A hash function is used to condense a variable-length message into a fixed-length code, known as a hash or message digest. Different algorithms will produce different length hashes. Some examples of hash functions are:

- Message Digest 5 (MD5) (128 bits)
- Secure Hash Algorithm-1 (SHA-1) (160 bits)
- Haval (variable length)

Hashes are cryptographic checksums used to provide an integrity check on messages. A change of just one character in the original message can produce a change in a significant number of the hash bits. A hash function is a one-way function, and it is mathematically infeasible to compute the original message from the hash. The sender computes a hash of the original message and sends it with the encrypted message. The receiver decrypts the message, and also computes a hash. If the original hash and the computed hash are the same, then the receiver is confident that the message is complete and unmodified.

Computing a hash of the message, and encrypting the hash with the sender's private key can create a digital signature. The sender attaches this digital signature to the message. The receiver separates the digital signature and decrypts it with the sender's public key. A hash of the message received is computed. If the two hash values match, then it verifies that this is the authentic message from the sender. This is also called nonrepudiation since the sender cannot deny sending the message.

Public Key Certificates

Public key certificates are data structures, signed by a trusted certificate authority (CA), that bind an identity to a public key and additional information. They provide a means of distributing public keys. The degree of trust that you put into the identity are dependent upon the procedures and trust that you place in the certificate authority. Public key certificates are used to support authentication, confidentiality, and integrity for such things as Web transactions, e-mail exchange, and IPSec. The certificate is signed with the private key of the certificate authority. The CA's public key is used to authenticate the certificate. Signed public key certificates, traceable via a hierarchical chain of trust, provide authentication and integrity of the public key and data included in the certificate.

The public key infrastructure provides a mechanism for generating keys, managing certificates, and ensuring integrity of the keys. Certificates are issued with expiration dates, after which they are no longer valid. Certificates may be revoked prior to the expiration date, for example due to personnel or organizational changes. Certificates are verified against recent certificate revocation lists (CRLs) or online query mechanisms to determine their validity. Certificate revocation lists can be downloaded from certificate authorities and used offline, but they need to be updated periodically.

Certificates are based on the formatting standards in X.509 v3. Version 3 improved the usefulness of certificates by adding standard and optional extension fields to the earlier formats. The standard extensions include such fields as Key Usage, Private Key Usage Period, Certificate Policies, and Policy Mappings.

Application Layer Security

Application layer security provides end-to-end security from an application running on one host through the network to the application on another host. It does not care about the underlying transport mechanism. Complete coverage of security requirements, integrity, confidentiality, and nonrepudiation can be provided at this layer. Applications have a fine granularity of control over the nature and content of the transactions. However, application layer security is not a general solution, because each application and client must be adapted to provide the security services. Several examples of application security extensions follow.

Pretty Good Privacy (PGP)

Phil Zimmermann created PGP in 1991. Individuals worldwide use it for privacy and digital signing of e-mail messages. PGP provides end-to-end security from the sender to the receiver. It can also be used to encrypt files. PGP has traditionally used RSA public key cryptography to exchange keys, and IDEA to encrypt messages.

PGP uses a *web of trust* or *network trust* model, where any users can vouch for the identity of other users. Getting the public keys of the intended person can be difficult to achieve in a secure manner. You can get a person's public key directly from that person, and then communicate the hash of the key in an out-of-band pathway. Keys are stored in files called key rings. There are some servers on the Internet with public key rings. These servers do not authenticate the keys, but merely store them. You should not trust keys that have an unknown heritage.

Secure Hypertext Transport Protocol (S-HTTP)

S-HTTP is not widely used, but it was designed to provide security for Web-based applications. Secure HTTP is a secure message-oriented communications protocol, and can transmit individual messages securely. It provides transaction confidentiality, authentication, and message integrity. It extends HTTP to include tags for encrypted and secure transactions.

S-HTTP is implemented in some commercial Web servers and most browsers. The S-HTTP server negotiates with the client for the type of encryption that will be used. Transactions can involve several types of encryption between a particular server and client.

S-HTTP does not require clients to have public key certificates because it can use symmetric keys to provide private transactions. The symmetric keys would be provided in advance using out-of-band communication.

Transport Layer Security

Transport layer security is directed at providing process-to-process security between hosts. Most schemes are designed for TCP to provide reliable, connection-oriented communication. Many transport layer security mechanisms require changes in applications to access the security benefits. The secure applications are replacements for standard unsecure applications and use different ports.

Secure Sockets Layer (SSL) and Transport Layer Security (TLS)

SSL was designed by Netscape and is used widely on the Internet for Web transactions such as sending credit card data. SSL can also be utilized for other protocols such as Telnet, FTP, LDAP, IMAP, and SMTP, but these are not commonly used. TLS is an open, IETF-proposed standard based on SSL 3.0. RFCs 2246, 2712, 2817, and 2818 define TLS. The two protocols are not interoperable, but TLS has the capability to drop down into SSL 3.0 mode for backwards compatibility. SSL and TLS provide security for a single TCP session.

SSL and TLS provide a connection between a client and a server, over which any amount of data can be sent securely. Server and browser must be SSL- or TLS-enabled to facilitate secure Web connections. Applications must be SSL- or TLS-enabled to allow their use of the secure connection.

For the browser and server to communicate securely, each needs to have the shared session key. SSL/TLS use public key encryption to exchange session keys during communication initialization. When a browser is installed on a workstation, it generates a unique private/public key pair.

Secure Shell (SSH)

Secure shell protocol is specified in a set of Internet draft documents. SSH provides secure remote login and other secure network services over an insecure network. SSH is being promoted free to colleges and universities as a means for reducing clear text passwords on networks. Middle and high-end Cisco routers support SSH, but only SSH version 1. SSH version 2 was rewritten completely to use different security protocols, and has added public key cryptography.

The SSH protocol provides channels for establishing secure, interactive shell sessions and tunnelling other TCP applications. There are three major components to SSH:

Transport layer protocol provides authentication, confidentiality, and integrity for the server. It can also compress the data stream. The SSH transport runs on top of TCP. The transport protocol negotiates key exchange method, public key, symmetric encryption, authentication, and hash algorithms.

User authentication protocol authenticates the user-level client to the server and runs on top of SSH transport layer. It assumes that the transport layer provides integrity and confidentiality. The method of authentication is negotiated between the server and the client.

Connection protocol multiplexes an encrypted tunnel into several channels. It is run on top of SSH transport and authentication protocols. The two ends negotiate the channel, window size, and type of data. The connection protocol can tunnel X11 or any arbitrary TCP port traffic.

Filtering

Packet filters can be implemented on routers and layer 3 devices to control the packets that will be blocked or forwarded at each interface. Routing decisions about whether to forward or drop the packet are made based on the rules in the access list. Standard access lists cannot filter on transport layer information. Only extended access lists can specify a protocol, and a parameter related to that protocol. TCP filtering options include established connections, port numbers or ranges of port numbers, and type of service values. UDP filter options specify only port numbers, since it is not a connection-oriented protocol.

Network Layer Security

Network layer security can be applied to secure traffic for all applications or transport protocols in the above layers. Applications do not need to be modified since they communicate with the transport layer above.

IP Security Protocols (IPSec)

IPSec protocols can supply access control, authentication, data integrity, and confidentiality for each IP packet between two participating network nodes. IPSec can be used between two hosts (including clients), a gateway and a host, or two gateways. No modification of network hardware or software is required to route IPSec. Applications and upper level protocols can be used unchanged.

IPSec adds two security protocols to IP, Authentication Header (AH) and Encapsulating Security Payload (ESP). AH provides connectionless integrity, data origin authentication, and antireplay service for the IP packet. AH does not encrypt the data, but any modification of the data would be detected. ESP provides confidentiality through the encryption of the payload. Access control is provided through the use and management of keys to control participation in traffic flows.

IPSec was designed to be flexible, so different security needs could be accommodated. The security services can be tailored to the particular needs of each connection by using AH or ESP separately for their individual functions, or combining the protocols to provide the full range of protection offered by IPSec. Multiple cryptographic algorithms are supported. The algorithms that must be present in any implementation of IPSec follow. The null algorithms provide no protection, but are used for consistent negotiation by the protocols. AH and ESP cannot both be null at the same time.

- DES in CBC (Cipher Block Chaining) mode
- HMAC (Hash Message Authentication Code) with MD5
- HMAC with SHA-1
- Null Authentication Algorithm
- Null Encryption Algorithm

A Security Association (SA) forms an agreement between two systems participating in an IPSec connection. An SA represents a simplex connection to provide a security service using a selected policy and keys, between two nodes. A Security Parameter Index (SPI), an IP destination address, and a protocol identifier are used to identify a particular SA. The SPI is an arbitrary 32-bit value selected by the destination system that uniquely identifies a particular Security Association among several associations that may exist on a particular node. The protocol identifier can indicate either AH or ESP, but not both. Separate SAs are created for each protocol, and for each direction between systems. If two systems were using AH and ESP in both directions, they would form four SAs.

Each protocol supports a transport mode and a tunnel mode of operation. The transport mode is between two hosts. These hosts are the endpoints for the cryptographic functions being used. Tunnel mode is an IP tunnel, and is used whenever either end of the SA is a security gateway. A security gateway is an intermediate system, such as a router or firewall, that implements IPSec protocols. A Security Association between a host and a security gateway must use tunnel mode. If the connection traffic is destined for the gateway itself, such as management traffic, then the gateway is treated as a host, because it is the endpoint of the communication.

In transport mode, the AH or ESP header are inserted after the IP header, but before any upper layer protocol headers. AH authenticates the original IP header. AH does not protect the fields that are modified in the course of routing IP packets. ESP protects only what comes after the ESP header. If the security policy between two nodes requires a combination of security services, the AH header appears first after the IP header, followed by the ESP header. This combination of Security Associations is called an SA bundle.

In tunnel mode, the original IP header and payload are encapsulated by the IPSec protocols. A new IP header that specifies the IPSec tunnel destination is prepended to the packet. The original IP header and its payload are protected by the AH or ESP headers. AH offers some protection for the entire packet. AH does not protect the fields that are modified in the course of routing IP packets between the IPSec tunnel endpoints, but it does completely protect the original IP header.

Key management is another major component of IPSec. Manual techniques are allowed in the IPSec standard, and might be acceptable for configuring one or two gateways, but typing in keys and data are not practical in most environments. The Internet Key Exchange (IKE) provides automated, bidirectional SA management, key generation, and key management. IKE negotiates in two phases. Phase 1 negotiates a secure, authenticated channel over which the two systems can communicate for further negotiations. They agree on the encryption algorithm, hash algorithm, authentication method, and Diffie-Hellman group to exchange keys and information. A single phase 1 association can be used for multiple phase 2 negotiations. Phase 2 negotiates the services that define the SAs used by IPSec. They agree on IPSec protocol, hash algorithm, and encryption algorithm. Multiple SAs will result from phase 2 negotiations. An SA is created for inbound and outbound of each protocol used.

Filtering (Access Control Lists)

Packet filters can be implemented on routers and layer 3 devices to control the source and destination IP addresses allowed to pass through the gateway. Standard access lists can filter on source address. Extended access lists can filter ICMP, Internet Group Message Protocol (IGMP), or IP protocols at the network layer. ICMP can be filtered based on the specific message. IP filtering can include port numbers at the transport layer to allow or disallow specific services between specific addresses. Access lists can also control other routed protocols such as AppleTalk or IPX.

Data-Link Layer Security

Data-link security is done point-to-point, such as over a leased line or frame relay permanent virtual circuit. Dedicated hardware devices attached to each end of the link do encryption and decryption. Military, government, and banking organizations are the most common users of this approach. It is not scalable to large internetworks, because the packets are not routable in their encrypted state. This method does have the advantage that an eavesdropper cannot determine the source or destination addresses in the packets. It can also be used for any upper layer protocols.

Authentication

Authentication can be provided locally on each device on your network, but using an authentication server offers improved scalability, flexibility, and control. Firewalls, routers, and remote access servers enforce network access security. Configuring these devices to use one centralized database of accounts is easier on the administrator and the users who may access the network through multiple pathways.

For example, a Cisco network access server (NAS), firewall, or router acts as the client and requests authentication from an authentication server. The access server or router will prompt the user for a username and password, and then verifies the password with the authentication server. TACACS+, RADIUS, and Kerberos are widely used authentication servers supported by Cisco. TACACS+ and RADIUS can also provide services for authorization and accounting.

Terminal Access Controller Access System Plus (TACACS+)

TACACS+ is an enhanced version of TACACS developed by Cisco. The enhancements include the separation of authentication, authorization, and accounting into three distinct functions. These services can be used independently or together. For example, Kerberos could be used for authentication, and TACACS+ used for authorization and accounting. Some of the characteristics of TACACS+ are:

- Whereas older versions of TACACS and RADIUS use UDP for transport, TACACS+ uses TCP (port 49) for reliable and acknowledged transport.

- TACACS+ can encrypt the entire payload of the packet, so it protects the password, username, and other information sent between the Cisco access client and the server. The encryption can be turned off for troubleshooting. Communication from the workstation to the Cisco client providing access services is not encrypted.

- TACACS+ supports multiple protocols such as IP, AppleTalk Remote Access (ARA), Novell, Asynchronous Services Interface (NASI), X.25 PAD connection, and NetBIOS.

- You can use TACACS+ to provide greater control over router management in either nonprivileged or privileged mode, because you can authenticate individual users or groups rather than a shared password. Router commands can be specified explicitly on the TACACS+ server to allow specific commands.

Remote Dial-In User Service (RADIUS)

RADIUS is an open standard and available from many vendors. RADIUS can be a good choice in a heterogeneous network environment because of its widespread support, but some vendors have implemented proprietary attributes in RADIUS that hinder interoperability.

- RADIUS uses UDP, so it offers only best-effort delivery.

- For authentication, RADIUS encrypts only the password sent between the Cisco access client and RADIUS server. RADIUS does not provide encryption between the workstation and the Cisco access client.

- RADIUS does not support multiple protocols, and works only on IP networks.

- RADIUS does not provide the ability to control the commands that can be executed on a router.

Kerberos

The Kerberos protocol can be used for network authentication and host authentication. Host-based applications must be adapted to use the Kerberos protocol. A Kerberos realm includes all users, hosts, and network services that are registered with a Kerberos server. Kerberos uses symmetric key cryptography and stores a shared key for each user and each network resource that is participating in its realm. Every user and network resource needs a Kerberos account. Knowing its shared key is proof of identity for each of those entities. Kerberos stores all passwords encrypted with a single system key. If that system key is compromised, all passwords need to be recreated.

The process of authenticating using Kerberos involves three systems: a client, a network resource, and the Kerberos server. The Kerberos server is called the Key Distribution Center (KDC). For remote network access, the client and network resource is the boundary network device, such as network access server or router. The remote user establishes a PPP connection to the boundary device, and the device prompts the user for username and password. The device, acting as the client, requests a ticket-granting ticket (TGT) from the Kerberos authentication server. If the user has an account, the authentication server generates a session key, and sends it to the ticket-granting server (TGS). The TGT is a credential that specifies the user's verified identity, the Kerberos server identity, and the expiration time of the ticket. By default, tickets expire after eight hours. The ticket-granting ticket is encrypted with a key known only to the ticket-granting server and the authentication server. The Kerberos server using a DES key generated from the users password encrypts the TGT, session key, and other information. Only the user and the Kerberos server should know the password. The Cisco access server will attempt to decrypt the TGT with the password that the user entered. If successful, the user is authenticated to the access server, and the user's workstation becomes part of the protected network.

Users who want to access services that are part of the Kerberos realm on the network must now authenticate against the Kerberos server and get authorization to access the services. The user first gets a ticket-granting ticket as described previously, which is used to request access to other services. The difference is that the client is now the user's workstation. The user then sends the TGT to the TGS to request access for a specific service on a specific server. The TGS generates a random session key and sends a server ticket containing the key to the client that requested the service. The client presents the new server ticket to the server in order to gain access. A server ticket must be created for each service that the client will access.

Summary

The growth of the Internet and its reach into the fabric of business and personal life has outdistanced most organizations' ability to protect the confidentiality and integrity of information. Many organizations are increasing their use of electronic commerce for business-to-business and business-to-consumer transactions. This increased exposure and the constant escalation of threats to network security have increased the need for effective controls that can restore availability, confidentiality, and integrity to information systems. Although no one product or system can provide complete protection, security can be layered to provide reasonable risk management reduction of vulnerabilities.

The TCP/IP protocol stack consists of four layers and provides data communications under a diversity of conditions. The application layer provides file transfer, print, message, terminal emulation, and database services. The transport layer provides duplex, end-to-end data transport services between applications. The TCP port determines which application on the end system is sending and receiving data. The Internet layer provides routing and delivery of datagrams to end nodes. The IP address determines the end system to send or receive communications. The network layer communicates directly with the network media. The hardware address is translated to an IP address to allow IP to traverse each network segment. Any of the protocol layers are vulnerable to attack.

Network security continues to be a very dynamic area as new protocols and technologies are evolving. Security can be provided in TCP/IP at any layer, but each approach has advantages and disadvantages. Application layer security protocols require modifications to each application that will use them, but they can provide fine granularity of control. Transport layer security protocols can also require modifications at the application layer and have been limited in practice to a few specific applications. Network layer security protocols promise to become widely used and will likely replace many of the more limited solutions in use today. Firewalls provide network access control at security zone perimeters.

FAQs

Q: How can I secure my systems against malicious attacks if my network is connected the Internet?

A: There are a number of technologies, policies, and procedures that need to be in place to provide adequate security in an Internet-connected environment. At the very minimum, you will need a firewall, which is software/hardware that allows or denies IP traffic between networks based on rules configured for various ports. It is also important to keep operating system and application software updated so that you have the latest security-related fixes available. This applies to both server and desktop applications.

Q: Why would a hacker want to conduct a Denial of Service attack?

A: The first reason is that it is easier to conduct a Denial of Service attack than it is to formulate an attack that allows a user to authenticate. Therefore, you tend to see a lot of script kiddies who gain a quick, cheap sense of satisfaction watching an e-mail server crash. However, more sophisticated reasons exist to conduct a Denial of Service attack. Should a malicious user want to hijack a connection between your e-mail server and a client logging in, they would want to conduct a Denial of Service attack against the client in order to take over the connection and log in. So, although many Denial of Service attacks are conducted just to watch the server die, there are times when a DoS attack is a step in a more sophisticated process.

Q: What is the difference between IPSec and IP Security?

A: IP Security is a broad term that describes securing communications at the IP protocol layer. For example, packet filtering could provide some level of IP Security. IPSec is IP Security Protocols, a standard architecture defined by the Internet Engineering Task Force in RFCs 2401–2411 and 2451. IPSec is the dominant security solution at the IP layer because it is a global standard supported by many vendors.

Q: Why should Telnet or other unencrypted protocols not be used to manage routers, firewalls, switches, servers, or other infrastructure devices?

A: If someone can acquire the passwords or community names to your network infrastructure devices, they have the keys to the kingdom. The dangers of packet sniffing on shared network media have been known for a long time, but many people mistakenly believe that switched networks protect from sniffing by reducing the collision domain to each port on the switch. Although limited to the same subnet as one of the communicating devices, ARP spoofing is an easy and effective technique that negates the protection of a switched network. It fools devices into communicating with a different hardware address than that of the intended IP destination. ARP spoofing allows the capture of clear text passwords, and other interesting information.

Q: While traveling, and using a VPN tunnel from my laptop to the corporate headquarters, is my e-mail protected from disclosure?

A: The encryption of the VPN would protect your e-mail and any other data in transit between the endpoints of the tunnel. Copies of the message stored on the mail server, your laptop, or the recipient's computer would not be protected unless some other measures are taken. PGP, S/MIME, or some other means of encrypting the message would protect it from end to end.

Chapter 2

Internetwork Security Concepts

Solutions in this chapter:

- **Choosing a Method for User Authentication**
- **Differentiating between Proxy Servers and Firewalls**
- **Setting up a Demilitarized Zone (DMZ)**
- **Protecting your Network with Dead Zones and Protocol Switching**
- **Implementing Port and Packet Filtering**
- **Avoiding Design Pitfalls**

Introduction

The key to network security can be found in understanding the choices and strategies available to you—look to the building blocks of network security. These include implementing user authentication, using proxy servers and firewalls, setting up demilitarized zones, and taking advantage of port- and packet-filtering technologies. The overview of these security solutions provided by this chapter will give you an understanding of the technology; you can then build on that knowledge as later chapters discuss how different vendors implement that technology.

User authentication, the first option discussed in this chapter, is the most basic component of network security, and its success depends on the method used (encrypted, plain text, and so forth), and on the ability to keep this information from unauthorized personnel. Some of the more popular versions of user authentication include the Password Authentication Protocol (PAP) and the Challenge Handshake Authentication Protocol (CHAP).

Proxy servers can provide multiple functions to your network. Not only can they provide security for your wide area network (WAN) connection, but they can also provide services like caching, port filtering, and in some products, reverse proxy. Firewalls can be software, hardware, or both, and they effectively block unauthorized access to your network just as proxy servers do. There are several types of firewalls that include software that enables them to act as a packet filter, circuit gateway, and application gateway. You should also keep in mind that the differences between these pieces of equipment are getting smaller very rapidly. The desire for an all-in-one security solution has created many hybrid devices with both capabilities.

Demilitarized zones (DMZs) allow you to set up a network between your internal network and the outside world to form an additional protective layer from outside access. Protocol switching, a self-explanatory function, can be very useful against specific types of protocol-based attacks. For instance, you can set up a *dead zone* with some other protocol (protocol switching) to help protect your network against specific protocol attacks.

Last, we have port and packet filtering. These two security methodologies allow you to block specific protocols or specific ports. There are numerous implementations of these technologies, and some of these will be detailed in later chapters.

User Authentication Methods

The most basic building block to any security model is user authentication. User authentication allows for verification that the user is who they say they are; it gives you, therefore, the ability to regulate who gains access to your network. Without any authentication mechanism in place, any user, theoretically, would be able to access your network and cause damage. Even for the most seasoned network administrator, providing and maintaining usernames and passwords can prove to be a challenge. Always remember that you are not only trying to protect your users from outside threats, but also from unwittingly enabling an attacker.

Password Design

There are several things that you can insist upon to ensure that your authentication methods will not be easily compromised:

- Do not base passwords on any word found in the dictionary. Avoid using combinations of small words or phonetic spellings of common words.

- Do not base passwords on anything that is familiar to the user like a spouse's name, a birth date, a phone number, names of pets, landmarks, nicknames, slang computer terms, book or movie titles, name of a child, or names of power (such as *God*, believe it or not). You would be surprised how many user names and passwords are easily guessed from these items.

- Use strong passwords for all user authentications where possible. A strong password consists of a combination of upper- and lowercase letters as well as numbers and special characters. Typically, passwords should consist of at least eight characters.

Authentication has become a somewhat standard feature of most networking software and operating systems. For this reason, it is imperative that you understand what potential issues you may face. In the following sections we will discuss types of encryption and authentication, and some of the common issues associated with their implementation.

Encryption

Authentication was designed to give an added boost to network security. However, some of the earlier specifications called for clear-text transmission of usernames and passwords. However, this allowed software programs, such as sniffers, to extract your username and password for future use. To correct this problem, vendors began to use encryption to protect usernames, passwords, and data as they traveled through the network.

Encryption is defined as the act of taking plain-text information and changing it using a mathematical algorithm, so that only those with the proper encryption key can decrypt the ciphertext. These mathematical algorithms are also referred to as *hashes*. At a very basic level, plain text is encrypted into ciphertext, and then transmitted to its destination. At the destination, the intended party has the key for the encryption algorithm, and the ciphertext is converted back into plain text. Think back to a time when Morse code was new. Anyone eavesdropping would hear a series of ticks or beeps. Without the proper tick-to-character translation the information would be useless.

A good example of encryption can be taken from the everyday configuration of a Cisco router. You can enter an **enable secret** password (that is encrypted), so that no one can get it by merely giving the command **show running-config**. Look at the following sample output.

```
Router#sho run
Building configuration...

Current configuration:
!
version 12.0
service timestamps debug uptime
service timestamps log uptime
no service password-encryption
!
hostname Router
!
enable secret 5 $1$bhND$YR6guXVV02lvoPnv8h21r/
enable password lab
-=snip=-
```

Just below the hostname, you can see the **enable secret** password in its encrypted form. This password happens to be *cisco*, but you would never know it from that string of characters. In the same text, you can see the **enable** password in an unencrypted format.

Some of the more popular terms you will see are 40-bit encryption, 56-bit encryption, and 128-bit encryption. All three are separate levels of the Data Encryption Standard (DES), created by the National Bureau of Standards. The algorithm uses a key that ranges from 40 up to 128 bits in length. The higher numbers have longer character strings, and therefore more possible key combinations. The key is then combined with the data using a mathematical algorithm. That serves as the encryption that the destination must reverse using the proper key combination (decoding).

It is not recommended to use 40-bit encryption for any type of corporate e-commerce security because the code can be broken fairly easily with the right program. The use of 56-bit encryption adds more to the DES algorithm, making it a bit more difficult to break, but not impossible. Because 56-bit DES was cracked a few years ago, you should not use it to secure anything critical within your network. However, 56-bit encryption is significant because it is currently the highest level of encryption allowed by the US government for exportation.

The use of 128-bit encryption has become the standard when using DES security. The 128-bit version of DES is strong enough that it would take someone a long time, with many high-end computers to break it. It would take the average person so long that it probably wouldn't be worth the hassle. This type of encryption is not allowed for exportation outside of the United States, but many other countries have comparable encryption methods in place.

There are other encryption algorithms on the market today. Many of them provide better security than the DES encryption algorithm. Some of these algorithms include Triple DES (3DES), Blowfish, and the International Data Encryption Algorithm (IDEA). Most of these algorithms use the block-cipher method for encryption. Block cipher takes user data and segments it into blocks of 64 bits before encoding. The block size can be anything up to 128 bits, but 64 is the standard.

3DES is a vast improvement upon its predecessor, DES. The 3DES algorithm uses three DES strings, each with its own key. This is a very secure encryption algorithm, but it is also very slow. 3DES does not have to use all three keys, however; it can use only two.

Bruce Schneier, author and industry expert, designed the Blowfish algorithm. This encryption algorithm is very fast and is resistant to both linear and differential analysis. Blowfish is designed on a 256-bit key, for very high security, and the data is broken into 64-bit blocks before it is encrypted (cipher block). Blowfish encryption has become the choice for many companies because of its strength and speed.

IDEA was designed by Xuejia Lai and James Massey of Switzerland. This algorithm is also resistant to linear and differential analysis, and is very fast. IDEA uses the block cipher method for the truncation of user data, and it operates with a 128-bit key.

Authentication Methods

There are many ways in which a user can be authenticated. The user can log into a network or system using an authentication protocol, a security key card, or even by allowing the Remote Access Service protocol (RAS) to use PPP dial-back for verification. In this section, we will focus on several of the main authentication protocols for PPP connections on the market. These protocols include PAP, Shiva Password Authentication Protocol (SPAP), CHAP, and Microsoft Challenge Handshake Authentication Protocol (MS-CHAP).

PAP is one of the most widely distributed authentication protocols to date. It's a very fast authentication mechanism, but it does have a few drawbacks. When you connect to a RAS using PAP, your username and password are sent in clear-text format. This would allow someone to intercept your password fairly easily. The client using PAP sends his or her username and password to the RAS, which has a table of mated username and password pairs with which it checks the inbound requests. The table is usually kept in an encrypted format so that you can't retrieve a whole listing of authentication.

SPAP is a proprietary authentication protocol from Shiva. SPAP works a lot like PAP, except that it doesn't transmit the password in a clear-text mode. When the Shiva Security Pack is added to Windows, there are some additional features added to the security session:

- Dial-back (roaming and fixed)
- Third-party security dialogs
- Grace login notification
- Change password
- Login banners

CHAP is an open standard for user authentication. This protocol differs from PAP in several ways. First of all, the CHAP authentication method uses a three-way handshake sequence to verify the user. The RAS will send a challenge on which the client will have to calculate a one-way hash. The client will send its calculated hash back to the RAS, which will also calculate a hash on the challenge. If the two match, the RAS will allow the client access—if not, the connection is dropped. After that occurs, the challenge can be reissued at any time during the session for user verification. CHAP is based on the Rivest, Shamir, and Adleman Message Digest 4 (RSA MD4) algorithm. This algorithm was named after the individuals who invented it.

MS-CHAP is based on the same premises as CHAP. There are a couple of differences that should be noted. Microsoft's implementation is also based on the RSA MD4 algorithm, but it adds data encryption to strengthen security. CHAP only encrypts the login information, so MS-CHAP may be a better choice in certain circumstances. As you might have guessed, MS-CHAP is a proprietary protocol that must be supported by your software or hardware.

Authentication Pitfalls

Authentication is used to help protect your network, but it is not infallible. You should make sure that you protect user information like your job depended on it—it just might. In the following paragraphs, we will look at a couple of the pitfalls associated with authentication and what you can do to protect yourself from them.

Social Engineering

There are plenty of software packages that allow crackers (malicious hackers) to cipher usernames and passwords, but the software doesn't pose the only threat to the integrity of your network. In recent years, the threat posed by *social engineering* has become more of a problem than ever before.

Social engineering is generally defined as an act by an outside party that acquires network or user information through such personal contact as a casual phone conversation. This type of thing occurs a lot more often than you might think. Social engineering can be as easy as someone calling and saying, "Hi, this is Jim, can you give me Bill Davis's phone number? I need to get in touch with him, and I left my computer at work." This is a very popular tactic of headhunters, who would love to recruit your top talent.

Although what is listed here may not seem like much, you would be surprised to discover what kind of information can be learned from these very innocent-sounding phone calls. It is possible to acquire just about any information desired if the caller is savvy enough to coax it out of you or your users.

It is certainly difficult to know when someone is truly asking for your help, and when that person is looking for personnel or corporate information. Does this mean that you shouldn't help anyone who calls you?

Certainly not, but it does mean that you should be cautious. You are more likely to encounter this sort of thing in a large successful company, but that does not mean than you won't run into it if you work for a startup. The shortage of qualified employees makes this an issue anywhere in corporate America.

There are several things that you can do to protect yourself from social engineering, beginning with educating your employees. Make sure that they know how to recognize it, and what to do if they do encounter an attempt at social engineering. You can direct personnel to transfer the call to a central location, such as a security desk.

If you are suspect of a call, check the caller's credentials after the call or check your caller ID to see if you can find out who it is. If the caller stated that he or she works in the engineering department, but the number shows up as "unavailable," that should send up a red flag. You may even want to consider making it corporate policy not to give out personnel or departmental information at all. If you have a corporate directory to which everyone has access, there shouldn't be a reason why they can't look the information up for themselves. Instruct your users to be educated and cautious, because the effects of social engineering can be disastrous.

One of the more notable computer deviants in recent history is Kevin Mitnick. A self-described master of the TELCO switch, he had been in and out of trouble with the authorities since the early 1980s. In his last escapade, Kevin eluded government officials for several years before being apprehended in 1996. His downfall came when he picked the pocket of the wrong person, Tsutomu Shimomura, who eventually tracked him down in Raleigh, NC. Shimomura, who is a senior fellow at the San Diego Supercomputer Center, is also a very well-respected network security advisor for the government.

Kevin baffled law enforcement authorities with how much he knew about the telephone infrastructure, and it was later discovered that his expertise at social engineering helped him significantly. According to Shimomura's book, *Take-Down; The Pursuit and Capture of Kevin Mitnick, America's Most Wanted Computer Outlaw—By the Man Who Did*, Kevin and a group of friends entered a Pacific Bell COSMOS phone center and talked their way past a night guard. Once inside, they planted phony names in the Rolodex to allow them to continue with the social engineering at a later time. It was at this time that Kevin also stole the switch-operating manuals, something that undoubtedly helped him in his endeavors.[1]

As you can see, if steps toward the proper education and preparation are not taken now, it can be too late by the time you realize you have been compromised. Admittedly, Kevin is a truly gifted hacker, but the point remains the same.

Password Management

The way that a lot of users manage (or mismanage) their login information has always struck me as funny. As the network administrator, you should be wary of your users storing their user names and passwords in obvious locations. There are several things that you should insist upon when thinking about password management:

- Passwords should not be stored in plain view. Cisco managers refer to this as the "Lion King Motif." Basically, this is the user that has a yellow "mane" of Post-Its all around the monitor edge. You will often find that the usernames and passwords will be listed along with what they go to.

- Passwords should not be saved to a text file on the desktop of the computer, or anywhere else for that matter. Just as you don't store your PIN to your bank card in your wallet (at least I hope you don't), you shouldn't store network authentication information on your computer.

- Require that the users on your network change their passwords at a regular interval. A lot of networks require this every 45 days or so, with the longest interval being about six months.

You may also want to consider setting up a team that checks for compliance with your management rules. In certain military installations, there are teams of individuals who do nothing but try to guess your passwords— you probably do not have the time or resources for this, but it is one way to verify the passwords have been changed and that they have used your requirements. It is also a good way to verify that strong passwords have been used. Most important is to define a set of standards for your network authentication model and then make sure that you enforce it.

Proxy Server Functionality

A proxy server is a software and/or hardware package that provides security plus many other functions such as Web and content caching. They are generally set up on a multihomed PC (dual network interface cards, or NICs), with one connection for the Internet and one connection for your network (see Figure 2.1).

Figure 2.1 A proxy server.

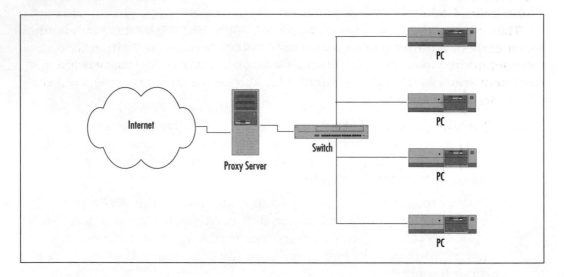

Caching is usually split into two groups, *active* and *passive*. With active caching, the proxy server will retrieve documents that it believes may be requested by the clients. Passive caching waits for a request before it retrieves a document and then the server will decide if the data should be cached.

An important concept to remember about proxy servers is that they act on Internet requests for the computers on the local area network (LAN).

When a PC on the LAN requests a file from the Internet, the request is taken by the proxy server, and then is retransmitted with the proxy's public address. This will cause the proxy server to look like the originating point of the request, and the destination will never know about the LAN behind the proxy.

Proxies can be deployed for several reasons, including these:

- A limited number of IP addresses are available for the Internet.

- Security is necessary, but high-end routers and firewalls are beyond budget range.

- It is necessary to speed up Web browsing for the users on the network.

First, proxy servers may be deployed if there are a limited number of Internet IP addresses available to you. Unless you have IP addresses to use for every machine in the network, you will need to find a way to manage them. A proxy server can take a single IP address and act as an interface to the rest of the Internet. This is achieved through a process known as

Network Address Translation (NAT). You may hear people talk about using NAT on their network when they actually mean Network Port Address Translation (NPAT).

The difference is that when using NAT, every IP address on the Internet has a corresponding address on the LAN. When using NPAT, there is one Internet address for multiple IP addresses on the LAN. The association is then kept track of with port assignments for each session opened from the LAN (refer to Figure 2.2).

Figure 2.2 NAT vs. NPAT.

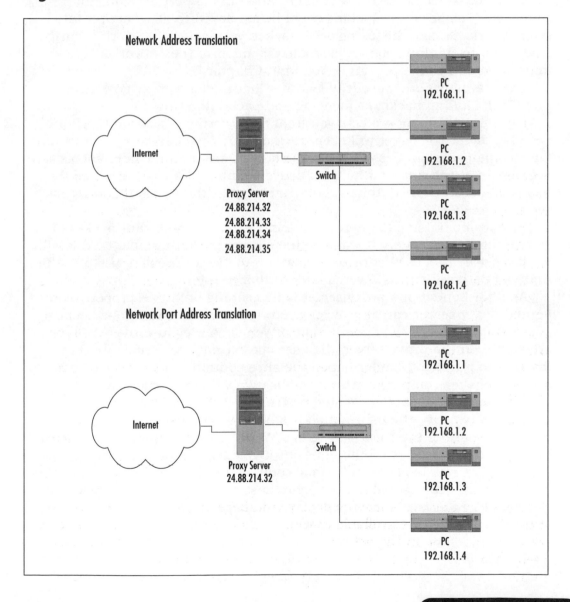

For more information on NAT or NPAT, please refer to Chapter 3.

Proxy servers can provide adequate security for a network used by small companies, or for companies on a strict budget. Many proxy servers today have features built into them to protect networks from outside aggression. NAT and NPAT, as previously discussed, act as a barrier to the Internet, effectively masking your network from the outside world.

Note that although NAT and NPAT can provide some security, you should not rely on them to provide the only security on your network. There are ways that NAT and NPAT can be circumvented, particularly NPAT. Since NPAT keeps track of information using port assignments, things such as session hijacking could be employed to allow access into the network. Session hijacking occurs when you fool the network security device(s) into thinking you are a trusted member of the network. More information on this topic can be found in Chapter 5.

There are also other security features that modern proxy servers can provide, including packet sequencing and packet filtering .

Packet sequencing protects you from many forms of session hijacking because the proxy server will keep track of which packets are to arrive next for the open session. Session hijacking occurs when an intruder spoofs the network into thinking that he is an active member of a session. Once that has been accomplished, the intruder can "hijack" the session, and receive the data freely.

If someone outside the network attempts to send an errant packet to gain access, chances are it won't be the correct packet number, and it will be discarded. Packet filtering will allow you to block specific types of traffic that you determine; it is covered later in this chapter.

Another benefit of a proxy server is its caching ability. A properly configured proxy server can appear to speed up Internet connections because of the ability to cache frequently visited Web sites. Because these Web sites are stored on the proxy server, the user doesn't have to connect to the Internet to retrieve the information the sites contain. This can also be a cost savings for companies with a per-use WAN billing structure.

One negative aspect to caching is a result of the very thing that also makes it a benefit—the information is stored locally instead of being retrieved from the Internet. If there is a Web site that is updated frequently and your users depend on the time-sensitive material (on stock quotes, for example, like nasdaq.com and etrade.com), you should make sure that the proxy server is configured not to cache those sites; otherwise, they will be viewing old material. This, of course, would depend on whether or not the sites allowed their data to be cached.

When Would You Need a Proxy Server?

Most corporate environments require Internet connectivity of some sort, and that makes it likely that you will need security. You may opt to choose a proxy server or you may choose a firewall. Please note that most modern proxy servers have some sort of firewall mechanism built in, but not all firewalls have the functionality of proxy servers (like Web caching).

Another popular configuration is to cache Web content with a proxy server and use a hardware-based firewall as the corporate security. It is also possible to secure your corporate network with a firewall, and then install a proxy server as a caching server and as a firewall. This way, you can implement a DMZ for e-mail and/or Web servers.

Best-Selling Proxy Servers

There are many proxy server packages currently on the market. Table 2.1 lists some of the best-selling packages, as well as some of their features.

Table 2.1 Popular Proxy Servers

Vendor/ Product	Protocols Supported	Platform	Features
Avirt Gateway	Hypertext Transfer Protocol (HTTP), HTTP Secure (HTTPS), File Transfer Protocol (FTP), Network News Transfer Protocol (NNTP), Post Office Protocol 3 (POP3), Simple Mail Transfer Protocol (SMTP), Telnet, SOCKS 4/5, Real Audio, Domain Name System (DNS), Point-to-Point Tunneling Protocol (PPTP), Internet Relay Chat (IRC), Proprietary Streaming video technology (VDO Live), Called Subscriber Identification (CSI) 3/4, WinCIM (CompuServe's GUI interface)	Windows 9x/NT/2000 Client support for Windows/ Mac/UNIX/Linux	■ Integration with Integrated Services Digital Network (ISDN), digital subscriber line (DSL), T1, or T3 ■ Automatic client configuration ■ Automatic proxy detection ■ Firewall security ■ Dial on Demand ■ Dynamic Host Configuration Protocol (DHCP) Server and DNS relay ■ NAT/NPAT

Continued

Table 2.1 Continued

Vendor/ Product	Protocols Supported	Platform	Features
Infopulse Pro GateKeeper	HTTP, FTP, Telnet, Real Audio, Socks 4/5, POP 3, Secure Sockets Layer (SSL), Mapped Link (Transmission Control Protocol or TCP), Mapped Port (User Datagram Protocol or UDP)	Windows NT Client support for Windows 9x/NT/2000	■ DHCP Server ■ NAT/NPAT ■ Customer Application Programming Interface (API): Allows customers to program their own proxy ■ Dial on Demand ■ Traffic tracking and management on a user/group basis
CSM Proxy Server	HTTP, FTP, SOCKS 4/5, Internet Mail Access Protocol (IMAP) 4, POP 3, Telnet, SSL	Windows NT	■ Firewall ■ Virus Scanning (McAfee) ■ Active-X Blocking ■ Java Blocking ■ Support for Sequel Net Access Manager ■ SMTP Command Filtering ■ NAT/NPAT ■ News Filtering ■ Support for Cache Array Routing Protocol (CARP) ■ Virtual private net-work (VPN)

Continued

Table 2.1 Continued

Vendor/Product	Protocols Supported	Platform	Features
Vicomsoft Internet Gateway	HTTP, FTP, SOCKS 4/5, IMAP 4, POP 3, Telnet, SSL, MacIP (IP encapsulated in AppleTalk)	Windows 9x/NT/2000 MacOS Client support for Win 9x/NT/2000/MacOS	■ Integration with ISDN, DSL, T1, Point-to-Point Protocol over Ethernet (PPPoE) ■ Firewall ■ DNS caching ■ Fallback server redundancy ■ DHCP server ■ RAS server ■ CyberNOT content filtering ■ NAT/NPAT ■ Multisite Web hosting
Microsoft Proxy Server 2.0 (see Chapter 7 for more information)	HTTP, FTP, SOCKS, Gopher, SSL, IMAP 4, NetShow, Real Audio, Telnet	Windows NT Client support for Windows 9x/NT/2000/MacOS/UNIX	■ Dynamic Packet Filtering ■ Firewall ■ Reverse Proxy ■ NAT/NPAT ■ Server proxy (shielded apps such as Exchange) ■ Web caching using CARP or daisy chaining ■ Hierarchical caching ■ SSL Tunneling ■ VPN

Please note that this is not an absolute listing of the features and functions of the proxy servers, just a subset. Additional information on any of these products may be obtained at the vendor's Web site:

- **Avirt Gateway** www.avirt.com/gateway
- **Infopulse Pro GateKeeper** www.proxy-pro.com
- **CSM Proxy Server** www.csm-usa.com/product/proxy
- **Vicomsoft Internet Gateway** www.vicomsoft.com/vig/vig.main.html
- **Microsoft Proxy Server 2.0** www.microsoft.com/proxy/default.asp

Pros and Cons of Proxy Servers

Like everything else, proxy servers have both good and bad points. The first good point, as discussed, is that they speed up Web access by caching downloaded content, which allows faster user access to information. They also provide network security with filters, NAT/NPAT, and other firewall features. They are available at a relatively low cost compared with other hardware-based firewall solutions. Last, they provide logging mechanisms for inbound and outbound data and connections.

The problem with proxy servers is that they can have high administration requirements in larger networks, especially if set up in a large array (Cache Array Routing Protocol, or CARP); they also add another point of failure into your network design, and can cause problems with proprietary network applications. In the instance of CARP, proxy networking can become complex quickly and the skill level of the administrator must be higher than average. This will also cause a higher price tag.

Firewall Functionality

The previous section discussed the function of the proxy server and that most have some sort of firewall mechanism built into them. A firewall is hardware and/or software that acts as a protective barrier from anything outside of your network. Firewalls can utilize a technology known as *stateful inspection*. Stateful inspection firewalls keep track of connections through sessions, and analyze incoming packets. These packets are accepted if they are in direct response to an active session. There are several types of firewalls including a packet-filtering firewall, application firewall, and circuit-level firewall. They are all slightly different from each other, but they provide the same basic functionality.

A packet-filtering firewall is designed to grant or deny traffic based on packet-level information, such as TCP or IP headers. Most packet-filtering gateways have the ability to block data based on source or destination address, port number, or protocol. Most routers employ this function, and are commonly referred to as *screening routers*. In Figure 2.3, if the aptly named intruder were to send any information to the network and he was on the packet filter list for source IP address, the packets would be dropped as shown. None of the data that the intruder sends destined for the LAN would ever make it.

Figure 2.3 Packet filtering firewall.

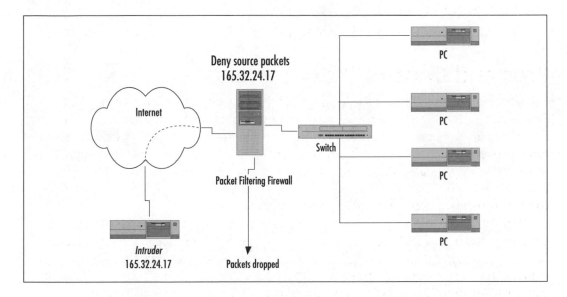

An application firewall, on the other hand, does filter, but it filters at the application level. Applications such as Telnet, FTP, or SMTP could be specifically granted or denied access. Routers can provide this service as well. If we were to deny a specific service, FTP for example, this could be done both inbound and outbound as shown in Figure 2.4. Most proxy servers provide this type of firewall, although some can do all three.

Something else that you will see with application firewalls is the read-dressing we spoke of with the proxy servers. Packets originating from nodes on the LAN will be readdressed so that they appear to originate from the firewall itself. In Figure 2.4, we can see both the denial of the FTP service as well as the readdressing of allowed information.

A circuit-level firewall protects your network in a slightly different way than other firewalls. The circuit-level firewall ensures that a host on the Internet does not have a direct connection to a host on your network. The firewall will accept service requests from local hosts, and will then check for service availability. After it has verified the availability, it will create the session but act as the "middle man," copying the endpoint information back and forth.

Figure 2.4 Application firewall.

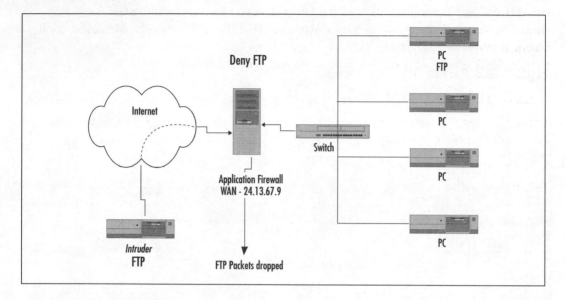

A lot of the firewalls on the market today have one, two, or all three of these functions so you will need to find the firewall that best fits your needs. Selecting a firewall can be tricky, so make sure that you know what kind of solution your network requires.

When Do You Need a Firewall?

Much like a proxy server, you will need to decide when your network requires a firewall solution. If your network requires security, you should think seriously about purchasing a firewall mechanism. There are a couple of questions you can ask yourself:

- What is the budget?
- Do I need Web and content caching ability?
- What applications on my network have proprietary needs?

The budget can play a key role in deciding whether you purchase a software solution, hardware solution, or both. Obviously some of the higher end units will cost you more money. NetBarrier for the Macintosh won't cost you nearly as much as the PIX Firewall from Cisco.

If Web or content caching is required, you may be able to select a proxy server with firewall capabilities. A lot of network administrators actually

opt to go with both. You could secure your network with a firewall, and then place a DMZ between your firewall and a proxy server that is protecting your LAN.

You'll notice that the question of proprietary applications keeps coming up. This is important—a lot of doctor's offices, law firms, banks, and hospitals have applications designed specifically for their needs. If these applications have the need for Internet connectivity, it will be up to you to integrate them into a new or existing infrastructure.

Best-Selling Firewalls

Table 2.2 details some of the popular firewalls, and some of their features. For a more complete listing of features, please refer to the vendor's homepage.

Table 2.2 Best-Selling Firewalls

Vendor/ Product	Protocols	Platform	Features
3Com Office Connect Internet Firewall 25	TCP/IP, DHCP, Internet Control Message Protocol (ICMP), NAT (Request for Comments—RFC— 1631)	Hardware Client support Windows 95, Windows 98, Windows for Workgroups, Windows NT, UNIX, and Mac OS 7.5.3	Protects against: ■ Denial of Service (DoS) ■ Ping of Death ■ SYN flood ■ LAND attack ■ IP spoofing ■ Teardrop ■ Bonk
Axent Technologies Raptor (see Chapter 10 for more information)	TCP/IP, DHCP, DNS, NAT, ICMP, HTTP, SSL, Gopher, SMTP, H.323, Telnet, SQL-Net, NNTP, Network Time Protocol (NTP), Real Audio	Client support Windows NT/ Sun/HP-UX/ Alpha Client support Windows 9x / NT/ MacOS/ UNIX	Protects against: ■ IP Address spoofing attacks TCP SYN Flood attacks ■ IP Source Route attacks ■ IP Fragmentation attacks ■ SMTP backdoor command attacks ■ SMTP buffer overrun attacks ■ Snooping of network traffic

Continued

Table 2.2 Continued

Vendor/ Product	Protocols	Platform	Features
Axent Technologies Raptor (see Chapter 10 for more information)	TCP/IP, DHCP, DNS, NAT, ICMP, HTTP, SSL, Gopher, SMTP, H.323, Telnet, SQL-Net, NNTP, Network Time Protocol (NTP), Real Audio	Client support Windows NT/ Sun/HP-UX/ Alpha Client support Windows 9x / NT/ MacOS/ UNIX	■ TCP Session Hijacking ■ Attacks via download of Java applets ■ TCP Sequence Number Prediction Attacks ■ Information leakage by means of finger, echo, packet internet groper (ping), SMTP and traceroute commands ■ Random port scanning of internal systems ■ Modification of network traffic ■ Large packet ping attacks ■ HTTP cgi-bin wildcard attacks and buffer overrun attacks ■ Password replay attacks
Checkpoint Software Firewall-1 (see Chapter 11 for more information)	TCP/IP, HTTP, FTP, Telnet, Gopher, SSL, S/Key, Terminal Access Controller Access Control System Plus (TACACS+), Remote Dial-In User Service (RADIUS), NAT, PPTP, Lightweight Directory Access Protocol (LDAP)	Client support Sun/Windows NT/HP-UX/ RedHat Linux Client support Microsoft Windows 9x/ NT/Sun Solaris SPARC/HP-UX 10.20 IBM AIX	Protects against: ■ IP Spoofing ■ DoS ■ SYNDefender (for SYN attacks) Employs stateful inspection of packets with Inspect

Continued

Table 2.2 Continued

Vendor/ Product	Protocols	Platform	Features
Cisco Systems Secure PIX Firewall (see Chapter 9 for more information)	TCP/IP, HTTP, FTP, Telnet, SSL, IPSec, VPN support (Layer 2 Forwarding/ Layer 2 Tunneling Protocol or L2F/L2TP), Internet Key Exchange (IKE), TACACS+, RADIUS, SMTP, NAT/NPAT, UDP, ICMP, generic route encapsulation (GRE), DNS, Address Resolution Protocol (ARP), SNMP, Trivial File Transfer Protocol (TFTP), Archie, Gopher, NetBIOS over IP, authentication, authorization, and accounting (AAA), SQL-Net, Real Audio, H.323	Client support Windows 95/NT Client support Microsoft Windows 9x/ NT/UNIX	Protects against: ■ DoS ■ SYN Floods ■ IP Spoofing ■ Filters Java, ActiveX, URLs ■ TCP Session Hijacking ■ Attacks via download of Java applets ■ TCP Sequence Number Prediction Attacks ■ Information leakage by means of finger, echo, ping, SMTP and traceroute
Novell BorderManager Firewall Services	TCP/IP, DHCP, DNS, NAT, HTTP, SSL, Gopher, SMTP, Telnet, ICMP, NNTP, NTP, Real Audio	Novell Client Support Microsoft Windows 9x/NT/MacOS	Protects against: ■ DoS ■ SYN Floods ■ IP Spoofing ■ Filters Java, ActiveX, URLs ■ TCP Session Hijacking

Not all functions of the selected devices have been listed. For more information on the firewalls listed in Table 2.2, you can visit the vendor homepages:

- **3Com Office Connect Internet Firewall 25** www.3com.com/smallbusiness/products/products_firewalls.html

- **Axent Technologies Raptor** www.axent.com

- **Check Point Software Firewall-1** www.checkpoint.com/products/firewall-1/index.html

- **Cisco Systems PIX** www.cisco.com/warp/public/cc/pd/fw/sqfw500/prodlit/pie_ds.htm

- **Novell BorderManager Firewall Services** www.novell.com/products/bordermanager/firewall

Pros and Cons of Firewalls

There are certain pros and cons associated with firewalls. Firewalls add very strong security to your network (if configured correctly), and they can be implemented in a variety of ways. On the other hand, they can be very cost prohibitive, and, because some firewalls require personnel to be very skilled, training could be an added cost. They also may cause problems with proprietary applications.

Setting Up a Demilitarized Zone (DMZ)

Now that we have touched on some technology, we can look at some of the network topology modifications used for security purposes. A DMZ is an area of a network that is separated from your LAN to provide services for the Internet, like a Web server. Refer to Figure 2.5 for a graphic representation of a DMZ.

There are a couple reasons why you could decide to set up a DMZ on your network, but the main reason is to provide different levels of security for different network services. Let's say that you have a Web server on your network that you want the Internet to be able to access. By setting up a DMZ, you can set whatever permissions you want for the Web server, and then lock down the rest of the network from outside access.

Figure 2.5 A demilitarized zone (DMZ).

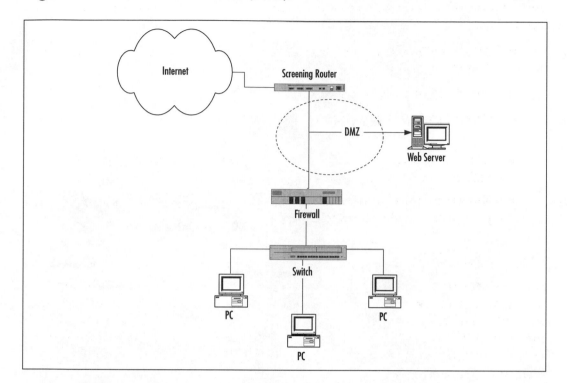

Dead Zones and Protocol Switching

A dead zone is defined as any network segment between two routers that is not running the TCP/IP protocol suite. Generally you will find dead zones used in conjunction with protocol switching.

Protocol switching can be an effective way to protect your network from certain types of attacks. It operates just as the name implies, by switching protocols between routing devices. Refer to Figure 2.6; if you were to switch protocols from IP to IPX, you would be able to thwart most IP-based attacks with that alone. You can also see from this image that we have integrated a firewall, proxy server, DMZ, protocol switching, and a dead zone in the same LAN topology.

Although protocol switching can't protect you from every type of malicious activity, it can help protect your network from attacks like the Ping of Death or SYN flooding because these attacks depend on the TCP/IP suite for operation. Unfortunately things such as distributed denial of service (DDoS) attacks cannot be prevented using protocol switching and dead zones.

Figure 2.6 A dead zone and protocol switching in a LAN.

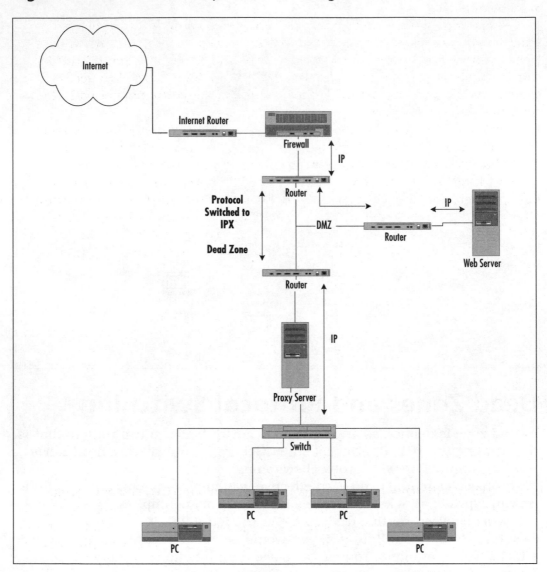

Implementing Port and Packet Filtering

Port and packet filtering can help prevent unauthorized access to your network from outside parties. Packet filtering is implemented at the network layer (Layer 3) of the Open Systems Interconnection (OSI) model, and can provide many ways to filter inbound or outbound packets. If you are using IP, you can filter packets based on many of the fields in the IP header like source address, destination address, source port number, and destination port number.

As previously discussed, packet filtering can allow you to specify exactly who accesses your network and who does not. Keep in mind that packet filters can be set up to work on inbound and/or outbound traffic. For instance, if you do not want IP address 153.26.157.5/16 to access your network, you can set up a packet filter to deny any packet with the specified source address.

You can also set up a packet filter, also on source IP address, to block traffic from an internal source from reaching the Internet. This is especially handy if you don't want certain users to have Internet address.

Port filtering will allow you to filter specific ports, and in essence, specific protocols or applications. For instance, if you want to block outbound FTP traffic, you would set up a port filter on port 20 and 21. Port 20 is used for data and port 21 is used for control. This would allow you to block all FTP requests regardless of the source or destination information within the IP header.

When To Use Packet Filtering

Packet filtering isn't an end-all solution for network security. If it is necessary for you to block a specific source or destination address, be aware of a few things: If the IP address in question is behind a firewall, you could just set up a packet filter for the address of the firewall. However, if you need to allow traffic from other addresses behind that firewall you will have effectively blocked traffic from them as well.

Most firewalls have an explicit deny built into their code, which means if the packet doesn't meet any of the permit requirements, the packet is discarded automatically. For this reason you may be better off setting up packet filters only for outbound access, and allowing the firewall to take care of inbound packets unless you are absolutely sure of the ramifications from your filters.

Table 2.3 lists some of the well-known ports with which you should be familiar.

Table 2.3 Well-known Ports

Protocol	TCP or UDP	Port(s)
HTTP	TCP	80
FTP	TCP	20/21
TFTP	UDP	69
Telnet	TCP	23
SMTP	TCP	25
DNS	TCP	53
POP3	TCP	110
Identd (IRC generally uses 6667-6670)	TCP	113
NNTP	TCP	119
IMAP v4	TCP	143
LDAP	TCP	389
HTTPS over SSL	TCP	443
Routing Information Protocol (RIP)	UDP	520

Design Pitfalls

There are some key points that you should keep in mind when setting up any of the discussed features in this chapter. No matter how obvious they may seem, some of them could prove devastating to your security model.

- Proxy servers or firewalls should never be connected through the same switch on both ports. If you connect the LAN and WAN ports to the same switch, you have just defeated your own network security.

- Public sites such as Web or FTP servers should not be placed on the same segment as the portion of the network that should remain secured. You can separate these by any of the methods we have discussed, such as a DMZ.

- Do not overload your firewall with filters. You should use only filters that are absolutely necessary because access problems become more likely to occur as the number of filters increase. Filters also require hardware time for processing.

- Apply access lists to the edge firewall to protect access to the DMZ, being careful not to overload it. This also applies to the screening router that is being used.

- Use data encryption where possible. Just because your network is secure does not mean that your data is.

- A single firewall or proxy server may not provide enough security. You should design a layered security model that includes multiple security measures for your network.

Design Scenario

Corporate management has asked that you design a network security model that will keep the Web server separate from the rest of the network, but also provides security for both. The requirements are as follows:

1. The Web server must be secure, but separated from the LAN.

2. The network must be able to stop TCP/IP-based attacks.

3. Web content must be cached for frequently accessed Web pages, except for the corporate dashboard (which is updated regularly).

4. (Optional) Ports for FTP, Telnet, and IRC must be disabled for the LAN.

How would you design your network?

Design Scenario Solution

The design is illustrated in Figure 2.7. The first thing to look at is the Web server. Because it needs to be separated from the rest of the network, a DMZ would be a good thing to implement. Next, setting up protocol switching on the network can help to stop most of the TCP/IP-based attacks on your network. Web content needs to be cached, so a proxy server can be put in place for this function. A filter will have to be set on the proxy server to keep from caching the corporate dashboard because it is updated regularly. The other solution would be to set up the dashboard so that it does not allow its content to be cached. Otherwise, you would run the risk of the users getting old information from the dashboard. Finally, block ports 20, 21, 23, and 6667–6670 on the proxy server to keep those protocols from functioning on the LAN. If necessary, you may also need to set up port filters on the switches to keep those same protocols from being used on a peer-to-peer basis.

Figure 2.7 Network security sample design.

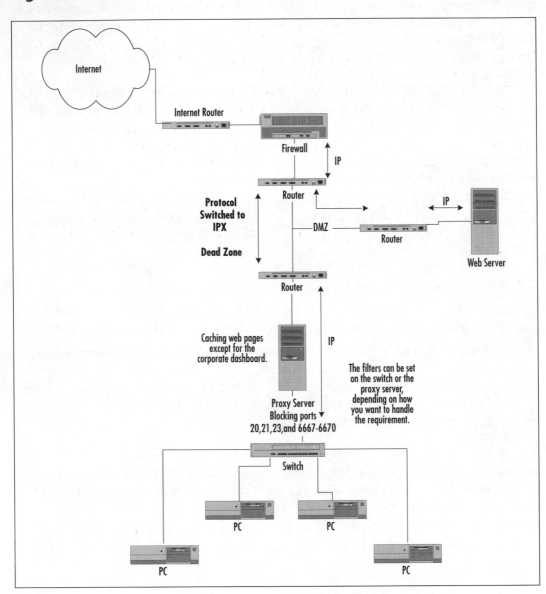

Summary

This chapter has covered some of the main components and techniques for securing your corporate network. Before you select which component(s) you need for your security model, decide how you want to lay it out, what protocols to use, and what hardware/software combinations are within your budget's grasp.

A proxy server can be useful if you are on a limited budget, and if your network requires security as well as Web or content caching. A firewall can be used if you do not need to cache Internet content, but you still require security for your Internet connection. Most security solutions today include both firewall and proxy capabilities, unless it is a specifically designed hardware firewall such as the Cisco PIX.

The use of protocol switching and dead zones, packet and port filtering, as well as DMZs, are several techniques for enabling security on your network at a very low cost. The main thing to remember is not to overload your network hardware with unnecessary protocol and port filters. The more you add, the more likely you are to have performance or connectivity problems from them.

Regardless of your current network status or your department's budget, insist on network security. Whether you get a high-end firewall mechanism or a lower end software package, it will make a huge difference in the event an unauthorized user attempts to get into your system.

FAQs

Q: What is the difference between a proxy server and a firewall?

A: Basically, a firewall is designed to act as a barrier between your network and an insecure network such as the Internet. A proxy server is designed to do the same, but it also adds functionality such as caching. Technically, the differences are becoming fewer and fewer. The newer proxy servers and firewalls are beginning to include the functionality of the other.

Q: I have set up an inbound access filter on a specific IP address and now nobody from the user's company can access our network. What could be causing this problem?

A: Make sure that the source address you have listed in the filter is not actually the edge firewall for that company. Using the firewall's address would effectively block all traffic behind it.

Q: Where can I find a listing of popular network security devices?

A: There are many Web pages out there that catalog and compare network security devices. One of the best listings that I have found is at www.thegild.com/firewall.

Q: Why should I use a DMZ on my network?

A: Why *shouldn't* you!? If your network has a Web server, FTP server, or a public mail server, chances are you should use a DMZ. The point here is that you do not want to have highly trafficked public servers inside your LAN. Allowing access in your LAN area introduces security problems that can easily be remedied by instituting a DMZ. The DMZ will keep high traffic public servers separate from your LAN.

Q: If I use protocol switching on my network, what protocol should I use in place of IP?

A: This decision is up to you. I suggest using something that you are familiar with, can set up easily, and can troubleshoot if necessary. It's common to use something like IPX because it is easy to use and it basically configures itself.

Chapter 3

IPSec

Solutions in this chapter:

- **Comparing IPv4 and IPv6**
- **Security Association (SA)**
- **Authentication Header (AH)**
- **Encapsulating Security Payload (ESP)**
- **Practical Usage**
- **IPSec Security Issues**

Introduction

The protocol that provides the addressing used on the Internet today is Internet Protocol (IP) version 4. In its original Request for Comments (RFC) 791, the designers of IP decided that it would be "specifically limited in scope to provide the functions necessary to deliver a package of bits (an internet datagram) from a source to a destination over an interconnected system of networks." Additionally, it was decided that there would be "no mechanisms to augment end-to-end data reliability, flow control, sequencing, or other services commonly found in host-to-host protocols. The Internet Protocol can capitalize on the services of its supporting networks to provide various types and qualities of service." (See www.ietf.org/rfc/rfc0791.txt?number=791.)

Obviously created during a time of free love and inherent trust for academic and military purposes, there are no mechanisms built into IP to secure the information that it is delivering. In an attempt to correct this *faux pas* for the increasingly security-sensitive corporate and commercial Internet, in November 1998 the Network Working Group of the Internet Engineering Task Force (IETF) put forth RFC 2401. RFC 2401, otherwise known as "Security Architecture for the Internet Protocol (IPSec)," is an attempt to provide security for both IPv4 and IPv6 at the network layer.

This "security" is designed to be highly interoperable and based on cryptographic mechanisms to provide access control, connectionless integrity, data origin authentication, protection against replays, confidentiality, and limited traffic flow confidentiality. By providing these security services at the IP or network layer, the higher layers (transport, session, presentation, and application) will benefit as well.

There are currently several versions of IPSec, due to the lack of a solidified standard from the IETF, but we will try in this chapter to focus on the components and abilities of the proposed IETF standard. It's important to note that since IPv4 was designed long before IPSec was put onto the standards track, it is not a required component of current IP networking. However, security features are already built into the IPv6 standard and should remain through to the final standard.

The IPSec standard is very detailed but its essence can be found in two main components: the Authentication Header (AH) and the Encapsulating Security Payload (ESP). Briefly, the Authentication Header provides authentication and integrity, but not confidentiality, as a means for providing security. The AH also encrypts the source and destination addresses in the IP header, which means that the sender cannot repudiate that it came from him, and the integrity is maintained by ensuring that the data has not been tampered with.

ESP provides authentication, integrity, and confidentiality. The addition here is that the ESP provides encryption on the user data to ensure that only the intended party can decipher the content. We look at both of these components in more depth later in the chapter; first let's review IPv4 and IPv6.

Comparing IPv4 and IPv6

The Internet Protocol is the backbone of the traditional Internet and was created during what I like to call the sticks-and-mud period of computing, the 1980s. Since that time, we've invented the wheel, learned how to toast bread, and discovered how ruthless some people can be in bending standards to their will. IP was never designed to be a protocol with security.

Because IPSec affects the way that IP datagrams look and act, it is important that you understand what IPv4 and IPv6 do. In the following sections, we will take a look at the IP protocol, IP terminology, and its basic operation.

An IPv4 Overview

Internet Protocol version 4 was first defined in IETF RFC 760 in 1980 (which was replaced by RFC 791 in 1981). Created for the Department of Defense in the United States for the Defense Advanced Research Projects Agency (DARPA), IP's original purpose was only to deliver bits from one node to another. IP doesn't care about how the data is sent, in what order, or how it is sequenced. IP would send its bits over interconnected networks and rely on the underlying networks to provide any quality of service mechanisms.

The two core functions of the Internet Protocol are *addressing* and *fragmentation*. A *datagram* (a piece of a message transmitted over a packet-switched network) is passed from one network host to another until it reaches the intended recipient of the data. This passing of data from network to network is called *routing* and is based on the Internet address that it is trying to reach. Sometimes, the datagrams need to pass through networks where the allowed packet size is smaller than the datagram size. Fragmentation is utilized to allow the data to pass through this network.

IP Addressing

IP addresses form the basis for how hosts speak to each other. Just like the address on your house or your phone number, an IP address is a mechanism that allows hosts to locate and speak with each other. In general there are three ways for hosts to find one another: by name, by address, and by route. Simply, a *name* lets us know what we are looking for (for example, MYDBServer), *addresses* tell us where we can find the server (that is, what network it's on), and a route tells us how to get there. IP is *address-based* and uses other protocols to determine how to get to its destination.

To include all the information that would be necessary in IP addresses, they were designed as 32-bit fixed-length binary numbers. Dealing with 32 bits all at once can be daunting; it is common practice to break up or segment it into four 8-bit fields called *octets*. Each octet is represented by a base-10 decimal number from 0 to 255 and separated by a dot (a period). This human readable format is useful for communicating addresses among other humans and machines, but is not useful for calculations for masks or subnets. These calculations need to be performed on the binary equivalent of the decimal address. For example, the IP address of 192.9.55.27 is equivalent to 11000000 00001001 00110111 00011011 in binary.

Each IP address is made up of a network number, and a local address and is divided into three classes based on the size of the network. In a *class A* network, the high-order bit is zero with the next 7 bits (for a total of 8 bits) for the network and last 24 bits (three groups of 8 bits) for the local address. A class A network can have 126 networks and approximately 16,700 hosts per network.

In a *class B* network, the high-order two bits are one-zero (1-0) with the next 14 bits (taking up the first two octets, for a total of 16 bits) representing the network and the last 16 bits for the local address. A class B network can have 16.3k networks with 65,000 hosts per network.

A *class C* network has three high-order bits at 1-1-0 with the next 21 bits for the network and the remaining 8 bits for the local address. A class C network can have over two million networks with 254 hosts per network.

In short, the fewer the bits allocated to the network, the more hosts you can have on that network.

IPv4 Header

The IP packet that is being transmitted across internetworks attaches its own information to help devices along the way to figure out what to do with the packet. The header is shown in Figure 3.1.

The first four-bit version field in the IPv4 header is used to indicate the current version of the Internet Protocol being used. The same field is used in the IPv6 header and is necessary in order to make IPv6 backward-compatible.

The four-bit header length field is necessary for the IPv4 header to indicate the length of the header since the total length of the IPv4 header is a variable length between 20 and 64 bytes, depending on the presence and the length of options in the option field. However, this field is not necessary in an IPv6 header, because an IPv6 header is a fixed length of 40 bytes.

Figure 3.1 The IPv4 header.

	0										1										2										3	
	0	1	2	3	4	5	6	7	8	9	0	1	2	3	4	5	6	7	8	9	0	1	2	3	4	5	6	7	8	9	0	1
0	Version				IHL				Type of Service								Total Length															
1	Identification																Flags			Fragmentation Offset												
2	Time To Live								Protocol								Sequence Number Field															
3	Source Address																															
4	Destination Address																															
5	Options																					Padding										
6	Data																															

The intent of this type of service field in IPv4 is similar to the traffic class field in the IPv6 header. Nevertheless, this field has not been widely accepted and used in IPv4 implementations.

Next, two fields in the IPv4 header—flags and fragmentation offset—are all related to the handling of fragmentation and the reassembly of packets in IPv4. In IPv4, an intermediate hop may further fragment a packet when the maximum transfer unit (MTU) on the outgoing link is smaller than the size of the packet that is to be transmitted on that link. Unlike IPv4, in IPv6, fragmentation processing takes place only at the source node, using a path MTU. Further, information related to fragmentation is encoded in the Fragmentation header as an extension header in an IPv6 packet. Therefore, identification, flags, and fragmentation offset fields are not necessary in the IPv6 header.

In the original design of IPv4, the Time To Live (TTL) field is used to indicate the number of seconds to live in a network, thus preventing packets from being circularly routed, if a circular route exists in a network. However, in implementations, this field is used to limit the number of hops the packet is allowed to visit. At each hop, a router decrements this field, and when this field reaches 0, the packet is removed from the network. In IPv6, this field is renamed to hop limit, a more accurate description of the implementation.

The protocol field, which is used to indicate the next protocol (header) following this IPv4 header, is similar to the Next Header field in the IPv6 header.

The header checksum field is used to maintain the integrity of the IPv4 header. However, the higher layer calculates the checksum again for the entire packet, thus making this field redundant. Therefore, this field is not used in IPv6 header. If applications require a higher degree of integrity, they can achieve it through appropriate use of Authentication Header and Encapsulating Security Payload extension headers.

The source and destination fields in the IPv4 header remain the same in the IPv6, except that the IPv4 node addresses are 32 bits, and the IPv6 node addresses are 128 bits.

The use of options in IPv4 implies that each intermediate node in the path needs to examine the option field in the IPv4 header, although the options may be pertinent only to the destination node. This leads to inefficient router performance when options are used. In IPv6, optional information is encoded in extension headers.

An IPv6 Overview

By the early 1990s, it was clear that the Internet was going to take off. The dramatic increase in usage of the Internet, which stemmed from outside the research community, was clearly not going to go away. Address space delegations increased at an alarming rate, and it was clear that the IPv4 had a foreseeable upper limit in terms of the number of entities it could connect to the ever-increasing worldwide Internet. The IETF, the standards group from which a large portion of Internet technologies emerge, was beginning to see this as a crucial issue. At present, for example, regional numbering authorities, such as the American Registry for Internet Numbers (ARIN), Réseaux IP Européens (RIPE), and the Asia Pacific Network Information Centre (APNIC) are delegating numbers from within the 216/8 network block. In 1996, by contrast, ARIN was delegating only in the 208/8 range. This would mean that just over 150 million hosts were added to the Internet in this three-year span (if delegations and address assignments were made efficiently). We calculate this by raising 2 to the power of 24 (for each /8) and multiplying by 9. Although the Internet *is* growing at an alarming rate, and slowly working its way into our daily life, it is clear that 150 million hosts were not added. There was a major problem with address allocation, even after the efforts of Classless Inter-Domain Routing (CIDR) were implemented. Address space was being wasted. Furthermore, we know that 224/8–239/8 is set aside for multicast, and that 240/8–255/8 is reserved. From this, we can see that we are nearing our end (although some of the addresses in the middle, from 64/8–128/8, are just now being delegated, so it will buy a little more time than expected).

Now we see that not only was there not enough space to take us far beyond the millennium, but also much of the current delegated address space was being wasted. Additionally, a greater need for enhanced network-layer (Layer 3 of the Open System Interconnection, or OSI, stack) features was beginning to emerge—for example, end-to-end encryption, authentication of packets, source-routing, and Quality of Service (QoS). For all of these reasons, it was becoming apparent that a new Internet Protocol was going to have to be conceived and adopted for the future of the Internet.

As people began to see these factors as a reality, many proposals for a new Internet Protocol emerged. The first draft that gained widespread notice was loosely based on the Connection-Less Network Protocol (CLNP), which was based upon another protocol suite, the OSI stack. This stack originally ran on the early Internet, but was quickly replaced by IPv4 when the Internet began to take on size and popularity. The proposal was coined TUBA (TCP/UDP over Bigger Addresses). CLNP does provide for a much larger address range than the current IPv4. Its Network Service Access Point (NSAP) address consisted of 20 octets, and would provide adequate addressing ranges for the Internet's foreseeable future. However, this proposal was rejected because CLNP lacked some of the value-added features that were already installed into the current IP (such as Quality of Service and multicast), and these were determined to be important to the Internet's future growth.

There was a proposal that attempted to create a packet format compatible with current IP, CLNP, and Internetwork Packet Exchange (IPX). Yet another proposal, known as Simple IP Plus (SIPP), simply advocated increasing the current IP addressing format to 64 bits, and fine-tuning some of the feature sets of IPv4, as well as establishing better routing strategies. SIPP turned out to be the closest match for what the Internet needed, after some modifications. The addressing range was changed from 64 to 128 bits, and the name was changed to IP version 6 (IPv5 was already delegated to another protocol). This would be the protocol to solve the Internet scalability problems, and put us into the next millennium. As of this writing, IPv6 is still on the standards track and has not been fully ratified. Refer to the IETF Web site for updated information on Internet Official Protocol Standards.

Expanded Addressing

IPv4 uses 32-bit addresses, which potentially can address up to 2^{32} nodes. However, the combination of network and local address hierarchy and reserved address space for special handling such as loopback and broadcast reduces the number of addressable nodes. At the same time, the exponential growth of computer networks in recent years indicates the outgrowth of addressable nodes using 32-bit addresses.

Furthermore, the network and local address hierarchy in IPv4 address architecture lead to inefficient use of address spaces. For instance, an organization that needs far fewer than 2^{16} hosts, but more than 2^8 hosts, may waste much usable address space when a using two-octet network address and a two-octet local address.

Despite the inefficiency of network address hierarchy, a flat network address (e.g., a sequential address assignment) is not realistic, since network operations such as routing would be impossible. When using a sequential address assignment, the size of routing tables would be unmanageable and routing would become a slow process because of the amount of data that needs to be scanned.

The IPv6 address size has been increased to 128 bits. The advantages of this increase are, first, more addressable nodes, and second, the ability to support more levels of addressing hierarchy. Better addressing hierarchy leads to more efficient network operations and network scaling. As more networks are added, the size of the routing table increases, and the routing process takes longer. A careful planning of addressing hierarchy can limit the growth of the size of the routing table, while routing packets efficiently. An organizational change often means configuration changes at each node that is affected. For instance, when an organization obtains a new Internet service provider (ISP) (which results most often in a network address change), each node in the organization must be reconfigured to reflect this. However, despite continuous efforts of developing autoconfiguration mechanisms such as Dynamic Host Configuration Protocol (DHCP), the reconfiguration process often needs to be done manually. The larger address space can support autoconfiguration better.

In addition to increased address size, IPv6 eliminated broadcast address and added the notion of an anycast address, which can be used to send a packet to any one of a group of nodes.

Simplified Header

IPv6 has evolved from the IPv4 technology; experiences learned from the IPv4 technology are reflected in the design of IPv6. The length of the IPv4 header varies between 20 and 60 bytes, and there are 11 fields within the first 20 bytes of the IPv4 header. The complexity of IPv4 can lead to inefficient router operations. By employing a simpler header, eight fields in 40 bytes, and fixed length of the header, IPv6 can enhance the performance of routers.

A couple of fields in the IPv4 header have been either removed or embedded in extension headers. Since options are embedded in extension headers, the length of the IPv6 header is no longer variable, thus eliminating the need for the Header Length field in the IPv6 header. In IPv6, only source node can perform fragmentation; therefore, the information necessary for fragmentation and reassembly is removed from IP header. Since the upper layer protocol such as Transmission Control Protocol (TCP) and User Datagram Protocol (UDP) calculates the checksum for the entire packet, the Checksum field also can be removed from the IP header.

Improved Support for Extension and Option

Since the total length of the IPv4 header is variable, the Header Length field is used to indicate its length. The number of bits in this field, four bits, determines the maximum length of the IPv4 header. In particular, 60 bytes is the largest size of the IPv4 header, for this field specifies the header length in four-octet units. Since the fixed portion of the IPv4 header is 20 bytes long, it places a stringent requirement on the length of options.

Length of Addressing Options in IPv4

The limit on the length of options has eliminated some options (such as the routing option), because they are ineffective in an IPv4 network.

Aside from the limit on their length, options are examined at every router on the path, when included. However, often these options include information applicable only to the destination node. Including such options in the IPv4 header forces each router on the path to examine the packet, thus leading to inefficient router operations.

By embedding options in extension headers, the option length limit has been relaxed greatly, and options can be used more effectively in IPv6. Use of a proper extension header in IPv6 allows a packet to carry optional information that is applicable only to its destination node as well as to all intermediate routers more efficiently. The proper extension also allows hardware memory lookups, since the headers are fixed.

Flow and Flow Labeling

IPv4 was designed to be connectionless (or stateless); in other words, each packet belonging to the same session is routed independently, and two packets from the same session may arrive at the destination via different paths.

This approach works well under error-prone networks, such as the time when IPv4 was being developed. There is a cost associated with this, however—processing each packet at every hop adds to the delay, and it is not trivial to provide special services for a communication between selected source and destination.

With technological advances in networking, network failures, especially hardware failures, have been drastically reduced in recent years. Also, new applications are more tolerant to errors, but more sensitive to fluctuations in delay. It is inevitable that networks support such applications. In the design of IPv6, the notion of a flow has been incorporated in order to facilitate special handling of data belonging to an application with special requirements.

RFC 1883 defines a *flow* as a sequence of packets sent from a particular source to a particular destination for which the source desires special handling by the intervening routers. IPv6 provides a framework for an easier per-flow handling. For example, a video application, which may have strict requirements on the maximum delay difference, may take advantage of flow and flow labeling in IPv6. The application marks each packet with a flow label, and routers on the path remember the state of packet transmissions on this flow. This state information will help a router to determine which packet to service next. A router may service a packet that has the largest elapse time since its previous packet in the flow, for instance.

IPv6 Header

The IPv6 header, illustrated in Figure 3.2, is fixed in length and aligned at eight-octet boundary, unlike the IPv4 header, which is variable length and aligned at four-octet boundary. Most modern computer architectures are optimized to read eight octets at a time. Thus, the length of the IPv6 header or extension headers is designed to be a multiple of eight-octets for eight-octet alignment. With a fixed IPv6 header, a router can efficiently process a packet. For instance, a router must decide if there are any options in an IPv4 packet by reading the Header Length field. Processing a variable length header leads to inefficient router implementation.

Figure 3.2 IPv6 header.

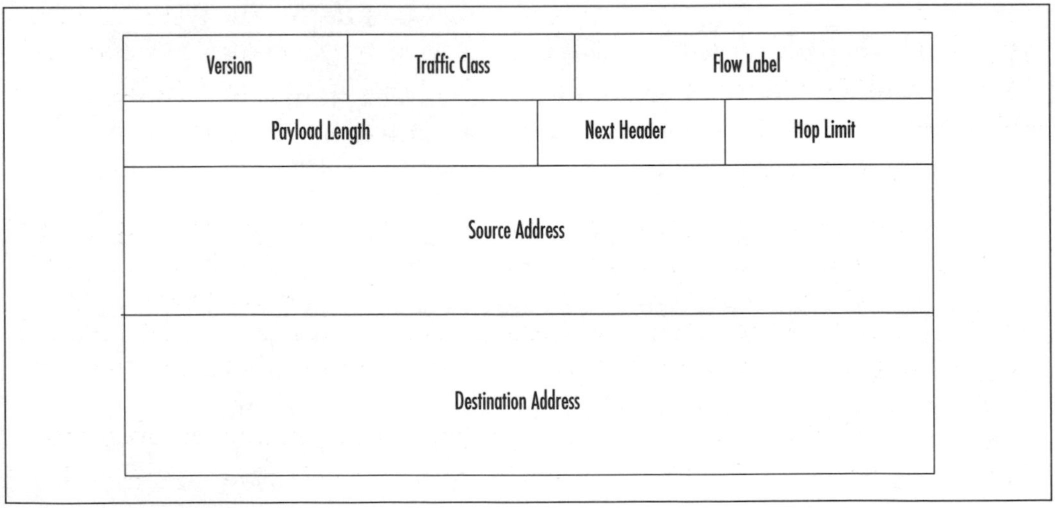

Version	Traffic Class	Flow Label	
Payload Length		Next Header	Hop Limit
Source Address			
Destination Address			

The IPv6 header stores the information necessary to route and deliver packets to their destination. The headers are processed by each node along the path. The first 4-bit field, *version*, indicates the version of the Internet Protocol being used, and its value is 6 for IPv6. This field is necessary because it allows both protocols to coexist on the same segment without conflicts. The next two fields, *traffic class* and *flow label*, are used to provide differentiated services and support applications requiring special handling per-flow. The 8-bit traffic class field can be used to provide differentiated services based on the nature of data being transmitted. This field is similar to the intended use of the type of service field in the IPv4 header. For instance, an organization may set up its network to prioritize network traffic based on applications, source and destination information, etc., and hosts and/or routers use the traffic class field to differentiate the priority. The values and the exact use of this field are yet to be determined. The flow label in combination with source and destination addresses can uniquely identify a flow that requires special handling by intermediate routers. When a router identifies a flow the first time, it remembers the flow and any special handling this flow requires. Once per-flow handling has been set up, the processing of subsequent packets belonging to this flow can be shorter than processing individual packets. The 16-bit *payload length* field, similar to the total length field in the IPv4 header, indicates the length of the packet, not including the length of the IPv6 header. The 8-bit *next header* field is used to indicate the next header following the IPv6 header. The intended use of this field is identical to the use of the protocol field in the IPv4 header. The *hop limit* can be used to limit the number of intermediate hops a packet is allowed to visit, which can prevent packets from being circularly routed in a network. In IPv4, the Time-To-Live field has been used to prevent packets from being routed circularly. The name of this field has been chosen to reflect accurately the purpose of this field. As in IPv4 headers, IPv6 headers contain *source* and *destination* IP addresses. Unlike IPv4 nodes, IPv6 nodes use 128-bit addresses.

Pros and Cons

Both IPv4 and IPv6 attempt to do similar jobs, but IPv6 has the advantage of being created at the cusp of the Internet revolution. IPv6 is a far superior protocol in that it has expanded the scope of addresses possible by jumping from 32-bit to 128-bit addresses. Along with a wider addressable range IPv6 improves on multicast routing and the introduction of the anycast.

From a technical perspective, the header is much simplified over IPv4 and it reduces the cost involved in processing and handling. Options in the header are more efficient and introduce less stringent limitations on their length. As we will talk about in more depth, IPv6 adds authentication and privacy capabilities supporting data integrity and data confidentiality.

A particularly troublesome feature of IPv4 is that it does not have any implicit support for flows. Because of this, routers along the pathway that a datagram is following must rely on TCP to identify the flow information.

Routers along the path that an IP datagram will traverse are required to identify packets from different data streams in order to process them according to their desired needs. The problem is that IPv4 does not directly support the concept of flows and intervening routers have to make use of the transport protocol or application level data to achieve proper packet classification.

Because routers should process data only at the network layer, they require information from the transport or application protocol (i.e., socket ports) to map packets on to their reserved resources. This introduces what is known as the *layer violation problem*.

The layer violation drastically affects network performance since accessing higher layer protocol information to distinguish different flows of the same host pair is an expensive operation, especially in IPv6 networks.

Additionally IPv4 has two main disadvantages over IPv6 with respect to end-to-end transmission performance. The first is the resource-intensive checksum handling that must be computed at every hop along the way; the second is the way in which the option field is processed. IPv6 introduces Extension Headers, which ensures that routers process only what they need to from the datagram, solving the version 4 shortcomings.

Security Association (SA)

Before any IPSec tunnel or authentication can be performed, the two hosts/gateways communicating with each other first must decide if IPSec is required and then negotiate how the encryption and other attributes will be handled. What is required is a protocol that can (as stated in RFC 2408, "Internet Security Association and Key Management Protocol" or ISAKMP) "negotiate, establish, modify and delete Security Associations and their attributes" for an environment, like the Internet, where a plethora of security mechanisms and options exist.

ISAKMP defines "the procedures for authentication a communicating peer, creation and management of Security Associations, key generation techniques, and threat mitigation." It is ISAKMP that defines, creates, and deletes *Security Associations* (SA)—which contain all the information necessary for the execution of network security services (e.g., IPSec Authentication Header).

Although ISAKMP is responsible for supplying the consistent framework under which encryption keys are transferred, it is *not* the same as a "key exchange" protocol. Additionally, the ISAKMP protocol is not responsible for key generation, encryption algorithms, or authentication mechanisms. ISAKMP is responsible for supporting the negotiation of SAs at all levels of the OSI model, and its centralization of management of SAs reduces the amount of duplicated functionality within each security protocol.

A Security Association is a one-way connection that defines the security services that the traffic traveling through it will be using. Security services are granted to an SA through the use of the *Authentication Header (AH)* or *Encrypting Security Payload (ESP)*, but not both. When using more than one security mechanism simultaneously, then two (or more) SAs are created to afford protection to the traffic stream. To secure typical, bi-directional communication between two hosts, or between two security gateways, two SAs (one in each direction) are required.

Because there are two types of IPSec tunnels that can be created (host to gateway and gateway to gateway) there are two distinct types of SAs that can be defined: *transport mode* and *tunnel mode*. A transport mode SA, or an SA between two hosts, the security header appears immediately after the IP header in IPv4 and after the base IP header and extensions in IPv6 (see the Authentication Header section for more information).

A tunnel mode SA is an SA applied to an IP tunnel. The general rule for tunnel mode is that if either end of the association is a security gateway the SA must be a tunnel mode SA. For the determination of what a "gateway" is you need to look at what activities the host is performing. If the host in question is transitioning traffic it is a *gateway*. If the host is the destination for the datagrams in question, it is a host and will not require the tunnel mode SA. This distinction is made due to packet fragmentation and reassembly. If there are multiple paths to an *inside* destination via different security gateways, the datagrams should be allowed to pass through without reassembly.

In a tunnel mode SA there are two IP headers—one for the outer portion that tells the datagram where the IPSec processing destination is, and an inner header that tells the datagram what the ultimate destination for the data is.

SA Functionality

What the SA does and how it operates is dependent on several factors: the security protocol selected, the SA mode, the endpoints of the SA, and on the optional services within the protocol. An example of this is the granularity of the security in an IP datagram. AH provides "data origin authentication and connectionless integrity," but the precision of the authentication service is determined by the SA with which the Authentication Header is employed.

Through the use of sequence integrity, AH offers anti-replay services at the discretion of the receiver (the receiver always determines if anti-replay is engaged, but regardless of whether it is used or not, the AH *sequence number* field is always set to zero when a communication starts and increments upwards by one). Because AH is not responsible for encrypting datagrams, it is a good choice for communications that need content integrity but not confidentiality.

IP packets transmitted via a single SA can either be protected by AH or ESP, but not both. When a combination of security policies is called for, multiple SAs must be employed in a "security association bundle." SAs in the bundle may terminate at different endpoints but they are combined typically in one of two ways:

- **Transport Adjacency** This refers to the application of more than one security protocol to the same IP datagram, without the use of a tunnel. As you can see in Figure 3.3, the use of two security protocols requires the use of two SAs, even though the communication channel exists between only two hosts.

Figure 3.3 Transport adjacency.

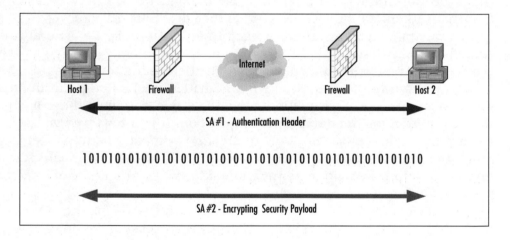

- **Iterated Tunneling** This refers to the application of multiple layers of security protocols through IP tunneling. As shown in Figure 3.4, SA 1 and SA 2 include discreet datastream between the endpoints, each within an IPSec tunnel of their own.

This section taught you that a Security Association is required for IPSec communications because it is what determines the security language that the hosts or gateways will use to converse with each other.

Figure 3.4 Iterated tunneling.

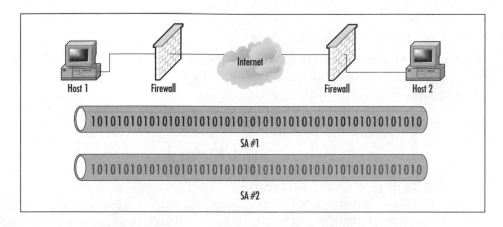

Concentrated ISAKMP

We already talked a little bit about ISAKMP, but it's important that we talk just a little bit more, to allow us to get a complete picture of the Security Association. Going back to our RFC resource for a minute, the ISAKMP protocol allows us to combine the security concepts of authentication, key management, and security associations to create the required security for communications over the Internet or other public networks. SAs are a core component of the key management protocol and are linked with the authentication and key exchange process. When hosts or gateways set up for secure communication, they must first come to an agreement on the initial security attributes. It's through this secure channel that ISAKMP communicates its subsequent messages. As stated by RFC 2408, this initial security also "indicates the authentication method and key exchange that will be performed as part of the ISAKMP protocol." After all the upfront and basic security attributes have been set up (identities authenticated, keys generated, and so on), this SA can be used for ongoing communications.

Strong authentication must be used in ISAKMP exchanges. A strong authenticator is something that is verifiable and difficult to impersonate or substitute. ISAKMP requires the use of digital certificates and digital signatures to provide the strong level of authentication required. Without being able to be certain of the authenticity of the entity at the other end of IPSec communication, the SA and session key established are suspect. Additionally, though encryption and integrity will protect all the session communications, without being able to properly authenticate the other end, you could be communicating securely with "the Enemy."

ISAKMP requires the use of digital certificates, but it also has the ability to allow secondary authentication through optional authentication mechanisms. It provides the protections for secure communications described in the following sections.

Prevention from Denial of Service Attacks

Denial of Service (DoS) attacks are very difficult to protect against since they use the basics of IP to overload devices listening for connections. (An attacker can send partially formed packets to a device listening for connections and cause it to be in a *wait* state until it times out the connection. Send a few thousand of these connections and you have effectively denied legitimate users from connecting.) ISAKMP uses a *cookie* or anti-clogging token (ACT) that is aimed at protecting the computing resources from attack, and it does so without spending excessive CPU resources to determine its authenticity. By performing an exchange prior to CPU-intensive public key operations, you can thwart some Denial of Service attempts (such as simple flooding with bogus IP source addresses). Absolute protection against Denial of Service is impossible, but this goes a long way for making it easier to handle

Connection Hijacking

Connection hijacking refers to the ability of attackers to insert themselves into a trusted data stream between two hosts, effectively negating the need to hack at accounts or passwords. Because the session is already established and the two hosts are communicating with each other, when the attackers insert themselves they can take over the connection or desynchronize the hosts, causing the connection to drop. ISAKMP can prevent this type of attack by linking the authentication, key exchange, and security association exchanges. This linking prevents an attacker from allowing the authentication to complete and then jumping in and impersonating one entity to the other during the key and security association exchanges.

Man-in-the-Middle Attacks

A man-in-the-middle (MITM) attack occurs when two hosts who are communicating with each other are actually talking with a third party, impersonating the other hosts. MITM attacks are difficult to pull off but are powerful because the middle-man can alter data and make it appear that it came from a legitimate communication partner. Consider a communication with your bank to transfer $100 between accounts. A MITM can alter the stream so that you just transferred $10,000 to his account. In summary, man-in-the-middle attacks include interception, insertion, deletion, and modification of messages; reflecting messages back at the sender; replaying old messages; and redirecting messages. ISAKMP can prevent these types of attacks from being successful by preventing the insertion of messages in the protocol exchange. ISAKMP requires the use of strong authentication and can prevent an SA from being established with anyone other than the intended party. Messages may be redirected to a different destination or modified but this will be detected and an SA will not be established. ISAKMP defines where abnormal processing has occurred and can notify the appropriate party of this abnormality.

Authentication Header (AH)

As defined in IETF RFC 2402 (www.ietf.org/rfc/rfc2402), the Authentication Header (AH) is "used to provide connectionless integrity and data origin authentication for IP datagrams and to provide protection against replays." In this section we will discuss how AH does what it does, and what it means to IPSec and your encrypted communications. In the process we will interleave information regarding *Encapsulating Security Payload* (ESP) and *Security Association* (SA).

IPSec tunnels have several methods of implementation, each requiring a slightly different security implementation. The two most common are host-to-gateway and gateway-to-gateway, the former being a tunnel created between a remote host machine and a network and the latter being two (or more) networks connected via a tunnel. Additionally, the industry has two phrases for the method in which IPSec has been implemented.

A "Bump-in-the-stack" (BITS) refers to when IPSec has been implemented below an existing IP stack—between it and the network drivers. This type of implementation is used with host-based tunnel creation since it easily slips into the communication channel via a third-party driver. When in host or *transport* mode, the AH is placed after the IP header, but before the upper layer protocol or any other IPSec headers (see Figure 3.5). When used with IPv6, AH is considered to be an *end-to-end* payload and will appear after routing and extension headers (see Figure 3.6).

Figure 3.5 IPv4 before and after AH insertion.

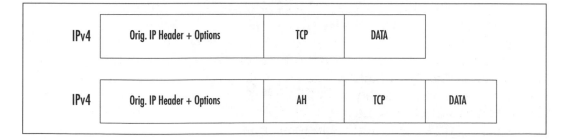

Figure 3.6 IPv6 before and after AH insertion.

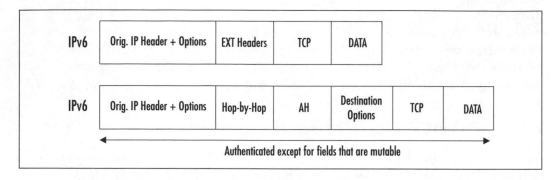

A "Bump-in-the-wire" (BITW) refers to when IPSec has been implemented as an outside process or device (such as a network encryptor). The device can service both gateways and hosts, and although it's reachable as a network node, its presence is similar to a gateway in that all traffic for the IPSec tunnel is passed through it with little intervention from the host. Regardless of where the tunnel is created (host or gateway), the datagram in question must be transformed with the AH so that it may be secured.

By placing the AH in the datagram prior to the data payload, it is possible to determine if the packet has been tampered with in transit. In the next section we will take a look at what is contained in the Authentication Header, and how you can prevent over-the-wire interference with your datagrams.

Authentication Header Format

The Authentication Header depicted in Figure 3.7 follows the same structure and format for implementations in IPv4 and 6. The changes between protocol versions are within the header fields themselves.

Figure 3.7 The AH Header.

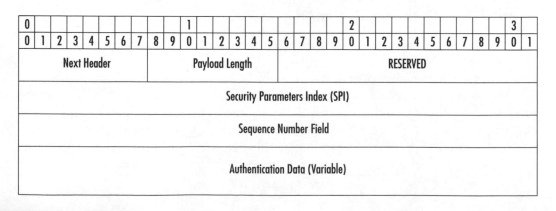

The basic breakdown of the header is as follows

Next Header An 8-bit field that identifies the type of the next payload after the Authentication Header.

Payload Length An 8-bit field composed of 32 bit-words describing the length of the AH.

Reserved A 16-bit field that is reserved for future use. Because of this, it must be set to zero or the packet will be dropped.

Security Parameters Index (SPI) A random 32-bit value that is used to identify the SA for a datagram when used in combination with the destination IP address and security protocol. It is ordinarily selected by the destination system upon establishment of an SA. This unsigned 32-bit field contains an increasing counter value or sequence number. This value is mandatory and is always present even if the receiver does not elect to enable the anti-replay service for a specific SA. The decision to use the Sequence Number field is determined by the receiver, so even if the sender sends it, the destination may choose to ignore it.

The counter values are all set to zero at the time of the establishment of the SA. If anti-replay is enabled (the default), the transmitted Sequence Number must never be allowed to cycle.

Authentication Data A variable-length field that contains the Integrity Check Value (ICV) for this packet. This field must always be an integer in multiples of 32 bits in length and can include padding. The padding is to ensure that the value length meets the 32-bit requirement.

Understanding the ICV

During the transit of the datagram, several of the header fields may be altered to reflect its progress to the final destination. The ICV, which is integral to determining tampering while in transit, is calculated from the immutable or predictable fields in the datagram header, the actual AH header, and upper level protocol data. For every header field that can be altered while in transit, the ICV gives it a zero value (for the purpose of the computation). For every header field that is alterable, but whose value is predictable, ICV uses that value for the computation.

ICV keeps mutable and unpredictable fields at a value of zero for two reasons. First, by keeping a value associated with alterable fields instead of removing a value all together, the ICV can keep the calculation aligned with the placement of the fields. Second, by including a zero value it defeats the insertion of a new value in the unused fields for the purpose of the ICV calculation.

Table 3.1 depicts the fields that are immutable, mutable but predictable, and mutable and zeroed out for the purposes of ICV calculations, for IPv4 and Ipv6.

Table 3.1 Mutable and Immutable Fields for IPv4 and IPv6

Field Type	Field	IP Version
Immutable	Version	v4, v6
	Internet Header Length	v4
	Total Length	v4
	Identification	v4
	Protocol	v4
	Source Address	v4, v6
	Destination Address	v4, v6
	Payload length	v6
	Next Header	v6
Mutable but Predictable	Destination Address	v4, v6
Zeroed Out	Type of Service	v4
	Flags	v4
	Fragment Offset	v4
	TTL	v4
	Header Checksum	v4
	Class	v6
	Flow Label	v6
	Hop Limit	v6

Packet Processing

During transmission, IP packets can be fragmented, but the Authentication Header is applied only to whole IP datagrams (so defragmentation must occur prior to processing).

When an IP datagram appears at the receiving host, if it is marked for AH processing it must be unfragmented or else it will be discarded. Packets marked for AH must be reassembled before reaching the IPSec host or gateway that will process the packet.

Once a proper packet that is marked for AH processing is received, the receiver must determine the appropriate SA (based on the destination IP address, the security protocol, and the SPI). If no SA can be determined for the packet, it must be discarded.

If sequence numbers are being used (the sequence number value is always calculated and updated, but the destination node determines if it will refer to that value) the receiving station resets the value in the SA to zero at the start of the conversation. Each packet that is received must be checked for the sequence number to make sure it has not been duplicated or that it is not out of order. Duplicate packets or packets with incorrect sequencing are rejected. If the packet appears to be correct (for example, it is not lower in sequence than the last received packet, and it falls within the window of acceptable sequence numbers), the receiving station performs ICV verification. Any failure while checking ICV will require the packet to be discarded. The sequence window is updated only if the packet passes ICV verification.

The receiver can validate the ICV by saving the ICV value, zeroing out all other fields modified in transit, and pushing the result through an algorithm. If the computed result equals the saved result, the ICV is validated.

Encapsulating Security Payload (ESP)

Encapsulating Security Payload (ESP) is documented in IETF RFC 2406 (www.ietf.org/rfc/2406) and is designed to provide confidentiality, authentication of the sender, data integrity, and anti-replay services. ESP can be used on its own or in conjunction with the Authentication Header in either IPv4 or IPv6. As with other IPSec protocols, what ESP provides is dependent on what the Security Association requires of it. It is important to note, however, that the use of confidentiality *without* the use of authentication could create a situation where you are securely sending data to a compromised or unintended recipient.

The ESP Header format, depicted in Figure 3.8, is broken out as follows:

Security Parameters Index (SPI) In conjunction with the destination IP address and security protocol to identify the Security Association for the datagram. This field is 32 bits and is set to zero for local functions. Zero means that there is no SA yet.

Sequence Number An unsigned 32-bit field that increments in a monotonic fashion. This field is mandatory and is always present, even if the destination host does not require sequencing for anti-replay. At the beginning of the conversation, the counter is set to zero and the first packet will receive a value of 1. If anti-replay is enabled (the default), the transmitted Sequence Number must never be allowed to cycle. The sender's counter and the receiver's counter *must* be reset (by establishing a new SA and thus a new key) prior to the transmission of the 2^{32} packet on an SA.

Payload Data A field of variable length that contains data described by the Next Header field. The Payload Data field is mandatory and is an integral number of bytes in length. In the case where the encryption algorithm used to encrypt the payload requires synchronization data (otherwise known as an Initialization Vector) then that data can be explicitly carried in the Payload field.

Figure 3.8 ESP Header format.

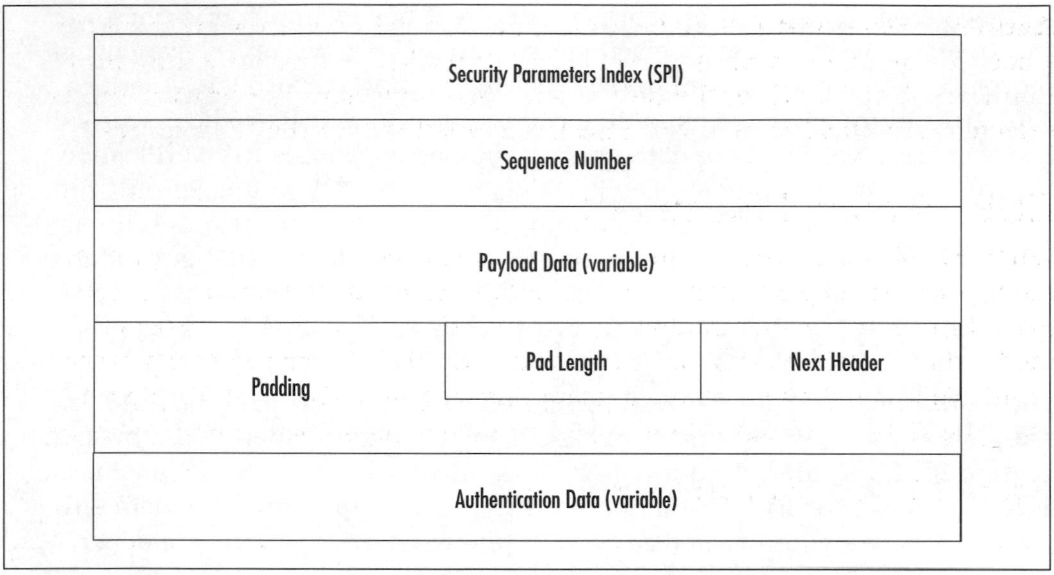

Security Parameters Index (SPI)		
Sequence Number		
Payload Data (variable)		
Padding	Pad Length	Next Header
Authentication Data (variable)		

Padding (for Encryption) There are several reasons that padding would be required:

- If an encryption algorithm is employed that requires the plain text to be a multiple of some number of bytes, for example, the block size of a block cipher, the Padding field is used to fill the plain text (consisting of the Payload Data, Pad Length, and Next Header fields, as well as the Padding) to the size required by the algorithm.

- Padding also may be required, irrespective of encryption algorithm requirements, to ensure that the resulting ciphertext terminates on a 4-byte boundary. Specifically, the Pad Length and Next Header fields must be right-aligned within a 4-byte word, as illustrated in the ESP packet format in Figure 3.8, to ensure that the Authentication Data field (if present) is aligned on a 4-byte boundary.

- Padding beyond that required for the algorithm or alignment reasons just cited may be used to conceal the actual length of the payload, in support of (partial) traffic flow confidentiality. However, inclusion of such additional padding has adverse bandwidth implications and thus its use should be undertaken with care.

Pad Length A mandatory field indicating how many bytes are immediately preceding it.

Next Header A mandatory field, 8 bits in length, indicating the type of data contained in the Payload field.

Authentication Data Variable in length, this field contains an Integrity Check Value (ICV) computed over the ESP packet minus the Authentication Data. The length of the field is specified by the authentication function selected. This field is optional, and is included only if the SA requires it.

ESP Header Placement

When ESP is employed on an IP datagram (either in transport or tunnel mode—see the explanation of these modes earlier in the chapter) it gets placed in the IP header similar to the way AH is. For IPv4 in transport mode (that is, host-to-host), ESP provides protection for the upper layer protocols but not the IP header itself. This requires that ESP be placed after the IP header and before upper protocols, as shown in Figure 3.9.

Figure 3.9 ESP Header placement in IPv4.

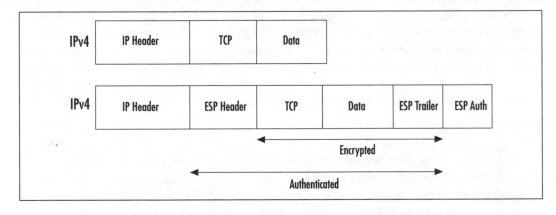

The IPv6 implementation is similar, but because ESP is an end-to-end payload, it needs to appear after the hop-by-hop, routing and extension headers (see Figure 3.10). ESP protects only fields after the ESP header.

ESP Encryption and Authentication

ESP, which is used for both confidentiality and authentication, uses encryption algorithms that have been specified in the SA. ESP uses *symmetric encryption* that is attached to every packet (because packets can arrive out of order) so that the receiving station can decrypt them. For clarity, encryption that is termed "symmetric" utilizes the same passphrase for the plain-text to ciphertext transition as for the ciphertext to plain-text transition.

Figure 3.10 ESP Header placement in IPv6.

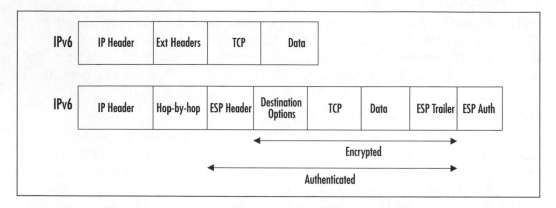

ESP encryption can be either *block* or *stream*, which refers to the way that the data becomes encrypted.

Block Cipher A block cipher is a type of symmetric-key encryption algorithm that encrypts a fixed-length block of unencrypted data into a block of encrypted data of the same length. Because of the nature of symmetric-key, this transformation takes place through the use of a user-provided secret key. Decryption is performed by applying the reverse transformation to the ciphertext block using the same secret key. The "block" refers to the fixed length, which is typically 64 bits.

Stream Cipher Another type of symmetric encryption is the stream cipher. Stream ciphers are exceptionally fast, much faster than any block cipher because they typically operate on smaller units of plain text, usually bits. The encryption of any particular plain text with a stream cipher will vary, depending on when they are encountered during the encryption process. Because of this, the ciphertext (or encrypted data) will be different every time, unlike a block cipher, which will create the same ciphertext every time.

A stream cipher generates a *keystream* (or a sequence of bits used as a key). Data becomes encrypted through the combination of the keystream with the plain text, typically with the bitwise XOR operation. The keystream can be generated independently of the plain- or ciphertext giving us what is called *synchronous* stream cipher. Most stream cipher designs are for synchronous stream ciphers.

ESP has the ability to use both Message Authentication Codes (MAC) like Data Encryption Standard (DES), or hash functions like Message Digest version 5 (MD5) or Secure Hash Algorithm version 1 (SHA-1). Let's take a quick look at each.

MAC

A message authentication code (MAC) is an authentication tag (also called a checksum) derived by applying an authentication scheme, together with a secret key, to a message. Unlike digital signatures, MACs are computed and verified with the same key, so that they can be verified only by the intended recipient.

DES

DES, or Data Encryption Standard, has been around in one form or another since the 1970s. Also know as the Data Encryption Algorithm, DEA utilizes a 64-bit block size along with a 56-bit key during execution. DEA is considered a symmetric cryptosystem and originally was designed for use in hardware. Both sender and receiver must know the same secret key, which can be used to encrypt and decrypt the message, or to generate and verify a message authentication code (MAC). DEA can also be used in a single user manner, such as to store files on a hard disk in encrypted form. In a multi-user environment, because of the symmetric nature of the algorithm the secret key must be distributed (it is used to both encrypt and decrypt), which may be difficult; public-key cryptography provides an ideal solution to this problem.

Recently (October 2, 2000) DES was replaced as the United States government's de facto encryption scheme. The *Advanced Encryption Standard (AES)* was created, and uses the *Rijndael* (pronounced Rhine-doll) data encryption formula. The selection process for this standard required that each of the candidate algorithms support key sizes of 128, 192, and 256 bits. For a 128-bit key size, there are approximately 340,000,000,000,000,000,000,000,000,000,000,000,000 (340 followed by 36 zeros) possible keys.

The message here is that DES is not considered to be safe or appropriate for most financial and government uses, which should be a factor you need to consider when deciding how to use ESP.

MD5

MD5 is a *message digest* algorithm invented by RSA and is meant for applications where a large "message" must be compressed in a secure manner prior to private key signing. MD5 can take an arbitrary length message and produce a 128-bit digest. This digest is used to verify that the contents of the message have not changed during transmission, by recreating the digest at the receiving end and comparing them.

The Encryption Process

The process of encrypting an IP packet with ESP is as follows:

- The sender encapsulates into the ESP Payload field the upper layer protocol information (for transport mode) or the entire IP datagram (for tunnel mode).

- Padding is added if necessary.

- The result is encrypted (payload data, padding, pad length, next header) using the key.

Any fragmentation that is necessary is performed *after* the encryption. Fragmentation en route must be reassembled prior to the receiving host decrypting the datagram. Should a packet reach the far end ESP processor before being reassembled, it will be dropped.

The process of decyrption for ESP is as follows:

- The receiver decrypts the payload data, padding, pad length, and next header using the key and algorithm indicated by the SA.

- Padding is processed.

- The original datagram is reconstructed.

Practical Usage

There are a great number of applications for IPSec in your everyday business and personal computing life. In this section we will take a look at how IPSec can be leveraged.

External VPNs

There are a thousand and one ways that you or your organization could use IPSec effectively, but the most popular is in the form of a virtual private network (VPN). VPNs allow hosts or networks to be connected to each other in a secure fashion over public networks, a design that eliminates the need for point-to-point or Frame Relay (virtualized via a permanent virtual circuit, or PVC) connections. Through the capabilities of the packet-switched Internet and IPSec, you can utilize the inherent connectedness of the Internet.

From a cost perspective, it's typically less expensive to have a connection to the Internet (via private line, digital subscriber lines or xDSL, or cable) than it is to support a private wide area network (WAN) through one of the long distance or Regional Bell Operating Companies (RBOCs). From a security perspective, an IPSec VPN is significantly more secure, as all data that travels over it is encrypted. In a traditional WAN, although you are running through a semiprivate network, all your data runs in the clear (unless you have taken steps to encrypt it at or after the router), readable to the host supplying the network.

Secure IP connectivity can be expressed as WANs, extranets, remote host connectivity, or even intranets. When using VPNs for these functions you gain the same types of protection that you would expect from IPSec: encryption, protection from impersonation, and protection of data integrity and data origin authentication. Certainly, VPNs are not foolproof or infallible if implemented without a complete understanding of the technology.

Internal VPNs

VPNs are also very useful over your internal semiprivate network, or LAN. I call the LAN *semiprivate* since, although the users on it are finite and known, each of them still has the ability to monitor other LAN traffic and perform many active and passive attacks. For example, communication with a sensitive server (for example, financial) could be done through an IPSec tunnel. This would enforce client authentication ("Is the right machine talking to me?"), encryption of client-server data stream, and protect against data tampering, redirection, or injection over the wire.

IPSec Security Issues

The biggest problems with IPSec and VPN implementations occur in the management and architecture arenas. It's critical that you fully plan and test your IPSec and VPN implementation before rolling it out to users or connecting it (in any large-scale way) to a public network. Let's take a look at some of the most critical IPSec implementation obstacles and how to be prepared for your IPSec/VPN implementation.

The Encryption Starts Here

Network-to-network IPSec VPNs are very widely used and help alleviate the cost and complexity of designing, installing, and managing point-to-point or virtualized WAN connectivity. In network-to-network designs, clients on each private network can securely talk with each other via a public network due to the fact that all the datagrams are encrypted while en route. However, because there is no client component in this setup, the data does not get encrypted until it reaches the security gateway at the network border. While the data is in transit to and from the gateway, it is "in the clear" and vulnerable to being compromised. Additionally, since the SA is only in effect between the gateways, there is no protection from attacks once the datagram is reassembled, decrypted, and placed on the receiving network.

Exploiting this communication chain is fairly simple and requires only standard network man-in-the-middle types of attacks. Additionally, passive attacks like wire sniffing, packet analysis, and identity capture are possible on either side. The lesson here is that although your network-to-network communications are protected after they have passed through the security gateway, you need to keep in mind that internal attacks or information-gathering is very likely. These attacks can come from any workstation this is connected to either local area network (LAN), in the form of an employee, a temporary or contract worker, or a device left clandestinely on the network. The best defense for this attack is first to have a policy regarding what is allowed on the private networks. Second, you need a mechanism to enforce your policy, like an Intrusion Detection System (IDS) that can find network cards in promiscuous mode or unexpected network traffic.

Who's Knocking?

One of the core principles of network security is to expect your attacker to use your design against you. For all the blocking and port restrictions that accompany traditional firewalls and security perimeters, 99 percent of all attacks occur over the ports that we *allow*. For example, just about every attack against Web servers that I've read about occurs over TCP/80 (the standard HTTP TCP port) on the Hypertext Transfer Protocol (HTTP), which is what you are explicitly allowing.

In a similar vein, the very nature of an IPSec VPN is to allow users to connect to it via a public network. Although your audience may be a known quantity, that is not always the case for their jumping-off points. Where are your users coming from?

Security can be viewed as an ever-expanding arrangement of concentric circles. The most secure is at the center, and the least secure points are the farthest. Having a single ring of security (your IPSec gateway) is not the best implementation of security and you will most likely have some uninvited guests.

If at all possible, try to keep the world of acceptable VPN users to a particular, identifiable group, so that you can restrict the majority of connection attempts to your service. In most cases, attackers will not be able to initiate a legitimate session with your security gateway, but who says they need to do that to penetrate your border?

He Sent Us What?

Attacks on systems are like dominoes. If you can topple the first one in the row, you have an excellent chance of toppling the rest simply due to proximity. You could have the best implementation of VPN technology, the most current and strongest encryption schemes, and a security architecture that rivals the National Security Agency's, but you still need to allow your remote users to connect. These users, the reason for the VPN in the first place, will most likely be the ones to bring your network to a complete stop.

The fact is that when users are outside the confines of the corporate enclosure, they are naturally susceptible to causes of system compromise. Once they are compromised with viruses, Trojan executables, or any of the things you seek to keep out, they will introduce them to your network the next time they connect to the VPN.

The only remedy for this type of unintentional attack is to have second- and third-level controls for VPN clients before they reach your core production network. Again, a security policy is needed to determine what is allowed and what is not (for example, what can the VPN clients do? Everything? Ping Flood? Send viruses?), and a mechanism is needed to enforce it. In may VPN installations, the VPN gateway is all that sits between the Internet and the core. A better design would be to place a firewall and IDS after the VPN gateway that is regulating what can and cannot come through (in either direction). A firewall (or other security device) in front of the VPN gateway is a good idea too, but it cannot be used to enforce VPN content policy since the traffic is encrypted until it gets to the security gateway.

Who Has the Certificate?

In many IPSec/VPN systems, a connection to the network requires a username and password combination along with a digital certificate to create the encrypted tunnel. All three of these mechanisms are somewhat weak, because usernames and passwords can be guessed easily, and because certificates authenticate the *machine* and not the user. It is entirely possible to export a certificate, install it on a separate machine, and connect to a "secure" VPN with the guessed or hacked personal access information.

Certificate "lifting" requires physical access to the client machine, but in most cases that is not a problem. Laptops get lost or stolen all the time, creating a window of opportunity before the certificate is revoked; machines left running and unlocked in corporate environments don't require any skill to penetrate.

Even with IPSec, there is a limitation to what the VPN can and cannot do; it's essential to have a good system of monitoring, auditing, protection, and enforcement to keep your network secure.

Summary

Although IPv4 was not designed for security like IPv6 was, IPSec is currently the best way to add authentication, confidentiality, and data integrity to both protocols. Through the use of cryptographic algorithms, anti-replay facilities, and security associations, any user or organization can use IPSec to enforce their communication security policy.

By leveraging these technologies in practical ways, such as a network-to-network or host-to-network VPN, or for secure intra-organizational communications, organizations can not only expand the reach of its employees and securely leverage public Internets, but they can also safeguard the mechanisms through which entities connect to them by requiring adherence to the IPSec security policy.

IPSec and VPNs are not foolproof however, and require you to have a good understanding of what you are creating and leveraging. Connecting any gateway up to a public network has its disadvantages, which must be mitigated with strong security policy, auditing, and enforcement.

FAQs

Q: I would like to set up a VPN architecture for my remote and traveling employees. What should I do first?

A: Before you read a single glossy, tri-fold handout from your local VPN vendor (you know the one, it's got IPSec in big letters on the front, probably right next to a cartoon padlock and a criminal looking very dejected) you need to write a security policy. This policy describes what you are allowing and disallowing and gives you a guide for selecting devices for enforcement. The bottom line is that you need to outline what it is you are protecting, and from whom, before you can effectively put a security infrastructure in place.

Q: My company has Check Point firewalls and our sister company has a different kind of firewall. Is it possible to set up an IPSec tunnel between them?

A: It is possible to create inter-vendor IPSec tunnels, but it will most likely create more work for you to perform. Vendors implement IPSec in different ways, and the common ground you find between vendors may not include the features you require. For example, an IPSec VPN between the Checkpoint Firewall and the Cisco PIX Firewall require creating manual keys, creating initialization vectors (IVs) and SPIs, and other tasks that would be performed automatically when using the same vendor's product. Not all IPSec implementations play nicely together, and you may encounter some significant hurdles.

Q: What ports are necessary for IPSec tunnels to pass through my firewall (it's not an endpoint)?

A: To allow IPSec traffic through your firewall, you should first put a sniffer on the outside of your network or keep a close eye on the firewall logs for the "deny" messages to determine what ports the VPN is asking for. Typically, you would need to open ESP (IP type 50), ISAKMP (UDP 500), and AH (IP type 51), as well as any IP specific filters you require to limit the audience that can speak to you over IPSec.

Q: Should I be placing my VPN gateway at the same level as my firewall?

A: Placement of your VPN gateway is very important and must correspond to your security policy. The important concept here is how you plan on monitoring usage of the VPN and enforcing your policy. Certainly, if you have remote users coming through, you will want to give them the same rights over the VPN as they have on the LAN. That requires an understanding of what they should be able to do and what you never want them to do. Can your users launch viruses or DoS attacks on your LAN? No? Then they should not be able to do that via your VPN, either. It is my feeling that both an Intrusion Detection System (IDS) and a firewall should be employed on all VPN infrastructures. The IDS could sit between the Internet and your VPN gateway, watching for anomalous behavior. This behavior could be attacks from users you don't want using your VPN, or leakage of internal IP addresses. The firewall would sit in front of your VPN gateway (after the traffic becomes unencrypted) and allow access only to servers and services that should be accessed by VPN users. By having a device to enforce your policy, you can keep track of what users are doing and protect your internal computing infrastructure.

Chapter 4

Internet Security Applications

Solutions in this chapter:

- **Using Digital Signatures**
- **Acquiring Digital Certificates**
- **Understanding SSL**
- **Understanding SSH**
- **Understanding PGP**
- **Understanding S/MIME**
- **Understanding Kerberos**

Introduction

This chapter will discuss Internet security applications and some of the more common methods used for securing Internet connections and e-mail messages. It will provide you with a good overview of the technology as well as some of the shortcomings that have been found and exploited.

Topics that will be covered in this chapter include Digital Signatures and Certificates, Secure Sockets Layer (SSL), Secure Shell (SSH), Pretty Good Privacy (PGP), Secure Multipurpose Internet Mail Extensions (S/MIME), and Kerberos; it will also provide information on protocols for authenticating users, for securing Internet transactions, and for secure messaging. All of these measures provide necessary services for a healthy and secure network. Not all of these applications have to be deployed, as there are many competing technologies, but you should be informed about what measures are available and how they work.

Integration of Internet Security Applications

You will find that different security applications can be used in different situations and there is even some overlap. For example, digital certificates can enable other technologies including S/MIME and SSL. Digital certificates are being integrated with Kerberos, and there are versions of SSH that support Kerberos authentication. All of the technologies discussed here should be considered complimentary, and part of a layered approach to enhancing the security in your environment. You may find that PGP is great for securing files, but it may not meet your requirements for secure e-mail as well as S/MIME. S/MIME, on the other hand, provides limited support for file encryption.

In a business scenario, different technologies address different security concerns. Let's take the example of a company with a Web commerce server. This company has a business need to protect customer data, which in this example happens to be credit card information. There is also a business need to securely administer this machine from the internal network, and to restrict access to specific administrators.

As mentioned, there is a stated business need to protect data between the Web browser application on a user's desktop and the Web server. SSL can be very effective for securing this connection by encrypting the session. It may not, however, be the right mechanism to provide secure administration to the server. In this case, the administrator needs to copy files securely back and forth from a workstation on the internal network to the Web server. The administrator also needs command shell access to start and stop server processes and to perform remote maintenance on the machine.

It is unlikely that you would want every employee in the company to be able to administer this machine. An error from a well-meaning employee or a malicious act from a disgruntled employee could expose your company to financial loss and public embarrassment. The stated business requirement is to provide a secure mechanism for administering the machine, while restricting access only to certain users. SSH can be used very effectively to address both of these concerns. Figure 4.1 details this scenario. Note that this figure also includes an internal and external firewall that can also help restrict access, in keeping with a layered approach to security.

Figure 4.1 A scenario using SSL and SSH together.

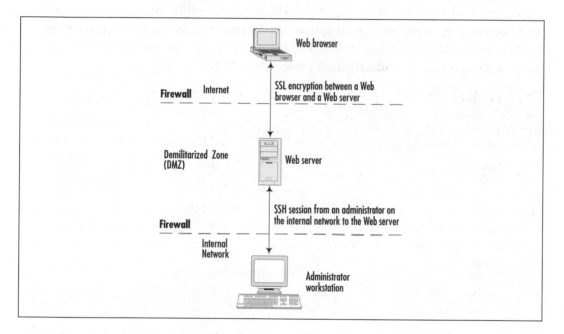

Security Concerns

Different applications discussed in this chapter address different security requirements. These protocols can provide a great deal of security when carefully implemented, but each comes with its own exploits, problems, and inherent limitations. Risks of implementing these protocols may be related to general use, specific vulnerabilities, or limitations of the technology.

You will notice by reading each Potential Security Risks section for each of the technologies covered that certain patterns emerge. For example, static user passwords rarely provide adequate security for a system. Public keys are relatively secureæso long as they are trusted. See if you notice other patterns, as this will help you to find flaws and spot limitations of new protocols and applications as they are introduced.

Security Services

Most security software can be discussed in terms of the general services it provides. Security software applications are installed to provide particular basic services or functions that enhance the operational security of an enterprise. Some of these services include the following:

Auditing A mechanism (usually a logging system) to record events that could include user and file access.

Authentication A mechanism to positively identify users by requesting credentials. Credentials could include a password, a smart card, or even a physical trait like a fingerprint as in the use of biometrics.

Authorization The resources a user is allowed to access after they have been authenticated.

Availability The accessibility of a resource. An attack on system availability is known as a Denial of Service (DoS) attack.

Confidentiality The protection of private or sensitive information. This information could include human resources records (such as payroll), medical records, or business plans.

Integrity The protection of data from unauthorized modification. This is especially important to financial institutions, as the modification of a monetary transaction could have a huge financial impact.

Nonrepudiation A fraud-prevention mechanism for proving that a user undeniably performed a specific action.

As you will see, many of the applications discussed in this chapter specifically address authentication, confidentiality, integrity, and nonrepudiation. All of these applications achieve their level of protection through the use of cryptography.

Cryptography

Cryptography is the art and science of keeping data secret. It is a complex subject involving mathematical concepts; this section was written with the assumption that the reader does not have a background in cryptography or in mathematics, but it will try to provide a functional understanding of cryptography, as well as a general understanding of some security programs that employ cryptography.

Data is encrypted through the use of a specific algorithm. An algorithm (also called a *cipher*) is simply a mathematical process or series of functions used to scramble data. Most encryption algorithms use keys, so that algorithms do not have to be unique for a transaction and so the details of an algorithm do not have to be kept secret.

Keys

In simple terms, the word *key* refers to the information needed to encrypt (scramble) or decrypt (un-scramble) data. The security of a key is often discussed in term of its length, or bits, but a large key length by itself is no guarantee of overall system security. There are two general types of cryptography defined by the type of keys being used: *secret key* cryptography and *public key* cryptography.

It is important to understand the principles of public key and secret key cryptography, as most security applications employ the use of one or both of these encryption types.

Secret Key Cryptography

Secret key encryption, also know as *symmetric encryption*, uses a single key to encrypt and decrypt data. The security of a symmetric key algorithm is often directly related to how well the secret key is protected and distributed. Secret key algorithms are usually categorized as either *block ciphers* that process data in measured blocks at a time, or as *stream ciphers* that process data a byte at a time. Block ciphers excel at encrypting fixed length data, whereas stream ciphers excel at encrypting random data streams, such as the network traffic between routers.

Some advantages of symmetric key encryption include the speed of the encryption process and the simplicity of its use. Drawbacks of symmetric key encryption are mostly related to secure key distribution and key management.

Examples of common symmetric key block algorithms include the Data Encryption Standard (DES), International Data Encryption Algorithm (IDEA), CAST-128 (named after its inventors: Carlisle, Adams, Stafford, and Tavares), and Blowfish. Examples of a symmetric key stream ciphers include Ron's Cipher 4 (RC4) and Software-Optimized Encryption Algorithm (SEAL).

Public Key Cryptography

Public key cryptography, or *asymmetric* cryptography, uses two encryption key pairs. One key, a public key, is published widely, whereas the other key must be guarded and kept secret. Given the public key, it is computationally infeasible (the cryptographer's way of saying "impossible in this lifetime") to derive the private key.

Even with modern computing hardware, public key algorithms are processor-intensive. There is an industry joke that refers to the RSA, a popular public key algorithm, as the Really Slow Algorithm (RSA stands for the last names of its creators, Rivest, Shamir, and Adelman).

Because of processing-speed issues, public key algorithms generally are not used for bulk data encryption—that is, encryption of large amounts of data. Instead, bulk data is usually encrypted with a symmetric algorithm.

Many of the technologies examined in this chapter use a hybrid public/secret key encryption method where public key cryptography is used to secure a symmetric key and the symmetric key is used for the bulk encryption of data. A symmetric key that has been secured using a public key algorithm is generally referred to as a *digital envelope*.

The private key half of the public/private key pair must always be protected. One mechanism for the secure storage of a private key is to use a *smart card*. A smart card is an electronic device that normally resembles a credit card. A cryptographic smart card has the ability to generate and store keys on the card itself, ensuring that the private key is never even exposed to the local machine. This greatly reduces the risk of key compromise. Smart cards may still be vulnerable to attack, but they do provide a great deal more security than storing a private key on a local machine.

Examples of common public key algorithms include RSA, ElGamal, and the Diffie-Hellman Key Exchange.

Key Management and the Key Distribution Problem

A fundamental problem in both public and private key cryptography systems is how to securely distribute and maintain the keys required to encrypt and decrypt data.

Secret key algorithms are dependant upon all parties involved to securely obtain a secret key. For example, e-mail would not be considered a secure mechanism to distribute a secret key, as third parties could intercept it while in transit. Another problem with secret key cryptography is that it does not scale as well as public key encryption. For example, if I wish to have ten recipients receive an encrypted message using secret key cryptography, I must securely distribute ten keys, all of which will be capable of decrypting my message. I must ensure that each of the ten recipients receives a key, that the key was not intercepted or compromised during delivery, and that the secret keys are kept secure once they reach their final destination. The next time I wish to send a message, I will need to repeat this process or else reuse the original key. Reusing the original key greatly increases the chances the key will be compromised. If I wish each recipient to have a unique secret key, the distribution system becomes almost completely unmanageable.

Using public key cryptography, only a single exchange of a public key for each recipient needs to take place. This can be automated by placing the public keys in a central depository such as a Lightweight Directory Access Protocol (LDAP) directory server. The public key, however, must be exchanged reliably and securely. You must be sure that a public key really belongs to the intended individual, and not to a third party masquerading as that individual. This problem will be further discussed in the Digital Certificates section of this chapter.

Hash Functions

A hash function provides a means of taking variable-length data and creating a fixed-length output. This is sometimes referred to as taking a *fingerprint* of the data, and the output is called a *message digest* or *hash*. If data changes in any way after the hash of a message is computed, the hash values will not match when computed the second time. Using a cryptographically strong hash algorithm, even small changes like deleting or adding a period at the end of a sentence will yield large differences between hash values. Using a cryptographically strong hash algorithm, it is computationally infeasible to produce an original message having only the message hash.

Hashing specifically addresses the security concern of integrity. That is, hashing can help verify that data has not been altered in any way.

Examples of some common hash algorithms include Secure Hash Algorithm 1 (SHA-1) and Message Digest 5 (MD5).

Key Length

The general security of both public and private keys can be discussed in terms of length. Again, a large key size is no guarantee of overall system security or sound key management. It also does not address other factors like random number generation. Poor use of random number generation compromised the original Netscape browser SSL implementation. By itself, a secure key length is only an indication that the encryption algorithm being used is strong.

At this point, it should be noted that the key length of public keys and secret keys differ in their size/security relationship. For example, a 512-bit RSA key actually provides less security than a 128-bit Blowfish key. Table 4.1 summarizes some generally agreed-upon public key lengths in relation to secret key block ciphers.

Table 4.1 Comparable Sizes of RSA Public Keys and Equivalent Secret Keys

Secret Key (Block Cipher)	Comparable RSA Key
56-bit	512-bit
80-bit	1024-bit
112-bit	2048-bit
128-bit	3072-bit
256-bit	15360-bit

Now that you have a basic understanding of the principles of cryptography, it is time to examine some applications that use cryptography to provide a high level of security protection under different scenarios. If you would like to learn more about cryptography and encryption algorithms, a good place to start is with Bruce Schneier's book, *Applied Cryptography: Protocols, Algorithms, and Source Code in C, 2nd Edition.*

Using Digital Signatures

With the signing of The Electronic Signatures in Global and National Commerce Act by President Clinton on June 30, 2000, digital signatures have become an increasingly important subject. The term *electronic signatures* has broad interpretations that could mean anything from a cryptographic digital signature to a scanned image of a handwritten signature. In either case, many people feel that this legislation paves the way for formally defining a legal use of digital signatures in electronic communications.

Digital signatures can help identify and authenticate people, organizations, and computers over the Internet. They can also be used to verify that data was not altered or tampered with in transit. To understand digital signatures and how they are used, it helps to first examine the use of a handwritten signature. Handwritten signatures are used every day to identify an individual in a legally binding manner. For example, when an individual agrees upon the terms outlined in a contract, the inclusion of a handwritten signature indicates that this individual has acknowledged and agrees to the terms outlined in the contract. The individual should not later be able to deny the fact that they signed the document or that they did not agree with its terms, except in the case of forgery.

Digital signatures, like handwritten signatures, can help identify the individual who signed a transaction or message. Unlike handwritten signatures, a digital signature can help verify that a document or transaction was not modified from its original state at the time of signing.

How Does a Digital Signature Add Security?

Unlike a handwritten signature, digital signatures are almost un-forgeable when implemented properly. Under ideal circumstances, this means that a digitally signed message must belong to the person whose digital signature appears in the message. The inability to deny that this message or transaction had been sent is referred to as *nonrepudiation*. Digital signatures provide three basic security services: authentication, integrity, and nonrepudiation.

Digital signatures achieve a high level of security through the use of two cryptographic technologies: public key encryption and hashing. Creating a digital signature involves hashing data, then encrypting the resulting message digest with a private key. Anyone with the public key half of the keypair will be able to verify that the hash corresponds to the original message.

The goal of digital signatures is to positively identify the originator of a message, and ensure that message data was not altered; however, problems can arise in deploying this complex technology securely. For example, a weak hashing algorithm used for digital signatures provides little security in relation to a cryptographically strong algorithm. Unfortunately, simply viewing the hash of a message is not sufficient to detect the use of a weak algorithm.

Potential Security Risks with Digital Signatures

Understanding the risks associated with using digital signatures means that you must first understand the limitations of the technology.

A digital signature, when not bound to a user's name with a digital certificate, is virtually meaningless. Secure distribution of a digital signature is the only way to guarantee its security. If large-scale distribution of public keys is needed to verify digital signatures, a database needs to be available that has highly available read access, but highly restricted write access.

Perhaps the greatest risk of digital signatures is putting too much reliance on the technology. In the real world, we put only so much trust in a handwritten signature. Real signatures can be forged or photocopied into a new document, but this should not be true with carefully implemented digital signatures. A handwritten signature can provide only so much assurance before the trust model breaks down. The problem with digital signatures is that we do not yet know where the trust model breaks down.

Acquiring Digital Certificates

A digital signature, by itself, does not provide a strong tie back to a person or entity. How do you know that a public key used to create a digital signature really belongs to a specific individual, and that the key is still valid? A mechanism is needed to provide a tie between a public key and a real individual. This is the function of *digital certificates*. A digital certificate in the Windows environment is shown in Figure 4.2.

Figure 4.2 A digital certificate in a Windows environment.

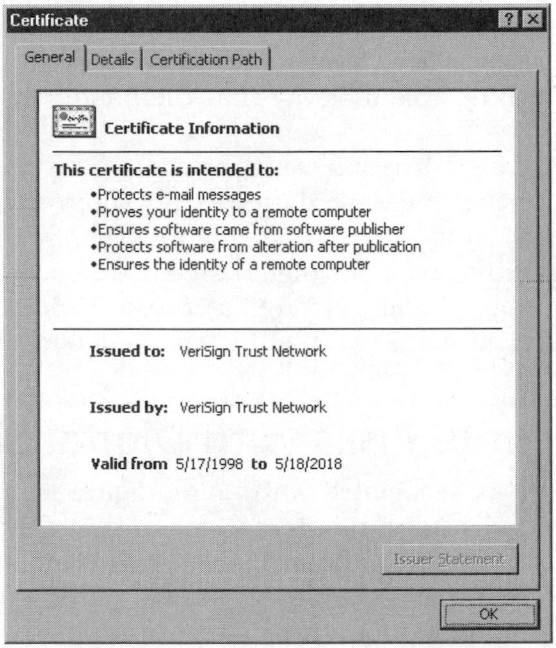

```
┌─────────────────────────────────────────────────┐
│ Certificate                              ? X     │
├─────────────────────────────────────────────────┤
│ General │ Details │ Certification Path │          │
│ ┌─────────────────────────────────────────────┐ │
│ │ [icon]  Certificate Information               │ │
│ │                                               │ │
│ │ This certificate is intended to:              │ │
│ │   •Protects e-mail messages                   │ │
│ │   •Proves your identity to a remote computer  │ │
│ │   •Ensures software came from software        │ │
│ │    publisher                                  │ │
│ │   •Protects software from alteration after    │ │
│ │    publication                                │ │
│ │   •Ensures the identity of a remote computer  │ │
│ │ ─────────────────────────────────────────     │ │
│ │   Issued to:  VeriSign Trust Network          │ │
│ │                                               │ │
│ │   Issued by:  VeriSign Trust Network          │ │
│ │                                               │ │
│ │   Valid from 5/17/1998 to 5/18/2018           │ │
│ │                                               │ │
│ │                          Issuer Statement     │ │
│ │                                ┌────────┐     │ │
│ │                                │   OK   │     │ │
│ └────────────────────────────────└────────┘───┘ │
└─────────────────────────────────────────────────┘
```

Digital certificates can provide a high level of trust that the person whose name appears on a certificate really belongs to the associated public key. This trust is accomplished through use of a third party, known as a certificate authority (CA). A CA signs a certificate as a means of "vouching" for the identity of a person whose name appears on the certificate. This end result, the certificate, is what binds an individual to a public key. The currently accepted format for digital certificates is X.509v3.

The X.509 Standard

The X.509v3 standard, defined in Request for Comments (RFC) 2459, describes an agreed-upon format for digital certificates. Version 1 and 2 digital certificates are not widely in use, so we will concentrate only on version 3.

This X.509v3 standard defines the elements of a digital certificate:

Certificate Version Indicates the version format of the certificate.

Serial number A unique number assigned by the issuing certificate authority (CA). Serial numbers can be used for tracking certificates.

Signature Identifies the encryption algorithms and message digest functions supported by the CA.

Issuer name The distinguished name (DN) of the CA.

Period of Validity The certificate's start and expiration dates. This does not include the possibility that the certificate has been revoked.

Subject The DN of the certificate owner.

Subject's Public Key Info The public key and algorithm associated with the subject field.

Issuer Unique ID An optional field used to identify the certificate issuer or certificate authority. Use of this field is generally not recommended by RFC 2459.

Subject Unique ID An optional field to identify the certificate subject. Use of this field is generally not recommended by RFC 2459.

Extensions An optional field used for private extensions. This field is not defined, but has included items such as alternate subject names, key usage information, and certificate revocation list (CRL) distribution points.

Encrypted This field contains the actual signature, the algorithm identifier, the secure hash of the other fields in the certificate, and a digital signature of the hash.

The format of a digital certificate is relatively straightforward, but exchanging certificates between individual users presents many challenges. Ensuring that a certificate really belongs to the intended user is difficult. For example, there could be many people named Jennifer Smith in an organization and only one of them is the intended recipient. Obtaining a certificate in a reliable fashion and storing them properly has proven difficult.

Without secured central storage, you would first have to contact the individuals with whom you wish to communicate, exchange certificates, and then begin communicating securely. Certificates require a means to manage certificate creation, distribution, central storage, revocation, key backup, and key update. This management system is collectively known as a *public key infrastructure* (PKI).

Certificate Authority (CA) and Public Key Infrastructure (PKI)

A PKI is a security architecture designed to facilitate the deployment of public key technology. Components of a PKI could include a certificate repository (usually an LDAP-compliant directory), digital certificates, CRLs, application software, and even the human aspect such as people and procedures. A public key infrastructure provides several core security services including user authentication, confidentiality, and integrity. PKI can help enable nonrepudiation.

A CA is one component of an overall public key infrastructure, and is a critical component of any large-scale PKI deployment. The primary function of a CA is to certify that a public/private key pair really does belong to a specific individual.

A helpful comparison is between a CA and the Department of Motor Vehicles, where you would normally go through a process of obtaining a license by identifying yourself, verifying your identity (by presenting a birth certificate, for example), and receiving a license that is good for specific purposes such as driving a car or verifying your age.

Actually, one of the problems regarding the use of digital certificates is verifying the intended *purpose* of the certificate. In our example, the fact that I have a driver's license does not necessarily mean that I am also licensed to drive a truck, practice medicine, or carry a handgun. In addition, I may not trust the DMV to provide a strong enough means of identification for providing access to sensitive government documents, since it is possible to obtain a fake driver's license.

How to Acquire a Digital Certificate

There are a number of ways to acquire a digital certificate, and where you obtain one may depend on what you want to use it for. For example, it is possible for developers to issue their own certificates through a product like Microsoft Certificate Services, but using self-issued certificates requires an additional step of installing a self-signed server certificate on each client machine or else the trust model breaks.

Another option is to obtain a certificate from an established certificate vendor. One of the largest providers of digital certificates is VeriSign (www.verisign.com). VeriSign sells digital certificates for S/MIME, SSL (client and server), server gated cryptography (SGC) certificates for financial institutions, Authenticode certificates for software publishing, and time stamp services. VeriSign is a well-established trusted root CA and comes predefined as a root CA in the Windows operating system. This means that certificates published by VeriSign do not require the additional step of installing a server certificate on each client machine.

The following section walks you through the steps of obtaining an S/MIME certificate for digitally signing e-mail. The e-mail client used is Outlook Express Version 5.5.

1. Click on the Tools | Options menu in Outlook Express.

2. Click the Security tab, then the Get Digital ID button. This will take you to a Web page with various certificate vendors.

3. Selecting VeriSign will take you to a form that you must fill out and submit. For a VeriSign Class 1 Digital ID trial, you will need to provide your name, e-mail address, zip code, and date of birth. For a full (non-trial) Class 1 Digital ID, you will need to provide your billing information.

4. After submitting the form, e-mail will be sent with instructions on how to install the digital ID. Installation is simple and generally involves launching a Web page, clicking on a few links, and verifying that the ID was successfully installed.

5. Once installed, signing a message involves composing the message and clicking the Digitally Sign Message button. Alternatively, you can also sign the message by selecting Tools | Digitally Sign.

Once your digital ID is installed, you will be able to digitally sign e-mail sent to other users. You will not, however, be able to encrypt e-mail to other users unless you first obtain the recipient's digital certificate.

Notice that the only means of authentication in this process of obtaining a certificate was the billing information (if I actually purchase a certificate) and e-mail address. The process of verifying an SSL Web server certificate is more complex and involves stronger verification of the certificate requestor.

Obtaining a digital certificate through Outlook Express and sending digitally signed e-mail, using the process outlined, uses S/MIME, which will be discussed later in this chapter.

Potential Security Risks with Digital Certificates

Digital certificates can be a strong authentication mechanism, especially when stored on a smart card. But for digital certificates to provide meaningful security, issues of trust must be carefully planned out beforehand. For example, a CA must have strong security mechanisms in place and must positively identify all principals that enroll for certificates. The question of how strongly a CA identifies a certificate holder before issuing a certificate determines the security of an overall PKI. A CA needs to be both physically and logically secured. If compromised, every certificate ever issued by the CA is in question.

If a digital certificate's purpose is to bind an individual to a digital signature, how do you know that the certificate really belongs to this individual and not to someone else masquerading as that user? Perhaps a certificate belongs to an unintended user with the same name as the intended recipient. Many certificates rely on the name that appears in the subject field as a means to positively identify the owner.

If a CA's function is to certify the identity of an individual and provide nonrepudiation services, this raises important liability issues. Public Key Infrastructure seems to be a prerequisite for the secure distribution and management of digital certificates. Operational issues and practices with a CA can impact the outcome of legal proceedings and take away much of the value provided by PKI.

Another problem with digital certificates is that certificate revocation lists (CRLs) are rarely checked by applications including Web browsers. A certificate could be revoked for any number of reasons including a key compromise, a CA compromise, or a changed affiliation. If these certificates are revoked, but their status is not checked, it could open a significant exposure. Issues regarding the distribution of CRLs have not been adequately resolved to date.

NOTE

Issues that you can explore further on your own include the possibility of identity theft and the privacy issues that arise by being able to positively tie a transaction to an individual.

Understanding SSL

Secure Sockets Layer (SSL) is a technology that is enabled by the use of digital certificates. SSL is a transport-level protocol that provides reliable end-to-end security. SSL can secure a session from the point of origin to its final destination. SSL addresses the security between two communicating entities. This could include communication between a Web browser and a Web server, an e-mail application and a mail server, or even server-to-server communication channels. SSL can also authenticate a server, and optionally a client. SSL has become the de facto method of securing commerce over the Web.

SSL is a connection-oriented protocol that requires both the application and server to be SSL-aware. If SSL is required on a server, applications that are not SSL-capable will not be able to communicate with that server.

SSL provides security services including privacy, authentication, and message integrity. SSL provides message integrity through the use of a security check known as a message authentication code (MAC). The MAC ensures that encrypted sessions are not tampered with in transit.

SSL provides server authentication using public key encryption technology, and is optionally capable of authenticating clients by requesting client-side digital certificates. In practice, client certificates are not widely deployed because they are not easily portable between machines, they are easily lost or destroyed, and they have been generally problematic to deploy in the real world. Many Web sites have found that the combination of SSL used with a username and password has provided adequate security for most purposes.

SSL or TLS?

The Internet Engineering Task Force (IETF) is responsible for the future development of the SSL standard, now known as Transport Layer Security (TLS). (The Netscape Communications Corporation originally developed TLS.) TLS 1.0, defined in RFC 2246, offers only minor enhancements to the SSL 3.0 protocol. Effectively, TLS is SSL version 3.1.

New enhancements to the TLS protocol include version number reported, differences in the alerting protocol message types, message authentication types, key generation, and certificate verification. Finally, TLS removes support for the Fortezza algorithm. Fortezza is a family of security products that includes Personal Computer Memory Card International Association (PCMCIA) card security solutions. Since TLS is an open standard, expect the Internet community to work together to continuously improve the security and performance of this protocol.

How SSL Is Related to HTTP

Standard Web sessions use the Hypertext Transfer Protocol (HTTP) to establish communication channels over Transmission Control Protocol/Internet Protocol (TCP/IP) networks. SSL was designed to be a separate security protocol that enhances the HTTP standard. Logically, SSL inserts itself between the HTTP application protocol and the TCP layer of a conversation. This means that SSL appears to be just another application protocol to TCP. Because SSL acts as an enhancement, it is a simple matter to add SSL to existing protocols without requiring a rewrite of the core protocol.

Because of this flexible design approach, SSL is capable of encrypting almost any TCP-based traffic. In fact, SSL has been used to provide session-level security of e-mail (SMTPS, IMAPS, and POP3S), news (NNTPS), LDAP (LDAPS), IRC (IRCS), Telnet (Telnets), and FTP (FTPS). SSL cannot, however, address security concerns with connectionless protocols like UDP.

Web-based SSL traffic generally is configured to use port 443, whereas HTTP traffic generally uses port 80. Web browsers request an SSL session by using HTTPS instead of the standard HTTP. Web browser software generally indicates when an SSL session is active by displaying a "closed lock" icon like the one in Figure 4.3.

Figure 4.3 Internet Explorer with lock indicating that an SSL session is active.

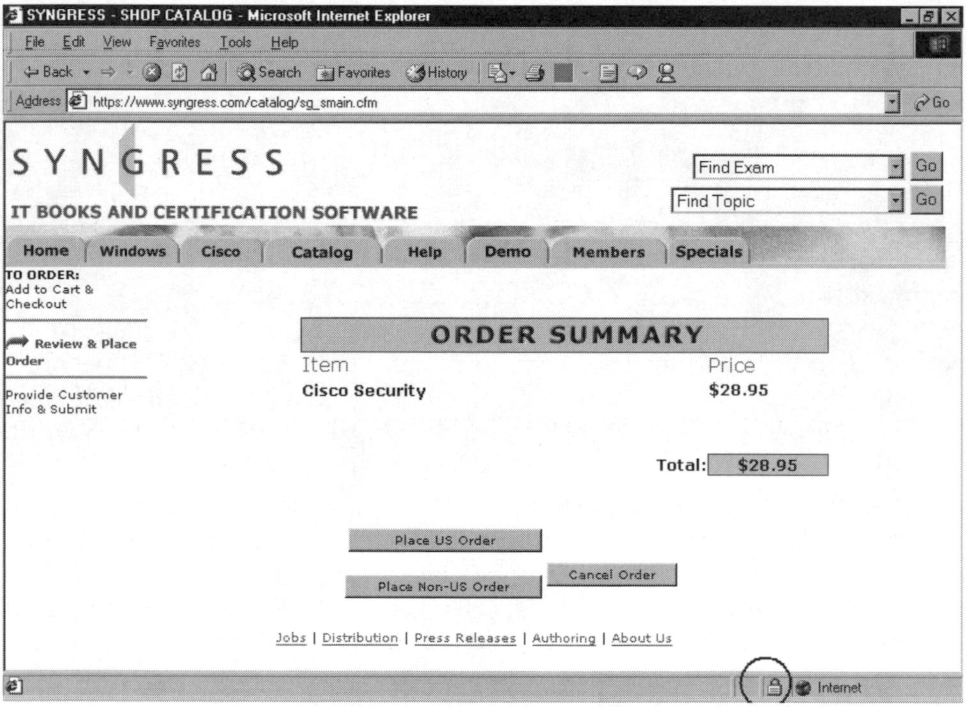

How Does SSL Work?

In order for an SSL session to take place, a number of elements must already be in place. First, the Web server requires a digital certificate with a corresponding private key. As mentioned earlier, the largest provider of server certificates is VeriSign. Obtaining and installing an SSL certificate from VeriSign typically involves a six-step process. This process includes generating a request, submitting a Certificate Signing Request (CSR), completing an application, authenticating the business or individual, installing the server ID, and finally enabling SSL on the Web server. Authentication by VeriSign can take three days or more, as it involves setting up an organizational contact and verifying that the company really exists and is not providing falsified information.

Before an SSL session can be established, the client also needs an SSL-capable Web browser, such as Internet Explorer or Netscape. When these elements are in place, both the client and server are ready to establish a secure connection.

Although the Web server can be set to require SSL, let's walk through the steps of a Web browser requesting an SSL session from a Web server. These steps are what typically might occur when making a secure online purchase. I will not discuss every detail of the SSL handshake, but instead will focus on the high-level steps that occur when establishing this connection.

Like many of the technologies discussed in this chapter, SSL uses a combination of public and secret key encryption. Bulk data of an SSL session is always encrypted with secret key cryptography, as it is far less processor-intensive than public key cryptography. The SSL/TLS protocol supports many secret key algorithms, including DES, Triple-DES, IDEA, RC2, and RC4. Key exchange algorithms supported include Diffie-Hellman and RSA.

The SSL handshake can best be described in the following nine steps.

1. **ClientHello** During the ClientHello stage, the client sends a server a message (ClientHello) requesting SSL options including protocol version number, cipher settings, randomly generated number data to seed cryptographic calculations, and the compression method being used.

2. **ServerHello** After receiving the ClientHello message, the server acknowledges its receipt by sending a ServerHello message. The ServerHello message contains the protocol version number, cipher settings, randomly generated number data used to seed cryptographic calculations, compression methods being used, and a session ID.

3. **ServerKeyExchange** Immediately following the ServerHello message, the server sends a ServerKeyExchange message to the client. This message contains the server's public key certificate. If client certificates are required, a request for the client certificate is generated at this stage of the communications.

4. **ServerHelloDone** Immediately following the ServerKeyExchange, the server sends a final message indicating that the initial handshake negotiations are complete.

5. **ClientKeyExchange** After receiving the ServerHelloDone message, the client responds with a ClientKeyExchange message. This message consists of the symmetric session key, encrypted with server's public key that was sent in step three.

6. **ChangeCipherSpec** At this point in the handshake, a preliminary SSL negotiation is complete. The client sends a ChangeCipherSpec message to the server that explicitly states which security options should be invoked.

7. **Finished** The client sends a finished message, allowing it to determine if the negotiation has been successful and that the security options have not been compromised at any stage.

8. **ChangeCipherSpec** The server then sends a ChangeCipherSpec message to the client activating the invoked security options.

9. **Finished** The server sends a finished message, allowing the client to check that the negotiated security options are in effect.

After the server finished message is sent, the handshake process is complete and the SSL session is established. From this point on, all communications are encrypted until the session is broken or completed.

Performance Issues with SSL

If SSL can provide such a great security boost, why not encrypt all traffic? Although this may sound like a good idea, a lot of overhead is involved in establishing an SSL session. Some Web servers experience as much as a 50 percent performance hit when using SSL. This can occur due to the nature of the HTTP protocol, which creates a new session for every object requested on a Web page.

For example, a simple transaction where a browser requests a single page of text with four images initiates five separate GET requests (one for the text page, and four for the images). Using SSL, each of these sessions must negotiate separate encryption keys, which puts a tremendous burden on the server. To make matters worse, users may get frustrated with response time and click the reload button on the Web browser, initiating even more SSL connections.

Some general tips on reducing the performance impact of SSL include:

- Use hardware encryption accelerators like those produced by nCipher (www.ncipher.com) or Rainbow Technologies (www.rainbow.com). This is the easiest single step you can take to increase SSL performance, as it does not involve rewriting Web pages or purchasing additional servers.

- Keep SSL pages simple, and use fewer images on SSL-encrypted pages.

- Use single-file animated GIFs instead of multifile animated GIFs. Using multifile GIFs requires a separate GET and SSL negotiation for each file. Better yet, avoid animated GIFs on SSL pages altogether and keep the image size of standard GIFs small.

- Use SSL only for selected Web pages, such as those that submit credit card information. Do not encrypt all Web traffic from a server unless this is dictated by the security requirements of the site.

- Consider using load balancing software or hardware.

It is possible to cache SSL connections for additional performance. Establishing a new SSL session takes five times as long as reconnecting to a cached session. However, enabling session caching of SSL is tricky to implement. If the timeout is set too long, the server may consume too much memory by simply preserving the state of unused connections. Caching SSL may not be desirable from a security viewpoint depending upon the site content. An online banking application, for example, should favor security over performance and should not cache SSL connections.

Although there are competing technologies, SSL has become the cornerstone of secure commerce over the Web. Since SSL is now an open standard, there should be significant security and performance improvements in the future and SSL should continue to be the dominant protocol used for securing Web-based transactions.

Potential Security Risks with SSL

Although SSL can provide a strong level of security when implemented correctly, you should understand its limitations. The best metaphor I have heard for SSL is that of an armored car. An armored car provides security from its origin to its final destination. When the armored car drives away, the security it provides ends. Using SSL as your only security mechanism is equivalent to an armored car leaving a sack of money on the curb (the server) and then driving away. SSL provides no protection beyond the session, and an SSL-enabled Web server cannot offer protection for data that is ultimately stored in a clear-text file on the server.

SSL provides no protection against Web-based attacks such as exploiting a flaw with a Common Gateway Interface (CGI) script. Web-based SSL also provides no mechanism to control security entitlements. Entitlements refer to what an individual is allowed to do once they have authenticated to a server. A number of third-party products are addressing this need, including Netegrity SiteMinder and Securant Technologies' ClearTrust SecureControl. Finally, SSL does not protect against denial of service (DoS) attacks and it remains vulnerable to traffic analysis.

To provide an adequate level of security, an SSL-enabled server should support 128-bit encryption with a 1024 bit public key on the server. If the server uses a 512-bit public key, the server's private key may be at risk. Although it may take some time to break an RSA 512-bit key, it is possible. The RSA keys are used to authenticate and exchange session keys. Once broken, all SSL-encrypted traffic would be at risk, as the mechanism for protecting session keys would be broken.

SSL 2.0 should not be used, as it is vulnerable to a "downgrade" attack where 40-bit encryption can be forced. This weak form of encryption would leave the session vulnerable to a brute force attack where every possible key is tried until the correct key is found. With current computer hardware, 40-bit encryption offers little or no protection against brute force attacks. In fact, brute force attacks on 56-bit encryption have become more practical over time.

Self-signed server certificates can provide security, but not authentication. A self-signed certificate is not considered trusted by a client machine without taking the extra steps of adding trust for the server certificate manually. By default, Windows computers trust root certificates only from specific CAs such as VeriSign.

On the client side, default settings for popular browsers such as Internet Explorer and Netscape do not check for certificate revocation and also accept SSL 2.0 sessions. In addition, default settings often allow SSL encrypted pages to be stored in the browser cache without encryption.

A recent survey of more than eight thousand Web servers using SSL as a security mechanism revealed that almost 32 percent of the servers surveyed had weak security because of expired certificates, use of self-signed certificates, use of SSL 2.0, use of weak (512-bit) RSA keys, or use of weak SSL3/TLS ciphersuites. Detailed information is available at www.lne.com/ericm/papers/ssl_server_stats.html. The Web sites examined in this survey appear to be providing security through encrypted channels, but they remain vulnerable to attack.

Understanding SSH

UNIX is a mature and sophisticated operating system that was developed by Bell Labs in the early 1970s. Over the years, UNIX has had its share of security problems, many of which have been addressed. Overall, UNIX is considered a secure and stable operating systemæwhen configured properly.

Some protocols, however, continue to tarnish UNIX's reputation as a secure operating system. These protocols include Telnet, FTP, and the infamous Berkeley "r*" commands (rcp, rsh, rlogin). Insecure programs and protocols continue to provide easy system access for administrators and malicious users alike. These protocols remain vulnerable largely due to the fact that authentication credentials are sent over the wire in clear text. This means that anyone using a network sniffer could obtain the username and password, and then exploit a service by masquerading as the legitimate user.

Developed by Tatu Ylönen in 1995, Secure Shell (SSH) provides session-based security services including authentication and confidentiality over insecure networks. It offers a secure replacement for rsh, rlogin, rcp, telnet, rexec, rcp, and ftp. The security of SSH is largely dependent on end-to-end encryption of a session between a client and server. SSH also has the ability to strongly authenticate machines before sending login information over the wire.

SSH is generally used to log in remotely to other computer systems and execute commands. SSH also allows for the secure transfer of files from one machine to another through the use of secure file copy (SCP) and secure ftp (SFTP). SSH can help secure X11 traffic by sending it through an encrypted tunnel. SSH has even been used to set up primitive virtual private networks (VPNs) between hosts.

SSH components include the server (SSHD), the client (SSH), secure file copy (SCP), and ssh-keygen. Ssh-keygen is an application used to create the public and private keys that are used for machine authentication. An SSH client for Windows is shown in Figure 4.4.

SSH provides basic port-forwarding features. Port forwarding allows users to tunnel protocols through an existing SSH connection. For example, POP mail (which normally sends the username and password in clear text) can be securely tunneled through an SSH session. There are limitations to port forwarding, however, because port ranges and dynamic ports cannot be specified. Although port forwarding can help secure protocols like POP, there are risks to enabling this feature. For example, allowing an outbound SSH connection could enable a user to bypass a firewall by tunneling inbound protocols not permitted by a firewall over the encrypted SSH session.

Figure 4.4 SSH Client for Windows.

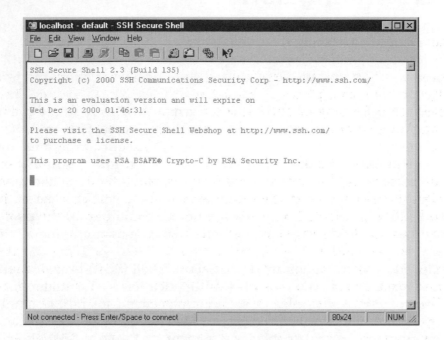

Using strong authentication options, SSH can protect against IP spoofing attacks, IP source routing, Domain Name System (DNS) spoofing, sniffing attacks, man-in-the-middle attacks, and attacks on the X-Window system.

SSH consists of three layers, the transport layer protocol, the authentication protocol, and the connection protocol. The SSH transport layer protocol is responsible for handling encryption key negotiation, handling key regeneration requests, handling service request messages, and handling service disconnect messages. The SSH authentication protocol is responsible for negotiating the authentication type, checking for secured channels before passing authentication information, and supporting password change requests. The SSH connection protocol controls the opening and closing of channels and also controls port forwarding.

Currently, there are two versions of SSH, v1 and v2. The official SSH program site is at ftp://ftp.ssh.com/pub/ssh and a commercial version is available from Data Fellows at www.datafellows.com. SSH clients are available on many platforms, including UNIX, Windows, Macintosh, and OS/2. A version of the server component, SSHD, is now available for Windows NT at www.gnac.com/techinfo/ssh_on_nt.

Network Sniffing

Network sniffers can be a security administrator's worst enemy, especially when insecure protocols like Telnet and FTP are being used. These protocols send username and password information in clear text format. In addition, some protocols like Telnet are vulnerable to session hijacking.

In nontechnical terms, a sniffer works by capturing all traffic seen by a machine over a network. Freeware, shareware, and commercial sniffers are available over the Internet and some commercial sniffers have been implemented as hardware devices. Network administrators should assume that sniffers are in use in their environment.

Several sniffers have been written to look exclusively for usernames and passwords and save this information to a file. This greatly increases the odds that a password will be compromised over time, as a sniffer could be introduced into a LAN environment and be left running for weeks. At the end of this time, an attacker would not have to sift through packet data to find username and password information, as that is all that would be present in the file. AntiSniff, a commercial tool from the L0pht, can help detect some (but not all) sniffers on a LAN. The tool is available at www.l0pht.com/antisniff.

Authentication and General Use

SSH1 provides several mechanisms for authenticating the user depending upon which version of SSH is being used. The weakest form of authentication is through the use of .rhosts files. This method should not be selected, as it is based on hostname and provides very little security.

Another authentication method is through the use of RSA encryption. Using this method, a user creates a public/private keypair by running the ssh-keygen program. The public key is stored in the user's home directory. When the client authenticates to the server, it sends a username and public key to the remote host. The server returns a session key encrypted with the user's public key. This encrypted session key is decrypted with the user's private key.

The primary means of authenticating to SSH is through the use of the .rhosts file combined with RSA authentication. This method authenticates the client and server and protects against some common attacks by preventing IP spoofing, DNS spoofing, and source routing attacks. Some people take an additional step of employing TCPWrappers instead of using .rhosts. This can provide a much greater level of control over who can connect to a service.

Finally, a user can be prompted with a username/password combination over an encrypted channel. Support for Kerberos, S/KEY, and SecurID also exist in various implementations.

Establishing an SSH connection is usually initiated by typing **slogin hostname** or **ssh hostname**. SSH connects to a server on TCP port 22. Once connected, public key authentication verifies both the server and client. Finally, a secure channel is established. General syntax of an SSH login is similar to that used in a Telnet session

SSH1

The original SSH, version 1, is generally distributed free for noncommercial use in source code format. It is available (at least in client form) on almost every computing platform ranging from UNIX to PalmOS.

SSH1 comes in three major variants, version 1.2, 1.3, and version 1.5. Although many security problems have been discovered with SSH, it is still considered secure provided that attention is paid to the authentication method and the ciphers being used. For example, SSH1 is vulnerable to a data insertion attack because it employs CRC for data integrity checking. Using the Triple-DES encryption algorithm solves this problem.

SSH1 actually supports a wider variety of authentication methods than version 2, including AFS (based on Carnegie-Mellon's Andrew File System) and Kerberos. SSH1 is still quite popular and is extensively in use. If you run SSH1, you should use the latest patched version of the server.

SSH2

SSH2 is a complete rewrite of SSH1 that also adds new features, including support for FTP and the TLS protocol. Because of differences in the protocol implementation, the two versions are not fully compatible. SSH2 provides improvements to security, performance, and portability.

SSH2 requires less code to run with root privileges. This means that an exploit such as a buffer overflow in the SSH server program will be less likely to leave an attacker with root privileges on the server.

SSH2 does not use the same networking implementation as SSH1, because it encrypts different parts of the packets. SSH2 does not support weak authentication using .rhosts files. In SSH2, the Digital Signature Algorithm (DSA) and the Diffie-Hellman key exchange replace the RSA algorithm, but since the RSA patents have now expired, expect support for this algorithm to return in future versions. SSH2 supports Triple-DES, Blowfish, CAST-128, and Arcfour.

Because of the differences between SSH1 and SSH2, and because of licensing restrictions, both versions will continue to be in use for some time. New development is happening primarily with SSH2, as it is in the process of becoming an IETF standard. For this reason, SSH2 should be preferred over SSH1. A free implementation of SSH2 has been developed by the OpenBSD community and is available from www.openssh.com.

Encryption Algorithms Used

When establishing an SSH session, both the SSH client and server negotiate encryption algorithms. The identity of the server is verified before sending any username and password information, a process that protects against Trojan applications that could accept connections and steal authentication information.

In order for a client to connect to a server using public key authentication, the public key must be securely distributed to the server.

Depending upon version, SSH supports several encryption algorithms, as shown in Table 4.2.

Table 4.2 Algorithms Supported by SSH

SSH1	SSH2
Triple-DES	Triple-DES
128-bit RC4	128-bit RC4
Blowfish	Blowfish
IDEA	Twofish
DES	Arcfour
RSA	CAST 128
—	DSA
—	Diffie-Hellman Key Exchange

The default algorithm for SSH1 is IDEA. For SSH2, the default algorithm is Triple-DES.

What SSH Can and Can't Protect You From

If you have to allow inbound connections to a server, SSH offers a secure and reliable mechanism for providing this access. SSH is so easy to deploy and use that it should be your only mechanism for providing FTP, Telnet, and rlogin-type functionality in secure environments. To the user, SSH use is nearly transparent.

SSH provides alternatives from using programs that authenticate based on IP address. When using public key authentication, it protects you from programs that use reusable passwords. It provides encryption of the data stream between client and server, which protects against session hijacking and clear-text password interception.

SSH offers protection from eavesdropping through its use of securely established session encryption. All data that flows between an SSH server and client, including authentication information, is encrypted. Providing that .rhosts authentication by itself is not used, SSH protects against IP address spoofing, DNS spoofing, and source routing attacks by authenticating both the client and server.

SSH suffers from a few limitations, including the inability to specify port ranges and the inability to forward dynamic ports. SSH can forward only individual ports. In addition, Windows versions usually do not implement secure file copy.

Potential Security Risks with SSH

Standard SSH1 distributions often include a clear-text option that should not be used or the program provides no security.

There are several version-specific bugs with early implementations of SSH. Always use the latest version with the latest patches applied. SSH1 may be vulnerable to man-in-the-middle attacks and supports a weak form of authentication through use of the .rhosts file. This stated, SSH1 supports authentication methods not supported by SSH2 including Kerberos. Authentication mechanisms should be chosen carefully, as they determine who may securely communicate with the SSH server. If you are using public key authentication, protect user home directories containing the key and do not export these directories by the Network File System (NFS).

SSH is one of the most popular Trojan applications for UNIX systems, so program binaries should be protected with an integrity assessment tool like Tripwire. SSH does not protect against incorrect configurations or an already compromised machine. SSH clients are vulnerable to keystroke recording, shoulder surfing, or the examination of core dumps that could contain passwords. Configuration is important; if SSH is going to replace rlogin and Telnet, these daemons must be shut down and disabled in the inetd.conf file.

Finally, consider disabling port forwarding. Port forwarding can provide an attacker access to resources they would not normally have the ability to access and it can be used to tunnel inbound connections through a firewall.

Understanding PGP

Sending an e-mail message over the Internet is very much like sending a postcard through the mail. Like a postcard, an e-mail message can be read by anyone with access to the transmission. This can occur without the knowledge of the sender or receiver of the message. In addition, a message could be intercepted, changed, and then resent.

Pretty Good Privacy (PGP) is a security program that provides strong e-mail and file security through the use of encryption and digital signatures. Implemented properly, PGP can provide several security services including confidentiality, integrity, and authentication.

Philip Zimmermann created the original PGP program. Though not personally responsible for posting PGP on an anonymous FTP site, Zimmermann became the subject of a three-year criminal investigation due to export restrictions on encryption software that were in effect at the time.

The stated intention of PGP was to provide a mechanism for communicating securely among individuals you've never met. The program uses both public and secret key encryption technologies. PGP uses the 128-bit IDEA algorithm for the symmetric encryption of messages. Versions 5 and above also supports CAST and Triple-DES algorithms. Version 7.0 implements a version of Twofish. A secret key is newly generated for each encrypted file or message. Not reusing a secret key is important, as it is more likely that the key will be compromised as it gets more exposure. It also enables a form of cryptanalysis known as a chosen-plain-text attack. Cryptanalysis is the study of recovering plain-text messages from encrypted format without access to the key.

PGP supports public key algorithms including RSA, DSA (Digital Signature Algorithm), and Diffie-Hellman. Hashing algorithms supported include MD5, RACE Integrity Primitives Evaluation-Message Digest (RIPE-MD), and SHA-1.

Network Associates distributes a commercial version of PGP available at www.pgp.com. The Massachusetts Institute of Technology (MIT) distributes a freeware distribution of PGP at http://web.mit.edu/network/pgp.html.

PGP Desktop Security, in version 7.0 at the time of this writing, includes security features beyond file and e-mail encryption. These features include a personal intrusion detection system (IDS), a personal firewall, a VPN based on IP Security (IPSec), PGP Disk encryption, and support for X.509v3 digital certificates.

Currently, PGP is going through the IETF standards process as OpenPGP. The current standard for OpenPGP is defined in RFC 2440. The GNU Project recently released a command line program called GNU Privacy Guard (GnuPG) based on the OpenPGP standard. This program is available as freeware from www.gnupg.org. GNU Privacy Guard is not as elegant as PGP Desktop Security and, as a command-line application, provides no integration with the operating system.

Using PGP

Network Associates product Pretty Good Privacy (PGP) provides high-level integration with the Microsoft Windows operating system and is available as a plug-in for most popular e-mail packages, including Outlook, Outlook Express, and Eudora. In theory, it is possible to use any Windows-based e-mail client with PGP, as PGP has the ability to encrypt the contents of the Windows clipboard. It can also encrypt a file-based message that can then be sent securely through any e-mail package capable of supporting attachments. In practice, however, these methods are clunky and you would be better off using PGP with a supported e-mail client.

During the installation of PGP, you will be prompted for an existing public/private keypair or you will be asked if you would like to generate new keys. The PGP Desktop Security program has a wizard that will take you through the key generation process. The wizard prompts you for algorithms, key sizes, expiration dates, and a passphrase. The passphrase protects access to the private key, so be sure to choose something sufficiently complex. In addition, the secret keyring (*secring.skr* in Windows) must be kept secure. Various Trojan applications have been designed to steal the secret keyring so an attacker can attempt to crack the passphrase offline. Also, keep in mind that if you lose or forget your passphrase you will not be able to access files or messages that have been encrypted with PGP.

After installing PGP, you have the option of sending your public key to a keyserver. You do not have to send your public key to the keyserver, but this makes it easier for other users to find your key. If you choose not to upload your public key, you will have to distribute it manually, though you also have the option of uploading your key to a keyserver at a later time.

Sending an encrypted PGP message is not complicated. First, the message is encrypted with a random symmetric session key. The session key is encrypted with the recipient's public key. If the message is signed, it is signed with the sender's private key. The encrypted session key is then sent along with the encrypted message to the recipient.

When a PGP-encrypted message is received, the reverse process takes place. PGP uses the recipient's private key to decrypt the session key. Finally, the session key is used to decrypt the message and the e-mail program displays the clear text message.

The Web of Trust

As stated earlier in this chapter, one of the problems with public key encryption is the issue of trust of the public key. In order for public key encryption to provide adequate security, you must be sure the public key you are encrypting to (the recipient) is really the intended recipient.

PGP addresses this issue with a model based on people trusting other people. This trust is expressed by signing someone's PGP key. In effect, any PGP user becomes a CA by signing other users' keys. In the PGP trust model, there is no difference between signing a key as a user or as a CA. This differs significantly from the public key infrastructure scenario described earlier in this chapter where only a CA can express trust of a public key. As other users sign your key, and you sign their keys in return, a "web of trust" is built.

This trust is based on whether or not you trust the public key as being genuine, and whether you trust the other people who have signed the key. This can be problematic, because keys should be trusted only if someone you know and trust has already signed the key. Otherwise, the only way to be sure a key is genuine is if you have obtained the key through a highly reliable mechanism like a face-to-face exchange. This trust model is suitable for informal messaging over the Internet, but it does not work well in a business scenario where nonrepudiation and user accountability would be required.

Just as CRLs are difficult to implement with a public key infrastructure, revocation of PGP keys that are no longer trusted can also be problematic. The only way to prevent use of a compromised PGP key is to send a key revocation certificate to everyone who could possibly be using the key in question. The revocation certificate can be placed on a keyserver to warn everyone from using a revoked key. Since keys can also be stored on a PGP key ring on the local machine, there is no guarantee that everyone will receive the revocation notice and discontinue use of the compromised key. PGP uses an application called PGPKeys, shown in Figure 4.5, to manage both public and private keys.

Version 7.0 of PGP Desktop Security introduces support for X.509v3 digital certificates, allowing PGP to participate in public key infrastructures, and allowing the PGP application to eventually start moving away from the web of trust security model.

There have been several implementation problems with PGP over the years, all of which have been addressed in the current version. The most notable was a bug discovered on August 24, 2000. This bug concerned the use of the additional decryption key (ADK) feature of PGP. This feature was intended to allow a business to recover encrypted data by including a second key during the encryption process. This feature was implemented to address the issue of key escrow, a mechanism for recovering encryption keys. This recovery could be required for a number of business reasons. For example, if an employee quits or is fired, the business may have a legitimate need to get at that person's encrypted data. If encryption keys are lost, say in a system crash, key escrow would provide the ability to recover the encrypted data.

Figure 4.5 PGPKeys key management application.

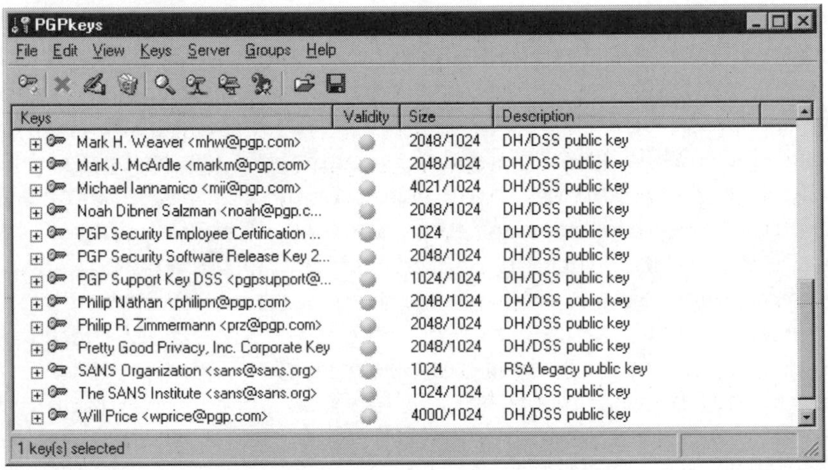

Under specific circumstances, this bug could have allowed a malicious user to add their own second key without the victim's consent or knowledge. Network Associates created a fix some 18 hours after hearing about the problem.

Potential Security Risks with PGP

Though cryptographically strong, there are many attacks against PGP that remain effective. One attack includes a dictionary attack on the PGP passphrase by attempting every word found in a dictionary and various combinations of these words. The strength of the passphrase and the protection of the private key are central to the security of PGP. In order for a passphrase to provide adequate security, it should be of sufficient length, it should not use common words found in a dictionary, and it should be changed with some frequency.

As long as a secret key is stored on the PC (and not, for example, on a smart card), the protection of the secret key file is also important. Clearly, the weakest point of attack in PGP is the protection of the secret key.

There are many applications that target the secret keyring and several programs like PGPCrack and PGPPass will run through dictionary-based attacks on the password.

Once a file or message has been decrypted, it is often kept in clear-text format on the machine. Obviously, PGP cannot offer protection in this scenario.

Almost any program that requires a user to type a password is vulnerable to certain attacks including keystroke monitoring, social engineering, or core dump/memory dump analysis. More obscure cryptographic attacks may be effective against PGP such as an attack on RSA timing or a chosen plain-text attack.

In addition, the PGP trust model is prone to error or outright deception. In order for this system to work, you must trust that the public key is genuine, belongs to the real owner, and has not been tampered with. For example, searching the MIT keyserver at pgpkeys.mit.edu yields several keys belonging to Santa Claus, and a few dozen keys claiming to belong to Bill Gates. One such key lists Bill Gate's e-mail address as god@microsoft.com. Many users have signed these and similar keys as being valid and belonging to the real owner.

Understanding S/MIME

Like PGP, Secure/Multipurpose Internet Mail Extensions (S/MIME) addresses the issue of secure messaging among parties who have never met. S/MIME addresses message confidentiality through encryption. It also addresses message integrity, message verification, and nonrepudiation through the use of digital signatures.

S/MIME does not provide session-level encryption, like SSL. Instead, S/MIME secures individual messages, making it preferable to use in an e-mail scenario where the receiver is not necessarily available at the time the message is sent. Using S/MIME, it is possible to encrypt a message, digitally sign a message, or both. Though S/MIME is not limited to securing only e-mail, this has been its primary use to date. S/MIME has also been applied to Electronic Data Interchange (EDI), online transactions, and secure application messaging.

S/MIME is based on technology created in 1995 by RSA Data Security in conjunction with a group of software vendors including Netscape, VeriSign, and others. S/MIME is based primarily on Public Key Cryptography Standards #7 (PKCS#7) for sending messages and the X.509v3 standard for digital certificates. PKCS is a set of standards used for the implementation of public key encryption systems.

S/MIME provides security enhancements to the MIME standard. Both MIME and S/MIME are defined in the following RFCs (Request for Comments).

RFC 1847: Security Multiparts for MIME

RFC 2045: MIME Part One: Format of Internet Message Bodies

RFC 2046: MIME Part Two: Media Types

RFC 2047: MIME Part Three: Message Header Extensions for Non-ASCII Text

RFC 2048: MIME Part Four: Registration Procedures

RFC 2049: MIME Part Five: Conformance Criteria and Examples

RFC 2183: Communicating Presentation Information in Internet Messages

RFC 2630: Cryptographic Message Syntax

RFC 2632: S/MIME Version 3 Certificate Handling

RFC 2633: S/MIME Version 3 Message Specification

RFC 2634: Enhanced Security Services for S/MIME

S/MIME version 3 is the preferred version to use due to its enhanced interoperability and security, so we will not discuss version 2.

Additions to MIME

S/MIME extends the MIME standard by providing security services including authentication and integrity through the use of digital signatures, and confidentiality through the use of encryption. Implemented properly, S/MIME can also help ensure nonrepudiation.

MIME is a common standard for transmitting files via Internet e-mail. It enables messages to be sent using languages with different character sets, and allows for the encoding and decoding of multimedia and binary objects that can then be sent through e-mail. Many predefined MIME types exist including Word documents, PostScript files, and WAV audio files.

MIME encodes files using various methods, and then decodes them back to their original format at the receiving end. A MIME header is added to the file, which includes the type of data contained and the encoding method used.

MIME is a rich and mature specification for sending a variety of content encoded over the Internet. It makes sense to add security features to this existing standard rather than creating a new and completely different standard. By extending MIME in the form of S/MIME, the standard is given a rich and capable foundation on which to add security features.

How S/MIME Works

In order to send an S/MIME secured message, both the sender and recipient must have an S/MIME-capable client such as Outlook, Outlook Express, or Netscape Communicator. Indeed, one of the advantages of S/MIME is that the sender and receiver of an e-mail do not need to run the same mail package. A list of products that have passed S/MIME interoperability testing is available at www.rsasecurity.com/standards/smime/interop_center.html. In addition, each user must obtain a digital certificate with a corresponding private key.

S/MIME is a hybrid encryption system that uses both public and private key algorithms. Public key cryptography is too slow to use for encrypting bulk data, but it is difficult to distribute private keys securely without public key cryptography. In the S/MIME standard, public key cryptography is used for symmetric key exchange and for digital signatures.

S/MIME requires the use of X.509 digital certificates discussed earlier in this chapter. The S/MIME specification recommends the use of three encryption algorithms: DES, Triple-DES, and RC2. The security of an S/MIME encrypted message largely depends upon the key size of the encryption algorithm. An interesting aspect of S/MIME is that the receiver, not the sender, of a message determines the encryption method used based on information provided in the digital certificate.

Sending an S/MIME message involves several steps. First, someone wishes to send an encrypted e-mail that will be safe from eavesdroppers. The message is encrypted with a randomly generated symmetric session key. Next, this session key is encrypted using the recipient's public key. This key was either previously exchanged or it was pulled from a directory such as an LDAP server. Next, the encrypted message, the session key, algorithm identifiers and other data are all packaged into a PKCS #7-formatted binary object. This object is then encoded into a MIME object using the *application/pkcs7-mime* content type. The message is then sent.

When the message is received, the digital envelope is opened and the recipient's private key decrypts the session key. The session key is then used to decrypt the message. The clear-text message can now be read.

Thanks primarily to vendor support, S/MIME seems to be emerging as the e-mail security standard of choice. S/MIME also plays a key role in Microsoft's Windows 2000/Exchange 2000 strategy.

S/MIME and PGP both provide reliable and secure methods for encrypting e-mail. PGP's trust model, until version 7.0, has relied on the web of trust security model. S/MIME, on the other hand, can take advantage of PKI and digital certificates, helping it to scale to much larger environments.

S/MIME is also integrated into many e-mail clients, whereas PGP requires the user to download an application and install e-mail application plug-ins.

Potential Security Risks with S/MIME

To be effective, S/MIME must use an adequate key length and strong encryption algorithm like Triple-DES. Many times when sending e-mail among various S/MIME-enabled applications, the only common encryption format is 40-bit RC4. This is not a sufficient key length to provide even minimal security. For example, Bruce Schneier, a noted cryptographer, created an S/MIME screen saver that cracks 40-bit RC2 keys using idle CPU cycles. This would not be a plausible attack against Triple-DES. The screen saver is available at www.counterpane.com/smime.html.

S/MIME has the same issues of trust as PGP. In order for secure communications to take place between a sender and recipient, you must have a level of assurance that you are encrypting to the correct public key. Like PGP, the secret key must be kept physically secure.

Since S/MIME uses digital certificates, many of the same issues apply, especially the handling of CRLs.

Understanding Kerberos

Originally developed at MIT, the Kerberos authentication protocol is capable of providing strong authentication services in a distributed computing environment. Kerberos provides mutual authentication of both the client and server.

With the inclusion of the Kerberos authentication protocol as the default authentication system in Windows 2000, interest in Kerberos and Kerberos application development have accelerated. For the purposes of this chapter, we will discuss version 5 of the Kerberos protocol, as the use of Kerberos version 4 is not generally recommended.

The principal behind Kerberos is that a client and server do not necessarily trust each other, but both machines trust a Kerberos KDC. Kerberos provides a system of encrypted messages called tickets, which securely establish trust between two machines on a network. Using Kerberos, passwords are never transmitted over the network, even in encrypted format. If a Kerberos ticket is intercepted, the ticket is still protected because it is encrypted.

Once a client machine has a ticket to a particular server, the ticket is cached on the local machine until it expires, making Kerberos a very efficient authentication system. Depending upon the implementation, a Kerberos ticket usually expires after eight hours.

By default, Kerberos uses DES symmetric key encryption.

Kerberos Components

A standard Kerberos implementation usually has the following components:

Principal A computer, user, or entity that will be authenticated.

Realm (Domain in Windows 2000) A logical grouping of principals that will be protected by Kerberos. All user accounts and protected resources reside within a Kerberos realm.

Key Distribution Center (KDC) The portion of a Kerberos implementation that authenticates principals. The Key Distribution Center distributes secret keys and mediates between a client computer and a network resource to set up secure communications. Secret keys are stored on the Key Distribution Center.

Ticket Granting Service (TGS) The Ticket Granting Service provides session tickets for accessing other resources in the Kerberos realm. The ticket granting service usually runs on the Key Distribution Center.

Ticket Granting Ticket (TGT, or user ticket in Windows 2000) A security token that verifies that an entity has been authenticated. The TGT ensures that users will not need to reenter their passwords after an initial login, until the ticket expires.

Session Ticket (ST, or service ticket in Windows 2000) A security token that allows a principal to access protected resources. A valid session ticket is required when accessing any Kerberos-enabled application.

How Kerberos Works

There are several functional steps that take place when a user authenticates to a Kerberos realm. First, a client requests a ticket from the Ticket Granting Service (TGS). Next, the server authenticates the client, and an encrypted ticket granting ticket (TGT) is sent back. This ticket is encrypted with the client's secret key, which is stored in a database on the server. Table 4.3 details the contents of a Kerberos ticket.

WARNING

Secret keys generated for the Kerberos ticket exchange are stored on a KDC, so the physical security of this machine is vital. If a KDC is compromised, the whole network could be at risk.

When the client accesses a protected resource on the network, a new request is sent to the Ticket Granting Service. During this request, the previously obtained ticket granting ticket is presented and a session ticket is requested. A Session Ticket (ST) is generated by the TGS and is sent to the client. The session ticket is then presented to the protected server and access is granted. The session ticket is cached on the client for later use.

The Kerberos authentication process is far more complex than what we have discussed here; however, the protocol is fast and efficient. In comparison, the user experience seems uneventful. After an initial authentication, usually in the form of entering a username and password, the rest of the process is transparent. When a Kerberos-enabled application (usually referred to as a *Kerberized* application) is launched, the authentication process happens without the user's knowledge. In an environment with many Kerberized applications, single-sign-on (SSO) becomes a possibility. Unfortunately, there is still a relative lack of Kerberized applications. This will hopefully change in the future, with the inclusion of Kerberos 5 as the default authentication mechanism in Windows 2000.

Table 4.3 Contents of a Kerberos Ticket

Name of Field	Contents of Field
Ticket Version	5
Realm Name	The name of the realm
Server Name	The name of the target server
Flags	The options for the ticket
Key	The session key
Client Realm	The initial realm that performed the authentication
Client Name	The name of the client
Transited	The names of the realm that have been crossed
Authentication Time	The time the ticket was created
Start Time	The time the ticket starts being valid
End Time	The time the ticket is no longer valid
Renew Till Time	The time the ticket absolutely expires
Client Address	The valid address(es) for the client
Authorization Data	The authorization data for the client
Extensions	An optional field for the use of application-specific data

Comparing Kerberos and Windows 2000

As the popularity and use of Windows NT 4.0 grew in the marketplace, so did interest in securing Windows NT systems. By adding Kerberos authentication into Windows 2000, Microsoft has increased the security capability of the operating system immensely. NT LAN Manager (NTLM) is provided for backward capability but should be disabled as soon as all the clients on the network can authenticate using Kerberos. As long as NTLM is available on the network, security is not at its strongest point.

Several benefits provided by Kerberos make it a better choice than NTLM for authentication. Kerberos is based on existing standards, so it allows Windows 2000 to interoperate on other networks that use Kerberos v5 as their authentication mechanism. NTLM cannot provide this functionality because it is proprietary to Microsoft operating systems. Connections to application and file servers are also faster when Kerberos authentication is used because the Kerberos server needs to examine only the credentials supplied by the client to determine whether access is allowed. The same credentials supplied by the client can be utilized for the entire network logon session. When NTLM is used, the application and file servers must contact a domain controller to determine whether access is allowed by the client. Kerberos authentication also provides authentication for both the client and server side, but NTLM provides authentication only of the client. NTLM clients do not know for sure that the server they are communicating with is not a rogue server. Kerberos is also beneficial for trusts. It is the basis for transitive domain trusts, and Windows 2000 uses transitive trusts by default with other Windows 2000 domains. A transitive trust is a two-way trust in which a shared interrealm key is created. The domains trust each other because they both have the shared key.

Many consider Microsoft's Kerberos implementation to be nonstandard, due to changes and extensions they made to the protocol. These changes primarily revolve around the marriage of Kerberos and public key technology, which allow users to replace their secret key authentication with a public key. This enables authentication to a Windows 2000 domain with a smart card, something that is considerably more secure than a static password.

Additionally, Microsoft terminology is slightly different than what is used in a standard implementation. For example, a traditional Kerberos Realm is referred to as a domain (similar to an NT domain). The ticket granting ticket (TGT) is called a *user ticket*, and a session ticket is called a *service ticket*. These differences aside, the Windows 2000 version of Kerberos has been demonstrated to be interoperable under several scenarios with the MIT Kerberos v5 distribution.

Keep in mind that in a Windows 2000 environment, every domain controller is also a KDC. This means that secret keys are stored on the server, so the physical and logical security of these machines is important.

Internet Information Services 5 (IIS 5), Internet Explorer 5, COM+, and SQL Server 2000 are all Kerberos-enabled.

How Microsoft Kerberos Interoperates with Other Kerberos Implementations

A key concern for managers planning to implement Windows 2000 into their existing networks that utilize Kerberos is the interoperability of the different flavors of Kerberos. Microsoft has tested various scenarios between Microsoft Kerberos and the MIT implementation of Kerberos. Their findings are:

- Clients that are not Windows-based can authenticate to a Windows 2000 KDC.

- Windows 2000 systems can authenticate to the KDC in an MIT-based Kerberos realm.

- Windows 2000 client applications can authenticate to Kerberos services running on systems that are not Windows-based as long as the service supports the Generic Security Service-Application Programming Interface (GSS-API). Windows 2000 uses the Security Support Provider Interface that is compatible with the GSS-API.

- Client applications on Kerberos systems that do not use Windows can authenticate to services on Windows 2000 systems as long as the client application supports the GSS-API.

- Windows 2000 domains can trust MIT-based Kerberos realms, and MIT-based Kerberos realms can trust Windows 2000 domains when everything is configured appropriately.

Potential Security Risks with Kerberos

There are several elements that can impact the security of a Kerberos implementation, and a great deal of design work should be performed before implementation. The primary weakness of Kerberos is that it remains vulnerable to password guessing attacks. If users select weak passwords, it is possible to collect tickets, decrypt them, and impersonate the user. Static passwords are typically the weakest point in any security system, as users generally do not pick strong passwords. The marriage of public key technology and Kerberos takes an important step toward addressing this weakness.

Kerberos stores keys on the Kerberos server. This makes the security of the server an important consideration. Kerberos is also dependent upon a reliable time mechanism, so this may be a point of attack, especially for Denial of Service (DoS).

Kerberos assumes that hosts have not been compromised. Essentially, the model is one of trusted hosts on an untrusted network.

If ticket lifetimes are set too long, the protocol becomes weak by exposing a session ticket for too much time. If the ticket lifetime is too short, it can impact usability and performance.

Certainly the use of DES in Kerberos may be cause for some concern, as DES is no longer considered a strong algorithm. Kerberos v5 allows for stronger encryption algorithms like Triple-DES, and this would be preferred.

Other issues I will mention in passing include the use of transitive trusts and the ability to forward tickets. Both may present implementation issues if not carefully considered beforehand.

Summary

In this chapter, we learned about several technologies that can help provide basic security services including auditing, authentication, authorization, availability, confidentiality, integrity, and nonrepudiation. We learned that different security applications meet different security requirements.

We discussed concepts of public and secret key cryptography. Secret key cryptography is generally used to secure large amounts of data, whereas public key cryptography is used mainly for securely distributing secret keys. The distribution and management of public keys can be facilitated through PKI.

We learned about digital signatures and how they are used to ensure data integrity. We also learned how digital signatures are tied to an individual through the use of digital certificates. There are still many legal and technical issues that need to be addressed before this technology can truly live up to its promise.

Some technologies help provide end-to-end session-based security like SSH and SSL. SSL is the most common mechanism for securing Web-based transactions; SSH provides a secure alternative for otherwise vulnerable protocols like Telnet and FTP.

Secure messaging and e-mail can be provided using applications like PGP and S/MIME. Both programs take very different approaches to the issue of trust.

Finally, we learned about secure user authentication using Kerberos. Kerberos can greatly enhance the security of a network by providing mutual authentication of both clients and servers.

Each one of these technologies meets different security needs, just as each comes with its own vulnerabilities and inherent limitations.

FAQs

Q: How can I be sure an application using encryption is really secure?

A: The first question to answer about a product whose security is at least partially dependent upon encryption is whether the product in question is using an industry-accepted algorithm like Triple-DES. Products that use proprietary algorithms rarely provide adequate security. You should also examine whether adequate key sizes have been used. DES, for example, is an industry-accepted algorithm, but at 56-bits does not provide sufficient key length to offer more than moderate security. You also need to examine how keys are managed. For example, if a secret key is stored on a local system, is access to the key protected? Other details you need to examine include the use of random number genera-tion, use of hash functions, adherence to applicable standards like PKCS or FIPS (Federal Information Processing Standards), and overall system operation. It is important to remember that when evaluating the security of a product or system, you need to know not only how each piece works, but also how they fail.

Q: Are there back doors in PGP?

A: Over the years, there have been many rumors about alleged "back doors" in PGP that would allow a third party—like the National Security Agency (NSA)—to intercept any communications made with the pro-gram. These rumors have all proven to be false. Philip Zimmermann is still actively involved in the development of the program, and it is unlikely that deliberate back doors have been placed in PGP with his knowledge. This stated, you should always ensure that you are obtaining your copy of PGP from a trusted source, such as directly from NAI. For the overly paranoid, it is possible to download PGP in source code format, perform a thorough code review, and compile a verified program. Source code is available at www.pgpi.com.

Q: Are there export restrictions on cryptographic software?

A: The export of cryptographic technology was formerly categorized under the International Traffic in Arms Regulations (ITAR). ITAR classified encryption under the same category as munitions, a category that includes firearms, missiles, nuclear weapons, and chemical agents. Recently, controls on the export of cryptographic technologies have been somewhat (though not completely) relaxed. If you are planning on exporting cryptographic software, one of the best Web sites to check is the Bureau of Export Administration US Department of Commerce at www.bxa.doc.gov/encryption. Also, there is a worldwide cryptography law survey available at http://cwis.kub.nl/~frw/people/koops/lawsurvy.htm.

Q: What is AES and why is it important?

A: The Advanced Encryption Standard (AES) will become a new Federal Information Processing Standard (FIPS) publication that will replace the aging DES algorithm. As a rule, I no longer consider products that use the DES algorithm to be secure. AES was planned with the idea that the algorithm would be secure for the next twenty to thirty years. The National Institute of Standards and Technology (NIST) recently sponsored a contest to determine a single AES algorithm and announced Rijndael as the winner. Further information about AES is available at http://csrc.nist.gov/encryption/aes.

Q: What are some issues I could face deploying e-mail encryption at my company?

A: There are many issues you may encounter if you decide to deploy encrypted e-mail services in a corporate environment. Some of these issues are technical in nature, and some of them involve user education. For example, users must be trained to recognize when an e-mail is sensitive and when to use encryption. I personally have found that a typical user has a great deal of difficulty understanding public key cryptography and why you must have a certificate or public key before you can encrypt a message. I have also had users question why the use of PGP requires a passphrase to access the secret key ring. Aside from the "people issues" you will encounter, you may also have a regulatory or business need to archive e-mail. Without proper escrow services, you will not be able to access encrypted communications. Clearly, virus scanning of encrypted content is not possible. This issue will become more prominent as technology like S/MIME is widely deployed.

Chapter 5

Attacks That Await Your Network

Solutions in this chapter:

- **Identifying Types of Attacks**
- **Protecting your Network from Specific Attacks**
- **Choosing an Intrusion Detection Package**

Introduction

Securing your corporate wide area network (WAN) connection will always be a challenge. There are numerous ways in which hackers can infiltrate your network and do damage. They can bypass your security measures, attach malicious code to an e-mail message, sniff your traffic to pick out passwords and whole e-mails, or even load drones onto unsuspecting systems and deny service by using your available bandwidth. New strategies are constantly being invented.

It's very unsettling to know that there are so many ways for people to get into your system. Some are as easy as scanning an open port and exploiting it. What you should know is that there are companies out there who work equally as hard to defend your network from those very threats. With every virus released today, there are teams of programmers at places like Symantec and Network Associates who act quickly to provide protection from them. Using a computer as a professional today is like being caught in the middle of a battle between hackers and security experts to see who is better at what they do.

This chapter will discuss several methods that hackers are actively employing to get into networks and cause damage. It will also discuss how you can protect your company from these threats. One thing to remember about this topic is that the hacks and solutions are constantly changing, so you need to make sure you keep ahead of the game. You can do this by updating your virus definitions regularly and keeping up with news about current security threats to your network systems.

Types of Attacks

Let's start with a simple analogy. Imagine you have spent time, money, and effort working to make your home just the way that you want it. Now you remove your curtains, leave the front door open, and leave the keys outside the front door. You've made everything inside perfect, so why enable strangers to get in, mess it up, and steal your property? Even if your home is secure, you might open the door to someone impersonating the telephone repairman.

As a measure to protect your home you would probably install a burglar alarm, motion detector lights, and maybe even install closed circuit TV. As an analogy to systems that take action against intruders you might even decide to install a trap door with metal spikes! It's definitely a good idea to check for any vulnerability, such as the old coal chute or cat flap.

The first step with network security is to identify what an attack or intrusion is. Any action that violates the security policy of your organization should be considered a threat, but broadly speaking, attacks and intrusions can be summarised as an exploitation of the following:

- Poor network perimeter/device security

- Poor physical security

- Application and operating software weaknesses

- Human failure

- Weaknesses in the Internet Protocol (IP) suite of protocols

Before we look at these threats in more detail let me suggest that you assume a devious mind—it helps when it comes to learning about intrusion detection.

Poor Network Perimeter/Device Security

This can be described as the ease of access to devices across the network. Without access control using a firewall or a packet filtering router, the network is vulnerable.

Network Sniffers

Network sniffer is actually an equivocal term because it refers to a general product as well as a specific brand: Network General owns a trademark on a product called "Sniffer," which analyzes network traffic for potential problems or specific protocol data. Since the release of Network General's product, many devices with promiscuous capabilities have been released. They range from software packages or hardware packages, to a combination of the two. Network Associates Inc. (NAI) now owns Network General, so technically it belongs to them. Several of the available applications are Sniffit, EtherPeek, and Sniffer Pro.

Sniffing soon became an affectionate term used by IT professionals to refer to many types of protocol or traffic monitoring on a corporate network. Because of the type of information that sniffing can provide (for example, IP information, usernames, and passwords), its use can be good or bad depending on the person at the other end of the line.

Normally, a system's network card will only receive packets destined to its specific network address (its Media Access Control, or MAC, address), and all other packets are ignored. Network cards, however, support a mode known as "promiscuous mode," which will allow them to receive all traffic that travels across the network. It is this mode that a sniffer uses to view all traffic. The sniffer, via an interface to the network card, places the card into promiscuous mode, and from that point on, all traffic is passed up to the operating system's TCP/IP stack.

Most operating systems, with a few important exceptions, provide an interface by which a user-level program has the ability to turn on promiscuous mode, and then read packets at this layer. This interface bypasses the operating system's TCP/IP stack, passing Ethernet (or other link layer packets) up to the application. Most UNIX operating systems provide a standard interface to accomplish this. Windows-based operating systems, however, require a kernel-level packet driver, as the operating system provides no standardized method to interface with this level of the networking layer.

For instance, I once worked in the IT department of a large investment house, and one day I was helping to tune an application that some developers were working on. The application contained sensitive information regarding the company's financial strategies. My role was to analyze the traffic to compare performance from one version of code to the next. In the network trace, I came across some frames containing usernames and clear-text passwords; I informed the application developers and they quickly fixed the problem. If it wasn't for my personal sense of ethics, I could have easily signed on to the application and then used that information to tamper with the records.

This method of intrusion is called *eavesdropping* or *packet snooping*, and the type of network technology implemented directly influences its susceptibility. For instance, it is easier to eavesdrop on shared networks than switched networks. Although you should keep in mind that just because you use a switched network does not mean that your network is automatically safe. The release of dsniff, which is a password sniffer, has made it possible to sniff on switched networks.

Scanner Programs

Certain types of software, such as those available from SolarWinds, are able to scan entire networks, produce detailed reports on what ports are in use, perform password cracking, and view account details on servers. Although this is a very useful tool if used for the purpose of legitimate network auditing, it could be devastating in the wrong hands. Scanning software commonly uses one or more of the following methods:

- Packet Internet groper (ping) sweep to obtain IP addresses.

- Simple Network Management Protocol (SNMP) sweep for compatible devices. An unprotected SNMP-capable device is dangerous because it can allow intruders to modify network configurations.

- Transmission Control Protocol/User Datagram Protocol (TCP/UDP) port scan to see which ports are open, in use, or available. Any of these ports can be used to obtain access to the network.

■ Scan logon accounts for usernames and passwords. This will allow an intruder legitimate access with a stolen account.

I once performed a global scan for a company using an SNMP sweep program. The objective was to ensure that all network devices were running at a millennium-compliant release of software. This was surprisingly easy and I even ended up accidentally scanning some devices outside the perimeter of our network inside the carrier's network. Incidentally one device in their network was not Y2K-compliant and was upgraded on our request!

Nmap is a UNIX-based port scanning tool that is designed to scan large networks for possible entry points. Although this is a good tool to see what others may be able to find, it is also a good tool for those same people to find openings on your network for you. This tool also has a stealth mode to allow it to bypass some firewall detection. Other features include TCP SYN scanning, ICMP scanning, and remote OS identification. This is a powerful tool that can help you secure your network, so use it wisely!

Network Topology

Shared networks are easier to eavesdrop on, because all traffic is visible from everywhere on that shared media. Switched networks, on the other hand, are more secure; by default there is no single viewpoint for traffic. On Cisco Catalyst switches there is a feature used for troubleshooting through which you can mirror traffic from virtual local area networks (VLANs) or switch ports to a single designated switch port called the Switched Port Analyzer (SPAN) port. Once you plug your sniffer into the SPAN port, you can easily view traffic in different VLANs by making configuration changes.

Thankfully, most organizations are moving away from shared media for multiple reasons, including improved security and performance.

Unattended Modems

Installing a modem on a PC for remote access allows a quick and easy way to access the network from home. Unfortunately this also means that the modem and PC may be prone to attack when you are not there. It is not generally possible to detect modems attached to PCs using most types of network auditing systems, so tighter software control and education of the user community is the best solution. If access is essential, you should explain the benefits of using the (secure) corporate remote access solution instead. This is an issue unless of course the modem has been set for Auto Answer (AA). You would see this if the machine has been set up to receive incoming faxes.

Poor Physical Security

There are simple security measures that can be taken in the physical world to ensure better security for your systems. Locking your doors is obviously a good common-sense start, but there are often a number of simple procedures and safeguards that companies could perform and implement that, for one reason or another, they do not.

I recently read an article in Packet magazine that described a theft in California of a file server that contained over 300,000 credit card numbers. The thief just unplugged the server and walked out with it. A simple tagging system would have done the trick, as alarms would have sounded when the machine was removed; even a paper authorization system would have worked. After all, it's pretty simple to bypass security on routers and switches if you can get to the console port, or in the case of servers you can remove the hard disks and reinstall them elsewhere.

Application and Operating Software Weaknesses

In this context, software is a term that describes the operating system as well as the packages that run under its control. Most software is or has been deficient at some point in its life and it is not always due to poor programming. Sometimes, for example, commercial pressures can force a company to release software early, before it is debugged completely.

Software Bugs

Most bugs are based on buffer overflows, unexpected input combinations, and the exploitation of multithread scheduling. An example of this is when a cracker tries to race the legitimate code in making modifications to files in the hope of updating a password file and *not* causing a software failure; this is called a *race* condition.

A buffer is a storage area, or memory of sorts, for software applications. If this buffer exceeds the allotted size limit, an overflow occurs that can render the software useless. Unexpected input combinations are exactly what they sound like: input that the software is not expecting that can lock up the processes and deny service to other users.

Web Server/Browser-Based Attacks

Because the Internet is such a quickly evolving arena, Web applications are often hastily written. General software bugs and browser configuration errors all provide vulnerabilities that allow a wily attacker to break in.

There are many reported issues with Web browsers on the market. Of course, in your travels you will most likely run across Microsoft's Internet Explorer, so we will focus on that. Internet Explorer has been found susceptible to many potential security flaws; the following examples are fairly common:

1. **Cached Web Credentials** A potential security risk that can occur if someone logs into a secure site that requires authentication. IE will send the cached username and password to unsecure pages within that same site. A potential intruder can acquire the username and password once it has been sent to the unsecured page.

2. **Virtual Machine ActiveX Component** Although most Java applets must be digitally signed or of a stand-alone format, if embedded in an HTML e-mail or on a Web page, this requirement can be circumvented. A malicious user can program a Java applet to execute code on the target machine, allowing for almost any desired result, including the retrieval or destruction of information.

3. **Secure Sockets Layer (SSL) Certificate Validation** IE ensures security with an SSL server by verifying that the certificate came from a trusted root. IE does not verify the name or expiration date for the certificate. Once more, IE does not authenticate a SSL connection if it is made to the same server during the same IE session. This potentially could allow an intruder access between SSL connections and could allow them to disrupt or destroy data.

For more information on IE security bulletins, or Microsoft security bulletins in general, please visit www.microsoft.com/technet/security/current.asp.

Getting Passwords: Easy Ways and Cracking Programs

Most people have at one time or another created a simple password based on objects that are easy for them to remember, such as a familiar name or favorite colour. In the dozen or so companies I've worked for, I don't recall seeing good password practices being enforced very often.

It's quite simple to get someone else's password; many times, all you have to do is ask. Some other ways that passwords might be obtained are:

■ Observation, over the shoulder

■ Gaining access to password files

■ Using a sniffer to look for clear-text passwords

- Replaying logon traffic recorded on a sniffer that contains the encrypted password

- Dictionary-based attacks, which use a software program to run through every word in a dictionary database

- Brute force attacks, in which the attacker runs a program that tries variations of letters, numbers and common words in the hope of getting the right combination

Human Failure

Henry Ford was quoted as saying, "If there is any one secret of success, it lies in the ability to get the other person's point of view and see things from that person's angle as well as from your own."

Everyone has individual thoughts, feelings, and moods. Of course the human failure factor spans far and wide across the security spectrum and is usually a common contributing cause for security breaches. These can be caused as a result of malicious motives or a simple innocent mistakes.

Poorly Configured Systems

The very first time I configured a Cisco router on a network I used the default password of *cisco*. If anyone had decided to choose that router to attack they could have logged on, looked at the routing tables, reloaded the router (causing user disruption), or changed the password.

Many new systems right out of the box use default accounts or passwords that are easy to obtain. Most allow you to decide whether or not to use security features without any guidance.

Some of the things you should be mindful of are:

- Careful planning before configuration

- Ample time to configure the product properly.

- Knowing the device you are configuring. As simple as it sounds, reading the manual can go a long way!

Leakage of Information

Leakage of information is usually a little more straightforward than a sinister individual selling secrets to the outside. You may have seen personal identification numbers (PINs) or passwords in diaries or written on Post-It notes. The list is long and an absolute feast for a nocturnal attacker wandering around the office. Not shredding sensitive documents and drawings can also be a risky practice. If someone gets hold of the network diagram then they can start targeting devices and choosing points for maximum impact.

I was sitting in an open-plan office once when the LAN administrator was asked by a colleague across the room what the supervisor account password was—so he shouted it back to him. Need I say more?

Malicious Users

There are people who, for various motives, will perform or facilitate intrusions and attacks into your network. For example, someone inside the company could perform an FTP download of all customer accounts information onto a laptop, and leave the building with it.

NOTE

An attacker can also be known as a *cracker*, someone responsible for negative and destructive attacks on systems. The term *hacker*, often used incorrectly in assuming malicious behavior, generally refers to people who have the knowledge and ability to infiltrate systems, whatever their ethics and intentions. Ethical hackers find the incorrect usage of this terminology extremely misleading and potentially damaging.

Weaknesses in the IP Suite of Protocols

Perhaps when the TCP/IP family of protocols was originally developed, the world was a nicer place! Perhaps there was not the need then for the security we have today. Nowadays it is possible to stroll into a bookshop and pick up a book on how to crack a network. The success of the Internet also makes this type of information readily available.

Because the TCP/IP stack is code written by programmers/developers, it is probable that some implementations will contain errors. If the implementation of TCP/IP is poor then the system can be compromised, in spite of the upper layer applications being used.

Taking advantage of these weaknesses requires an in-depth awareness of TCP/IP protocols. Flaws exploited by attackers are being countered by software developers and then recountered by attackers again.

One example of improvement is IP Security (IPSec), which is an addition to the IP Protocol suite. IPSec provides privacy and authentication methods, creating traffic security on a network. (For more information on IPSec, refer to Chapter 3.)

NOTE

Although we discuss TCP/IP weaknesses in this section, application programs can also be poorly written or badly designed in the way that they interface with the lower layer protocols. Bad application software can provide the attacker with a foothold to penetrate a system.

Conversely, a server running well-written applications with solid code but using a bad TCP/IP implementation can still be compromised, since the application relies on the TCP/IP stack for network services.

Any member of the TCP/IP suite can be the target of an attack. Some have flaws that are easier to exploit by a cracker than others.

In order to understand this section a little better, the specific attacks will be broken down according to the Open Systems Interconnection (OSI) model layer. The OSI model is an open systems reference model, created by the International Standards Organization (ISO) in 1984, to allow different vendors to interoperate with each other. The OSI reference model provides a hierarchical tool for understanding networking technology, as well as a basis for current and future network development. The OSI model is broken down into seven layers, which are as follows:

1. Physical
2. Data-Link
3. Network
4. Transport
5. Session
6. Presentation
7. Application

Another model that is widely used is the TCP/IP model. The TCP/IP model is broken down into four separate layers instead of seven, but they all loosely map to OSI model layers.

In descending order, the application layer is represented first. The application layer or the TCP/IP model maps to the application, presentation, and session layers of the OSI model. It's responsible for application-to-application communication, presentation of data, and the creation and tear-down of sessions. The transport layer maps to the transport layer of the OSI model. The transport layer is responsible for the end-to-end integrity of the network connection and can also provide such services as flow control and error correction.

The network layer of the TCP/IP model maps to the network layer of the OSI model. The network layer is responsible for the routing and delivery of the packets through the network. Addressing at this level is handled logically by each individual protocol (IP addresses, IPX addresses, and the like).

The Host-to-Host layer (also sometimes referred to as the Host-to-Network layer), loosely maps to the OSI model's physical and data-link layers. Some of the associated protocols are ARP, RARP, SLIP, L2TP, and SDLC. Table 5.1 and Figure 5.1 map some of the more common protocols to their proper layer within their respective models.

Table 5.1 TCP/IP Model Layers and Commonly Associated Protocols

TCP/IP Model Layer	Commonly Associated Protocols
Application	FTP
	Telnet
	SMTP
	TACACS+
	SNMP
	TFTP
	NNTP
	HTTP
	DNS
Transport	TCP
	UDP
	SPX
Internet	IP
	IPX
	RIP
	IGRP
	SNA
	RTP
	X.25
	DDP
Host to Host	ARP
	RARP
	SLIP
	L2TP

Figure 5.1 TCP/IP Protocol Suite.

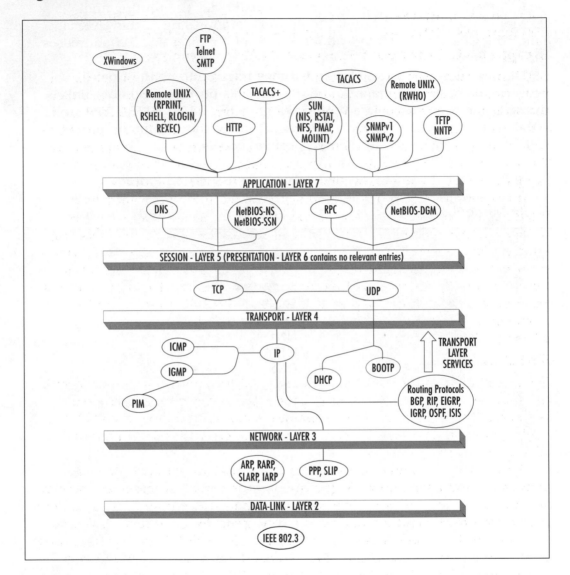

The next sections highlight some examples of the more common attacks to date; for the purpose of our discussion I've assumed that an attacker (Station C) can see traffic returning from his victims (Stations A and B). In practice this may not be the case, but the attack can still succeed, it just takes more skill on the part of the attacker. For each type of attack, I've listed the URL of a related CERT document (CERT is a central coordination center for Internet security problems worldwide; see www.cert.org).

Layer 7 Attacks

Some common attacks that can occur at the application layer include SMTP attacks, SMTP spam, FTP attacks, and SNMP attacks.

Simple Mail Transport Protocol (SMTP) Attacks

SMTP has been used to send mail by a wide variety of mail programs for many years. A common method of attack is the *buffer overflow*, in which the attacker enters a larger number of characters in an e-mail field than expected by the e-mail server. The extra characters contain executable code that is run by the e-mail server following an error in the application. The code could then facilitate further cracking. Installing the latest security patches for the e-mail system may avoid this kind of attack.

It is good practice to use digital signatures and cryptography techniques in cases where sensitive information is to be sent across shared networks. These methods can offer you good protection against spoofing attacks. Digital signatures will ensure that each message is signed and verified and encryption techniques will ensure that the mail content is viewable only by the intended receiving e-mail address. Digital signatures are covered in detail in Chapter 4. Details of spoofing attacks can be found at www.cert.org/tech_tips/email_spoofing.html and www.cert.org/advisories/CA-1997-05.html.

SMTP Spam

Spam is similar to the junk mail you receive through the postal service; it is e-mail sent to a large number of people but not personally directed at any one of them. Internet service providers can restrict spamming by the implementation of rules that govern the number of destination addresses allowed for a single message.

Spam can take many forms, but the end result is always the same—annoyance and aggravation. Think about your e-mail, whether at home or at work, and I will bet you have come across it—the e-mail that says "I'm a good luck e-mail, send me to everyone you know for good luck. If you do not forward this, you will have bad luck for 10 years." Oddly enough, those used to circulate via the United States Postal Service under a different guise. They used to be called chain letters. Chain letters can cause an inordinate amount of SMTP traffic if you have a large address book.

Some of the larger Global Service Providers (GSPs) have a severe problem with spam e-mail. Basically what happens when you sign up for their service is that your name is cataloged as a member. That member list is distributed or sold to third-party marketers that can deluge you with e-mail for just about anything. It usually has to do with a service that they want you to try or a product they want you to buy.

One of the more popular spam e-mails floating around today is the virus hoax. You may have seen a message that talks about a virus that can destroy your computer hardware. There are several of them out there, but my favorite one states that your motherboard, video card, and your hard drive will be destroyed if you are infected with this "super virus." The e-mail also states that the effects are so bad, Symantec has urged everyone to forward the message to everyone they know warning them of the potential danger. First of all, Symantec posts virus warnings and patches to their Web site. They won't ever e-mail you asking that you forward this message to everyone you know. Sound familiar? This type of message is similar to chain mail, but it is spread by the paranoia of the recipients.

You should also be aware of the possibility of e-mail bombing. E-mail bombing is actually a flood of e-mails from one or multiple sources that can overload your system or the e-mail server. Several years ago, the easiest way to do this was to get a hold of someone's e-mail address and sign him or her up for several thousand mailing lists. By standard operation, mailing lists can send out several thousand e-mails to a group per day. If you amplify that by several thousand, you have just created a very bad situation. Most mailing daemons now require you to respond to them in for verification that you did want to sign up for the list. On the other hand, if you are signed up for that many lists, the verification requests alone can be a problem.

One of the problems that you face as an administrator is the fact that spam takes a lot of bandwidth to circulate. Not only can it clog your WAN connection, but it can also bring down e-mail servers if the load is heavy enough. This type of flooding can cause a Denial of Service (DoS) to e-mail and/or Internet connectivity for your company.

For further information, go to www.cert.org/tech_tips/ email_bombing_spamming.html.

File Transfer Protocol (FTP) Attacks

Anonymous connections to servers running the FTP process allow the attacking Station C to download a virus, overwrite a file, or abuse trusts that the FTP server has in the same domain.

FTP attacks are best avoided by preventing anonymous logins, stopping unused services on the server, as well as creating router access lists and firewall rules. If you require the use of anonymous logons, then the best course of action is to update the FTP software to the latest revision and to keep an eye on related advisories. It's a good idea to adopt a general policy of regular checks of advisories for all software for which you are responsible. For further information go to www.cert.org/advisories/ CA-1993-10.html.

Simple Network Management Protocol (SNMP) Attacks

Using **SNMP get** queries it is possible to gain detailed information about a device. Armed with this information the cracker can facilitate further types of attack. By using an "SNMP set" program it is also possible to change the values of Management Information Base (MIB) instances.

WARNING

A few years ago I had to modify the outbound ISDN number called by a non-Cisco router in Korea. Based in London, I had no access to the configuration utility or any onsite engineers.

However, by viewing the entries in the MIB tree and performing multiple SNMP sets I was able to change the phone number to the correct string. This allowed calls to be made successfully to the London router.

I'm no attacker, but if default community strings of *public* and *private* are used for SNMP configuration without SNMP access lists, the door is left wide open for attack.

All applications and services can leak information that an attacker can use. In this section we have reviewed a few common ones but there are hundreds that have been reported, with many more that remain unreported or undiscovered. Security personnel must keep up-to-date with advisories on all software (and operating systems) so that they are best prepared against attacks: in other words, build security through prevention.

Layer 5 Attacks

Common attacks that occur at the session layer of the OSI model include Domain Name System (DNS) attacks and NetBIOS Win Nuke.

Domain Name System (DNS) Attacks

Within the TCP/IP network structure, all nodes attached to the network will be issued an IP address. In smaller networks it is fairly easy to keep track of what devices have what IP addresses assigned to them. However, in the largest network of all (the Internet), keeping track of what IP address the Web server at Cisco Systems has would be very difficult. DNS alleviates this issue by allowing us to associate names with IP addresses. So, instead of having to remember 198.133.219.25, you can type in www.cisco.com and get to the same page.

The DNS service in most companies is vital. Nothing works as it should without it. For example, e-mail, Web services, and most communications applications use DNS names. One method of attack is to infiltrate the server in order to modify DNS entries directly. Another is where station C would pretend to be another DNS server responding to a request from a real DNS server. In this way the DNS cache on all DNS servers could be "poisoned," which would affect the whole network. This works by making a DNS server think it needs an update, act as its peer, and then send it a blank database. This will wipe out the DNS capacity of the server until it is rebuilt.

Modern DNS software has the capability of using authentication between servers. For further information go to www.cert.org/advisories/CA-2000-03.html.

NetBIOS Win Nuke

In a NetBIOS Win Nuke attack, Station C would send Out Of Band (OOB) data to station B with an Urgent (URG) flag on port 139 (NetBIOS Session Service). This could cause station B to fail. There are vendor software patches available to overcome these types of issues. For further information, go to www.cert.org/vul_notes/VN-2000-03.html.

If you have been around for a couple of years you should have at least heard about Win Nuking. When it was released, the ability was introduced to lock up a remote system by sending this packet to a Windows-based machine. This type of attack quickly became a favorite way to knock people off of Internet Relay Chat (IRC), the Internet, or lock up their machine all together. For a time, this was a weapon used by staunch Macintosh supporters.

Microsoft has released updates for their stack that will protect your systems from such attacks. You should make sure that you download the patches and get them applied to systems on your network.

Win Nuke affects only specific versions of the Microsoft OS. Older versions such as Windows 95 are affected, but the security issue was corrected prior to the release of Windows 98, so Windows 98 is not affected. Windows NT resolved this issue with a service pack, and all later versions of the Microsoft OS are not affected (i.e., Windows Me and Windows 2000).

Layer 3/4 Attacks

Layer 3 and Layer 4 attacks occur at the network and transport layers of the OSI model; some of the more common attacks include TCP SYN flooding, Smurf IP spoofing, TCP/IP sequence number spoofing or session hijacking, Denial of Service (DoS) and Distributed Denial of Service attacks (DDoS), such as Ping of Death, teardrop and land attacks.

TCP SYN Flooding

A TCP SYN flooding attack is best described in stages:

1. Attacking Station C sends lots of SYN packets to Station B in rapid succession from nonexistent host addresses (see Figure 5.2).

Figure 5.2 TCP SYN flooding attack: Step 1.

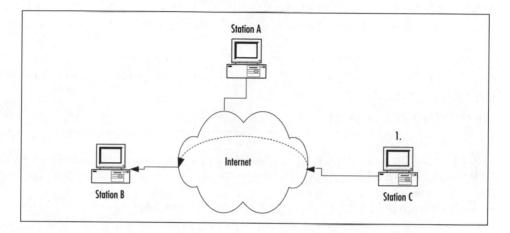

2. Station B sends back SYN/ACKs and maintains the half-opened connections in a queue as it waits for ACKs from the nonexistent hosts at the source addresses (see Figure 5.3).

Figure 5.3 TCP SYN flooding attack: Step 2.

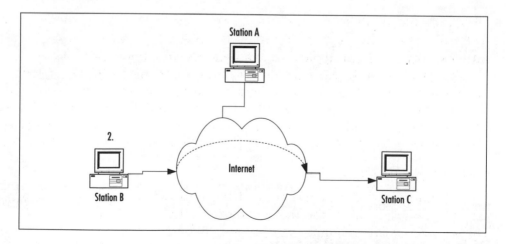

3. Station B runs out of resources waiting for ACKs back from nonexistent hosts (see Figure 5.4).

Figure 5.4 TCP SYN flooding attack: Step 3.

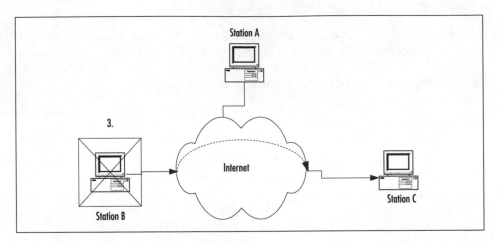

4. At this point Station B drops legitimate connections and is likely to hang/crash (see Figure 5.5).

Figure 5.5 TCP SYN flooding attack: Step 4.

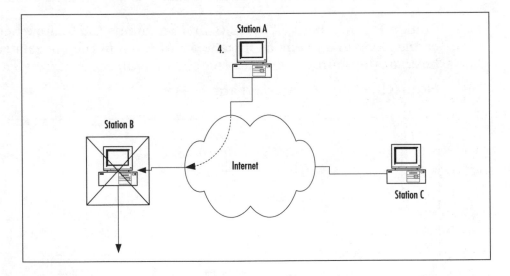

There is no widely accepted solution for this problem. On Cisco routers, however, it is possible to configure TCP Intercept, which protects against SYN floods.

TCP Intercept Configuration

The TCP Intercept feature is available on Cisco routers that have Cisco Secure IS (Firewall Feature Set) installed; it is configured as follows:

1. Ensure that you have the necessary IOS Firewall Feature Set installed.

2. Create an extended access list where the source is **any** and designate internal networks to protect against SYN flooding attack.

3. In global configuration mode enter the following command:

```
ip tcp intercept list <access-list number>
```

4. Choose which mode you want to operate in. If you don't specify, it will be in *Intercept* mode. In *Watch* mode the router monitors TCP connection requests; if they do not become established within 30 seconds, the router sends a TCP RST to the receiving station, thus allowing it to free its resources. When operating in *Intercept* mode, the router acts as a middle-man in the TCP handshake. It will keep the original SYN request; respond back to the originator with a SYN/ACK pending the final ACK. Once this happens, the router sends the original SYN and performs a three-way handshake with the destination. It then drops out of the way to allow direct communications between source and destination. To choose the mode, enter the following command:

```
ip tcp intercept mode intercept|watch
```

TCP Intercept will monitor for the number of incomplete connections; when this figure goes over 1100, or if a surge of over 1100 connections is received within 60 seconds, then the router deletes the oldest connection request (like a conveyor belt) and then reduces TCP retransmission time by 50 percent. The aggressiveness of this behavior can be adjusted to fit security policy. For further information on TCP SYN flooding, go to www.cert.org/advisories/CA-1996-21.html.

SMURF IP Spoofing Attack

This is based on IP spoofing where multiple broadcast pings are sent out by Station C with Station A's IP address as the source. Station A could be overwhelmed with Internet Control Message Protocol (ICMP) response packets. Recommended solutions are as follows:

- Disable IP-directed broadcasts at the router by entering the global command **no ip directed-broadcast** in the router configuration.

- If possible, configure the operating system not to respond to broadcast pings. For more information go to www.cert.org/advisories/CA-1998-01.html.

- Use the global command ip **verify unicast reverse-path** on the router. This will match the routing entries in the Cisco Express Forwarding (CEF) table against the source IP addresses of incoming packets. If there is no route back out of the interface then the router drops the packet. This will work only if CEF is enabled on the router.

- Use Committed Access Rate (CAR) on the Cisco routers to limit the inbound levels of ICMP traffic. Note that CAR configurations can also reduce the amount of SYN traffic to help against SYN flooding and DDoS attacks (discussed later in this section)

TCP/IP Sequence Number Spoofing/ Session Hijacking

Let's imagine Station C wants to spoof Station B into thinking it is Station A.

1. Station C initiates a Denial of Service (DoS) attack on Station A and then impersonates Station A by spoofing its IP address. The purpose of this is to prevent the real Station A from interfering with the attack.

2. Station C initiates a connection to Station B and tries to guess the sequence number from frames it has sniffed.

3. If Station B is fooled into believing Station C is actually Station A, then data will flow freely between the two.

Some TCP/IP implementations increment SEQ numbers in a predictable manner, which makes the exchange easier to intercept and spoof.

NOTE

Modern TCP/IP implementations are able to take advantage of a SYN cookie. If this were in place, Station B would create a cookie to store the sequence number and forget about it. This would free up Station B's resources and avoid it crashing. The same cookie could be referenced when traffic arrives back at Station B. This method prevents a hijacking station from using a "guessed" sequence number as the cookie controls (the validity of) all TCP/IP exchanges.

Applying an access list to the WAN interfaces of the company router can prevent hijack attacks from outside the network. This prevents traffic with internal source addresses from being accepted from the outside. This type of filtering is known as input filtering and does not protect against attempts to hijack connections between hosts inside the network.

Another access list to prevent unknown source addresses from leaving the internal network should also be applied. This is to prevent attacks to outside networks from within the company. For more information on spoofing and session hijacking go to www.cert.org/advisories/CA-1995-01.html.

Denial of Service Type Attacks

A Denial of Service attack occurs when the victim is left paralyzed and unable to provide services or is overwhelmed by attack traffic.

Ping of Death This type of attack takes advantage of an inability of poor IP implementations to cope with abnormally large IP packets. During this attack, ICMP packets transmitted by the attacking station would exceed 65535 bytes (the maximum IP packet size). The packet would then be fragmented and the receiving station could fail the re-assembly process and then crash or hang.

Several vendors have released software patches to overcome this problem. For more information, go to www.cert.org/advisories/CA-1996-26.html.

Teardrop Attack A teardrop attack targets a specific weakness in some TCP/IP implementations where the re-assembly fails to work correctly when incorrect offset values are injected into IP traffic. The attack is based on the same principle as the Ping of Death attack.

Land Attack Land is an IP spoofing type attack—here's how it works:

1. Station C sends a SYN packet to Station B using Station B's IP address and identical source and destination port numbers.

2. Station B will never be able to complete this connection and may go into an infinite loop.

3. If Station B is susceptible to this type of attack it will hang or crash.

The recommended solution is to install vendor patches. For Land it is also advisable to install ingress filters to combat IP spoofing. For more information, go to www.cert.org/advisories/CA-1997-28.html.

Distributed Denial of Service Attacks (DDoS) Recently DDoS-types of attacks have become more common. Typical tools used by crackers are Trinoo, Tribal Flood Network (TFN), TFN2K, and Stacheldraht. Refer to Figure 5.6 to see how a DDoS attack works.

Figure 5.6 Simplified DDoS attack scenario.

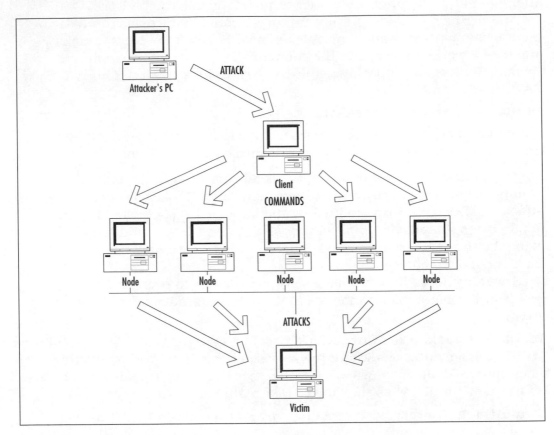

As illustrated in Figure 5.6, the attacker gains access to a client PC. From there, he or she can use tools to send commands to the nodes. These nodes then flood or send malformed packets to the victim. Coordinated traceroutes from several sources can be used to probe the same target to construct a table of routes for the network. This information can be used as the basis for further attacks. So what makes this so nasty? In practice there may be thousands of nodes. Billions of packets can be directed at the victim, taking up all available bandwidth or causing DoS. At present there is no solution to the problem, nor is it easy to trace the attack origin. A list of general suggestions is as follows:

- Prevent initial compromise of the client, through good security practice.
- Keep software up-to-date with patches and upgrades.

- Keep all antivirus software up-to-date.

- Run desktop firewall software where available.

- Use CAR to limit ICMP and SYN packets inbound.

- For more information go to www.cert.org/advisories/
  CA-1999-17.html and www.cert.org/reports/dsit_workshop.pdf.

Trojan Horse Attacks

Legend says that the Greeks won the Trojan War by hiding soldiers in an enormous wooden horse before offering it as a gift, in order to sneak past the gates of Troy. At night the Greeks leapt out and seized control to win the war—brilliant! Today, some malicious computer programmers write software *Trojan horses*. These are disguised as something quite innocent such as an e-mail attachment or a game, but once initialized, start other hidden programs that proceed to wreak havoc.

A recent example of this would be the Love Letter virus that caused huge disruption worldwide. An e-mail attachment was sent out which, once opened, would infect files on the hard disk, read your address book, and then propagate the same e-mail to everyone telling them that you love them. I was quite touched by the number of e-mails I received, until I read the news.

A primary effect of this Trojan was an overload of mail servers as they struggled to keep up with the exponential rise in e-mail traffic. The attack had a sizeable impact on the global business community.

Virus or Worm Attacks

Viruses are programs that target files on your computer and worms are viruses that have the ability to propagate themselves. These types of attacks are often contained within Trojans.

Specific Attacks and How to Protect Yourself from Them

Now that we have learned about some of the attacks out there, we should discuss how you could protect your network from them. Not all attacks can be prevented, but you can take measures to ensure that your whole network isn't taken down. For instance, a DoS or DDoS attack is almost impossible to prevent because of the spoofing of IP addresses involved.

Back Orifice and NetBus

Back Orifice is a client/server program that allows an intruder to control a remote system. NetBus is a program with many of the same features, and can be protected against in the same way. The server program must be installed on a target machine in order for Back Orifice to work. Once installed, the hacker's machine will run the client program and be able to delete files, lock up the remote machine, install a screen-saver password, and several other destructive things.

Protection

Believe it or not, Back Orifice and NetBus are fairly easy to guard against. There are several things that limit the functionality of this program:

- The target system's IP address must be known, and the server program must be installed either by the hacker or the target user.

- The nature of this attack is stopped by most firewall mechanisms, so merely having one correctly installed will probably protect you.

- Many of the commercially available antivirus packages detect and remove these two programs from your system.

Melissa, Love Letter, and Life Stages

Of late, there has been a sudden increase of automated worm and macro viruses that can do a range of things on your system. A couple of the more notable are the Melissa Macro virus, Love Letter, and Life Stages.

The Melissa virus is actually a macro virus that affects Microsoft's Word application. The virus will appear as "An important message from <user>." If the payload is executed, it will attempt to e-mail itself to 50 people using your Outlook address book. This virus is also capable of disabling the security features in Microsoft Word 2000, so that after the first time you open a document it no longer prompts you for permission to run macros.

The Love Letter worm is a very destructive and highly distributed Visual Basic Script (VBS). If you were in corporate America just a few short months ago, you probably heard about it or experienced it for yourself. This worm was by far the most quickly distributed virus I have ever seen. It was first detected on a Friday at about 3 P.M., and I had already seen it by 7:30 P.M. that same day. There are several differences that set this apart from most other worms.

If the VBS payload is executed, the Love Letter worm will attempt to e-mail a copy to everyone it can find in the Outlook address book. This contrasts with the 50 people to whom Melissa was sent. The VBS was designed to delete all files of the following types: .vbs, .vbe, .js, .jse, .css, .wsh, .sct, .hta, .jpg, .jpeg, .wav, .txt, .gif, .doc, .htm, .html, .xls, .ini, .bat, and .com. The payload will then replace them with virus code. MP2 and MP3 files are hidden instead of being deleted. Needless to say, this can cause *huge* problems with any computer system that is infected.

The VBS payload also looked for common Internet Relay Chat (IRC) programs, such as mIRC, and then wrote code into the .INI file to send a copy of itself to users over IRC.

The Life Stages worm is a Microsoft SHS (or *scrap*) file that replicates itself to 100 entries selected randomly from your address book. Although not particularly destructive, you should keep in mind that any of these worms could cause severe network capacity problems. If Windows 2000 users are sending 100 e-mails at the same time you may have some server problems.

Don't Play with Fire

Although you can view the code of this worm by removing the .VBS extension, it is never recommended that you do so. It is best if you just remove the file and keep others from modifying the file as well. This worm spreads so quickly that you don't want to run the risk of another outbreak.

Protection

There are several ways in which you can protect yourself from these types of viruses/worms. First of all, it is absolutely imperative that your network has updated virus definitions. I have gone to many companies that do not keep them updated, and that are commonly infected with these sorts of viruses. Most of the commercially available antivirus packages have regular definition updates either by subscription or download.

It may also be necessary to write filters to strip off any unused file types before they enter your network. Some of the more common file types you may not need in e-mail are .shs, .vbs, .com, .bat, .exe, or ActiveX controls and Java applets. Writing filters will surely affect the users on your network, but this is an option that many have taken after the recent outbreak of destructive worms. Please keep in mind that you should also set the filters to look inside of compressed files. Without that feature, the payload can be hidden from your security measures.

As we have seen, there are many attacks that pose a potential security risk to your network. We have looked at many of the more popular ones, but there are many more where these came from. To this point, we have been discussing a defensive posture with network security—but you can protect your network more proactively by detecting, cataloging, and tracking attacks, by exploring the options of intrusion detection.

The World of Intrusion Detection

Intrusion Detection Systems (IDSs) have become a necessary component of any corporate network security model. An IDS can be deployed to look for specific attacks by searching for known patterns, or to look for any behavior that is not deemed normal.

There has been a large amount of market hype around what IDSs are capable of. Cisco and other reputable IDS vendors maintain that the IDS is a key component to be used in conjunction with other tools to provide an end-to-end secure system.

Why Was it Developed?

The main reason that intrusion detection was developed was to help in the diagnosis and correction of network security failures. Intrusion detection can do a lot to aid in closing exploited holes, notifying administrator groups, or even authorities.

What Intrusion Detection Can Do for You

The IT community is undecided on the best way to perform intrusion detection. Should it be network-based? Or host-based? The truth of the matter is that a combined approach is probably best. Let's describe both of these methods in order to understand their particular strengths and weaknesses.

Network IDS

The network-based IDS is usually composed of a sniffer or a sensor that examines frames on the wire and a reporting or analysis engine. The sensor and analysis engine can be packaged in a single host or as a distributed system. In the same way that you have a signature or thumbprint by which you are identified, an attack will display a unique signature or pattern, hopefully. The sensors in this type of system are promiscuous and will look at all traffic that passes by. The moment they spot something suspicious they will send notification messages to an analysis or management station.

The advantages are:

- They can be configured to be nonobtrusive. You can pick up intrusion attempts, create log entries, and inform security staff of the event without the intruder's knowledge.

- You don't need application passwords, network operating system rights, or system logons in order for the software to run and return results.

- They are not dependent on OS or application types as they work at a packet level, identifying attack patterns or signatures.

- No infrastructure changes are usually required; the network IDS can just slip into the existing network.

- There are no overheads or changes on servers and workstations; the network IDS does not require any software to be installed on these devices.

The disadvantages are:

- Some vendors' systems are unable to collect data at higher speeds. Because collection and analysis is key, the network IDS must not drop or miss packets. Some network IDSs running at speeds of 100 Mbps or above may experience this problem.

- They are able to sniff only on the local segment. Ideally the network IDS must be connected to a promiscuous hub or a span port on a switch. If "visibility" is limited then its capacity will be too.

- They are based on predefined attack signatures, and as a result could be out of date or miss more complex types of attacks. Although every effort is made by authorities like the Cisco Countermeasure Research Team (C-CRT) and CERT to keep the signature databases up to date, new attacks can be protected against only after the event has occurred.

- They perform impersonal analysis and resulting actions can therefore be impersonal too. Due to the level at which the network IDS works, it cannot "see" who the user is or what the business value of a service is, so this can result in a secure but sometimes severe action (for upper layer services) being taken.

- Depending upon the configuration, large amounts of data can be sent from collection devices back to the central management station. The more granular the collection is, the more traffic there will be.

- The reporting engine can generate a lot of events. Trained personnel will need to spend time tuning the system by analyzing the reports and filtering out false positives.

- They have difficulty in dealing with attacks within encrypted sessions. The network IDS relies on being able to identify attack signatures. If the traffic is encrypted, then the signature will be hidden too, rendering the IDS ineffective.

False Positives, False Negatives

A *positive* is reported when a detection has been made. If the attack is real, then appropriate action must be taken—but what if it isn't a real attack? This scenario is known as a *false positive*.

A perfectly legitimate transaction could trigger an IDS to believe that an attack was in progress. The solution is to investigate and review the IDS configuration to prevent the false positive from occurring again; this is possible if you use Cisco's Secure IDS (this product was formerly known as NetRanger).

When an attack takes place and the IDS doesn't detect, the situation is called a *false negative*. How do you know that you've had a false negative? Usually only one tier of security in your defense would have been compromised, and the attack would be detected through another line of defense. Responsible IDS vendors like Cisco make every effort to keep their IDS detection database up to date.

Host IDS

Host IDSs will use system, audit, and event logs from different operating systems and applications. They are able to generate reports based on user/system process activity and can highlight any suspicious behavior based on a set of rules.

The advantages are:

- They provide specific information about who did what, when, and to whom! This is great because there are no speculations or deductions to be made. Meaningful actions can be taken according to specific individuals or applications.

- Host IDSs are less likely to generate false positives because information is directly related to people and applications.

- They produce much less traffic than Network IDSs; there is little emphasis on multiple separate sensors and centralized management stations.

- They do not suffer from network visibility problems (like network IDSs).

A disadvantage is that there is a lack of portability between operating systems, and multiple software installations are required as a result. Also, host IDSs are usually written for one operating system only.

What Can't IDSs Do?

Let's eliminate some of the common misunderstandings regarding IDSs. They are not "silver bullets" and cannot perform magic when it comes to stopping intruders. They cannot provide investigations without human assistance—like a good tool, the IDS is most effective when in the right hands. They are not intuitive to company security policies, and have to be configured to match. They are not self-correcting—if we don't take the time to configure the IDS properly we will get poor results (the "garbage in, garbage out" principle still applies). They cannot necessarily sustain direct attacks (on the IDS itself): just like any other system the IDS itself can be compromised. They cannot track and defend against all types of attack. They cannot always analyze all traffic on a network; sometimes the IDS is unable to keep up with all the traffic or the location of the IDS is such that it has a limited view of the network. And finally, they cannot improve a poor security strategy.

Deploying in a Network

The placement of a network IDS requires careful planning. Cisco's Secure IDS product Secure IDS is made up of a Sensor and a central management station called a Director. Let's look at the best place to put the Sensor (see Figure 5.7).

Sensor Placement

Most companies have a firewall that separates the internal network from the outside world; the network outside the firewall is known as the demilitarized zone (DMZ).

Should we place the Sensor outside or inside? If the Sensor is outside, then it can monitor external traffic. This is useful against attacks from the outside, but does not allow for detection of internal attacks. Also, the Sensor itself may become the target of an attack so it must be protected.

If you place the Sensor inside, then it will be unaware of violations that have occurred that were prevented by the firewall. On the plus side it will detect internally initiated attacks and can highlight firewall rules that are not working properly or are incorrectly configured.

Figure 5.7 Distributed network IDS deployment example.

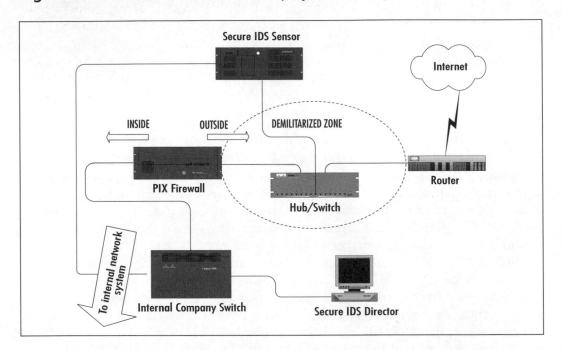

So which one do we choose? The answer is to install the Sensor so that one of its two interfaces is connected to the DMZ (monitoring port) and the other (control and communication port) is connected on the inside. The Sensor can then manage the outermost Cisco router in order to protect itself and the rest of the internal network while communicating back to the Director.

When you review your security policy you may decide that you need to install more Sensors at different points in the network according to security risks and requirements.

Some example locations are:

- Accounts department's LAN

- Company strategic networks, for example, Development LAN

- Technical department's LAN

- LANs where staff turnover is rapid or where hotdesk/temp locations exist

- Server LAN

NOTE

It is important that the firewall allow the Sensor to manage the router in the DMZ and the Director (behind the firewall) to communicate with the Sensor. Depending upon your firewall setup this may involve rules to allow communication on UDP port 514 for syslog traffic from the router to the Sensor, Telnet from the Sensor control interface to the router, and communication on UDP port 45000 between the Sensor and the Director.

Network Vulnerability Analysis Tools

Some time ago I bought a 20-year-old car for a small sum. The only way that I could achieve peace of mind was by taking it to a specialist, a mechanic who performed a full safety check. After this I had a long list of risks, armed with this knowledge I was able to repair, remove, and replace components in order to make my vehicle secure.

It is important to proactively scan for weaknesses in the network before they are exploited.

Intrusion Detection Packages

Since we have discussed what intrusion detection is and what it can do for you, it is a good idea also to know what products are available on the market. The following list details some of the available packages, and what features they have.

ICEpac Security Suite

The ICEpac security package is available from Network ICE, and it comes with quite a few features. It is a relatively small package, but it is extremely versatile and it can be integrated with other vendor products very easily.

This package is broken down into several key components:

- ICEpac Manager
- BlackICE Agent
- BlackICE Sentry
- BlackICE Guard
- Installpac

The ICEpac Manager is a Web-based management tool for all of the components included in the suite. The manager allows for very easy deployment of agents, guards, and sentries, as well as real-time collection of logs and security intrusion attempts for forwarding to proper systems or databases.

BlackICE Agent is a software package that deploys the functions of a firewall with the added feature set of a seven-layer protocol decode. This allows the agent to protect your network from malicious code, whereas firewalls generally cannot. It's nice to note that this product takes up only a mere 10MB of space for installation, considering that some other packages are becoming quite hefty. Some of the features of BlackICE are as follows:

Alerting Alerts are communicated by visual, audible, SNMP e-mail, or pager notification.

IP Address Blocking BlackICE Agent can block attacking addresses automatically or manually.

Evidence Logging BlackICE Agent logs malicious packets and hacking attempts into a central database for internal, civil, or criminal investigations.

Trusted IP Addresses Indicates trusted IP addresses to reduce false positives.

Back Trace ID BlackICE Agent can identify a hostile IP address to track down the origin of the attack, and help determine if the attacker is inside or outside your organization.

BlackICE Sentry is the intrusion detection package that is included in the security suite. BlackICE Sentry monitors the network traffic and sends detected intrusion back to the ICEpac Manager for cataloging. The BlackICE Sentry can also be configured in a stand-alone arrangement in which you can use this product without the rest of the package. This product boasts the ability to run at gigabit and Fast Ethernet speeds without dropping a single packet.

BlackICE Guard is a protection tool that can sit out in front of a network server or on the internal side of a firewall and filter suspect packets, so that they never reach their destination.

More information can be found at www.networkice.com.

Cisco Secure Intrusion Detection System (Secure IDS)

Secure IDS originally was developed by Wheelgroup, Inc. but is now owned by Cisco Systems. Secure IDS is a solution that can be added to your network to perform dynamic intrusion detection. It will monitor for and respond to intrusions in real time. A simple Secure IDS solution is made up of a distributed model with three main components: the Sensor, the Director, and the Post Office.

The Sensor

The Sensor is a specialized device that uses a rule-based inference engine to process large volumes of traffic in order to identify security issues in real time. You can purchase a ready-made appliance from Cisco or purchase a software-based package to install on an x86 or SPARC Solaris 2.5.1/2.6 station. The software to create your own Sensor can be found on the Secure IDS CD. The Sensor can either capture traffic itself or monitor syslog traffic from a Cisco router. Once an attack or security event is detected, the Sensor can respond by generating alarms, logging the event, resetting TCP connections or "shunning" the attack (by reconfiguration of managed router ACLs). Sensor events are forwarded to a central facility called *the Director* via a control/command interface.

Sensors have two interfaces, one for monitoring and one for control. The monitoring interface of the Sensor does not have an IP address and will not respond to detection attempts. There are several types of monitor interfaces available from Cisco, each selected for a particular network scenario. An example is the IDS 4230 Sensor, which is capable of supporting LAN speeds of up to 100 Mbps LAN or T3 WAN speeds. Another is the Catalyst 6000 IDS module, which is designed for switched networks.

The Director

The Director is a GUI software solution used to "direct" or manage Secure IDS from an HP OpenView platform; it is installed on a HP UX or Solaris workstation. Directors are used to complete initial Sensor configuration, process and present information sent from Sensors (in HP OpenView), and specify Sensor behavior. The Director contains drivers for the Oracle Relational Database Management Systems (RDBMS) and the Remedy trouble ticket system. It is possible to modify these drivers to interface with Sybase or Informix systems if required. When the Director receives information from the Sensors it initially logs to a flat file and then pushes the data to a relational database. Once the data are stored in the database, RDBMS tools such as SQL can be used to interrogate the data. Database details such as location of files and account information have to be configured using the nrConfigure utility (discussed later in this chapter). Systems such as Oracle contain tools to generate reports containing graphical as well as numerical representation of data. To get you started, each Director ships with a sample set of SQL queries that can be modified easily and run from within your RDBMS. It is possible to define custom actions based on events too; this is covered in more detail later in this section. The Director also provides you with access to the Network Security Database (NSDB) for reference material on exploits.

NOTE

Cisco recommends that no more than 25 Sensors should be configured to send information to a single Director. If more Sensors are required in your network then you should install multiple Directors and build a hierarchical structure of Sensors and Directors.

The Post Office

The Post Office is a messaging facility between Directors and Sensors that uses a proprietary UDP transport protocol for communication. Rather than being unacknowledged, the protocol guarantees transmissions, maintains connection status and provides acknowledgement for packets received with lower overhead than TCP/IP. It uses an enhanced addressing structure upon which it is ideal for building hierarchical fault tolerant structures. Up to 255 alternate routes between each Sensor and its Director can be supported. The structures are composed of multiple Directors and Sensors; in this way you can support a theoretically unlimited number of Sensors. Sensors can forward updates onto one or more directors that can then propagate the message to other Directors in the hierarchy.

NOTE

If you need to perform any traffic filtering on routers between Directors and Sensor (control interface) then you must allow traffic using UDP port 45000 to pass between the two.

Figure 5.8 shows these basic components in context.

You can see the Secure IDS components with the main daemons that are responsible for the running of the system. Each daemon performs a specific function.

Figure 5.8 Secure IDS daemons and associated components.

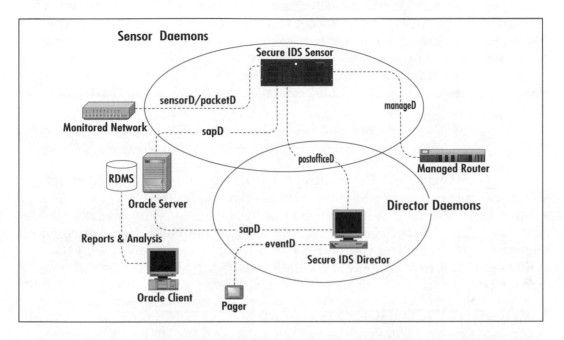

sensord/packetd sensord is used to relay intrusion detection information that is sent from other devices capable of detecting attacks and sending data; packetd is used when the Sensor itself does the intrusion detection.

loggerd is used to write to log files to record events such as alarms and command instructions.

sapd provides file and data management functions including the transfer of data to database systems such as Oracle.

postofficed manages and provides all communications between the Director and Sensors.

eventd performs notification management on events to pager and e-mail systems.

managed controls configuration of managed Cisco routers.

Here are some other daemons not displayed on the diagram:

smid is a Director daemon that converts raw information into data that **ndirmap** uses.

nrdirmap displays icons for Secure IDS components, and events such as alarms and status conditions for other daemons.

configd interprets and manages commands entered through **ndirmap** to interface with the other daemons.

Now that we understand the components, let's discuss some of the more general features. Secure IDS is a network-based IDS system that captures packets and then performs signature analysis using an inferencing engine. The analysis involves examination of each packet's payload for content-based attacks and examination of the header for patterns of misuse. Secure IDS classifies the types of attacks into two types: *atomic* (single, directed at one victim) and *composite* (multiple, over a period of time involving many victims).

The Director uses an internal (upgradeable) security database (Network Security Database, or NSDB) for signature analysis that provides information about exploits and matching countermeasures.

There are two types of signatures, *embedded* and *string matching*. As the name suggests, embedded signatures are contained within the Sensors system files, they cannot be modified and protect against misuse by matches against the packet header fields. String matching signatures, on the other hand, are user configurable and work by examining the payload of the packet. A description of how to do this is included later in this section.

General Operation

The Director runs under HP OpenView; the top-level icon is "Secure IDS" which, once double-clicked, shows submaps containing Secure IDS nodes. As more Directors and Sensors are configured, they will also become visible. Each submap can represent different security regions across the company. Once you select the Director or Sensor icon, the application daemons running on that machine are displayed. These can be selected in turn to show alarm icons generated by each. Each type of icon describes a different classification of attack based on the signatures found in the NSDB.

From HP OpenView, selecting the Security option displays further Secure IDS options. Some of the more significant are:

- **Show** (select icon first) Provides information on devices, configuration, alarms, the NSDB and others.

- **Configure** (select sensor first) Starts nrConfigure, which is used to configure Sensors and Directors.

- **Network Device** (select device first) Starts network device configuration utility.

- **Shun** (select alarm first) Allows you to shun devices and networks.

- **Advanced** (select Sensor first) Allows various options, one of the most useful being the Statistics, Show option.

Cisco IOS Firewall Intrusion Detection System

The Cisco IOS IDS is a feature that puts the Cisco solution "streets ahead" of the competition, because intrusion detection is integrated into the router IOS. Any traffic that passes through the router can be scrutinized for intrusions, with the router acting as a sensor that checks for intrusions in a similar fashion to a Secure IDS Sensor device. It's a way to have a firewall IDS without having to buy the whole IDS system that Cisco offers.

IOS IDS is useful to install at network perimeters such as intranet/extranet borders or branch office routers. You may decide to deploy this method of intrusion detection where a Secure IDS Sensor is not financially viable or where a reduced set of signatures to be checked will suffice. Despite not having the same level of granularity during signature identification and checking against a much smaller signature base than Secure IDS, it is still capable of detecting severe breaches of security, reconnaissance scans, and common network attacks. The signatures it uses constitute a broad cross-section selected from the NSDB. IOS IDS will protect against 59 different types of network intrusions. It is possible to disable checking for individual signatures through modification of the router config in order to avoid false positives. The signatures can be categorized into two main types: Info and Attack. Info refers to reconnaissance scans for information gathering and Attack refers to DoS or other intrusions. Each type can also be further divided into atomic (directed at an individual station) or compound (directed at a group of stations perhaps over an extended period of time).

IOS IDS is fully compatible with Secure IDS and can appear as an icon on the Director GUI. The router can send alarms back to a syslog server, a Secure IDS Sensor, or take action through dropping unwanted packets/terminating a TCP/IP sessions. Dropping of packets happens transparently without the router interacting with end stations, but session termination involves the router sending a TCP RST to source and destination devices; it is usually best to use both these actions together when configuring the router.

One important consideration is that of the impact of IOS IDS on the router. This will vary depending upon the specification of the router, the number of signatures configured, as well as how busy the router is. The most significant impact on the router is caused by audit rules that refer to access control lists. It is probably a good idea to keep an eye on the router memory by using the **sh proc mem** command from the privileged exec prompt after configuration.

Unlike Secure IDS, IOS IDS (as the name suggests) contains the signatures within the image. For future updates to the IOS IDS signature base, the image on the router flash has to be upgraded. It is not possible to modify or add new signatures to the existing set (which is a useful feature available on Secure IDS). A sample running-config output and integration with the Cisco Secure IDS can be found in Figure 5.9.

Figure 5.9 Sample running-config from a router with the Cisco Firewall IDS IOS installed (shown with integration with the Cisco Secure IDS).

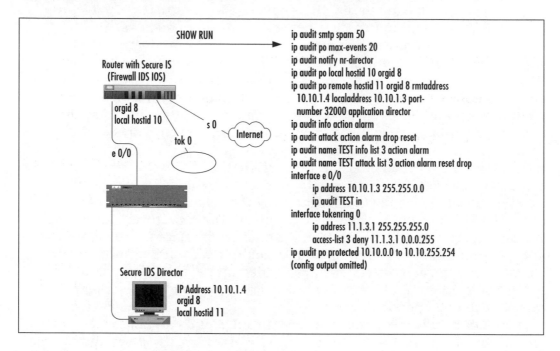

Cisco Secure Integrated Software (Firewall Feature Set)

The Firewall Feature Set contains IOS features that allow you to configure the router as a firewall, as well as provide intrusion detection services. Apart from IDS, the Firewall feature set also contains the following features:

Access Control Lists   Standard, Extended, Dynamic (to provide temporary access) and Reflexive (to permit/deny traffic based on its direction).

TCP Intercept   See the earlier section on protection against SYN flood attacks.

Authentication Proxy Service   Implementing user access security policies.

Port to Application Mapping (PAM)   Allows TCP/UDP port customization.

Security Server Support For Radius, TACACS+ and Kerberos.

Network Address Translation (NAT) Translation of unregistered addresses.

IPSec Network Security Cryptography techniques across untrusted networks.

Neighbor Authentication Checking of routing updates for authenticity.

Event Logging Can be sent to the console, virtual terminals, and syslog servers.

User Authentication and Authorization Protects against unauthorized access.

Context-Based Access Control See the following section.

CBAC (Context-based Access Control)

The CBAC component of the feature set is particularly relevant to this section as it provides protection against attacks by inspecting traffic and taking action. CBAC can inspect a variety of traffic types and is able to disconnect idle sessions, drop packets, or log inspection results to a server.

CBAC can protect against Denial of Service attacks through dynamic monitoring, interception, and response to DoS-type network attacks. For example, the router can drop suspicious packets and notify the administrator. The router should also be configured with TCP Intercept to protect against SYN floods, as discussed earlier in the chapter.

CBAC also blocks unauthorized or malicious Java applets. Java has gained popularity with developers over the last few years. Java applets can be embedded within Hyper Text Transfer Protocol (HTTP) traffic, so CBAC will permit or deny Web sites to send traffic to your network using access lists on boundary routers.

CBAC provides a comprehensive audit trail showing source, destination, timestamps, duration of connection, and bytes transmitted. This is configurable to highlight specific applications and features.

CyberCOP Intrusion Detection Package

The Intrusion Detection Package from CyberCOP includes a high-quality set of features. There are several components that make up this package:

- CyberCOP Scanner
- CyberCOP Monitor
- CyberCOP Sting
- CASL

The CyberCOP Scanner is a set of scanning tools that will allow you to identify potential security issues before they become a problem, and will also give you advice on how to correct them. An in-depth firewall test mechanism is included to help provide feedback for your firewall configurations.

The CyberCOP Monitor is a multitiered monitoring agent with the ability to maintain real-time intrusion detection for areas of the network with less security. It can operate in a high-speed switched network, and can inspect packets individually for possible threats.

CyberCOP Sting is a very intelligent system architecture that acts like a Windows NT server, SUN server, or a Cisco router to potential intruders. This type of system is called a *honey pot*; the premise behind this design is to decoy hackers by providing them a system with seemingly bountiful exploits. When an intrusion is detected, this system will redirect the intruder to a system that collects all of the evidence from the intrusion.

Custom Audit Scripting Language (CASL) allows users to design custom scripts for Intrusion Vulnerability Detection. This architecture will allow you or your team of developers to scan for unknown holes in your security fabric.

Summary

There are many forms of security breaches that can be encountered on your network. This chapter has detailed how some of the most common attacks occur, and what can be done to protect you from them. Some important points to remember are:

- DoS attacks are very hard to track or prevent.

- Most TCP/IP based attacks can be defeated using protocol switching.

- LAND attacks can be defeated by filtering IP Spoofing, because LAND depends heavily on IP Spoofing for operation.

Attacks such as the Ping of Death can send an improperly sized IP packet to a host, with a weak TCP/IP stack, and can cause that system to hang or crash.

It is most important to keep your server software up-to-date with all necessary patches. It is also good practice to verify proper configuration of firewalls, and make sure that all network virus definitions are updated regularly.

Intrusion Detection Systems (IDSs) have been developed to assist with securing and monitoring network equipment. Some IDS systems have the ability to probe network components for possible security holes, and either close them or notify the network administrator of such issues.

FAQs

Q: If I have a firewall, why do I need an IDS? Isn't it just a waste of money?

A: Let's go back to the analogy of the house. Look upon the firewalls as being guards at the front and back garden gates. They will do their best to stop any obviously nasty individuals from coming to your door. But how will they be able to stop the postman who's carrying a hatchet in his mailbag? Also, what if someone jumps the fence, or tunnels under it? The firewall is pretty rigid in its security. If you knew that the server had a rule that allowed Web cookies to pass then you could take advantage of it with an embedded file upload program. On the other hand, the IDS is a much more flexible and comprehensive solution. There are cameras, trap doors, a central control team, and a security patrol. The IDS is integrated into the very heart of the networking infrastructure (through Secure IDS). It is complemented by a comprehensive vulnerability and attack scanning solution. Cost-wise, you could save money in the short term by leaving out the IDS, but you need to ask yourself whether it is worth leaving yourself exposed. Consider the IDS as an insurance policy that works for you and helps you live longer.

Q: I need to make my network secure. What do I do and where do I start?

A: Gain senior management approval first for your initiative. The next step is to implement a change "freeze" so that all network related documentation can be brought up to date and compiled. Bad documentation is usually the "road to ruin." Once this stage is complete you can start an investigation to classify the types of protocols, devices, and software applications/revisions in use. This does not need to be extensive, just enough to get a good feel for what you have. Assemble a security team and evaluate the real risks; hire expert consultancy if required. On the basis of your findings, make a proposal for an IDS and firewall security solution. Implement other sound security practices as suggested in this book. Once the solution is in place tie other procedures, such as change control and new project designs, into the security process.

Q: What should I do if my IDS detects a serious security breach?

A: Ideally you should be prepared for the worst well before the event. But if security is compromised, stay cool and work through these steps:

1. Verify that it is not a false positive.

2. Establish a working party made up of key people from across the company. There should be representatives from senior management, technical departments, human resources, and of course, your security experts. Present the security capabilities of your system and the impact of the attack to the team.

3. Gather and discuss information regarding the attack; investigate and correlate information. Involve outside authorities such as the Police, if necessary.

4. Based upon severity decide whether to monitor for recurring attacks (if they are non-destructive) or remove access entirely to protect the company. Gain authority to take draconian measures to protect the network if required.

5. Design a plan that all relevant teams will execute upon intrusion.

6. Document all incident handling procedures, including actions according to severity. This should include responses to attacks from your IDS.

7. Record all suspicious activity. Take further advice from law enforcement on the next steps to take. Review the outcome in a meeting with the working party—update any procedural documentation as required.

Q: Would a firewall or other security product interfere with the IDS?

A: In short, not if the system is configured correctly. Sensors should be made aware of Cisco Secure Scanner scans for example; this prevents unnecessary auditing. Likewise a firewall should not be configured to restrict the IDS from performing its function properly. Because this is a detection system we would expect it to pick up all intrusions including other legitimate operations from security products.

Q: What is Signature Analysis?

A: Signatures are identifiable attack patterns, either strings within data or more complex events. The signature can be defined as an event or process with a resulting outcome. Systems that are compromised can be monitored to identify what types of attacks are in progress. The analysis portion involves pattern matching against a database. For further details, have a look at www.cisco.com/univercd/cc/td/doc/product/iaabu/csids/csids2/index.htm.

Chapter 6

Microsoft RAS and VPN for Windows 2000

Solutions in this chapter:

- What's New in Windows 2000

- Discovering the Great Link: Kerberos Trusts between Domains

- Understanding EAP, RADIUS, and IPSec

- Configuring Microsoft RAS and VPN for Windows 2000

- Avoiding Possible Security Risks

Introduction

The latest release of Microsoft's network operating system (NOS) is Windows 2000. Many employees will use Windows 2000 at home to access their corporate networks. One thing that you must make sure of is that their connection will be safe for your network. Allowing access into your network from anywhere outside your security measures creates an opportunity for someone to exploit any weaknesses in the software and gain access to your network.

Invariably, Microsoft had to provide solutions to this problem, so they incorporated a host of new security features in Windows 2000. The most notable addition to Windows 2000 could quite possibly be Active Directory (AD). AD is a new environment for Windows 2000, and is based on the open standard of Lightweight Directory Access Protocol (LDAP) instead of the more proprietary Users, Groups, and Domains. A single sign-on method has also been incorporated to allow for a single sign-on process for access to network resources.

This new directory structure brings several key security pieces to the table. The addition of Kerberos v5 allows, again, for an open standard approach, and NT LAN Manager (NTLM) provides compatibility with previous OS versions. Some of the other open standards embraced in Windows 2000 include:

- **IP Security (IPSec)** Allows for secure transmissions within IP networks. Incorporates security using an Encapsulating Security Payload (ESP) or an Authentication Header (AH).

- **Extensible Authentication Protocol (EAP)** Provides support for third-party authentication products, to be used with PPP. EAP allows for support of Kerberos, Secure Key (S/Key), and Public Key.

- **Remote Access Dial-In User Service (RADIUS)** A client/server authentication method that provides a way to offload the Windows 2000 server of authentication duties.

With this in mind, the objective of this chapter is to introduce you to some of the new features with the Remote Access Service (RAS) and virtual private network (VPN) technology in Windows 2000. After you have completed this chapter, you should be familiar with Microsoft's new security features, the implementation of RAS and VPN, as well as how they all work together.

What's New in Windows 2000

Like every other operating system on the market, Microsoft needed to create a secure networked environment for Windows users. Microsoft responded to the need for security by increasing its attention to security issues in the Windows NT operating system as the product matured (in fact, many of its service packs have addressed just that issue), but security has always been considered by many to be one of Windows NT's less-than-strong points when compared to alternative network operating systems. The NT LAN Manager (NTLM) security protocol used in NT, although providing a reasonable level of security for most purposes, has several drawbacks:

- It is proprietary, not an industry-wide standard, and not popular outside Microsoft networking.

- It does not provide mutual authentication; that is, although the server authenticates the client, there is no reciprocal authentication on the part of the client. It is just assumed that the server's credentials are valid. This has been a weak spot, leaving NT networks vulnerable to hackers and crackers whose programs, by masquerading as servers, could gain access to the system.

One of the enhancements to the security in Windows 2000 Server is that Windows 2000 Server supports two authentication protocols, Kerberos v5 and NTLM. Kerberos v5 is the default authentication method for Windows 2000 domains, and NTLM is provided for backward compatibility with Windows NT 4.0 and earlier operating systems.

Another security enhancement is the addition of the Encrypting File System (EFS). EFS allows users to encrypt and decrypt files on their system on the fly. This provides an even higher degree of protection for files than was previously available using NTFS (NT File System) security only.

The inclusion of IP Security (IPSec) in Windows 2000 enhances security by protecting the integrity and confidentiality of data as it travels over the network. It is easy to see why IPSec is important; today's networks consist of not only intranets, but also branch offices, remote access for telecommuters, and, of course, the Internet.

Each object in the Active Directory can have the permissions controlled at a very high granularity level. This per-property level of permissions is available at all levels of the Active Directory.

Smart cards are supported in Windows 2000 to provide an additional layer of protection for client authentication as well as providing secure e-mail. The additional layer of protection comes from an adversary's needing not only the smart card but also the Personal Identification Number (PIN) of the user to activate the card.

Transitive trust relationships are a feature of Kerberos v5 that is established and maintained automatically. Transitive trusts rely on Kerberos v5, so they are applicable only to Windows 2000 Server–only domains.

Windows 2000 depends heavily on Public Key Infrastructure (PKI). PKI consists of several components: public keys, private keys, certificates, and certificate authorities (CAs).

Where Is the User Manager for Domains?

There are several changes to the tools used to administer the network in Active Directory. Users, and groups are administered in a new way. Everyone who is familiar with User Manager for Domains available in Windows NT 4.0 and earlier versions now must get used to the Active Directory Users and Computers snap-in for the Microsoft Management Console (MMC) when they manage users in a pure Windows 2000 domain. The MMC houses several new tools used for managing the Windows 2000 Server environment such as the Quality of Service (QoS) Admission Control and Distributed File System. The MMC also includes old tools such as the Performance Monitor and Event Viewer. Table 6.1 shows the differences between some of the tools used in Windows NT 4.0 and those used in Windows 2000 Server.

Table 6.1 Tools Used in Windows NT 4.0 and Windows 2000 Server

Windows NT 4.0	Windows 2000 Server
User Manager for Domains	Active Directory Users and Computers is used for modification of user accounts. The Security Configuration Editor is used to set security policy.

Continued

Table 6.1 Continued

Windows NT 4.0	Windows 2000 Server
System Policy Editor	The Administrative Templates extension to Group Policy is used for registry-based policy configuration.
Add User Accounts (Administrative Wizard)	Active Directory Users and Computers is used to add users.
Group Management (Administrative Wizard)	Active Directory Users and Computers is used to add groups. Group policy enforces policies.
Server Manager	Replaced by Active Directory Users and Computers.

Problems and Limitations

Windows 2000 Server maintains compatibility with down-level clients (Windows NT 4.0, Windows 95, and Windows 98), so it uses the NTLM and LM authentication protocol for logins. This means that the stronger Kerberos v5 authentication is not used for those systems. NTLM and LM are still used, so the passwords for those users can be compromised. Figure 6.1 shows a packet capture of a Windows 98 client logging on a Windows 2000 domain. The Windows 98 machine is sending out a broadcast LM1.0/2.0 logon request.

Figure 6.2 shows a Windows 2000 server responding to the request sent by the Windows 98 client. The Windows 2000 server responds with a LM2.0 response to the logon request.

NTLM is also used to authenticate Windows NT 4.0, but LM is used to authenticate Windows 95 and Windows 98 systems. NTLM is used to authenticate logons in the following cases:

- Users in a Windows NT 4.0 domain authenticating to a Windows 2000 domain

- A Windows NT 4.0 Workstation system authenticating to a Windows 2000 domain controller

- A Windows 2000 Professional system authenticating to a Windows NT 4.0 primary or backup domain controller

- A Windows NT 4.0 Workstation system authenticating to a Windows NT 4.0 primary or backup domain controller

Figure 6.1 A Windows 98 client sends a LM1.0/2.0 logon request.

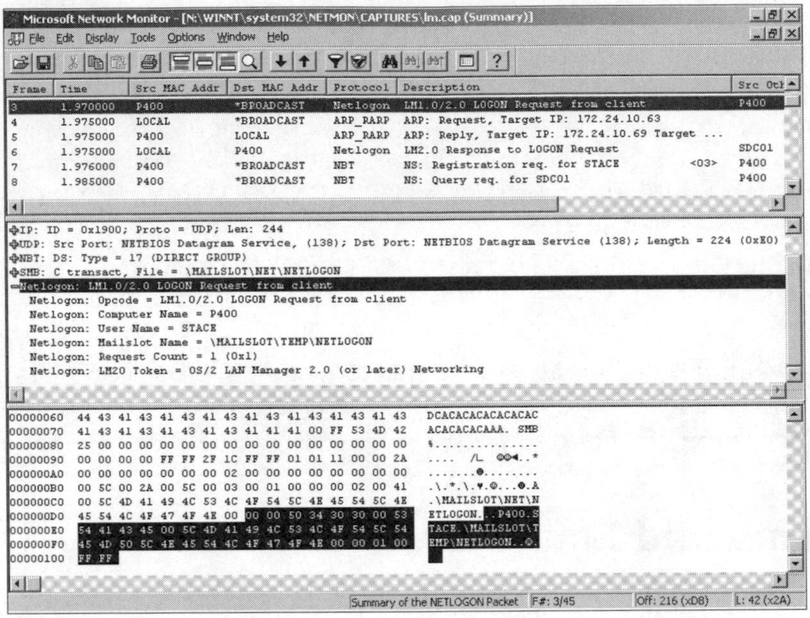

Figure 6.2 Windows 2000 server responds with a LM2.0 response to the Windows 98 client logon request.

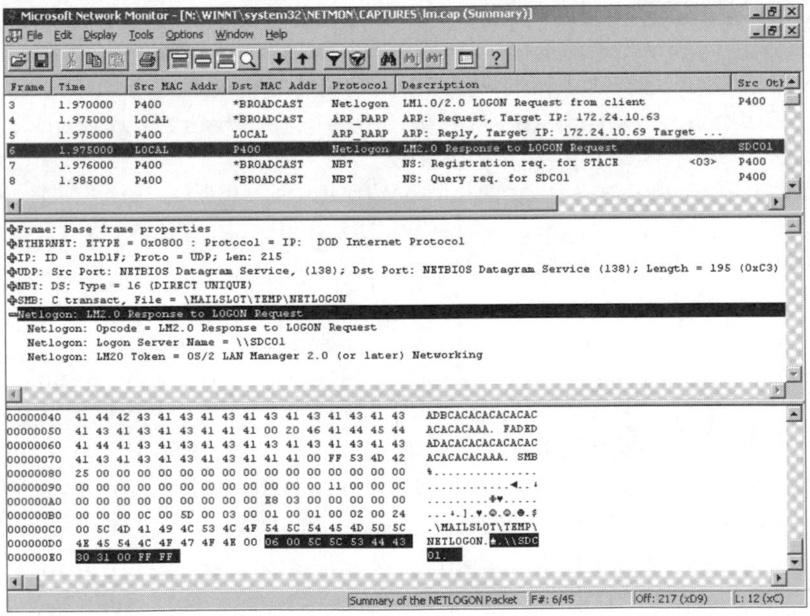

The difficulty with using NTLM or LM as an authentication protocol cannot be overcome easily. The only way to get around using NTLM or LM at the moment is to replace the systems using earlier versions of Windows with Windows 2000 systems. This probably is not economically feasible for most organizations.

Windows NT 3.51 presents another problem. Even though it is possible to upgrade Windows NT 3.51 to Windows 2000 Server, Microsoft does not recommend running Windows NT Server 3.51 in a Windows 2000 Server domain, because Windows NT 3.51 has problems with authentication of groups and users in domains other than the logon domain.

What Is the Same?

Windows 2000 Server has grown by several million lines of code over the earlier versions of Windows NT, so it may be hard to believe that anything is the same as in the earlier versions. NTLM is the same as it was in earlier versions because it has to support down-level clients.

Global groups and local groups are still present in Windows 2000 Server, with an added group. Otherwise, for security purposes, this is a new operating system with many new security features and functions for system administrators to learn about.

Windows 2000's security protocols (note the plural; the new operating system's support for multiple protocols is one of its strongest features) are different; they are part of what is known as the distributed services. *Distributed services* is a term that pops up frequently when we discuss network operating systems, and it seems to be mentioned even more often as we familiarize ourselves with the Windows 2000 Server family. Most network administrators have a vague idea of what it means, but probably have never really sat down and tried to define it, especially in terms of security.

Distributed Services

Distributed services are those components that are spread (or distributed) throughout the network, and that are highly dependent upon one another. The high-profile member of this group of Windows 2000 subsystems is Active Directory, but the Windows 2000 security subsystem is another of the operating system's distributed services. In fact, in keeping with the interdependency of the distributed services, there is a fundamental relationship between the Active Directory service and Windows 2000's security subsystem.

Open Standards

Windows 2000 signals a big change in direction for Microsoft, away from the proprietary nature of many of Windows NT's features, and moving toward the adoption of industry standards. This new path is demonstrated most prominently in the area of distributed services. Active Directory itself is based on the Lightweight Directory Access Protocol (LDAP), thus making it compatible with other directory services, such as Novell's Netware Directory Services (NDS), which adhere to this open Internet standard.

NOTE

LDAP standards are established by working groups of the Internet Engineering Task Force (IETF).

Active Directory is also compatible (although not fully compliant) with the International Standards Organization's X.500 standards for distributed directory services. With this commitment to supporting widespread standards, Microsoft is demonstrating its serious intent to make Windows a true enterprise-capable network operating system.

One of the primary requirements of an enterprise level NOS is the ability to protect the integrity and privacy of the network's data. So it is no surprise that there have been major, drastic changes made to the security subsystem in the latest implementation of Windows server software.

Much as it has adopted open directory services standards, Microsoft has incorporated into Windows 2000 support for the widely utilized and respected Kerberos security protocol developed at the Massachusetts Institute of Technology (MIT), and the ISO's X.509 v3 public key security, another accepted standard. These are in addition to the NTLM security protocol used in Windows NT, which is included in Windows 2000 for compatibility with down-level clients. Figure 6.3 gives an overview of the Windows 2000 security structure.

The following section examines Windows 2000's distributed security services in detail, with the focus on how intimately the security and directory services are intertwined, and how Active Directory's objects can be secured in a granular manner that was never possible in Windows NT. It also looks at the security protocols themselves, and the role and function of each. Finally, it addresses the special area of Internet security, and the added level of protection from unauthorized outside access provided by the Windows 2000 distributed security subsystem.

Figure 6.3 The Windows 2000 security structure.

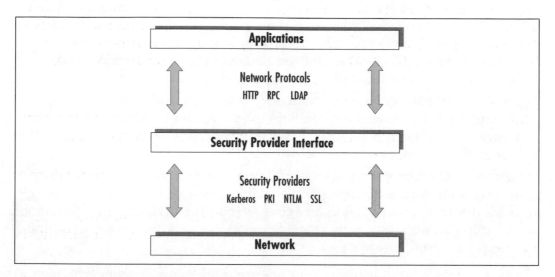

Windows 2000 Distributed Security Services

What exactly are these security services that are distributed throughout the network, and how do they work together to ensure more robust protection for user passwords and other confidential data? A number of security features, which together make up the distributed security services, are built into Windows 2000:

Active Directory security This includes the new concept of transitive trusts, which allows user account authentication to be distributed across the enterprise, as well as the granular assignment of access rights and the new ability to delegate administration below the domain level.

Multiple security protocols Windows 2000 implements the popular Kerberos security protocol, supports PKI, and has backward compatibility with Windows NT and Windows 9x through the use of NTLM.

Security Support Provider Interface (SSPI) This component of the security subsystem reduces the amount of code needed at the application level to support multiple security protocols by providing a generic interface for the authentication mechanisms that are based on shared-secret or public key protocols.

Secure Sockets Layer (SSL) This protocol is used by Internet browsers and servers, and is designed to provide for secure communications over the Internet by using a combination of public and secret key technology.

Microsoft Certificate Server This service was included with IIS 4.0 in the NT 4.0 Option Pack and has been upgraded and made a part of Windows 2000 Server. It is used to issue and manage the certificates for applications that use public key cryptography to provide secure communications over the Internet, as well as within the company's intranet. Within Windows 2000, it has been renamed to Certificate Services.

CryptoAPI (CAPI) As its name indicates, this is an application programming interface that allows applications to encrypt data using independent modules known as cryptographic service providers (CSPs), and protects the user's private key data during the process.

Single Sign-On (SSO) This is a key feature of Windows 2000 authentication, which allows a user to log on the domain just one time, using a single password, and authenticate to any computer in the domain, thus reducing user confusion and improving efficiency, and at the same time decreasing the need for administrative support.

As a network administrator, you are probably not most concerned with the intricacies of how the various cryptographic algorithms work (although that can be an interesting sideline course of study, especially if you are mathematically inclined). This jumble of acronyms can be used to keep your organization's sensitive data secure. This chapter emphasizes just that—combining the distributed security services of Windows 2000 in a way that balances security and ease of accessibility in your enterprise network.

Active Directory and Security

It should come as no surprise, given the amount of time and care Microsoft has put into developing its directory services for Windows 2000, that a great deal of attention was paid to making Active Directory a feature-rich service that will be able to compete with other established directory services in the marketplace. After extensive study of what network administrators out in the field want and need in a directory service, Active Directory was designed with security as a high priority item.

These are some of the important components of Active Directory's security functions:

- Storage of security credentials for users and computers in Active Directory, and the authentication of computers on the network when the network is started.

- The transitive trust model, in which all other domains in the domain tree accept security credentials that are valid for one domain.

- Secure single sign-on to the enterprise (because security credentials are stored in Active Directory, making them available to domain controllers throughout the network).

- Replication of all Active Directory objects to every domain controller in a domain.

- Management and accessibility of user and computer accounts, policies, and resources at the "nearest" (in terms of network connectivity) domain controller.

- Inheritance of Active Directory object properties from parent objects.

- Creation of account and policy properties at the group level, which can then be applied to all new and existing members.

- Delegation of specific administrative responsibilities to specific users or groups.

- Ability of servers to authenticate on behalf of clients.

- Ability of these features to work together, as part of Active Directory and the security subsystem. Compared to Windows NT, this is a whole new (and better) way of doing things.

- Management of user and computer accounts in the enterprise.

Advantages of Active Directory Account Management

Windows NT, as it came out of the box, was not a particularly secure operating system, for several reasons. First, during the timeframe in which Windows NT was initially developed, security was not as big a concern in the corporate environment as it has become in the past several years. Second, security is not traditionally as crucial in smaller network environments as in large ones, and Windows NT was not in widespread use in large-enterprise situations. Finally, Microsoft's focus in designing Windows NT was ease of use; there will always be a trade-off between security level and accessibility. With Windows 2000, security is built right into Active Directory.

Active Directory will support a much larger number of user objects (more than a million) with better performance than the Windows NT Registry-based domain model. Maximum domain size is no longer limited by the performance of the security account repository. A domain tree can support much larger, complex organizational structures, making Windows truly suitable for enterprise networking.

Since account management is the foundation of any Windows NT or Windows 2000 security plan, it stands to reason that the easier and more specific management of user accounts is, the better it will be for security purposes.

Account management is an important issue. Every user initially enters the network through a user account; this is the beginning point for assignment of user rights and permissions to access resources, individually or (as Microsoft recommends) through membership in security groups (see Figure 6.4).

Figure 6.4 The user account is the entry point to the network and the basis for security.

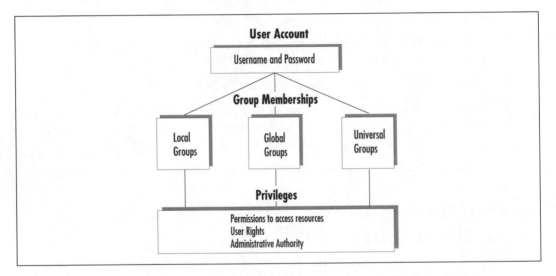

In Windows NT 4.0 Server, user accounts were administered from the User Manager for Domains and computer accounts were managed via Server Manager. In a Windows 2000 domain, both types of accounts are managed from a single point, the Active Directory Users and Computers MMC snap-in. To access this tool, follow this path: Start menu | Programs | Administrative Tools | Active Directory Users and Computers.

Figure 6.5 shows the separate folders for computers and users (showing the Users folder expanded).

This one-stop account management setup makes it easier for the network administrator to address the issues that arise in connection with the security-oriented administration of users, computers, and resources.

Figure 6.5 Accounts can be managed with the Active Directory Users and Computers snap-in.

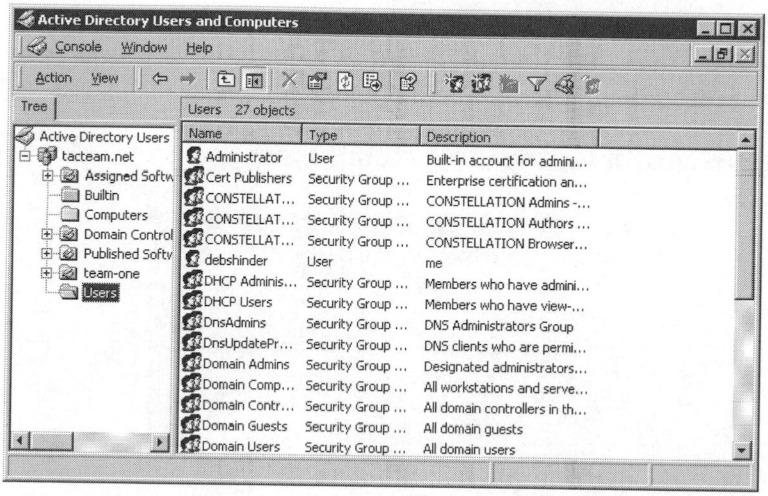

TIP

Group names, as well as individual user accounts, are included in the Users folder.

Managing Security via Object Properties

In Active Directory, everything is an object, and every object has properties, also called attributes. The attributes of a user account include security-related information. In the case of a user account, this would include memberships in security groups and password and authentication requirements. Windows 2000 makes it easy for the administrator to access the attributes of an object (and allows for the recording of much more information than was possible with Windows NT). Figure 6.6 shows the Account property sheet of a user account and some of the optional settings that can be applied.

It is possible to specify the use of Data Encryption Standard (DES) encryption or no requirement for Kerberos preauthentication, along with other security criteria for this user account, simply by clicking on a check box. The same is true of trusting the account for delegation or prohibiting the account from being delegated. Other options that can be selected here (not shown in Figure 6.6, but available by scrolling up the list) include:

- Requirement that the user change the password at next logon
- Prohibition on the user's changing the password
- Specification that the password is never to expire
- Specification that the password is to be stored using reversible encryption

Figure 6.6 This is the user account properties sheet (Account tab).

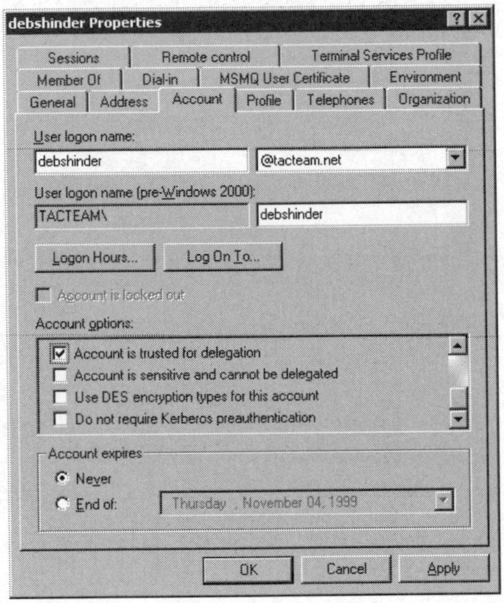

Some of the settings in the user account properties sheet (such as password expiration properties and logon hours) could be set in Windows NT through the User Manager for Domains. Others are new to Windows 2000.

Managing Security via Group Memberships

In most cases, in a Windows 2000 domain, access to resources is assigned to groups, and then user accounts are placed into those groups. This makes access permissions much easier to handle, especially in a large and constantly changing network.

Assigning and maintaining group memberships is another important aspect of user account management, and Active Directory makes this easy as well. Group memberships are managed through another tab on the property sheet, the Member Of tab (see Figure 6.7).

As Figure 6.7 shows, you can add or remove the groups associated with this user's account with the click of a mouse.

Figure 6.7 Security can be managed through group membership assignments.

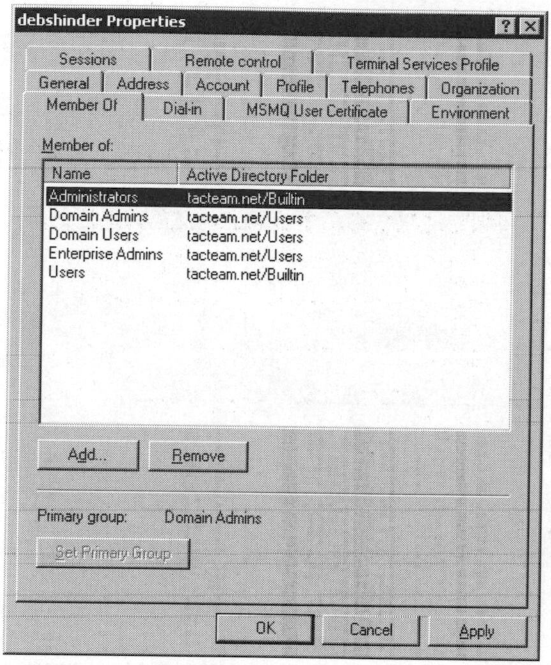

Active Directory Object Permissions

Permissions can be applied to any object in Active Directory, but the majority of permissions should be granted to groups, rather than to individual users. This eases the task of managing permissions on objects.

You can assign permissions for objects to:

- Groups, users, and special identities in the domain
- Groups and users in that domain and any trusted domains
- Local groups and users on the computer where the object resides

To assign Active Directory permissions to a directory object, do one of these things:

- Open the Active Directory Domains and Trusts tool by following this path: Start | Programs | Administrative Tools | Active Directory Domains and Trusts. Right-click the selected domain and choose Manage.
- Open the Active Directory Users and Computers tool directly, and expand the tree for the domain you wish to manage.

In the View menu, be sure Advanced Features is checked (see Figure 6.8).

Figure 6.8 The Advanced Features option on the View menu must be selected in order to set Active Directory permissions on an object.

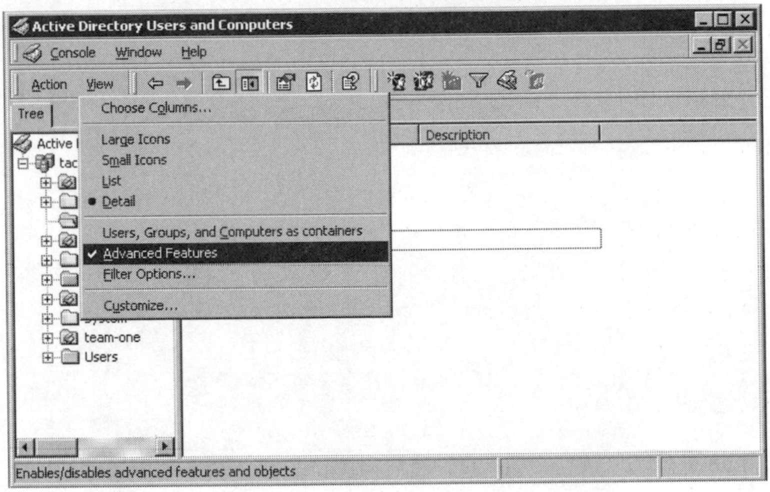

WARNING

If the Advanced Features selection is not checked, you will not see the Security tab in the next step.

Now choose an Active Directory object and right-click it, then select Properties. The Security tab (see Figure 6.9) will provide you with the available permissions for this type of object. In the example, we've selected a computer object named Excelsior.

To view additional special permissions that may be set on this object, click the Advanced button at the bottom left of the dialog box. Figure 6.10 shows that the resultant dialog box allows you to choose permissions entries to view or edit.

Now select the entry that you wish to view, and click View | Edit. The special permissions are shown in Figure 6.11.

Finally, to view the permissions for specific attributes, click the Properties tab (see Figure 6.12).

Active Directory permissions can be fine-tuned to an extraordinary degree. But remember, especially as you begin to deploy your security plan using Windows 2000's new features, just because you *can* do something, this does not mean you *should* do it.

Figure 6.9 Active Directory permissions are assigned in the Security section of the Properties sheet.

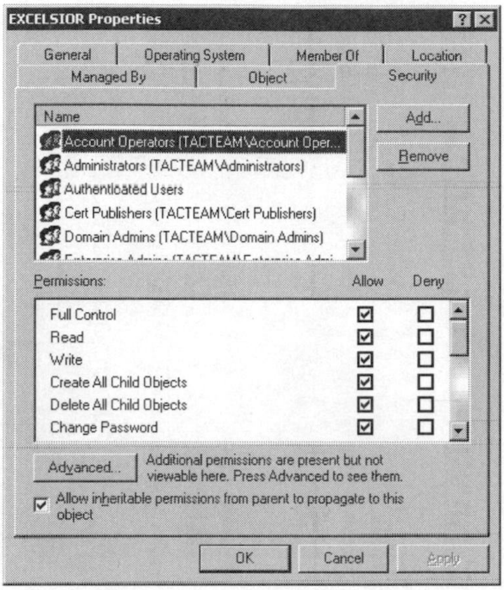

Figure 6.10 The Access Control Settings dialog box.

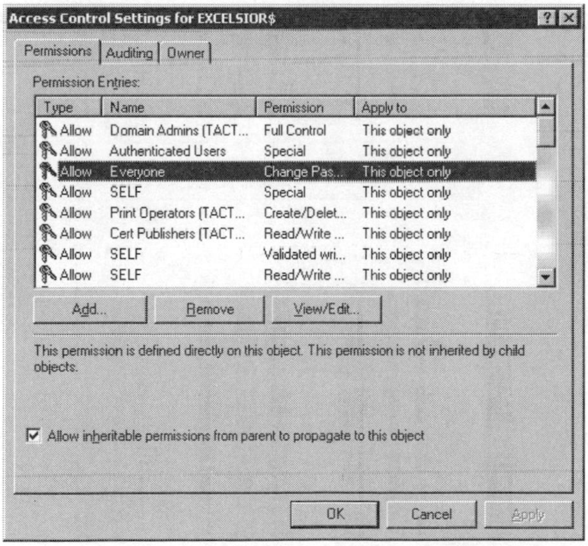

Figure 6.11 Special permissions for an Active Directory object.

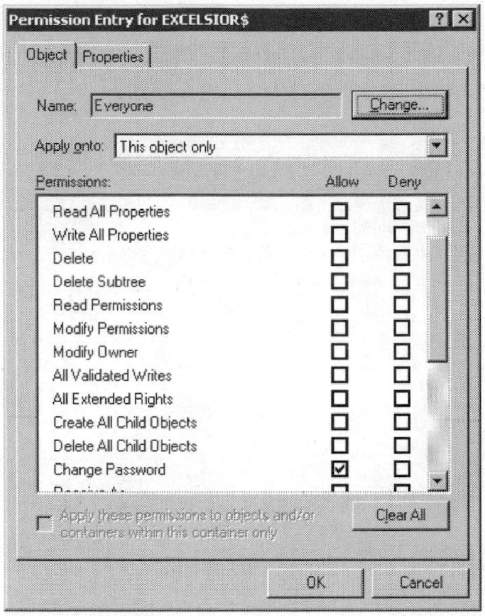

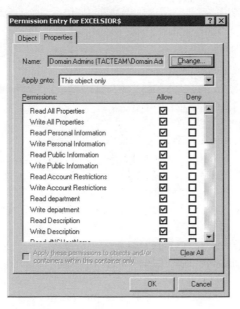

Figure 6.12 The Properties tab on the Permission Entry box shows permissions that can be granted for specific property attributes.

Although Windows 2000 gives you the ability to assign Active Directory permissions not only to objects themselves but to their individual attributes, Microsoft recommends in general that you should not grant permissions for specific object attributes, because this can complicate administrative tasks and disrupt normal operations.

WARNING

You should use Active Directory Permissions only when absolutely necessary, and only when you are absolutely sure of the effects your actions will have.

Relationship between Directory and Security Services

Every object in Active Directory has a unique security descriptor that defines the access permissions that are required in order to read or update the object properties. Active Directory uses Windows 2000 access verification to determine whether an Active Directory client can read or update a particular object. Because of this, LDAP client requests to the directory require that the operating system enforce access control, instead of having Active Directory make the access-control decisions.

In Windows 2000, security is directly integrated with the directory services. This differs from the Windows NT model. In Windows NT 4.0, the SAM (Security Accounts Manager) database and the characteristics of the NTLM trust relationship combined to limit security to three levels within the domain: global and local groups, and individual users. With Active Directory, the database is distributed throughout the enterprise.

The result is that security can be administered with much more granularity and flexibility. One example is the ability to delegate administrative authority at the organizational unit (OU) level. In NT, assignment of administrative privileges made that user an administrator throughout the entire domain.

Windows 2000 Distributed Security Services use Active Directory as the central repository for account information and domain security policy. This is a big improvement over the registry-based implementation in terms of both performance and scalability. It is also easier to manage. Active Directory provides replication and availability of account information to multiple Domain Controllers, and can be administered remotely.

In addition, Windows 2000 employs a new domain model that uses Active Directory to support a multilevel hierarchy tree of domains. Managing the trust relationships between domains has been enormously simplified by the treewide transitive trust model that extends throughout the domain tree.

Windows 2000's trusts work differently from those in Windows NT, and this affects security issues and administration in the Active Directory environment.

Domain Trust Relationships

The Kerberos security protocol is the basis for the trust relationships between domains in a Windows 2000 network. For the purposes of this chapter, it is important to understand that Kerberos is what makes the two-way transitive trusts of Windows 2000 work.

For an Active Directory namespace, when the first Windows 2000 server computer in a network is promoted to domain controller, this creates the internal root domain for your organization. It will have a hierarchical name, like *mycompany.com.*

Microsoft calls this the *root domain.* I use the term *internal root domain* to distinguish it from the Internet root domain, which is represented by a dot. On the Internet, mycompany.com, although referred to as a *second-level* domain, resides below both the Internet root and the external *top-level* domain "com").

When additional domains are created in your company's network (by promoting other Windows 2000 servers to domain controllers and designating them as DCs for the new domains), there are two options:

- They can be created as children of the internal root domain, if they include the internal root's namespace in their own; for instance, sales.mycompany.com is a child domain of mycompany.com.

- They can be created as root domains for new domain trees in the forest, if they use an unrelated namespace (also called a noncontiguous namespace); for example, the creation of a domain named yourcompany.com would start a new domain tree that can exist in the same forest as the tree for which mycompany.com is the root.

Figure 6.13 illustrates the relationships of parent and child domains within a tree, and trees within a forest.

Figure 6.13 Relationships of domains within a tree and trees within a forest.

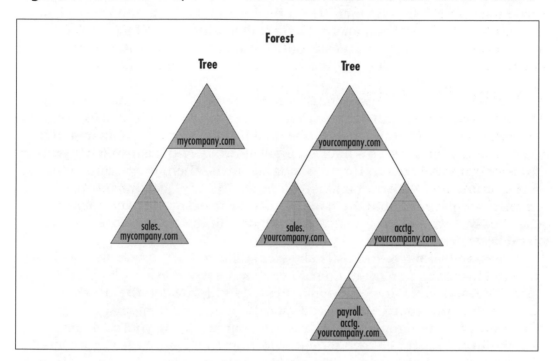

In Figure 6.13, two domain trees exist in the forest. The internal root domains are mycompany.com and yourcompany.com; each has one or more child domains that include the parents' namespace, and as you can see, the child domains can have children of their own (to continue the analogy, these would be the grandchildren of the internal root domain).

The Great Link: Kerberos Trusts between Domains

In Windows NT networks, every domain was an island. In order for users in one domain to access resources in another, administrators of the two domains had to set up an explicit trust relationship. Moreover, these trusts were one-way; if the administrators wanted a reciprocal relationship, two separate trusts had to be created, because these trusts were based on the NTLM security protocol, which does not include mutual authentication.

In Windows 2000 networks, that has been changed. With the Kerberos protocol, all trust relationships are two-way, and an implicit, automatic trust exists between every parent and child domain; it is not necessary for administrators to create them. Finally, these trusts are transitive, which means that if the first domain trusts the second domain, and the second domain trusts the third domain, the first domain will trust the third domain, and so on. This comes about through the use of the Kerberos referral, and as a result every domain in a tree implicitly trusts every other domain in that tree.

All this would be cause enough for celebration for those administrators who have struggled with the trust nightmares inherent in the Windows NT way of doing things, but there is one final benefit. The root domains in a forest of domain trees also have an implicit two-way transitive trust relationship with each other. By traversing the trees, then, every domain in the forest trusts every other domain. As long as a user's account has the appropriate permissions, the user has access to resources anywhere on the network, without worrying about the domain in which those resources reside.

For practical purposes, as is shown in Figure 6.13, a user in the payroll.acctg.yourcompany.com domain who needs to access a file or printer in the sales.mycompany.com domain can do so (provided the user's account has the appropriate permissions). The user's domain, payroll.acctg.yourcompany.com, trusts its parent, acctg.yourcompany.com, which in turn trusts its own parent, yourcompany.com. Since yourcompany.com is an internal root domain in the same forest as mycompany.com, those two domains have an implicit two-way transitive trust; thus mycompany.com trusts sales.mycompany.com—and the chain of Kerberos referrals has gone up one tree and down the other to demonstrate the path of the trust that exists between payroll.acctg.yourcompany.com and sales.mycompany.com .

On the other hand, these Kerberos trusts apply only to Windows 2000 domains. If the network includes down-level (Windows NT) domains, they must still use the old NTLM one-way explicit trusts in order to share resources to or from the Windows 2000 domains.

NOTE

Despite the transitive trust relationships between domains in a Windows 2000 network, administrative authority is not transitive; the domain is still an administrative boundary.

Extensible Authentication Protocol (EAP)

Extensible Authentication Protocol (EAP) is an open standard defined in Request for Comments (RFC) 2284, and is used by Microsoft to allow for developers to add support for third-party security features in Windows 2000's RAS or VPN service sets. EAP, a Layer 2 protocol, adds support for the integration of services such as Biometric authentication devices (finger or voice printing), Message Digest 5-Challenge Handshake Authentication Protocol (MD5-CHAP), or Transport Level Security (TLS). TLS allows the deployment of devices such as Token or Smart cards. Instead of choosing an authentication type during the link control protocol (LCP) function, EAP leaves that up to the client and server during the authentication phase.

EAP was proposed by the IETF, as an addition to Point-to-Point Protocol (PPP), so that vendors could add support for any of the security devices that will be developed in the future. In essence, this works as follows: ACME company designs a fingerprint security system that will probably be used with Windows 2000. After the product is developed, ACME can use EAP to create a plug-in security module for both the client and the server sides of the connection.

NOTE

EAP does not work in a Windows NT 4.0 environment.

Remote Authentication Dial-in User Service (RADIUS)

Remote Authentication Dial-in User Service (RADIUS) is used by Windows 2000 as a way to offload the authorization, accounting, and auditing (AAA) functions from the server. In the older Windows NT 4.0 model, the Domain Controller handles all of these features.

RADIUS accounting systems can be used to show how much time a user was connected, how many packets were sent, or how many bytes were sent. By utilizing RADIUS, you can take a lot of burden off of your servers so that they can be used for other network functions.

Figure 6.14 shows how RADIUS works in a Windows 2000 environment.

Figure 6.14 RADIUS utilized in a Windows 2000 environment.

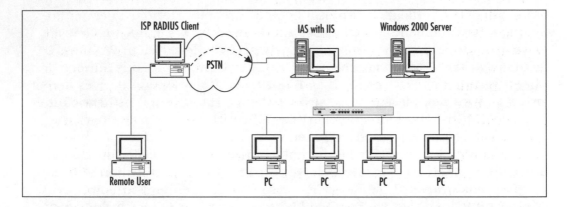

First, the Remote User will dial into his or her ISP's RADIUS client system. The ISP client system will not make any determination of authentication credentials, but will instead forward the request to the remote RADIUS server for processing.

Next, the RADIUS server (represented in Figure 6.14 as the system named "IAS with IIS") will determine what services the Remote User's request will be allowed to have. The Internet Authentication Server (IAS) provides the authentication offload for the network servers, and may also provide the accounting and auditing services listed earlier.

Once authentication is complete, the Remote User's session will be active with the network.

Internet Protocol Security (IPSec)

The IETF RFC (RFC 2401), IPSec tunnel protocol specifications did not include mechanisms suitable for remote access VPN clients. Omitted features include user authentication options or client IP address configuration. To use IPSec tunnel mode for remote access, some vendors chose to extend the protocol in proprietary ways to solve these issues. Although a few of these extensions are documented as Internet drafts, they lack standards status and are not generally interoperable. As a result, customers must seriously consider whether such implementations offer suitable multivendor interoperability.

Building an IPSec Policy

IPSec uses policy to determine how and when secure communications are employed. IPSec policy is built either at the local machine, or in the Active

Directory. IPSec policies created in the Active Directory take precedence over local IPSec policies. The IPSec policies themselves are driven by Filter Lists, Filter Rules, and Filter Actions.

Each IPSec policy can contain multiple rules that determine the security settings of a secure connection when the link matches parameters set in the rule. For example, we can create a policy called "Secure from Legal to Accounting." In this policy we can create a list of rules to apply. Each rule contains its own "Filter List." The filter list determines when the rule is applied. Rules can be set up for IP Address, Network ID, or Domain Name System (DNS) name.

You could set up a filter list that includes the Network IDs of the legal and accounting departments. Whenever the source and destination IP address of a communication matches this filter, the authentication methods, filter actions, and tunnel settings for that rule go into effect.

Building an IPSec MMC Console

Let's take a look at how we can configure a custom IPSec console that we can use to configure IPSec policy and monitor significant IPSec-related events.

1. Click the run command and type **mmc**. Click OK.

2. Click the console menu, then click Add/Remove Snap in. Click the Add button, select Computer Management and click Add. A dialog box will appear that will want to know what computer the snap-in will manage. Select Local computer (the computer this console is running on). Click Finish.

3. Scroll through the list of available snap-ins and select Group Policy and click Add. At this point the wizard will query you on what group policy object you want to manage. Confirm that it says Local Computer in the text box and click Finish.

4. Scroll through the list of group policy objects again, and select Certificates. Click Add. The Certificate Snap-in dialog box asks for the kind of certificate you want to manage (Figure 6.15). Select Computer Account, click Next, and then select Local Computer for the computer you want the Snap-in to manage. Click Finish.

5. Click close on the Add Standalone Snap-in dialog box and then click OK in the Add/Remove Snap-in dialog box. Expand the first level of each of the snap-ins. You should see something similar to Figure 6.16.

Figure 6.15 Certificate Management Plug-in for local computer.

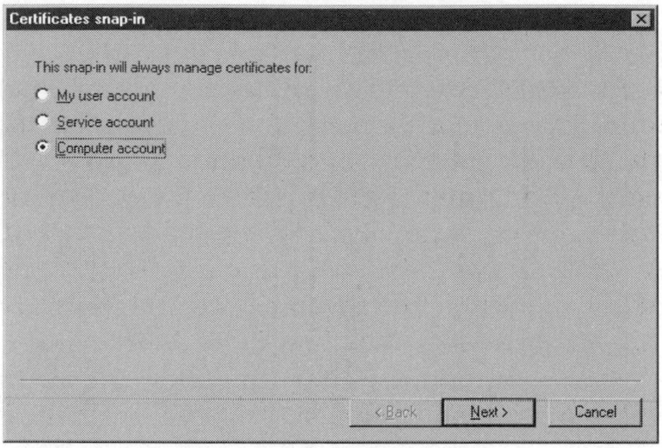

Figure 6.16 Custom IPSec Security Management Console.

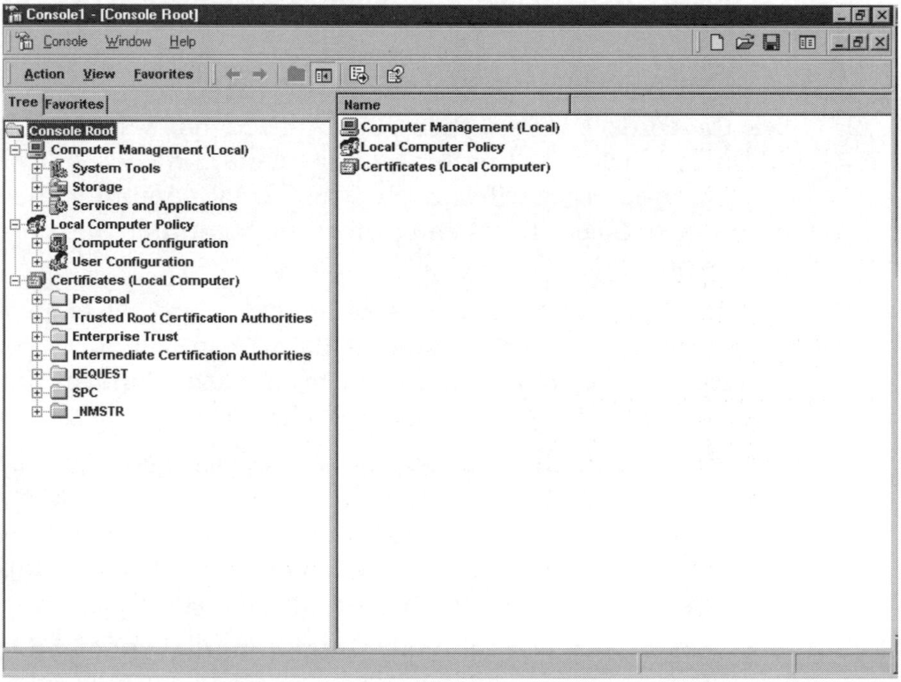

We can configure and manage IPSec policy from the custom console. Note that in this example, we've chosen to manage IPSec policy for this single machine. This might be appropriate if you were configuring IPSec policy for a file or application server. If you wanted to manage policy for an entire domain or organizational unit, you would make the appropriate selection in the Group Policy snap-in configuration.

Security Policies

We can build our own IPSec policy or choose from one of the three built-in polices. Let's take a moment to understand the built-in policies.

To find where IPSec policies are defined, expand the Local Computer Policy, expand the Computer Configuration object, expand the Windows Settings object, and then click on IP Security Policies on Local Machine. In the right pane you will see listed the three built-in IPSec Policies: Client (Respond Only), Secure Server (Require Security), and Server (Request Security). Your screen should look like Figure 6.17.

Figure 6.17 The IPSec Security Console with the three built-in IPSec Policies.

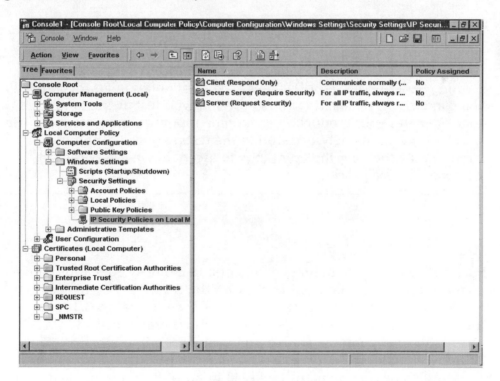

The Client (Respond Only) policy allows you to have a computer use IPSec when another computer requests it to use IPSec. For example, you want to connect to a file server that requires IPSec connections. The workstation that has the built-in client policy enabled will negotiate an IPSec security association. However, the workstation never demands IPSec itself; it will only use IPSec to secure communications when another computer asks it to use IPSec.

The Server (Request Security) policy is used to request IPSec security for all connections. The Server policy would be used when you need to enable IPSec aware and unaware clients access to the server. If an IPSec aware client establishes a connection, the session is secured. Unsecured sessions will be established with non-IPSec aware computers. This policy can be used for networks transitioning from Windows NT to Windows 2000 and finds its best use in a mixed environment.

Use the Secure Server (Require Security) policy to demand that all connections to the machine use IPSec. Examples include file servers with highly sensitive information, and security gateways at each end of a Layer 2 Tunneling Protocol (L2TP)/IPSec tunnel. Secure Server policy will always request a secure channel. Connections are denied to computers unable to respond to the request.

NOTE

Security policies are bidirectional. If a Secure Server attempts to connect to non-IPSec-aware network servers such as DNS, Windows Internet Naming Service (WINS), or Dynamic Host Configuration Protocol (DHCP), the connection will fail. It is imperative that you test all scenarios in a lab that simulates your production environment prior to implementing IPSec policies on your life network. During the testing phase, you must be assiduous at checking the event logs to ascertain what services fail because of IPSec policies.

Rules

An IPSec policy has three main components: IP Security Rules, IP Filter Lists, and IP Filter Actions. Double-click on the Server Policy to see the Server (Request Security) Properties sheet, as seen in Figure 6.18.

Rules are applied to computers that match criteria specified in a Filter List. An IP filter list contains source and destination IP addresses. These can be individual host IP addresses or network IDs. When a communication is identified as a participant included in an IP filter list, a particular filter action will be applied that is specific for that connection.

The All IP Traffic filter list includes all computers that communicate with the server via Transmission Control Protocol/Internet Protocol (TCP/IP). Any instructions in the Filter Action associated with All IP Traffic will be applied. Let's look at some of these actions.

Figure 6.18 The Server (Request Security) Properties sheet.

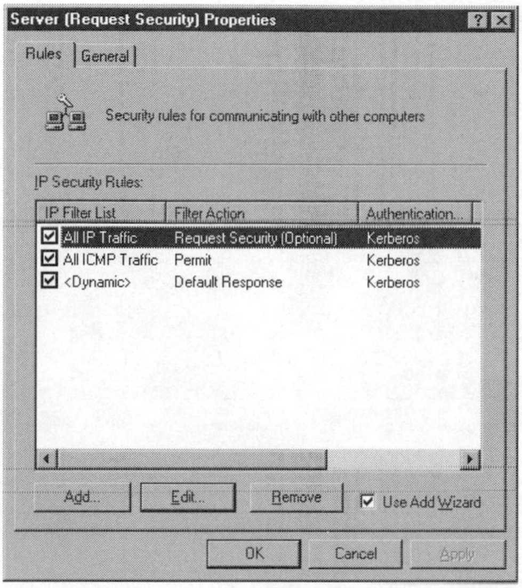

First, double-click on the All IP Traffic filter list. This opens up the Edit Rule Properties dialog box for the All IP Traffic filter. You should see a tabbed dialog box consisting of five tabs, as seen in Figure 6.19.

Figure 6.19 The All IP Traffic Edit Rule Properties dialog box.

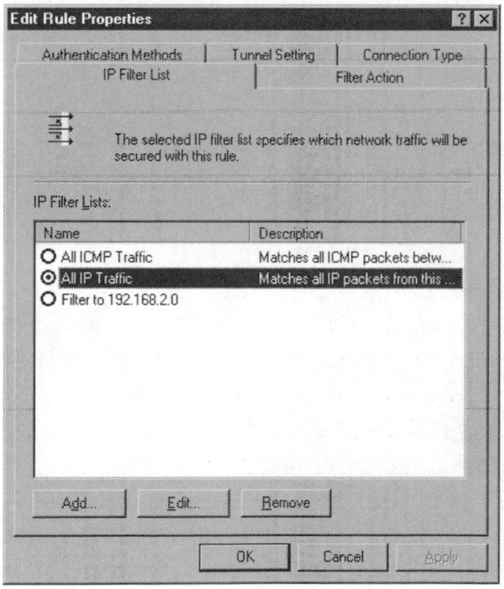

The option button for the IP filter list is selected and a description is included, which explains the purpose of the list. Double-click on the All IP Traffic filter list to see the details of the All IP Traffic Filter. The name, description, and the details of the filter are displayed here, as depicted in Figure 6.20.

Figure 6.20 The IP Filter List Details dialog box.

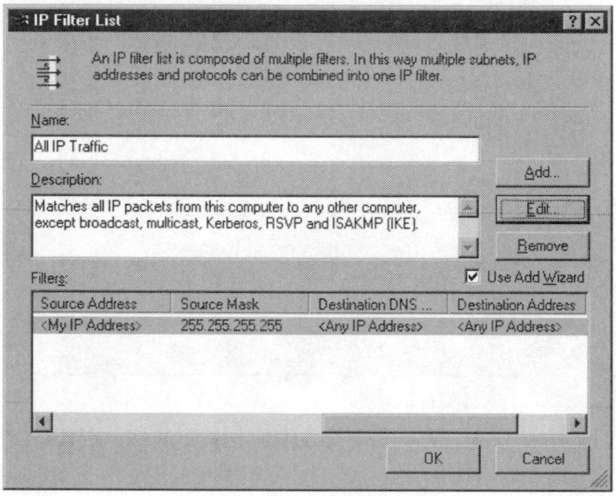

If you want to see more details regarding the addressing, protocol, and description of the filter, you can click on the Edit button. Click Cancel twice to return to the Edit Rules Properties dialog box.

Walkthrough

The next section is designed to walk you through a step-by-step configuration of IPSec in a Windows 2000 environment. If you are doing this exercise on a corporate network, you must obtain permission from your network administrator. Installing an unauthorized server on your network can have severe negative consequences on network function and reliability. For the most part, sessions like this should not be done in a production environment. Lab sessions should be specific to a lab environment.

Set Up IPSec Conversation between Two Computers

In these practice exercises, we will perform a packet analysis of IPSec secured communications. To complete these exercises you will need two Windows 2000 computers. Be sure that neither of these computers needs to be accessed by others on your network while completing these exercises.

Down-level operating systems do not support IPSec; therefore, you must use Windows 2000 machines.

Before we start analyzing IPSec communications in the Network Monitor, let's set up a custom console to use for the exercises.

1. Click Start | Run. Type mmc in the run command text box.

2. Click the Console menu, then click Add/Remove Snap-in.

3. In the Add/Remove Snap-in dialog box, click the Add button. In the Add Standalone Snap-in dialog box, select Computer Management and click the Add button.

4. You are asked whether the snap-in will manage a local or remote computer. Select Local computer: (the computer this console is running on) option button, and click Finish.

5. You are returned to the Add Standalone Snap-in dialog box. Scroll through the list and select Group Policy, then click Add. You are presented with the Select Group Policy Object dialog box. Make sure that Local Computer is listed in the Group Policy Object text box. Click Finish.

6. You are back at the Add Standalone Snap-in dialog box again. Scroll through the list and select Certificates and click Add. The snap-in will manage certificates for the local computer, so select the Computer account option button and click Finish.

7. Click Close to close the Add Standalone Snap-in dialog box.

8. Click OK to close the Add/Remove Snap-in dialog box.

9. Click the Console menu and click Save. In the Save As dialog box, name the file *IPSecPractice* and save it to your desktop to make it easy to find.

Enabling Auditing of Logons

When IPSec communications take place, an event will be written to the event log. We can use the event log to see if IPSec is working properly and to troubleshoot IPSec-related events. Perform the following steps so that logons are recorded to the event log. If both computers are part of the same domain, be aware that domain policies override local policies. In this example, both computers will be handled as if they are stand-alone servers. Perform the following steps on both computers:

1. In the IPSecPractice Console, expand the Local Computer Policy node, expand the Computer Configuration node, expand the Windows Settings node, and expand the Security Settings node. Click on the Audit Policy node.

2. Double-click on the Audit logon events policy in the right pane. In the Local Security Policy Setting dialog box, put a checkmark in both the Success and Failure checkboxes.

3. Double-click on the Audit object access policy in the right pane. In the Local Security Policy Setting dialog box, put a checkmark in both the Success and Failure checkboxes.

Create a Custom IPSec Policy

In this exercise we will create a custom IPSec policy. This policy will insure secure communications between the two computers. The computer on which we will run network monitor is referred to as NETMON. The other computer is called NETCLIENT. You do not need to change the names of your computers. The names are used to distinguish the two computers for monitoring purposes.

Perform the following steps on the NETMON machine:

1. In the IPSecPractice Console, expand Local Computer Policy, expand Computer Configuration, expand Windows Settings, expand Security Settings, and click on IP Security Policies. In the right pane you will see the built-in Security Policies.

2. Right-click on IP Security Policies and click on Create IP Security Policy.

3. The IP Security Policy Wizard welcome screen appears. Click Next.

4. Enter the name and a description of the Security Policy, as seen in Figure 6.21. Click Next.

Figure 6.21 Naming the IP Security Policy.

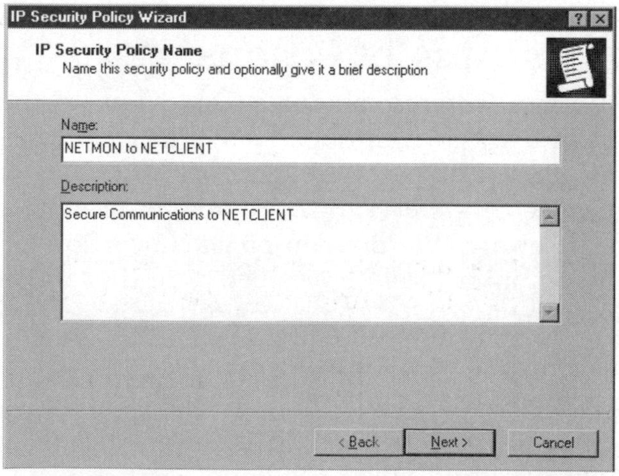

5. You are asked if you want to Activate the default response rule. Remove the checkmark from the checkbox for this option. We will create our own rule that will secure communications with NET-CLIENT. Click Next.

6. The wizard is done. Be sure there is a checkmark in the Edit properties checkbox. Click Finish.

7. You now see the NETMON to NETCLIENT Properties dialog box, as seen in Figure 6.22.

Figure 6.22 The NETMON to NETCLIENT Properties dialog box.

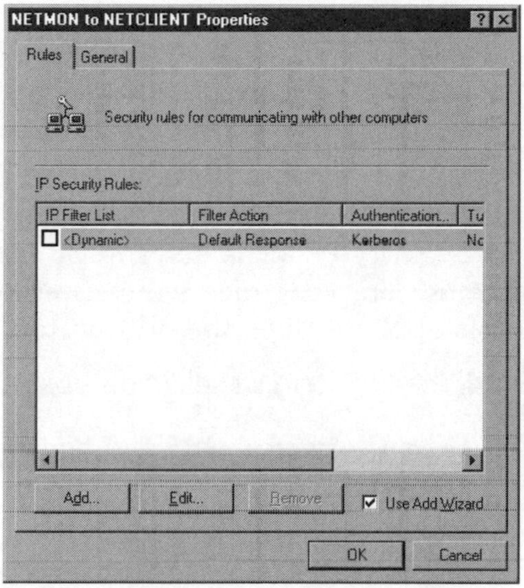

8. Click the Add button to add a new IP Security Rule. Be sure there is a checkmark in the Use Add Wizard checkbox.

9. You see the Welcome screen for the Security Rule Wizard. Click Next.

10. The wizard asks if you want to specify a tunnel endpoint. We will not be using IPSec tunneling in the exercise. Select This rule does not specify a tunnel. Click Next.

11. The wizard now asks for the type of network connections that should use this IP Security Rule. Select the All network connections option button and click Next.

12. Now we need to decide the initial authentication method. The default is Kerberos V5. Select the Use this string to protect the key exchange (preshared key) option button. In the text box below, type 12345 as seen in Figure 6.23. Click Next.

Figure 6.23 Defining a preshared Master Key.

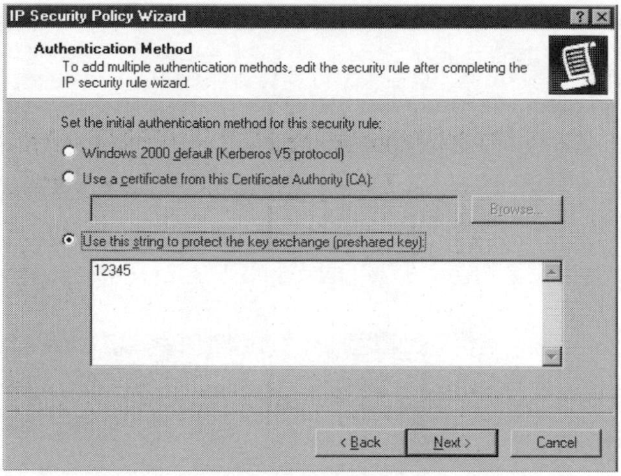

13. Define when the Security Policy will be applied. The decision to apply an IP Security Policy is determined by a Filter List. If the communicating computer meets the criteria on the Filter List, the IP Security is applied. Click the Add button as seen in Figure 6.24.

Figure 6.24 The IP Filter List selection box.

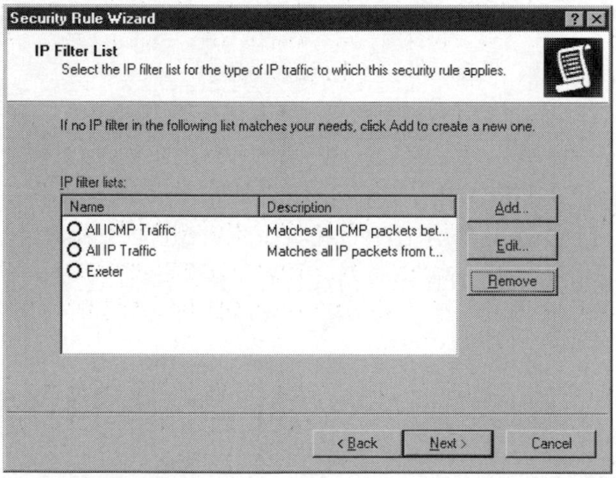

14. This opens the IP Filter List dialog box depicted in Figure 6.25. Here you can create multiple filters that can be combined into a single applied filter. We want to create a new filter so that our IP Security Policy is applied when communicating with NETCLIENT.

In the Name text box type NETCLIENT. Type a description in the Description text box. Insure that the checkmark is in the Use Add Wizard and click the Add button.

Figure 6.25 The IP Filter List dialog box.

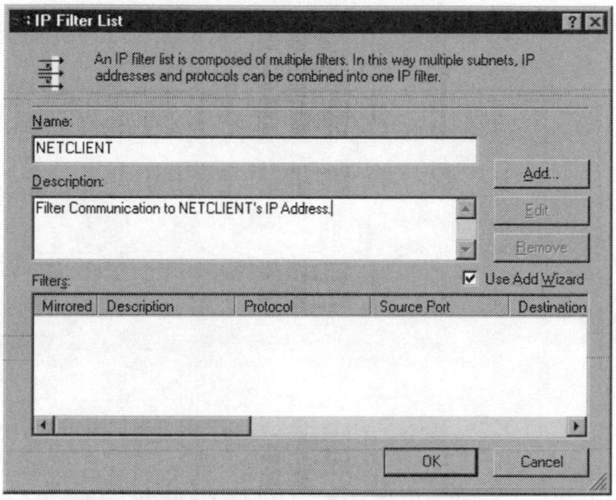

15. This starts the IP Filter Wizard and you are presented with a Welcome screen. Click Next.

16. The wizard asks what the source address of IP traffic should be. In the Source Address drop-down list box, click the down arrow and select My IP Address. Click Next.

17. Now enter the destination IP address of NETCLIENT. In the Destination address drop-down list box click the down arrow and select A specific IP Address. Enter the IP address of the NET-CLIENT computer as seen in Figure 6.26.

18. The wizard now needs to know what protocols should trigger the IP Security Policy. In the Select a protocol type drop-down list box, select Any. Click Next.

19. The wizard has finished collecting information. Click Finish. Your IP Filter List dialog box should appear as in Figure 6.27. Click Close to close the IP Filter List dialog box and return to the Security Rule Wizard.

20. The Security Rule Wizard dialog box now has an entry for NET-CLIENT. Click on the option button next to the NETCLIENT entry and click Next.

Figure 6.26 Entering the IP address of IP traffic.

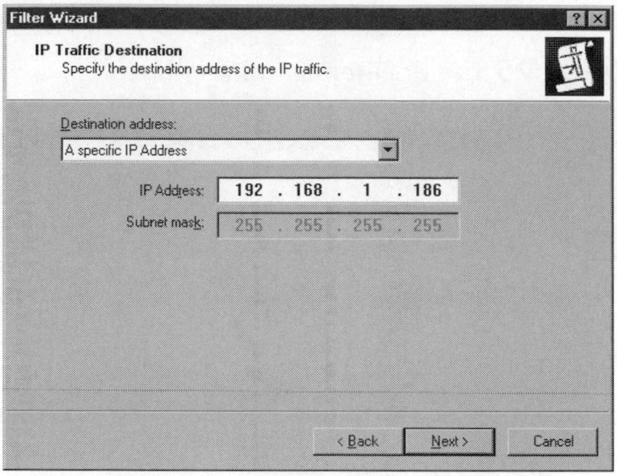

Figure 6.27 The completed IP Filter List dialog box.

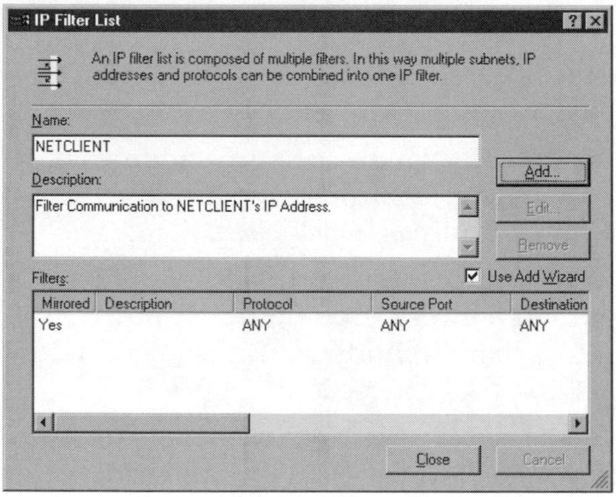

21. Decide on what action is to be taken when the Security Rule is activated. Select the option button next to Request Security (Optional) as seen in Figure 6.28. Click Next.

22. The Security Rule Wizard has completed gathering information. Click Finish. You are returned to the NETMON to NETCLIENT Properties dialog box as seen in Figure 6.29. If there is a check-mark in the <Dynamic> IP Filter List, remove it now. Click Close.

Figure 6.28 Defining the Filter Action.

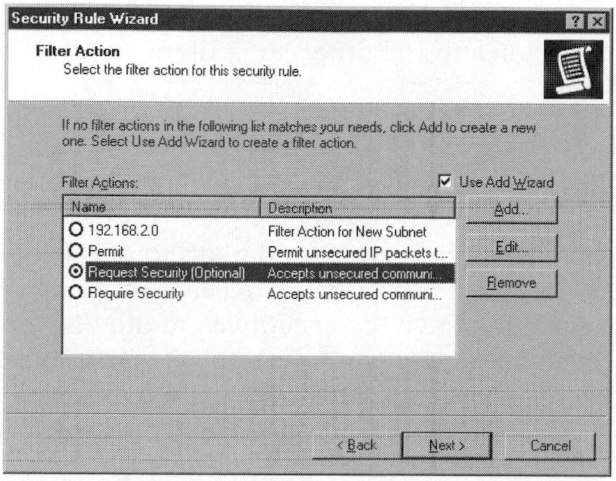

Figure 6.29 The completed NETMON to NETCLIENT Properties box.

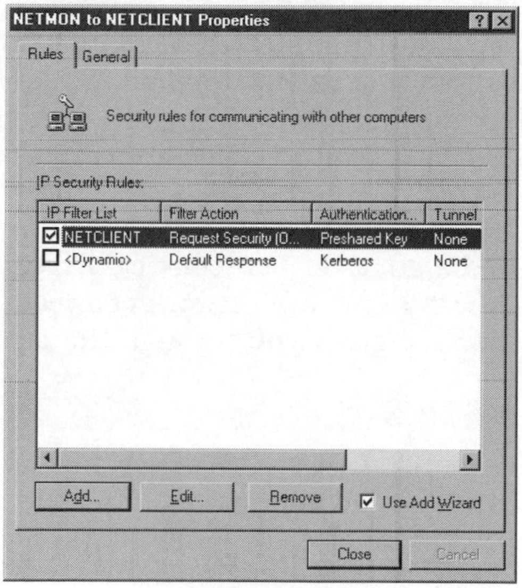

Now that you are back at the IPSec Practice Console, you should see an entry for your new IPSec Security Policy. In order for that policy to take effect, you have to "assign" it. To assign the policy, do the following:

1. Right-click on the NETMON to NETCLIENT Policy.

2. Click Assign.

In the right pane you will see Yes in the Policy Assigned column. This completes the IPSec Policy setup on the NETMON computer. The preparation of the NETCLIENT computer will be much simpler. We will assign one of the Built-in Policies to the other computer.

Configuring Microsoft RAS and VPN for Windows 2000

Remote connectivity is becoming a popular solution to a variety of problems: the need for sales personnel to access company databases while on the road, the need for traveling executives to stay in touch with the office, the need for telecommuting employees to view and manipulate files on the corporate servers. The ability to connect to a local area network from off-site locations is becoming not just a luxury, but a necessity in today's business world.

There are several ways to establish a remote connection to a private network. One option is to dial in directly over the public telephone lines, using a modem on the remote computer to connect to a modem on the company server. Another possibility is to have dedicated leased lines installed from one point to another. A third, increasingly attractive solution, is to take advantage of the widespread availability of Internet connectivity to establish a virtual private network, which circumvents long distance charges, doesn't require expensive capital outlays, and can be done from virtually anywhere.

In the past, a VPN was looked upon as a somewhat exotic, high-tech option that required a great deal of technical expertise. With Windows 2000, setting up a virtual private network connection is much easier—there is even a wizard to guide you through the process.

Tunneling Basics

A VPN can use the public network (Internet) infrastructure, yet maintain privacy and security through encryption and encapsulation of the data being transmitted, or "tunneled" through the public communications system.

VPN Definitions and Terminology

To understand how a VPN works, it's important first to define the terms used in conjunction with this technology.

Tunneling Protocol

A *tunneling protocol* is used to create a private pathway or "tunnel" through an internetwork (typically the Internet) in which data packets are encapsulated and encrypted prior to transmission to ensure privacy of the communication. Windows 2000 supports two tunneling protocols: Point-to-Point Tunneling Protocol (PPTP) and L2TP.

NOTE

PPTP and L2TP are the tunneling protocols supported by and included with Windows 2000. However, other technologies exist for establishing tunnels, as well as non-Microsoft implementations of PPTP and L2TP. In fact, IPSec can perform Layer 3 tunneling for cases in which L2TP cannot be used.

For more information on PPTP and L2TP, and the differences between the two, see the section, "Windows 2000 Tunneling Protocols," later in this chapter.

Data Encryption

The earliest virtual private networking technologies attempted to provide security through encrypting every packet, using encryption hardware that sat between the LAN and the WAN router. There were many drawbacks to this solution, including the fact that private (unregistered) IP addresses on the LAN generally were not supported.

Modern VPN technologies use both encryption and encapsulation to provide an easier-to-implement and more flexible way to transmit private data over the public network.

In a Windows 2000 VPN using the Point-to-Point Tunneling Protocol (PPTP), encryption keys are generated by the MS-CHAP or EAP-TLS authentication process, and Microsoft Point-to-Point Encryption (MPPE) is used to encrypt a PPP frame.

Data Encapsulation

Encapsulation means putting one data structure inside another. VPN technology encapsulates private data with a header that provides routing information that allows the data to travel over the Internet to the private network. Figure 6.30 illustrates the data encryption process.

Figure 6.30 Data encapsulation

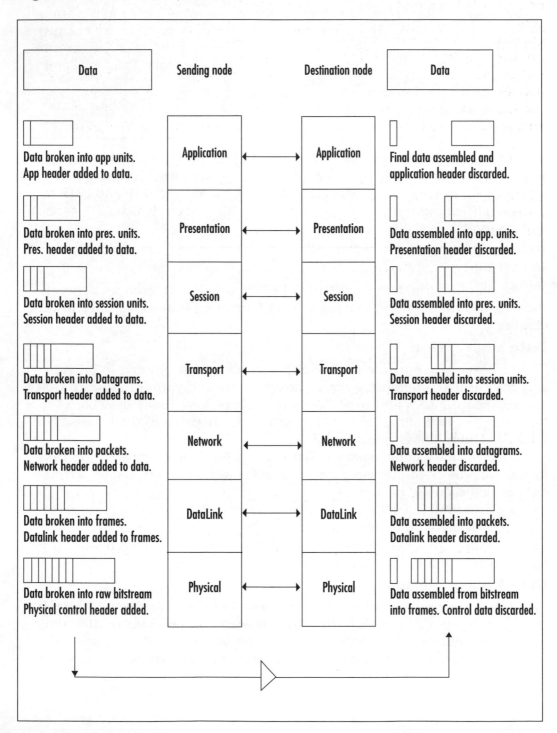

In a VPN, the data packets (IP, Internetwork Packet Exchange (IPX), or NetBIOS Extended User Interface (NetBEUI), depending on the LAN protocol used by the private network to which you are connecting) are encapsulated in a tunneling protocol such as PPTP or L2TP; these packets are then packaged by an IP packet that contains the address of the destination private network. The local Internet service provider (ISP) or other access provider will assign the user an IP address, so the user can keep the unregistered internal address for communications on the LAN. The encapsulated packets can be encrypted using IPSec or another security protocol.

The encapsulation process conceals the original packet inside a new packet. Then the new packet provides the routing information to allow it to go through the Internet or another internetwork without regard to the final destination address that is contained in the original packet header. When the encapsulated packet arrives at its destination, the encapsulation header will be removed and the original packet header will be used to route the packet to its final destination. Tunneling protocols are sometimes referred to as encapsulation protocols.

NOTE

See RFC 1483 for more detailed information on protocol encapsulation.

How Tunneling Works

Tunneling emulates a point-to-point connection by wrapping the datagram with a header that contains addressing information to get it across the public network to the destination private network (see Figure 6.31, Step 1). The data is also encrypted to further protect the privacy of the communication. The "tunnel" is the part of the connection in which the data is encapsulated and encrypted; this becomes the "virtual private network" (see Figure 6.31, Step 2). Figure 6.31 is a visual representation of the tunneling process.

Data encryption is performed between the VPN client and the VPN server; thus the connection from the client to the Internet Service Provider does not need to be encrypted.

Figure 6.31 Tunneling process.

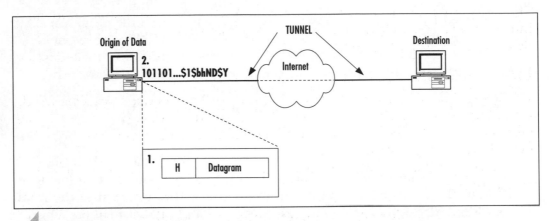

> **NOTE**
>
> It is possible to send a PPP frame through a tunnel in plain text, with no encryption, but this is not recommended for VPN connections over the public Internet, as the confidentiality of the communication would be compromised. This would actually be considered a "virtual" network, although technically it is not a VPN because the element of privacy is missing.

IP Addressing

The VPN connection will use a valid public IP address, usually supplied by the ISP's DHCP server, to route the data. This data packet, containing internal IP addresses of the sending and destination computers, is inside the "envelope" of the VPN, so even if you are using private (nonregistered) IP addresses on the private network, they will never be "seen" on the Internet. Encryption and encapsulation protect the addresses of the computers on the private network.

Security Issues Pertaining to VPNs

The concept of using an open, public network like the vast global Internet to transfer sensitive data presents obvious security concerns. For virtual networking to be feasible for security-conscious organizations, the privacy component must be ensured. Security over a VPN connection involves encapsulation, authentication of the user, and security of the data.

Encapsulation

The encapsulation of the original data packet inside a tunneling protocol hides its headers as it travels over the internetwork, and is the first line of defense in securing the communication.

User Authentication

Windows 2000 VPN solutions use the same authentication protocols used when connecting to the network locally; authentication is performed at the destination, so the security accounts database information is not transmitted onto the public network.

Windows 2000 can use the following authentication methods for VPN connections:

- **CHAP** Challenge Handshake Authentication Protocol, which uses challenge-response with one-way hashing on the response, allows the user to prove to the server that he or she knows the password without actually sending the password itself over the network.

- **MS-CHAP** Microsoft CHAP, which also uses a challenge-response authentication method with one-way encryption on the response.

- **MS-CHAPv2** An enhanced version of Microsoft-CHAP, which is a mutual authentication protocol requiring both the client and the server to prove their identities.

- **EAP/TLS** Extensible Authentication Protocol/Transport Level Security, which provides support for adding authentication schemes such as token cards, one-time passwords, the Kerberos V5 protocol, public key authentication using smart cards, certificates, and others.

NOTE

Data will be encrypted by MPPE in a PPTP connection only if MS-CHAP, MS-CHAPv2, or EAP/TLS authentication is used, as these are the only authentication protocols that generate their own initial encryption keys.

Data Security

Data security is provided through encapsulation and encryption, but the higher the security, the more overhead and the lower the performance. IPSec was designed to work with different encryption levels and provide different levels of data security based on the organization's needs.

NOTE

PPTP uses Microsoft Point-to-Point Encryption (MPPE) to encrypt data. When using L2TP for VPN connections, data is encrypted by using IPSec.

L2TP over IPSec uses certificate-based authentication, which is the strongest authentication type used in Windows 2000. A machine-level certificate is issued by a Certificate Authority, and installed on the VPN client and the VPN server. This can be done through the Windows 2000 Certificate Manager or by configuring the CA to issue certificates automatically to the computers in the Windows 2000 domain.

Windows 2000 Security Options

Windows 2000 provides the network administrator with a great deal of flexibility in setting authentication and data encryption requirements for VPN communications. Microsoft has compiled a chart of possible security settings combinations for both PPTP and L2TP, shown in Table 6.2 and also available at www.windows.com/windows2000/en/datacenter/help/Sec_vpn.htm.

Table 6.2 Authentication and Encryption Requirement Settings

Validate my identity using	Require data encryption	Authentication methods negotiated	Encryption enforcement
PPTP			
Require secured password	No	CHAP, MS-CHAP, MS-CHAP v2	Optional encryption (connect even if no encryption)
Require secured password	Yes	MS-CHAP, MS-CHAP v2	Require encryption (disconnect if server declines)
Smart card	No	EAP/TLS	Optional encryption (connect even if no encryption)
Smart card	Yes	EAP/TLS	Require encryption (disconnect if server declines)

Continued

Table 6.2 Continued

Validate my identity using	Require data encryption	Authentication methods negotiated	Encryption enforcement
L2TP			
Require secured password	No	CHAP, MS-CHAP, MS-CHAP v2	Optional encryption (connect even if no encryption)
Require secured password	Yes	CHAP, MS-CHAP, MS-CHAP v2	Require encryption (disconnect if server declines)
Smart card	No	EAP/TLS	Optional encryption (connect even if no encryption)
Smart card	Yes	EAP/TLS	Require encryption (disconnect if server declines)

These settings are configured by using the Security tab of the Properties sheet for the VPN connection, as shown in Figure 6.32. To access this dialog box, from the Start menu select Settings | Network and Dialup Connections | [name of your VPN connection].

Figure 6.32 To customize security settings for a VPN connection, select Advanced and click the Settings button.

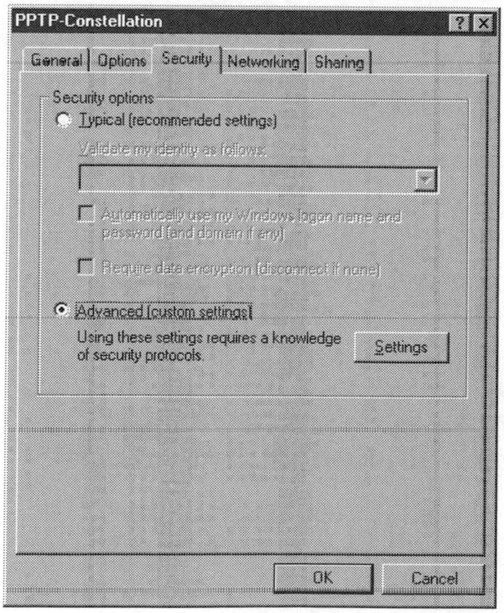

Then click on the Properties button and select the Security tab.

Selecting the Advanced radio button and clicking on the Settings button displays the Advanced Security Settings dialog box shown in Figure 6.33, where the authentication and encryption setting combinations can be adjusted.

Figure 6.33 Selecting the desired custom security settings in the Advanced Security Settings dialog box.

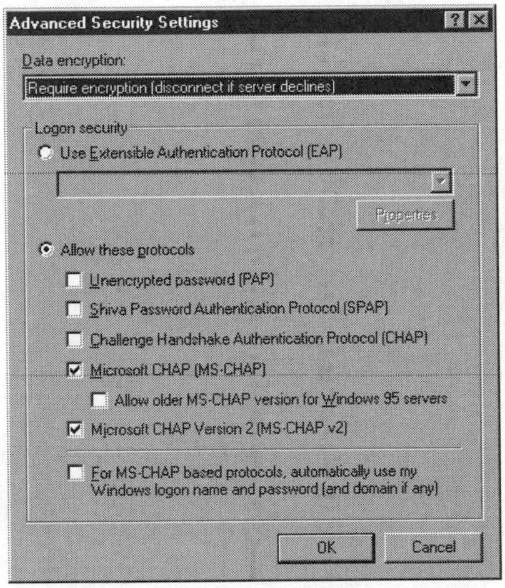

This dialog box allows you to select whether encryption is optional, required, or not allowed, whether to use EAP or allow other designated protocols, and whether to automatically enter the logged on account's Windows username and password for MS-CHAP authentication.

WARNING

The advanced security settings should not be changed from the Typical (recommended) settings unless you thoroughly understand the security protocols and what effects your changes may have.

If you choose to use EAP (for instance, to enable authentication via smart card), you will need to configure the properties for the smart card or other certificate authentication as shown in Figure 6.34.

You can choose from a list of recognized root certificate authorities (CAs).

Figure 6.34 Setting Smart Card or Certificate properties when using EAP.

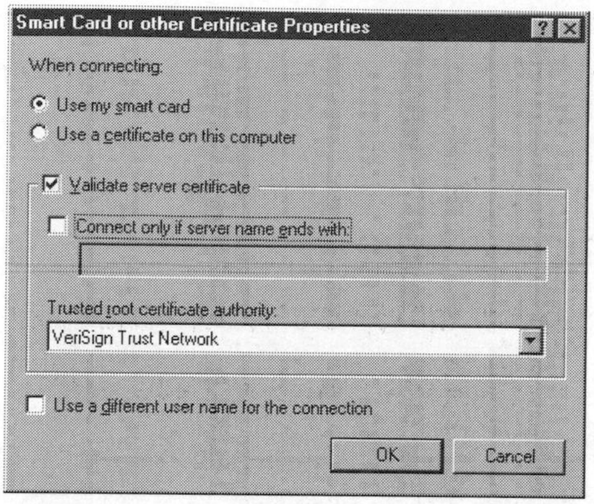

> **NOTE**
>
> A CA is an entity entrusted to issue certificates to individuals, computers, or organizations that affirm the identity and other attributes of the certificate. VeriSign is an example of a remote third-party CA recognized as trustworthy throughout the industry.

Common Uses of VPNs

Virtual private networks are commonly used by companies to provide a more cost-effective way for employees, customers, and other authorized users to connect to their private networks. The VPN is a viable alternative to direct dial-in, which incurs long-distance charges, or to the hefty initial and monthly expense of a dedicated leased line.

VPNs are typically used to allow a standalone remote user to connect a computer, such as a home desktop system or a laptop/notebook computer when on the road, to the corporate network. However, VPNs can also connect two distant LANs to one another using their local Internet connections, or connect two computers over an intranet within the company.

We will take a look at each of these situations and discuss special considerations and best practices for each.

Remote User Access over the Internet

A typical scenario is the telecommuter, traveling employee, or executive who takes work home and needs to connect to the company's network from a remote location. The traditional way to do so was to dial in to the company RAS server's modem. That works, but often was costly if the remote user was not in the company's local calling area. If the remote user has an Internet Service Provider local to his location, however, he can avoid long distance charges by dialing the ISP instead of the company's modem, and setting up a VPN through the Internet.

See Figure 6.35 for an illustration of this common situation.

Figure 6.35 A user can access the company network from home through a VPN.

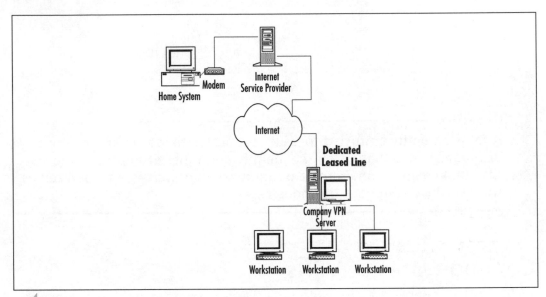

NOTE

An active Winsock Proxy client will interfere with the creation of a VPN by redirecting data to the proxy server before the data can be processed by the VPN. You must first disable the Winsock Proxy client before attempting to create a VPN connection.

Connecting Networks over the Internet

Another use of the VPN is to connect two networks through the Internet. If you have offices in two cities with a Local Area Network at each office location, you may find it advantageous to connect the two LANs so users at both locations can share one another's resources. One way to do that would be to purchase a leased line such as a T1 line to connect the two networks, but this would be expensive.

Sharing a Remote Access VPN Connection

If both offices already have Internet connections, perhaps through dedicated Integrated Services Digital Network (ISDN) lines or Digital Subscriber Line (DSL) service, you can use the existing connection to the Internet to set up a VPN between the two offices and transfer data securely.

Figure 6.36 illustrates a situation where the VPN would be used to connect two distant networks.

Figure 6.36 A VPN connection can connect two LANs in distant locations.

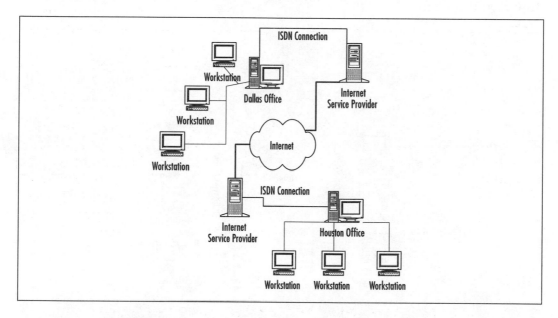

In this case, setup will be slightly more complicated than connecting a single remote computer to a company network.

To give all the computers on both LANs access to the resources they need, you can set up a VPN server on each side of the connection, then configure a VPN client connection on each side as well. The VPN client connection can then be shared with the rest of the LAN via Internet Connection Sharing.

You can also, if you wish, restrict access by remote access VPN clients to only the shared resources on the VPN server and not allow access to the network to which the VPN server is attached.

Using a Router-to-Router Connection

Another way to connect two networks via a VPN is to use a router-to-router VPN connection with a demand-dial interface. The VPN server then provides a routed connection to the network of which it is a part. Routing and Remote Access Service (RRAS) is used to create a router-to-router VPN connection, so the VPN servers acting as routers must be Windows 2000 servers or NT 4.0 servers with RRAS.

Mutual authentication is supported, so that the calling router (VPN client) and answering router (VPN server) authenticate themselves to one another. Figure 6.37 illustrates how a router-to-router connection can be used to connect two networks.

Figure 6.37 The VPN server can provide a routed connection to the network to which it belongs.

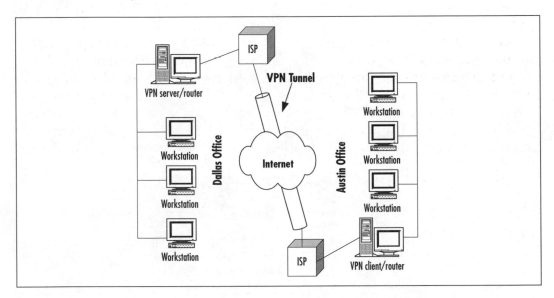

In a router-to-router connection, the VPN works as a data link layer link between the two networks. In the illustration, the Windows 2000 computer acting as a router to the Austin office is the VPN client that initiates the connection to the VPN server, which is the computer acting as a router to the Dallas office.

NOTE

The VPN server will need to have a dedicated connection to the Internet, unless the ISP supports demand-dial routing to customers, which is not common.

The endpoints of a router-to-router connection are the routers, and the tunnel extends from one router to the other. This is the part of the connection in which the data is encapsulated.

Connecting Computers over an Intranet

A less common scenario, but one that will be useful in some instances, is to provide for a virtual private network over an internal intranet. This is appropriate when you have certain departments or divisions that deal with particularly sensitive data and as a result are not physically connected to the company's intranet. This provides the necessary security but also prevents authorized users from accessing the department's data from computers physically located outside the department.

One way to solve this problem is to physically connect the department to the intranet but set up a VPN server between the department and the rest of the network. In this way, users who have permissions to do so can use the VPN connection to access resources in the high-security department, and the encapsulation and encryption will protect their communications used by the tunneling protocol. The department's resources will not show up as network resources to users outside the department who do not have permissions to access them.

Figure 6.38 illustrates this use of VPN connectivity.

Figure 6.38 Using a VPN connection to hide a high-sensitivity department from the intranet.

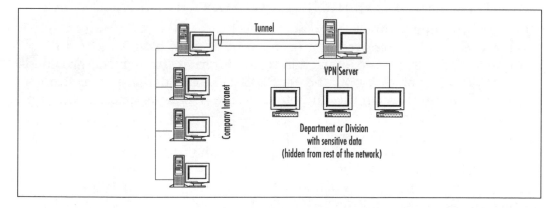

The VPN connection in this example uses the network's IP connectivity, so you don't have to establish the connection over phone lines or a public network.

TIP

You can restrict access to intranet resources for IP traffic by using packet filters based on a remote access policy profile.

Tunneling Protocols and the Basic Tunneling Requirements

Establishment of a secure tunnel through a public or other internetwork requires that computers on both ends of the connection be configured to use Virtual Private Networking, and they must both be running a common tunneling protocol. Windows 2000 Server can be a VPN client, or it can be a VPN server accepting PPTP connections from both Microsoft and non-Microsoft PPTP clients.

Windows 2000 Tunneling Protocols

As mentioned earlier, Windows 2000 supports two tunneling protocols for establishment of VPNs: PPTP and L2TP. A primary difference between the two is the encryption method: PPTP uses MPPE to encrypt data, whereas L2TP uses certificates with IPSec.

Point-to-Point Tunneling Protocol (PPTP)

The Point-to-Point Tunneling Protocol (PPTP) was developed as an extension to the popular Point-to-Point Protocol (PPP) used by most ISPs to establish a remote access connection to the Internet through the provider's network. PPTP allows IP, IPX, and NetBIOS/NetBEUI datagrams or frames to be transferred through the tunnel. From the user's perspective, the tunneling is transparent.

PPTP allows for NT 4.0 secure authentication, using Password Authentication Protocol (PAP), Challenge Handshake Authentication Protocol (CHAP), and Microsoft's version of CHAP, MS-CHAP.

PPTP support became available in Windows NT Server in 1996, and client software is available for DOS, Windows, and most PPP clients. The PPTP specifications were developed by the PPTP Forum, made up of Microsoft and networking equipment vendors such as Ascend, 3Com/Primary Access, ECI-Telematics, and US Robotics. PPTP is an open standard.

Layer 2 Tunneling Protocol (L2TP)

The Layer 2 Tunneling Protocol (L2TP) provides the same functionality as PPTP, but overcomes some of the limitations of the Point to Point Tunneling Protocol. It does not require IP connectivity between the client workstation and the server as PPTP does. L2TP can be used as long as the tunnel medium provides packet-oriented point-to-point connectivity, which means it works with such media as Asynchronous Transfer Mode (ATM), Frame Relay, and X.25. L2TP can authenticate the tunnel endpoints, and can be used in conjunction with secure ID cards on the client side and with firewalls on the server side.

L2TP is an Internet Engineering Task Force (IETF) standard, which was developed in a cooperative effort by Microsoft, Cisco Systems, Ascend, 3Com, and other networking industry leaders. It combines features of Cisco's Layer 2 Forwarding (L2F) protocol with Microsoft's PPTP implementation.

L2TP can utilize IPSec to provide end-to-end security (see the section on IPSec for more information).

Using PPTP with Windows 2000

PPTP is installed with the Routing and Remote Access Service (RRAS). It is configured by default for five PPTP ports. You can enable PPTP ports with the Routing and Remote Access wizard. The PPTP ports will be displayed as WAN miniports in the RRAS console, as shown in Figure 6.39.

Figure 6.39 PPTP ports in the Routing and Remote Access (RRAS) console.

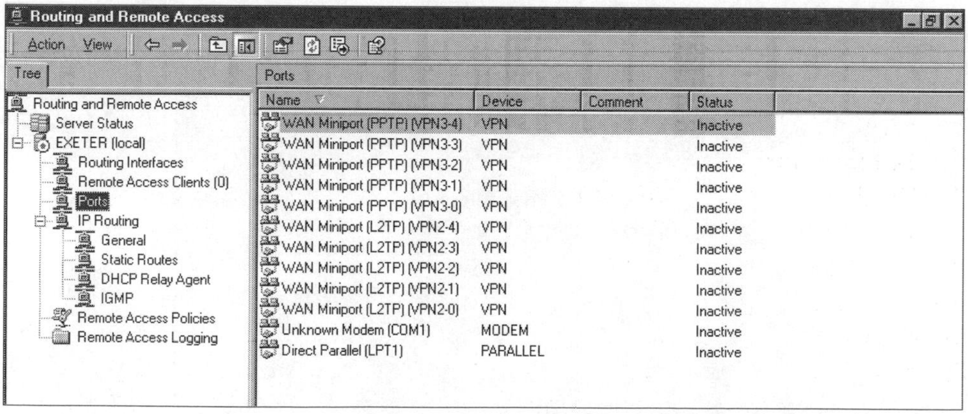

You can view the status of each VPN port, and refresh or reset it by double-clicking on the port name to display the status sheet and clicking on the appropriate button.

How to Configure a PPTP Device

To configure a port device, right-click on Ports in the left panel of the console and select Properties. A dialog box similar to Figure 6.40 is displayed.

Figure 6.40 Configuring the properties of a PPTP port device.

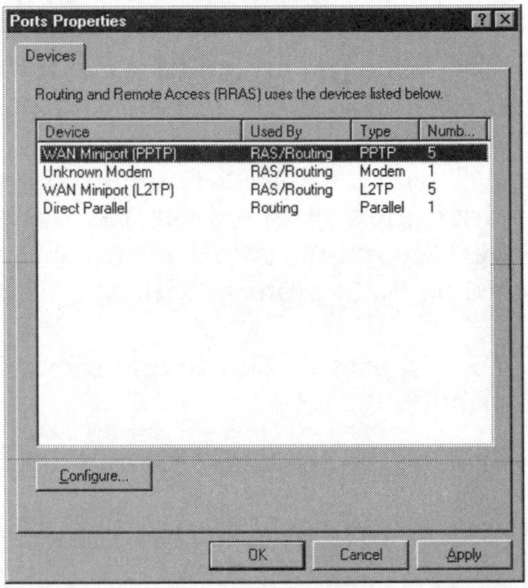

Highlight the RRAS device you wish to configure and then click the Configure button. You will see a dialog box like the one in Figure 6.41.

Figure 6.41 Using the WAN miniport (PPTP) configuration dialog box.

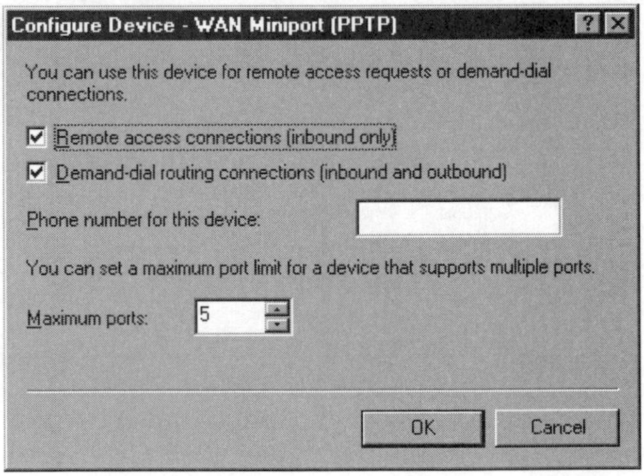

In the device configuration dialog box, you can set up the port to be used for inbound RAS connections and/or inbound and outbound demand-dial routing connections.

NOTE

A device can be physical, representing hardware (such as a modem), or virtual, representing software (such as the PPTP protocol). A device can create physical or logical point-to-point connections, and the device provides a port, or communication channel, which supports a point-to-point connection.

A standard modem is a single port device. PPTP and L2TP are virtual multiport devices. You can set up to 1000 ports for PPTP and L2TP devices (five is the default number of ports).

TIP

When you change the number of ports on the PPTP or L2TP WAN miniport device, the computer must be rebooted before the change will take effect.

Using L2TP with Windows 2000

Layer 2 Tunneling Protocol (L2TP) over IPSec gives administrators a way to provide end-to-end security for a VPN connection. L2TP doesn't rely on vendor-specific encryption methods to create a completely secured virtual networking connection.

How to Configure L2TP

To enable the server to be a VPN server for L2TP clients, you must first install Routing and Remote Access (RRAS) if you haven't already.

1. Open the RRAS console: Start | Programs | Administrative Tools | Routing and Remote Access.

2. In the left pane of the console tree, right-click the server you want to enable, and click Configure and Enable Routing and Remote Access. This will start the wizard, which will guide you through the process.

3. After the service is installed and started, configure the properties of the server by right-clicking on the server name and selecting Properties. You will see a properties sheet similar to the one in Figure 6.42.

Figure 6.42 The RRAS properties sheet for the selected remote access server.

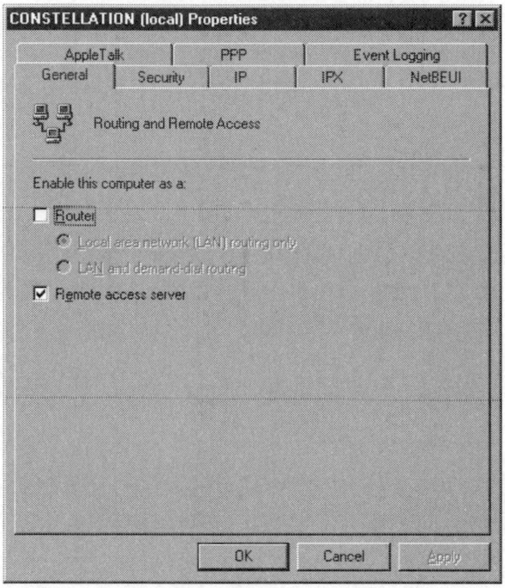

4. On the General tab, be sure that the Remote access server check box is selected.

5. On the Security tab, under Authentication Provider, you can confirm the credentials of RRAS clients by using either Windows 2000 security (Windows Authentication) or a RADIUS server (see Figure 6.43). If RADIUS is selected, you need to configure RADIUS server settings for your RADIUS server or RADIUS proxy.

6. In the Accounting Provider drop-down box, choose Windows or RADIUS accounting. You can then record remote access client activity for analysis or accounting purposes.

7. Click the Authentication Methods button, and choose the authentication methods that are supported by the RRAS server to authenticate the credentials of remote access clients, as shown in Figure 6.44.

Figure 6.43 Choose either Windows Authentication or RADIUS as your authentication provider.

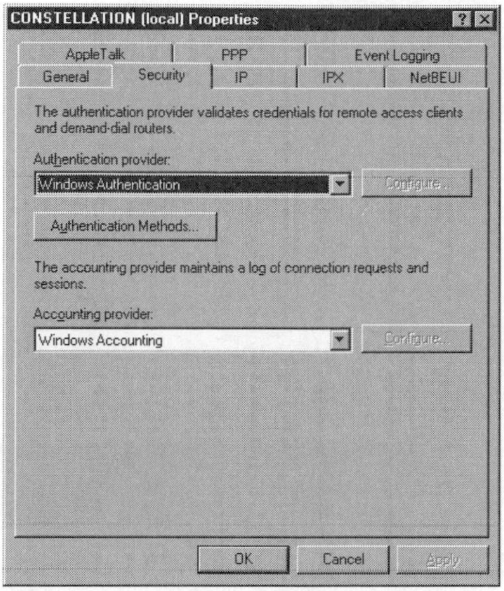

Figure 6.44 Select the authentication method that will be used by the RRAS clients.

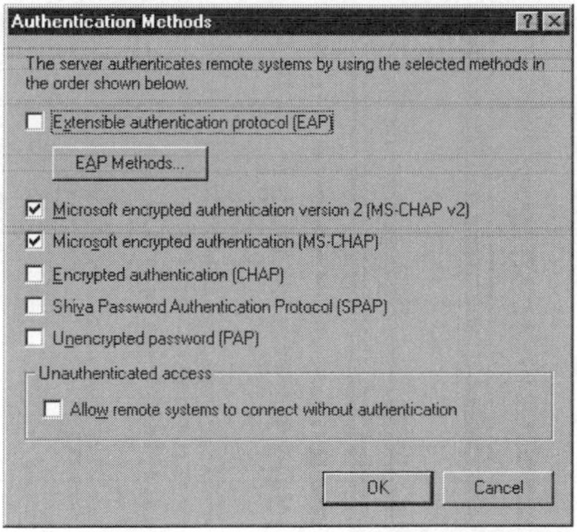

TIP

Microsoft remote access clients generally will use MS-CHAP authentication. If you want to enable smart card support, you need to use EAP authentication.

8. On the IP tab, verify that the Enable IP routing and Allow IP-based remote access and demand-dial connections check boxes are both checked, as shown in Figure 6.45.

Figure 6.45 Enable IP routing and allow IP-based remote access and demand-dial connections.

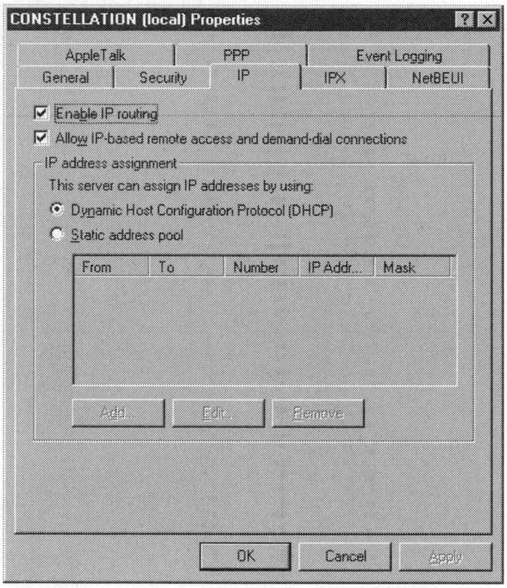

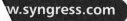

9. Configure the L2TP ports for remote access. In the RRAS console, right-click on Ports and select Properties. Select the L2TP ports as shown in Figure 6.46.

10. Click on the Configure button and you will see the dialog box displayed in Figure 6.47.

You can also configure remote access policies to control access to the VPN server.

Figure 6.46 Select the WAN Miniport (L2TP) for configuration.

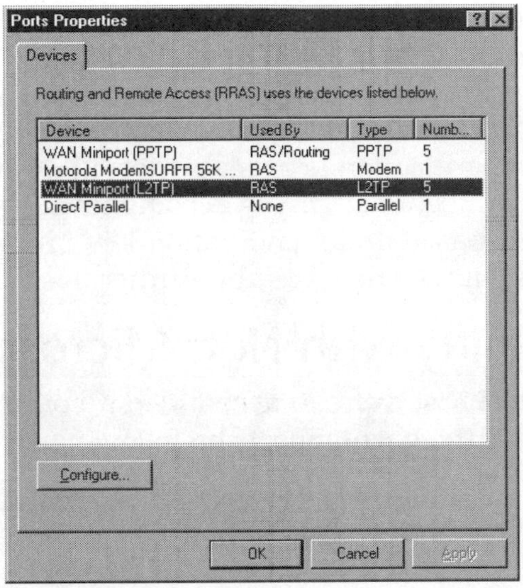

Figure 6.47 Configuring the L2TP ports to allow remote access and/or demand-dial connections.

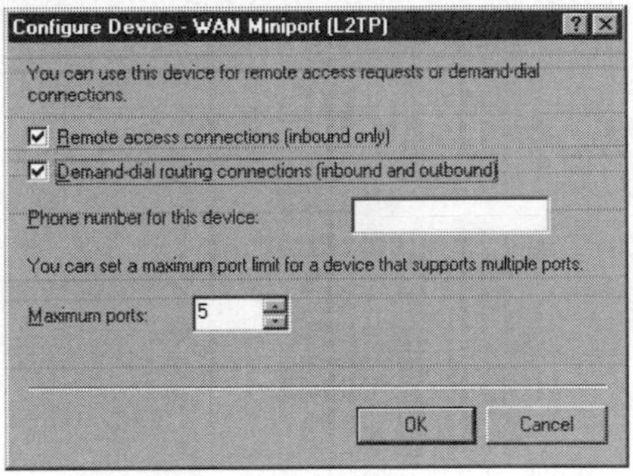

How L2TP Security Differs from that of PPTP

L2TP is similar to PPTP in many ways. They both support multiprotocol VPN links and can be used to create secure tunnels through the Internet or another public network to connect to a private network that also has a connection to the internetwork. L2TP can be used over IPSec to provide for greater security, including end-to-end encryption, whereas Microsoft's PPTP connections are dependent upon MPPE for encryption. L2TP is derived from L2F, a Cisco Systems tunneling protocol.

With L2TP over IPSec, encapsulation involves two layers: L2TP encapsulation and IPSec encapsulation. First L2TP wraps its header and a User

Datagram Protocol (UDP) header around a PPP frame. Then IPSec wraps an ESP (Encapsulating Security Payload) header and trailer around the package, and adds an IPSec authentication trailer. Finally an IP header is added, which contains the addresses of the source (VPN client) and destination (VPN server) computers. IPSec encrypts all the data inside the IPSec ESP header and authentication trailer, including the PPP, UDP, and L2TP headers. Data authentication is available for L2TP over IPSec connections, unlike for PPTP connections. This is accomplished by the use of a cryptographic checksum based on an encryption key known only to the sender and the receiver. This is known as the Authentication Header (AH).

Interoperability with Non-Microsoft VPN Clients

A Windows 2000 VPN server can accept client connections from non-Microsoft clients, if the clients meet the following requirements:

- The clients must use PPTP or L2TP tunneling protocol.
- For PPTP connections, the client must support MPPE.
- For L2TP connections, the client must support IPSec.

If these requirements are met, the non-Microsoft clients will be able to make a secure VPN connection. You do not have to make any special configuration changes on the VPN server to allow non-Microsoft clients to connect.

Possible Security Risks

Several of the preceding sections detail security services available to you in Windows 2000. You should also know about some of the potential security issues you face, and what impact they can have on your network. For this reason, there are several things that you should make sure you do to help protect your VPN:

- Make sure that Windows 2000 is set up with the latest patches, hot fixes, and service packs. As of this writing, Service Pack 1 for Windows 2000 has been released.
- Make sure that you disable all inbound and outbound traffic on your firewall to TCP and UDP ports 135, 137, 139, and UDP port 138. This will keep anyone from snooping around on your network to see what services are available (user names, computer names, etc.). This solution will only truly protect you from outside users. Users internal to your network can still snoop around your network as much as they want.

Summary

In this chapter, we have discussed some of the new security features available in Windows 2000. Kerberos, EAP, and RADIUS, add a lot to the flexibility of the security model in Windows 2000. The most important thing to remember about the direction of Windows 2000 is the movement toward industry standards. By embracing industry standards, Microsoft will be able to enter into markets that it was previously locked out of because of proprietary network models. AD comes a long way from the Domain models of NT4 by using LDAP as its foundation.

Windows 2000 adds a lot of security features into the default configuration, especially when compared to Windows NT 4.0. EAP is an open standard that allows vendors to integrate proprietary security software or equipment into Windows 2000. RADIUS allows Windows 2000 to offload AAA functions from the network servers by providing a dedicated authentication interface on separate network equipment.

IPSec, although a powerful security feature included with Windows 2000, has some drawbacks. Remember that the RFC did not include mechanisms suitable for remote access. This makes it difficult to deploy a multi-vendor solution without care for interoperability. Microsoft has embedded significant support for IPSec, which can be set up through the MMC.

VPN support allows clients to tunnel over a dial-up connection to a specific destination, such as a corporate network, using protocols like PPTP and L2TP. This tunneling feature creates a virtual private network between the client and server. IPSec can be used to tunnel client connections at Layer 3 when PPTP and L2TP are not options.

FAQs

Q: Why can't I use L2TP/IPSec when running NAT?

A: You cannot use IPSec on the inside of a NAT network. NAT (Network Address Translation) allows an intranet to use IP addresses assigned to Private Networks to work on the Internet. A Private IP Address is not recognized as valid by Internet routers, and therefore cannot be used for direct Internet communications. A server running a Network Address Translator will map intranet client's IP addresses to a request, and then forward the request to the destination using its valid Internet address. The destination Internet Host responds to the NAT server by sending the requested information to its IP address. The NAT server then inserts the intranet client's IP address into the destination header, and forwards this response to the client.

Incoming packets are sent to a single IP address, which NAT maps to a private IP address. When using ESP, or AH, or both, IPSec must be able to access the Security Parameters Index associated with each internal connection. The problem is, when NAT changes the destination IP address of the packet, this changes the SPI, which invalidates the information in the Auth trailer. IPSec interprets this as a breach, and the packet is dropped.

Q: Can I use IPSec to secure communications with my Win 9x machines?

A: No. At this time, only Windows 2000 clients and servers can participate in IPSec secured communications. Microsoft source material suggests that Windows CE may support IPSec in the future, but there are no plans to support other down-level clients.

Q: Does my VPN server require a dedicated connection to the Internet?

A: Your VPN server requires a dedicated IP address. In most instances, this means your VPN server needs to be connected to the Internet at all times. A small number of ISPs support "on demand" routing, which will cause the ISP to dial up your VPN server when incoming requests are received for its IP address. However, to ensure highest availability, it is best to have a dedicated connection. Remember that the VPN clients will dial-in to your server using its IP address, and therefore that IP address must be constant.

Q: Is there a way to force the use of strong authentication and encryption for VPN users and a different set of authentication and encryption constraints for dial-up users?

A: Yes—you can do this by setting remote access policies. With remote access policies, you can grant or deny authorization based on the type of connection being requested (dial-up networking or virtual private network connection).

Q: Is there a way for me to monitor the IPSec connections to my server?

A: Yes. Microsoft provides a tool called ipsecmon.exe. You can start this tool from the **run** command. Figure 6.48 shows the ipsecmon window.
The IP Security Monitor allows you to assess when failures take place in negotiating security associations, when bad Security Parameters Index packets are passed, and many other statistics. The Oakley Main Modes number indicates the number of Master Keys exchanged, and the Oakley Quick Modes number indicates the number of session keys. The Options button allows you to configure the update interval of the displayed statistics.

Figure 6.48 Main screen from the IP Security Monitor.

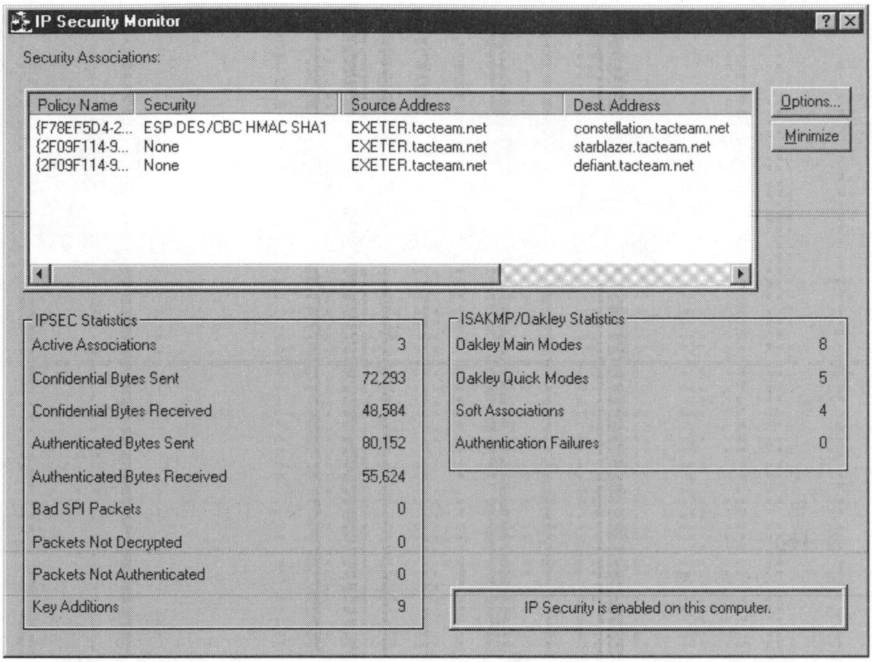

Q: My VPN clients cannot access network resources beyond my VPN server. What might be causing this?

A: There are several reasons why this might happen. One possibility is that the clients are not running the same LAN protocols used by the internal network. For example, the VPN client is running only the TCP/IP protocol. The internal network runs only NWLink. The VPN client is able to connect to the VPN server because they both run TCP/IP. However, when the VPN client tries to access a server on the internal network, the connection fails because the internal server runs only NWLink.

Another circumstance that can lead to VPN client access failures is when VPN clients are assigned IP addresses via DHCP, and the DHCP server becomes unavailable. If the VPN server has Automatic Private IP Addressing enabled, VPN clients will be assigned IP addresses in the Class B address class 169.254.0.0. Unless there is a route for this network ID in the VPN servers routing table, communication with the internal network will fail.

Also, make sure that your RRAS policies do not filter TCP/IP incoming and outgoing packets to and from the VPN clients. Be careful to open the Ports for the control channels used for your VPN connections as well.

Chapter 7

Securing Your Network with Microsoft Proxy Server 2.0

Solutions in this chapter:

- **Understanding the Core Components of Proxy Server 2.0**

- **Setting Up Proxy Server 2.0**

- **Troubleshooting Proxy Server 2.0**

- **Configuring Proxy Server Applications**

- **Understanding the Security Issues**

Introduction

Microsoft has produced many products to aid in securing your network—a notable security product is Proxy Server 2.0. Proxy Server 2.0 is not only designed to secure your network, but it is also designed to help speed up your Internet connections. Proxy Server 2.0 is designed to allow you to manage network security in a number of ways, through inbound and outbound access control, packet filtering, and even dial-in access.

Proxy Server 2.0 can cache frequently visited Web pages, speeding up browsing access for your users, and it can even be integrated in Novell environments. This Microsoft package is very versatile in its application on your network. This chapter will discuss the components of MS Proxy Server 2.0, how to configure and troubleshoot it, some common applications, and potential security risks associated with it.

Components of Microsoft Proxy Server 2.0

Microsoft Proxy Server 2.0 consists of many different components and services, including Web Proxy Service, Winsock Proxy Service, SOCKS Proxy Service, Reverse Proxy, and Reverse Hosting. As an administrator, you'll have to decide which of these services you'll employ on your network, and your decision will need to be based on the infrastructure of the network as well as what each service offers. Each of the following services has limitations on protocols offered, clients serviced, and browsers that are supported. In order to make an informed and appropriate decision, you'll need to know the facts about all of them. Each of these components will be described in detail in their respective sections within the chapter, and information on design issues and platform compatibility will also be discussed. Figure 7.1 shows how a proxy server sits "between" the Internet and the internal network.

Web Proxy Service

Web Proxy Service is a core component of MS Proxy Server 2.0 that will suit the needs of multiple network types because of its many features and its compatibility with various operating systems. Internet Service Manager administers this service, and the Web Proxy service can be used with almost any browser, and on almost any operating system platform.

Figure 7.1 How Proxy Server 2.0 protects a network.

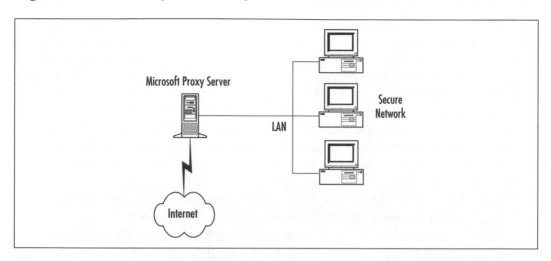

Choosing between Passive or Active Caching

Choosing between passive or active caching is a choice you will make depending upon the infrastructure of your network. With passive caching, everything is stored in cache, and each of these objects has a Time to Live (TTL). No objects will be updated at their originating site until their TTL has expired. The TTL is determined by configuring settings in the cache properties of Proxy Server 2.0, or are defined by the source HTML.

Active caching, on the other hand, is configured such that the cache automatically updates itself when an object's TTL is close to expiring. Most of the caching is done during off-peak times, when the network is not busy. This is accomplished through an algorithm that calculates the popularity of an object, its TTL, and current server load.

Both active and passive caching offer configuration settings that enable administrators to control how and when data is cached, thus adding even more opportunities to tweak the server and make it more efficient and reliable.

Web Proxy Service is the only service of the three offered that supports caching and routing of data. Caching can be passive or active, the administrator can set cache size, and cache filters can be defined. Routing can be used to define primary and secondary routes, and resolving them within an array before routing upstream can also be enabled. The Web Proxy service also offers Web publishing, reverse proxying, and reverse hosting, to assist in securing the internal servers from unwanted attacks from hackers or unwanted guests from outside the local network. These services are described later in the chapter. Clients can be logged and monitored by checking protocols used, date and time of requests, domain names of the computer responding to requests, as well as the contents of the URL request.

The Web Proxy service is a powerful utility that offers CERN (European Laboratory for Particle Physics)-compliant communications and works with both Microsoft Internet Explorer as well as Netscape Navigator. Permissions can be applied to secure communication through the proxy server for File Transfer Protocol (FTP)-Read, Gopher, Secure (Secure Sockets Layer), and WWW protocols. Transmission Control Protocol/Internet Protocol (TCP/IP) is used as the protocol of choice, and Internetwork Packet Exchange/Sequenced Packet Exchange (IPX/SPX) is not supported.

Winsock Proxy Service

Winsock Proxy service is the only service offered that supports IPX/SPX as well as TCP/IP as a protocol of choice. When IPX is used, conversion of IPX to IP is done twice, once when the information leaves the network for the Internet, and once on its return. This is necessary since the Internet is solely a TCP/IP-based network. Winsock Proxy is compatible with Windows Sockets applications and operates with them as if they had a straight connection to the Internet. Winsock Proxy service does not cache Internet addresses or support routing like the Web Proxy service does, but it does offer the ability to add protocols other than FTP, Gopher, Secure, and WWW. With Winsock Proxy service, protocols such as Post Office Protocol 3 (POP3), Hypertext Transfer Protocol (HTTP), and Real Audio can be added simply by configuring them through the Internet Service Manager.

With Winsock Proxy service, both inbound and outbound access can be secured by placing permissions on protocols, port numbers, users, or groups. IP addresses, domain names, and IP address ranges can also be used to restrict users' access to the Internet. External users can be blocked from accessing the internal network using this service.

Clients that use the Winsock Proxy service must be using a Windows operating system. This rules out this service for many networks since there are usually other clients like Novell or UNIX. As with the other services, logging is enabled and can be used to track client usage.

SOCKS Proxy Service

SOCKS Proxy service is very similar to the Winsock Proxy service, but it can be used by most popular client operating systems. With SOCKS Proxy, by default, all SOCKS requests are denied. You can allow or disallow requests to and from Domains or Zones, IP subnets, or All. Logging can be used to track clients as in the previous services. SOCKS provides secure communication between the client and server and can provide redirection for non-Windows platforms. It uses TCP/IP as the protocol.

TIP

When working with SOCKS Proxy and Winsock Proxy services, make sure that you've enabled access control! This is simply a checkbox on the permissions tab of the service you're using. If this is not enabled, you will not see an option for selecting permissions for these services.

Reverse Proxy

Reverse Proxy is offered by Proxy Server 2.0 to increase the security level for internal servers on the network. Reverse Proxy works by listening for HTTP requests by enabling the proxy server to capture incoming requests to an internal Web server and to reply for that server. This provides a measure of security for an internal Web server that might contain sensitive information or be vulnerable to hackers' attacks. Since the proxy server handles requests, the outside user never sees the internal server. Configuring the Web server to sit behind the protection of the proxy server provides an essential layer of defense against hackers. See Figure 7.2 for a visual example of how Reverse Proxy works. Enabling reverse proxying is discussed in a later section.

Reverse Hosting

Reverse hosting is similar to reverse proxying except that in addition to protecting the servers sitting behind it, it also keeps a list of those servers on the network that are permitted to publish to the Internet. The proxy server listens for requests from those servers and responds for them, thus protecting them from unwanted visitors. The proxy server hides all internal servers.

Figure 7.2 How Reverse Proxy works.

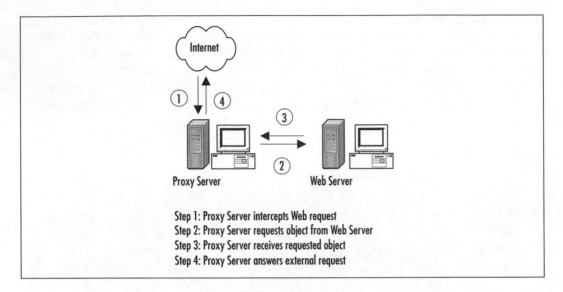

Step 1: Proxy Server intercepts Web request
Step 2: Proxy Server requests object from Web Server
Step 3: Proxy Server receives requested object
Step 4: Proxy Server answers external request

When configuring reverse hosting, ensure that all incoming Web requests will be discarded by default. This is done through the properties pages of the Web Proxy service under the Publishing tab. Mappings will be added that provide paths to the servers "downstream" or behind the proxy server, and these mappings will connect virtual paths that belong to the proxy server to the actual path of the Web server. Again, for the protection of the internal servers on the network, proxy is the gatekeeper so to speak, inspecting what comes in or goes out, and making sure that its internal network is safe.

Setting Up Proxy Server 2.0

This section covers the installation and configuration of Proxy Server 2.0. As with any installation, there are requirements that must be met, and crucial configuration parameters. Proxy Server 2.0 must be installed on a server in the network, which can be a stand-alone, primary, or backup domain controller, or a Windows 2000 server. However, don't try to install Proxy Server 2.0 on a Windows 2000 Professional machine, or on a Windows NT Workstation machine, because you'll get error messages galore! On a Windows NT 4.0 Server, you'll need at least Service Pack 3 and Internet Information Server 3. You should also have disk configuration issues resolved, and the drive should contain at least 10MB of disk space for the installation of Proxy Server 2.0 itself, and 100MB plus 0.5MB for each user in order for caching to be used efficiently. There must be at one NTFS partition on the proxy server of 5MB for caching to be configured. If it is possible to install multiple drives, cache access speed will be improved noticeably. Caching is the only part of Proxy Server that requires an NTFS partition, as Proxy Server itself can be installed on a FAT partition if necessary.

Potential Installation Problems

Before installing Proxy Server on any machine, and certainly before buying a new machine to be a proxy server, make sure that the computer you are buying is going to be compatible with both Windows NT Server products as well as Windows 2000 products. Even though most newer computers are compatible, there will be a few that won't have a modem on the Hardware Compatibility List (HCL), a network interface card (NIC) on the HCL, or even a basic input/output system (BIOS) that supports the Windows 2000 operating system. I recently tried to install Windows 2000 Server on a laptop computer, only to find out that this was exactly the case. Neither the modem nor the video card had drivers available for them for Windows 2000. Upon further inspection, there wasn't even an update for the computer's BIOS on the manufacturer's Web site. This being the situation, it would have been a bad idea to install Proxy Server 2.0 on this machine, since one of the requirements for installation is Windows 2000 Server or Windows NT 4.0 Server with SP3 installed, and components like modems and video cards are pretty important!

There are also suggested requirements for the amount of space available for caching. Although the official word is that you should have a minimum of 5MB free hard drive space available, it is recommended that you have 100MB plus 0.5MB per client on the network.

There are other less obvious requirements before beginning the installation. The internal adapter on the server machine must be configured such that the gateway is left blank, that an appropriate protocol (either TCP/IP or IPX/SPX) is configured and bound to the adapter, and that all other protocols that are not going to be used are disabled. You wouldn't want the proxy server's internal adapter to offer the gateway address! The internal adapter will also need a static IP address, and should not be configured to use Dynamic Host Configuration Protocol (DHCP). IP forwarding should also be disabled to prevent problems associated with users having the ability to access a particular site even though filters have been set in place to prevent access. When IP forwarding is enabled, clients' Web browsers can be configured not to use the proxy server and to bypass access controls.

The external adapter should be using only TCP/IP; all other protocols should be disabled. The external network adapter will need to be configured with an IP address, subnet mask, default gateway, Domain Name System (DNS) server, and Domain Name. Once you begin installing the Proxy Server, one of the first screens you'll see will ask you to create a Local Address Table (LAT). (See Figure 7.3.) The LAT is very important; take great care when constructing it. If any external addresses are included in the LAT, it will cause security features such as packet filtering not to be applied, making the proxy server vulnerable to attack and reducing the effectiveness of security controls. The LAT can be constructed in a number of ways. You can enter the addresses of the internal adapters manually, by adding a scope of addresses in the LAT configuration screen, or you can choose to let the installation process construct the table for you by clicking on Construct Table on the same screen (see Figure 7.4). If the latter is used, the addresses can be added automatically using the internal Windows NT routing table, by loading known address ranges from all IP interface cards, or by inputting the addresses manually. After the LAT is complete, double-check it for external addresses that could compromise your network.

Figure 7.3 An empty LAT.

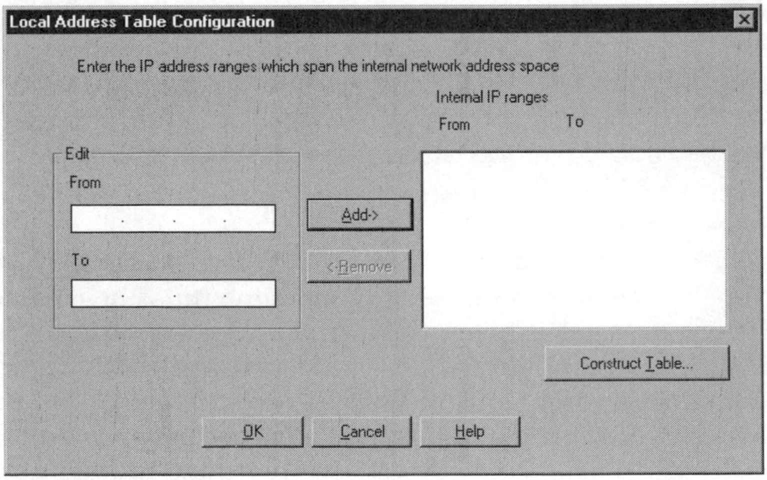

Figure 7.4 Constructing the LAT.

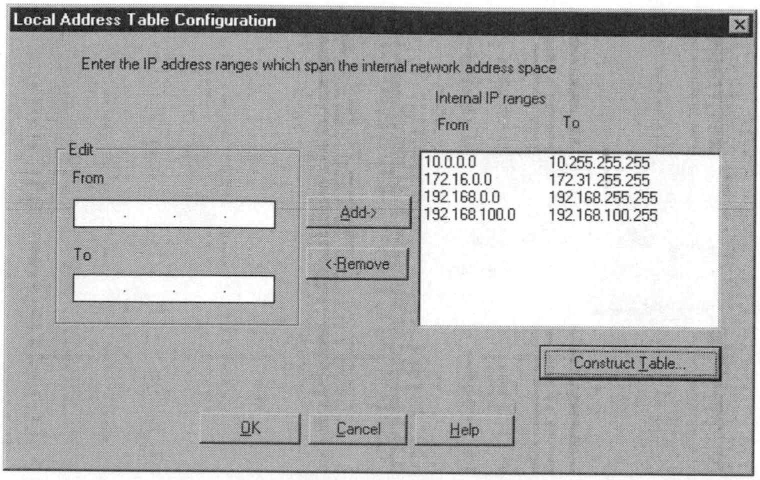

After installation of Proxy Server 2.0 is complete, the proxy server services mentioned previously must be configured. From the Internet Services Manager, the Web Proxy service, WinSock Proxy service, and the SOCKS Proxy service can all be configured. The Web Proxy Service Properties page has six tabs: Service, Permissions, Caching, Routing, Publishing, and Logging. The WinSock Proxy Service Properties page has three tabs: Protocols, Permissions, and Logging. The SOCKS Proxy Service Properties page has only two configuration tabs: Permissions and Logging. For our discussion, we'll focus on the Web Proxy service, since this service's properties page contains the most configuration options. WinSock and SOCKS configurations will be similar.

The first tab on the Web Proxy Service Properties page is the Service tab, shown in Figure 7.5. This tab allows you to make configuration changes that are common to all services including security, configuring arrays, setting up and using auto dial, and configuring plug-ins. These are located in the Shared Services section of this page. The Security option on this page can be used to set up packet filtering, dynamic filtering, alerting, and logging. It is here that packet filtering is enabled and custom packet filters are added. The Arrays section allows you to join an array simply by typing the name of the computer you'd like to be in an array with. This can also be done at the command line with the command **REMOTMSP <common options> <command> <command parameters>**. An example of such a command is **remotmsp join –member:mainproxy**. The third shared service that is common to all services is AutoDial. From AutoDial you can enable dialing for any of the services offered (Web Proxy, Winsock,

SOCKS), define dialing hours, and configure the RAS phone book entry. The last option in this area is the plug-ins button and allows the configuration of add-on components.

Figure 7.5 The Service tab.

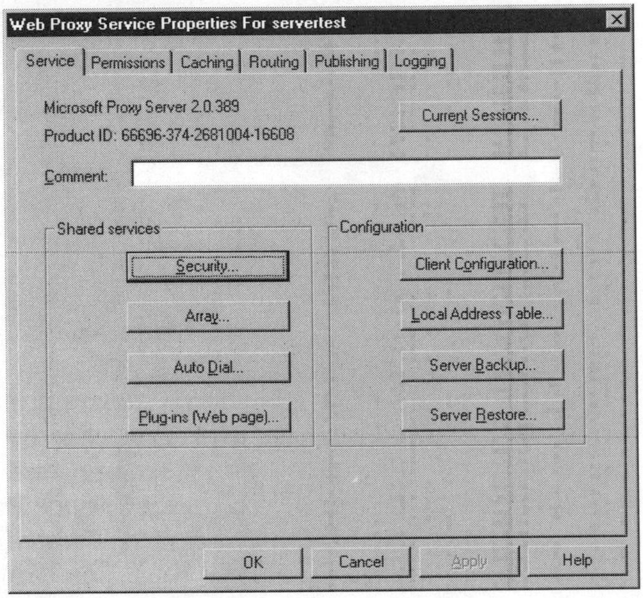

The second tab on the Web Proxy Service properties page is Permissions. Each of the three services has a permission page. The Web Proxy service page offers configuration parameters for FTP Read, Gopher, Secure, and WWW. To access these options, you must enable access control. For the FTP Read or Gopher permissions, read access can be granted, and for Secure and WWW, full access can be granted. The permissions pages for WinSock and SOCKS are slightly different, allowing or denying access by domains, zones, IP addresses, ports, destinations, or all objects. Figure 7.6 shows the Web Proxy Properties page and the Permissions tab.

The third tab is the Caching tab. Caching is unique to the Web Proxy Service; none of the other services offer caching as an option. Figure 7.7 shows the Caching tab of the Web Proxy Service. To use the caching options, check the Enable caching box, and passive caching will be used. You can also configure active caching by checking the Enable active caching box. Caching parameters can be set here that define how often an object should be updated once it has been cached. Known as an object's Time to Live (TTL), expiration can be set as: Updates Are More Important, Equal Importance, or Fewer Network Accesses Are More Important.

Figure 7.6 The Web Proxy Properties page, Permissions tab.

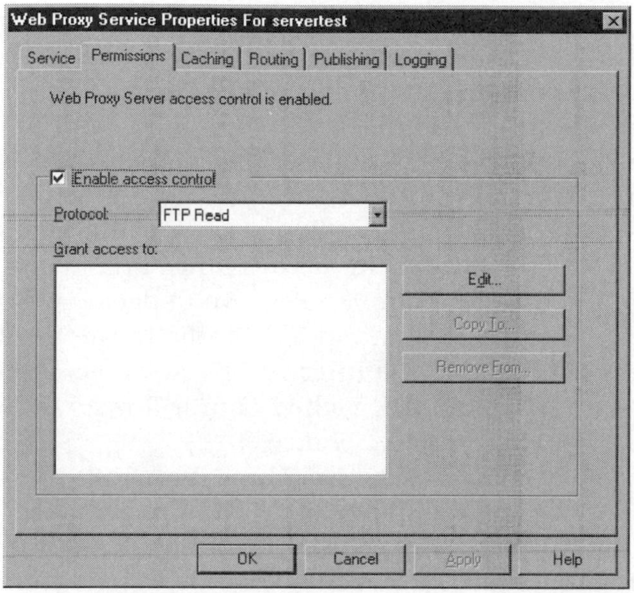

Figure 7.7 The Caching tab of the Web Proxy Service Properties page.

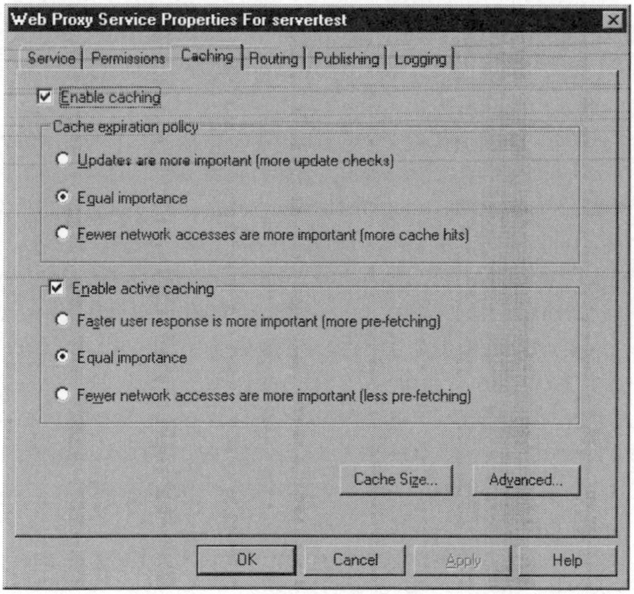

The first option under passive caching, Updates Are More Important, sets the TTL for all objects to 0 minutes. If information must be updated very often, for instance a site that offers stock quotes, this would be an appropriate setting. Although this lowers cache performance, it keeps important and often-used pages updated. The second option, Equal Importance, specifies a minimum TTL of 15 minutes and maximum of 1440. Using this option balances cache performance with cache updates. If the third option, Fewer Network Accesses Are More Important, is chosen, then the TTL is set to a minimum of 30 minutes and a maximum of 2880. This setting provides the best cache performance and allows more cache hits than any of the other options. You'll have to decide what is important to your network, more cache hits and less traffic to the Internet, or fewer cache hits and more traffic to the Internet. These choices will also need to be weighed against how often the cached data will need to be refreshed, or if active caching would be a better choice.

If Enable active caching is checked, three more options are available: Faster User Response Is More Important, Equal Importance, and Fewer Network Accesses Are More Important. The option, Faster User Response Is More Important causes more users to access their sites from the Internet directly instead of accessing the information from cache; however, the cache updates itself often, keeping the cache fresh. Equal Importance again balances cache performance with cache updates as seen earlier. The option, Fewer Network Accesses Are More Important lets the least amount of Internet traffic occur by keeping information in cache longer; however, cache is not updated as often as the other options. These options are similar to the ones described earlier. Advanced options can be selected to set cache filters, such as adding, editing, and deleting specific URLs that will always be cached or never be cached.

The fourth tab, Routing, is also unique to the Web Proxy Service. Routing can be configured one of two ways and provides fault tolerance by providing alternate routes to the Internet or other network. Either configure the proxy server to route user requests to a proxy server or array upstream from itself, or configure it to route user requests directly to the Internet. Note that no routing will take place if the object needed is in cache. You can also configure the server to resolve requests in an array before looking upstream. The routing tab is shown in Figure 7.8. To see how proxy server routing provides fault tolerance for a network, see Figure 7.9.

Arrays can be configured by choosing the Modify button on the Routing tab of the Web Proxy Services Properties page (again, see Figure 7.8). This is where multiple proxy servers can be configured to provide a single logical cache that is very large. These servers can further be configured to communicate with each other so that none of the information in cache is repeated among servers. Arrays such as these use Cache Array Routing Protocol (CARP), and communicate using HTTP. Routing can then be configured to forward requests downstream to another proxy or upstream if those proxies cannot give the required information.

Figure 7.8 The Routing tab of the Web Proxy Service page.

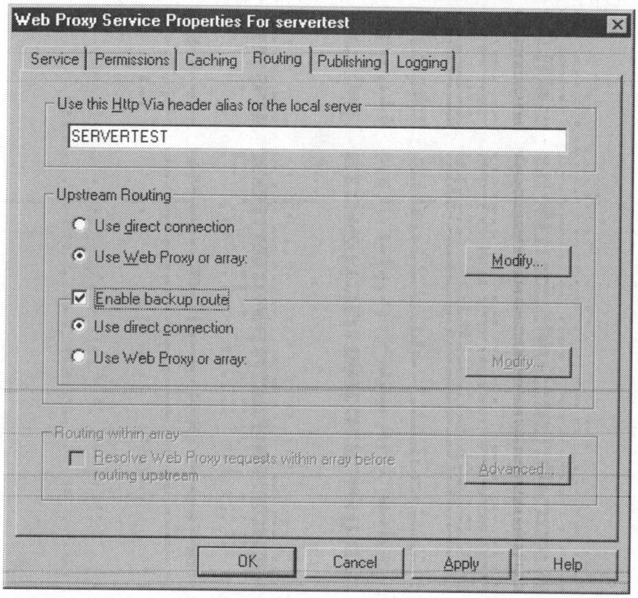

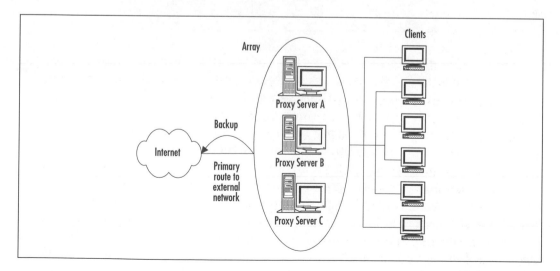

Figure 7.9 Using Proxy Server Routing for Fault Tolerance.

The fifth tab is the Publishing tab (see Figure 7.10). Web publishing was mentioned earlier and is a way to keep external users from actually "seeing" the Web server they are accessing. This protects the identity of the Web servers on the network, thus reducing unwanted attacks. Once publishing is enabled there will be three ways to configure it to deal with incoming Web requests: all requests can be discarded, all requests can be sent to a local Web server, or all requests can be sent to a specified Web server not local to the network.

Figure 7.10 The Publishing tab of the Web Proxy Service properties page.

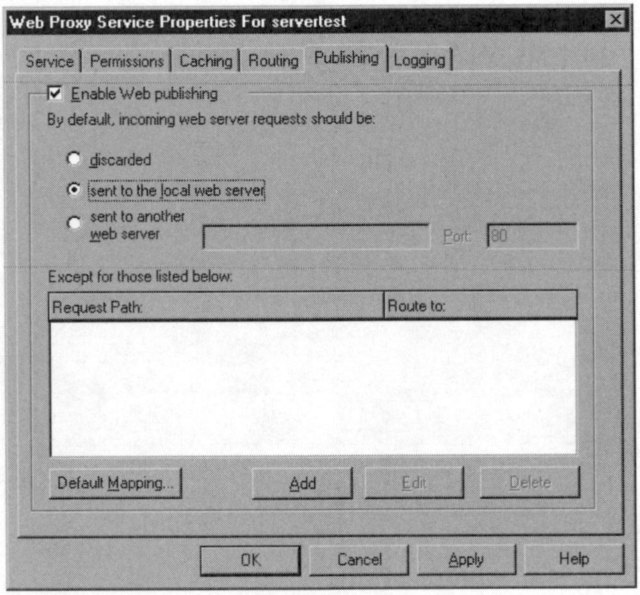

Discarding all requests is the safest of the three if network security is the biggest issue on your network. By choosing to discard every request that comes in to the network, there is no chance that unwanted visitors could come on to the network. If incoming requests do need to be accepted however, they can be configuring to be sent to a local Web server, or another server completely. When deciding which of these to choose, compare the needs of the network verses the importance of allowing outside users access to your proxy servers. You may even decide to set up a Demilitarized Zone (DMZ) for extra protection. That will be discussed later in the chapter.

Logging is the last tab available on the Web Proxy Service Properties page. Logging can be configured to keep track of information such as what protocols are being used, to track which protocols a certain user is using, to track time and date of requests, and in some cases, port numbers, which users are making requests, and their destination addresses. This could be helpful if you suspect inappropriate behavior on the network. Logging can be configured to log in regular or verbose format. It can also be saved as a text file that can be tied to a Structured Query Language/ Open DataBase Connectivity (SQL/ODBC) database. These log files can be configured to log daily, weekly, or monthly, and configuration of how old logs will be dealt and what will happen when the log files becomes full are configured here also. See Figure 7.11 for the Logging tab.

Figure 7.11 The Logging tab of the Web Proxy Properties page.

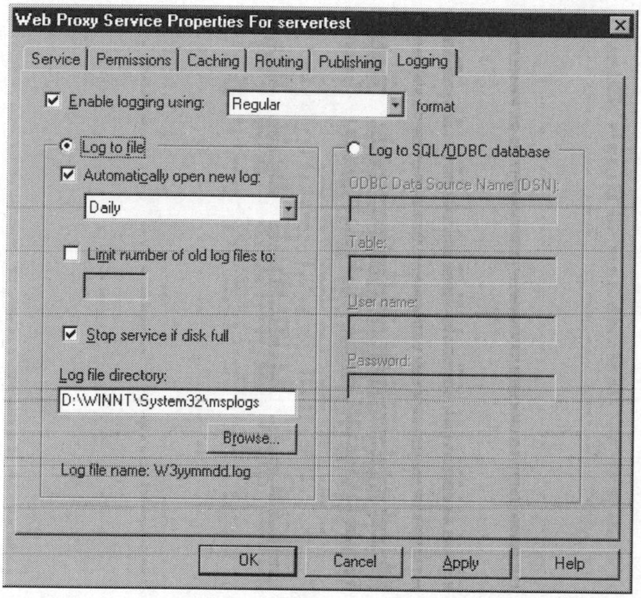

If you are planning to enable logging, you'll need to know where to locate the files once they've begun logging information. These logs are stored in the C:\WINNT\SYSTEM32\MSPLOGS\ directory by default. Each service has a specific log name:

- The Web Proxy service log is called W3*filename*.LOG
- The WinSock Proxy service log is called WS*filename*.LOG
- The SOCKS Proxy service log is called SP*filename*.LOG
- The packet filters log is called PF*filename*.LOG

The *filename* is in the form of yymmxx, where yy is the year, mm is the month, and xx is the day, week, or month of the log, depending on the logging options set.

TIP

If you are concerned about the resources necessary for the log files, then choose to log in text format. Logging to a database takes more resources. If you do plan to log to a database, make sure that you have an ODBC driver installed on the proxy server, and that you take advantage of the tools available to you that are included in Proxy Server. MPKLOG.EXE will assist you in creating SQL tables for proxy server logging.

The Protocols tab (see Figure 7.12) on the WinSock Proxy Service Properties page is the only page not yet mentioned. Besides the protocols like FTP, Gopher, Secure, and WWW, other protocols can be added when using this service. For example, HTTP, Real Audio, and POP3 might be added. This is a simple procedure that is accomplished simply by clicking on Add and typing the protocol name, port number, and whether it is TCP or User Datagram Protocol (UDP). You can then define how the protocol should be used; for example, only for inbound traffic, outbound traffic, or both.

Figure 7.12 The Protocols tab of the WinSock Proxy Service Properties page.

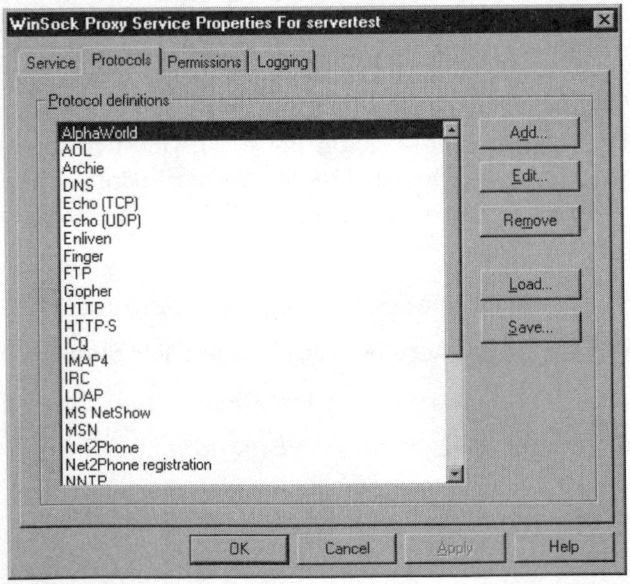

Some of the port numbers that you should familiarize yourself with are:

- FTP-Port 21
- Telnet-Port 23
- Simple Mail Transfer Protocol (SMTP)-Port 25
- Gopher-Port 70
- HTTP-Port 80
- POP3-Port 110
- Point-to-Point Tunneling Protocol (PPTP)-Port 1723

Access Control

Proxy Server 2.0 offers numerous ways to control access into and out of a network. Packet filtering, dynamic filtering, applying permissions, reverse proxy, and/or reverse hosting can assist in controlling inbound and outbound traffic and thus securing the network. Reverse proxy and reverse hosting were described earlier. Packet filtering can be used to allow or deny packets based on protocol, port number, by source address, and even by destination address. This provides a security filter that can be used to protect the network against attacks by hackers and unwanted guests. Packet types that will be accepted can be listed, and all others will be rejected. There are 16 predefined packet filters that can be used to secure a network. Some of these filters are Internet Control Message Protocol (ICMP) filters, PPTP filters, SMTP, POP3, and NetBIOS filters. Custom filters can also be defined. Figure 7.13 shows the dialog box for enabling access controls for various services.

NOTE

To use packet filtering, you must configure an external adapter. If you are using a modem, Digital Subscriber Line (DSL), or an Integrated Services Digital Network (ISDN) adapter for access to the Internet or other external network, Auto Dial must be configured before packet filtering can be enabled. In addition, packet filtering can be applied only to the external interface.

Dynamic filtering is used to configure security and filter access when you need ports to be opened and closed when transmission occurs. If dynamic filtering is used, the ports are opened when data is sent or received, and closed when the transmission ends. This reduces administration, but if applications that use the Internet are being run from the Proxy Server, static filtering designations are required.

Figure 7.13 The Protocols tab of the WinSock Proxy Service Properties page.

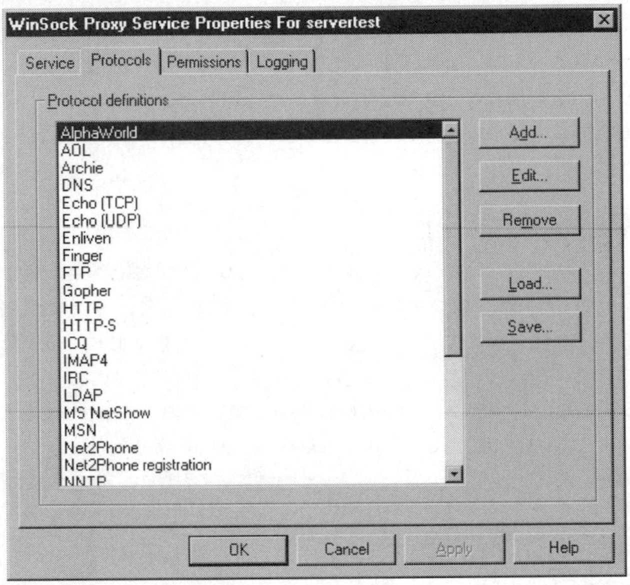

Authentication Types

Authentication types for user logins can also be configured to assist in the administration and security of a network. Password authentication can be configured in Internet Services Manager under the Properties page of the WWW service.

There are three available choices for authentication. Basic authentication is available but should not be chosen under most circumstances. It offers very weak security compared to the other options, and is usually not required for most clients or browsers. Basic authentication is the weakest of all of the available authentication methods because the passwords are only encoded, and they are not securely encrypted. Because of this, simple network sniffers can decode the encryption and obtain the real password. If there does become a need for such authentication, for instance if you have UNIX-based Web browsers on the network, apply this authentication configuration only to those users.

Windows NT Challenge/Response authentication is a more secure option because it does not transmit the user's password across the network.

However, only Windows-based clients who use Microsoft Internet Explorer can use this type of authentication method, and the client and server must both be in the same domain or in trusted domains. This may be a deterrent for using this configuration for the clients on your network, but again, this can be applied to certain sets of users and does not have to be applied to the entire network. To authenticate users under this method requires a series of complex calculations to be calculated on both the server and the client, and the software then allows access to the site instead of having the user input his or her name and/or password.

The last type of authentication, Allow Anonymous, is also discouraged. Anonymous logins are a security threat, allowing anyone to access a particular site or server.

MS Proxy Client Setup

Just because you've gotten Proxy Server 2.0 installed and configured doesn't mean that anyone is able to use it. The clients on your network will need to be configured, and these clients may not all have the same operating system or Web browser. For Windows-based computers, setup is fairly easy, and the setup program can automate most of the process of client configuration. However, there will be clients that are not Windows-based that will need special consideration. These clients might include IPX clients, Netscape Navigator users, Macintosh or UNIX users, or any other number of configurations.

As mentioned earlier, most of the Windows-based computers client setup can be automated and is simple to configure. Use Internet Service Manager to open the Properties page of any of the proxy services, and choose Client Configuration. (On the Web Proxy Services Properties page, this is the Services tab, Configuration area of the page—see Figure 7.14.) The three sections on this page are WinSock Proxy client, Web browsers, and Web Proxy clients. This last section is also where automatic configuration scripts are configured, which can be used by Web browsers like Internet Explorer or Netscape Navigator.

To configure WinSock Proxy clients, configure them to connect to the proxy server using either the computer name, DNS name, or IP address, or by manually entering an array name or a group of IP address that an array uses on the network. You can also choose to configure these clients automatically by checking the Automatically Configure Web Browser During Client Setup box. Several changes will be made to the client's machine during the configuration and setup of the client. These changes include installation of the Proxy Server client application, a new version of the WINSOCK.DLL file, a program to uninstall or reinstall the proxy client if necessary, a new control panel icon, the WinSock Proxy (WSP) Client, and

Figure 7.14 The Client Installation and Configuration dialog box.

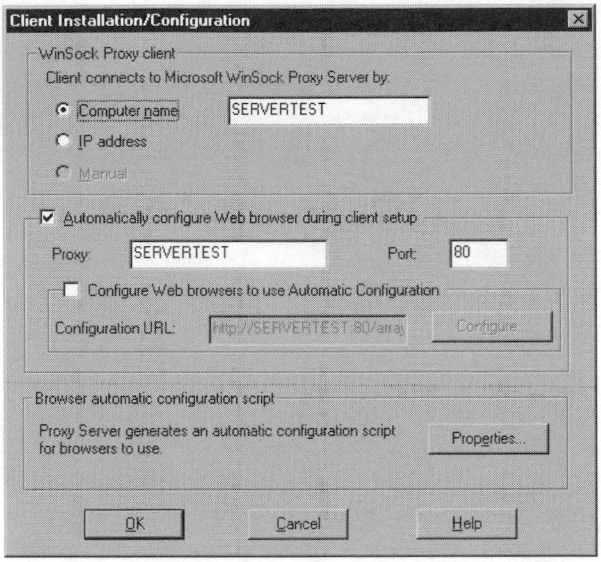

a copy of the LAT to the directory C:\MSPCLNT. If you check the Configure Web Browsers To Use Automatic Configuration box, client Web browsers will be configured automatically when the proxy client is installed. The configuration script's URL can be changed to any location, and configuration information can be accessed from there. The automatic configuration script will have information that configures the client to do one of four things: to force all traffic to go through the proxy server, force requests to specified IP addresses to bypass the proxy server, force requests for specified domains to bypass the proxy server, and finally, to reroute the request if the current proxy server is down by either routing traffic directly to the Internet or to another proxy server.

NOTE

There are numerous options for accessing the Setup program for the client. They can also be achieved by going through the MSPCLNT share on the proxy server or by using the Web browser and accessing http://servername/Msproxy.

Users that employ Netscape Navigator or Internet Explorer can be configured manually or automatically as Web Proxy clients. To configure a client that uses Internet Explorer as the default browser, start Internet Explorer and click on Tools | Internet Options | Connection tab, then select LAN settings to see the screens in Figures 7.15 and 7.16.

Figure 7.15 The Automatic Configuration screen.

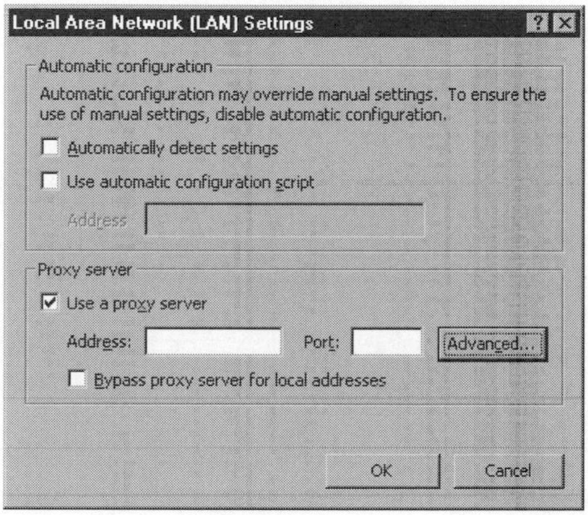

Click the Advanced button to see other options (Figure 7.16).

Figure 7.16 Configure Proxy settings.

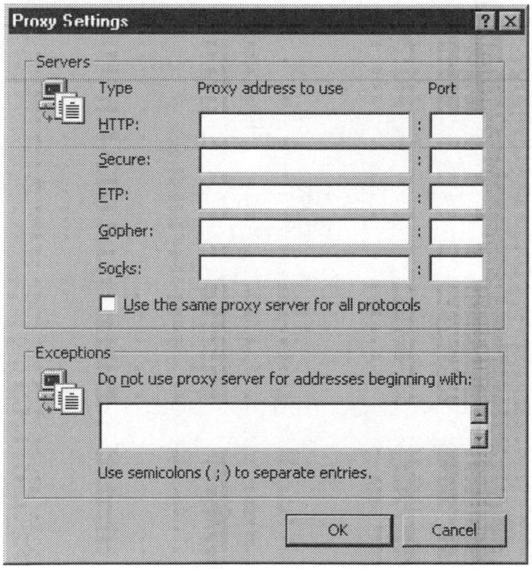

NOTE

Older versions of Internet Explorer may require a different path to Internet Options. Internet Options may need to be accessed by choosing the View | Internet Options | Connection tab.

To configure Netscape Navigator 2.x and 3.x as Web Proxy clients, start Netscape Navigator, go to Options | Network Preferences. Setup is similar to Internet Explorer from here. You can choose No Proxies, Manual Proxy Configuration, or Automatic Proxy Configuration from this page. For Netscape Navigator 4.0x and higher, Select Edit | Preferences, then click on the plus sign to the left of the word *Advanced*. Click on Proxies to see the Preferences screen and choose either manual or automatic proxy configuration.

Enabling Reverse Proxy

As mentioned previously, Proxy Server can be configured to intercept incoming requests to a Web server and respond for that server, thus increasing the level of security on the network and keeping the internal Web server hidden from the outside world. This is an important and useful feature in Proxy Server that is almost mandatory these days, with the number of Denial of Service attacks, viruses, and hackers. Proxy Server 2.0 can be configured to deal with incoming requests in any of the following ways: All requests can be discarded immediately upon arrival, all requests can be forwarded to the local Web server, or all requests can be sent to a specified Web server outside the local network. The steps required for enabling and configuring reverse proxying are as follows:

1. Start Internet Service Manager by selecting Start | Programs | Microsoft Proxy Server | Internet Service Manager.

2. Select the Web Proxy Properties page and choose the Publishing tab. This tab is shown in Figure 7.17. (Note that the other two services, WinSock and SOCKS, do not offer a Publishing page.)

3. Check the Enable Web publishing box.

4. Choose to send requests either to a local Web server or another Web server.

5. Click OK or choose Apply, then OK.

Figure 7.17 The Publishing tab.

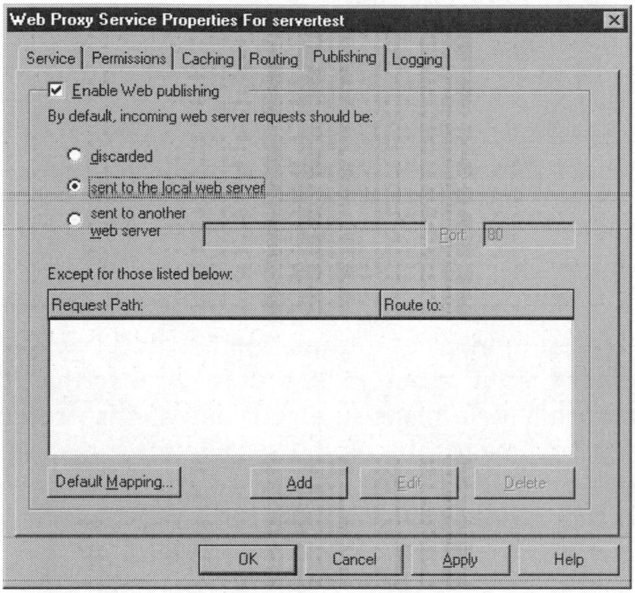

Troubleshooting Proxy Server 2.0

Proxy Server is almost always installed and configured successfully and without any problems. It is the day-to-day activities that require troubleshooting, as is true of many other network applications of this magnitude. In this section, we'll discuss some of the most common installation errors and their solutions, as well as client access and caching problems that you may encounter while using Proxy Server. Later, we'll discuss how alerts and log files are used to troubleshoot these problems, as well as security issues to be aware of, and how to monitor and enhance the performance of the proxy server.

Installation problems usually occur when the minimum requirements have not been met, hard disk configuration is not recognized, there isn't enough memory, or IIS isn't installed correctly. Simply making sure the requirements for installation have been met prior to beginning the installation of proxy easily solves these problems.

Some of the hardware and software requirements for Proxy Server have been mentioned earlier; here is a complete list:

- 486 DX/33 or higher CPU
- 24MB RAM if an Intel processor is used

- 32MB RAM if a RISC processor is used

- 10MB free hard drive space

- 5MB hard drive space for caching although it is recommended that you have 100MB plus 0.5MB per client.

- NT Server 4.0 with Service Pack 3 or higher installed

- Internet Information Server 3.0 or higher installed

WARNING

If you are using Internet Information Server 3.0 with Proxy Server 2.0, be aware that there is a bug in IIS that may cause the Web service to terminate abnormally. To make sure your network is protected from this bug, go to ftp://ftp.microsoft.com/bussys/winnt/winnt-public/fixes/usa/nt40/hotfixes-postSP3/iis-fix/ to download a fix.

Other less noticeable installation problems occur when general recommended requirements have not been considered. One important recommendation is the installation of two network adapters for the proxy server, one for internal communications, and one for external communications. If a problem occurs where the proxy server can be configured only as a caching-only server, it is because there is only one network interface card. Other problems can occur if the external card is not configured with the appropriate IP address information. If the external card is a NIC, it must be configured with two IP addresses: one for an external DNS server, and one that is a valid Internet IP address. If the external card is a modem, it must be configured with Dial-up network phone book entry configured to connect to the Internet service provider (ISP) and contain proper DNS information. Another problem occurs if the internal card is set up incorrectly. A common mistake is to configure the internal card with the required TCP/IP address and its appropriate subnet mask, but to then include the gateway address as well. If the gateway is defined for the internal card, a route to the internal network can be created.

Client access problems can be investigated with a tool from Microsoft called MSPDIAG.EXE located in the C:\MSP directory. This program can be used to verify the following common problems associated with client access.

- Proxy version

- Operating System requirements such as NT version or IIS version

- IPX and Service Access Protocol (SAP) configurations
- Invalid LAT entries
- IIS status
- The settings of the MSPCLNT.INI file
- IP forwarding and default gateway configurations

The Importance of Disabling IP Forwarding and Proper Configuration of the LAT

IP forwarding must be disabled and the LAT must not contain any external addresses. Understanding this is important to ensure the security of your network.

IP forwarding enables packets to be forwarded across both internal and external networks. The purpose of Proxy Server 2.0 is to monitor and secure a network from this type of activity. Disabling IP forwarding allows you to secure the network by controlling IP routing.

When configuring the LAT, it is important to make positively sure that there are no external addresses in the table. The LAT is used to decide from whom to answer requests. Having external addresses in the LAT would cause security risks from hackers.

This information can be used to troubleshoot almost any client access problem that arises.

TIP

For WinSock Proxy client problems try CHKWSP32.EXE or CHKWSP16.EXE for 32-bit and 16-bit systems, respectively. These files can be found in the MSPCLNT directory and will check for connectivity with the proxy server.

Caching is usually automatic and trouble-free once configured correctly. Problems occur when there is not enough disk space to cache required information, or if the configuration of caching was not done properly. Other problems occur if the cache becomes corrupted, if the Web

Proxy service fails to initialize cache, or if the hard disk that is used by the Web Proxy server to cache URLs is full. These problems can be corrected by stopping the WWW service and restarting, by deleting cached objects from the hard disk, or by running chkdsk/r at a Command Prompt and looking for disk errors. Other common problems that are not system events include out-of-date Web pages or using old addresses.

Special Windows 2000 Issues

Microsoft's Proxy Server requires an update to run on Windows 2000 Servers. You can obtain the MS Proxy 2.0 Update Wizard at http://download.microsoft.com/download/proxy20/SP/1/NT5/EN-US/msp2wizi.exe. The wizard can be used to install Proxy Server 2.0 on Microsoft Windows 2000 or when upgrading a Windows NT Server computer already running Proxy Server 2.0 to Windows 2000.

Alerts

Performance Monitor in Windows NT and the System Monitor in the Performance Console in Windows 2000 have a scheme in place that can be used to alert administrators when thresholds have been exceeded or security is at risk due to abnormally high attempts at logons, protocols, or any other number of events. These alerts can be sent via e-mail, Event Viewer, or written to a system event log. As an administrator, you probably have some alerts already configured.

Packet filtering alerting is configured under the Properties page of any of the three services, by choosing the Shared Services section, Security page, Alerting tab. Three types of events can be configured to generate alerts in this section. These alerts are sent based on a threshold of a number of events that happen per second:

- **Rejected Packets** These are dropped IP packets on the external network adapter.

- **Protocol Violations** These are illegal IP packets on the external network adapter.

- **Disk Full** These are caused when the disk that holds the service logs or packet logs becomes full.

By setting alerts, the network administrator can be informed immediately of potential security problems, risks, or holes in the proxy server defense.

TIP

To receive an e-mail when an alert is issued, you'll need to configure the e-mail settings so that the proxy server will know where to send the alert. You can do this by clicking on the Configure Mail Alerting dialog box and inputting the necessary information. Make sure you have an e-mail client installed on this machine, an e-mail account, and that the e-mail client is running.

Monitoring and Performance

Performance Monitor in Windows NT and the System Monitor in the Performance Console in Windows 2000 offer powerful ways to monitor the performance of the proxy server as well as other servers on the network. Counters are added to these applications when Proxy Server is installed. These include Web Proxy Server Service counters, cache counters, packet filtering counters, and WinSock Proxy Server Service counters. Using these counters in addition to counters offered by the performance monitor applications enables an administrator to manage Proxy Server and configure its optimal performance. The following list includes some of the most common counters and their uses when monitoring Proxy Server.

- Use the %Processor Time-Process counter (INETINFO instance) to measure how much of the processor's time is spent on IIS processes.

- Use the % Processor Time-Process (WSPSrv instance) to measure how much of the processor's time is spent on the WinSock Proxy service.

- Use Cache Hit Ratio (%) to compare the percentage of requests that are served from cache to the actual number of total requests. Using this counter can help you determine if cache size is appropriate or if cache filters are needed.

- Use FTP Requests or HTTP Requests to monitor the number of requests received for these protocols.

- Use the Frames Dropped Due to Protocol Violations to alert you to potential attempted security violations.

- Use Packet Filtering counters such as Frames Dropped Due to Filter Denial, Frames Dropped Due to Protocol Violations, Total Dropped Frames, and Total Incoming Connections to monitor possible security violations and generally give a feel for the state of security of the network.

Figure 7.18 is an example of the System Monitor in Windows 2000.

Figure 7.18 System Monitor.

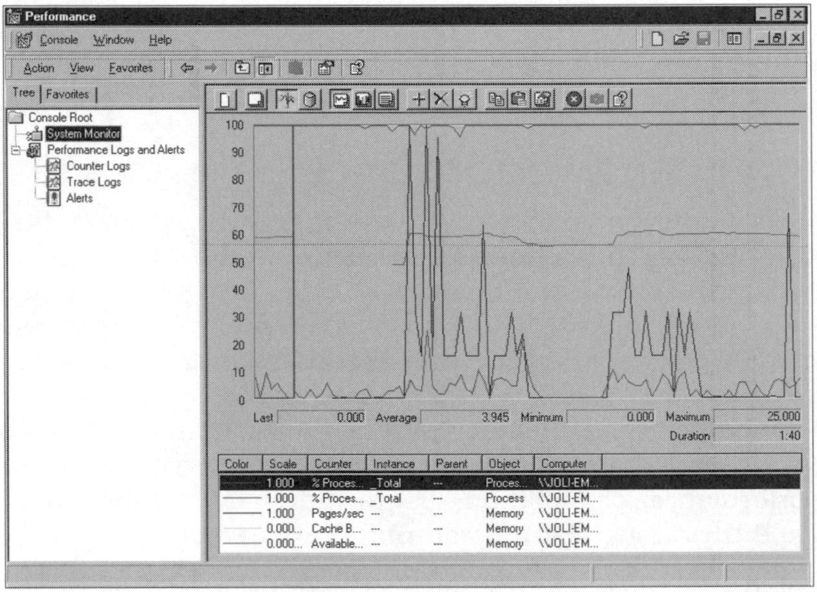

Of course, these are only a few of the events that can be logged, and enabling performance counters can slow down a network. Identifying bottlenecks, disk-related performance issues, CPU-performance issues, and memory-related issues are all important things that you should already be monitoring in your NT or 2000 network. Any bottlenecks or performance problems that the network server(s) have will adversely affect the performance of your proxy server. Consider this when deciding what to monitor. Make sure you know what you'd like to keep a log of, what you need to be alerted of, and if logging any packet-filtering counters, make sure that packet filtering is enabled for them.

Transaction Log Files

Proxy Server 2.0 offers three available logs, one for each of the three services. These logs can be used to track events such as protocol use, date and time of requests, specific user requests and protocol use, and successful completion of requests. This log information is stored in the C:\WINNT\SYSTEM32\MSPLOGS file by default, and is enabled for each server when Proxy Server is installed.

Logging and packet filtering are configured in the Internet Service Manager under the Properties page of the service to be logged. On the logging tab, there are options to log the data in regular or verbose format, and to open new log files daily, weekly, or monthly (see Figure 7.19). This is also where you can configure how old files will be dealt with and where log files are stored. Packet filtering logging is configured under the Security section of the Properties page.

Figure 7.19 The Logging tab.

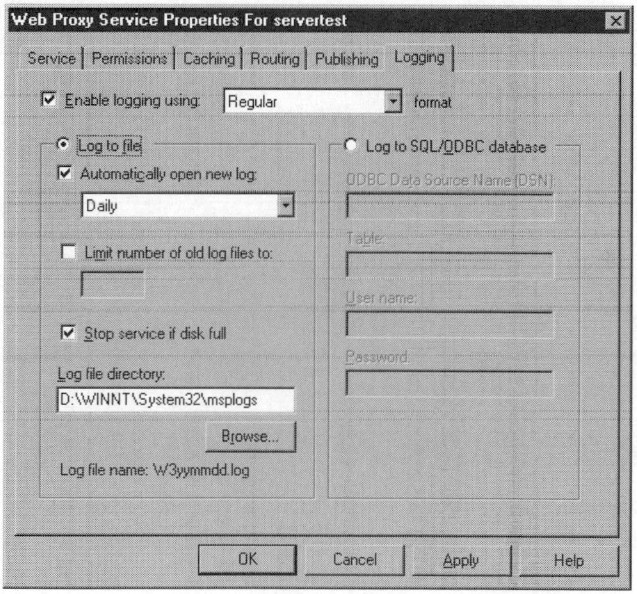

If Web Proxy, WinSock Proxy, or SOCKS Proxy are configured to log in Regular format, a great deal of information can be gathered and logged. For all services, the current user of the request, the domain name for the responding computer, the port number on the remote computer service making the connection, and the date and time of the request can be logged. For the Web Proxy service, these additional objects can be logged:

the source used to serve the request, the protocol used for transfer, and special error codes. If logging in verbose format, all of the previous information is logged as well as additional information such as if the request is using an authenticated client connection, the number of bytes sent and received to and from the remote computer (only for the Web Proxy service), and various other information such as client platforms, processing times, proxy names, and destination IP addresses.

When packet-filtering logging is enabled, it can also be configured to log in regular or verbose formats. In regular format the following can be logged: the IP address of the destination computer, the port number used by the local computer, dropped packets, date and time the packet was received, the protocol used, the IP address of the source computer, and, the port number of that source. With verbose logging, the information logged can contain all of these, but can also include the IP header of the packet that generated an alert event, the payload value of the data packet that generated the alert event, and the TCP flag value in the header of a TCP packet.

Applications

There are many ways to use and configure a proxy server in your network. Up to this point, we've been concerned mostly with the installation and configuration of the proxy server, and monitoring its performance. Many networks, however, have hundreds if not thousands of clients to serve, and to send all of their requests to one proxy server will not pan out to be a good configuration for these users. However, load balancing, using multiple proxy servers in a chain, using arrays, employing reverse proxy and multiple web servers, as well as using a proxy server in a DMZ can be, and therefore should be discussed here.

Distributed Caching

One way to configure a network to handle a large amount of requests is to configure the proxy server to share its workload with other proxy servers on the network. Load balancing techniques only work with the Web Proxy service because load balancing involves using the cache files of multiple servers on the network. If you remember, WinSock and SOCKS Proxy services do not cache data.

One way to configure and employ load balancing is to use Distributed Caching. Distributed caching allows multiple Proxy Servers to distribute and simultaneously cache information. This type of setup offers not only fast response time for clients, but also fault tolerance. Distributed caching offers many advantages over other caching configurations by distributing the load on the proxy server to other proxy servers on the network. This type of caching could be configured if a corporate office wants to configure proxy services with its branch offices. The branch offices would be considered "downstream" and could benefit from the cache hits made by the main office. Increased cache space is also an advantage to distributed caching.

Distributed caching is configured as an array. An array is a set of proxy servers that are configured and treated as one large proxy server configured as one large cache. Arrays are configured in the Internet Service Manager, Web Proxy, in the Properties page. It is here that you'll have the option of joining an array as discussed earlier. See Figure 7.20 to understand how a simple proxy array is used to distribute caching among multiple servers.

Figure 7.20 Simple proxy array.

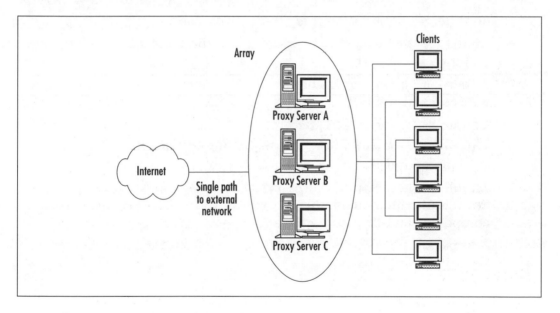

A second technique for implementing load balancing is to employ chaining. Proxy servers that are chained together are configured with direct connections to their local proxy server. If the local proxy server does not have what is needed in its cache, the request is forwarded to the next proxy server in line. These servers, configured in a line or hierarchical fashion, forward requests until resolution is made. Each server can be configured to check its cache before the request is finally sent out to the Internet for resolution.

Demilitarized Zone (DMZ)

Demilitarized Zones are created and used for the same purpose as proxy servers, for simply protecting the internal network from outsiders and potential problems. Think of a DMZ as a cushion of sorts, a network between your internal network and the Internet. DMZs are generally used when Reverse Proxy features cannot be employed, as is the case when using Apple or UNIX and when not publishing HTTP.

DMZs are configured with these three networks in mind: the Internet, the internal network, and the DMZ. The steps to implementing a DMZ are as follows:

1. Select a computer that has three NICs: one for the Internet, one for the internal network, and one for the DMZ. Disable packet filtering.

2. Make sure to give the DMZ and Internet NICs valid IP addresses on different subnets, so that routing will work.

3. Configure the internal network NIC and the DMZ addresses to be included in the LAT.

4. If there are other servers on the DMZ segment, do not include their addresses in the LAT.

5. Enable IP forwarding on the proxy server

6. The computers on the DMZ segment should have their default gateway addresses set as the DMZ NIC of the proxy server.

7. Enable packet filtering on the proxy server computer and open relevant static filters to enable the flow of traffic between the DMZ computers and the Internet.

8. Add packet filter exceptions as necessary from the Proxy Server Security Dialog box.

Reverse Proxy

Using Reverse Proxy is another way to configure a proxy server to protect a network. As mentioned earlier, Reverse Proxy is a way for small businesses to publish to the Web without compromising the security of the network. The proxy server can be configured to intercept all incoming requests from the Web, get the needed information from the internal Web servers, and respond for those servers without exposing the internal network to the outside world. You can configure how incoming requests will be dealt with by either discarding all requests, sending requests to the local Web server, or sending the requests to another Web server. See Figure 7.21.

Figure 7.21 The Publishing tab.

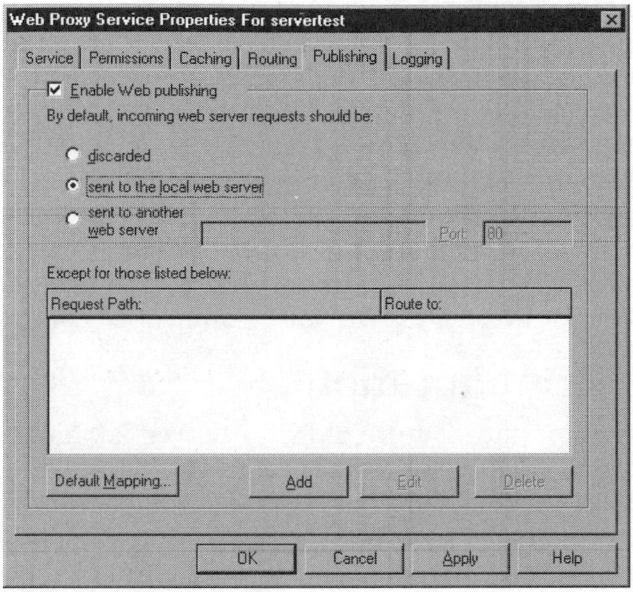

> **NOTE**
>
> If you want to use reverse proxying with only a single network interface card you must configure that network card to have two IP addresses bound to it. Each of these adapters must be on different IP subnets and only one of the IP addresses should be listed in the proxy server's local address table.

Security Issues

As with any product, there will be security issues and holes found in defense mechanisms. Microsoft tries to keep abreast of this situation and keep its customers protected by sending out security bulletins like the Virtualized Universal Naming Convention (UNC) Share Vulnerability Bulletin released in March of 2000, described in the next section. Administrators, or anyone for that matter, can sign up for updates and bulletins for any of Microsoft's products simply by sending an e-mail requesting the information, as described in the Microsoft Security Bulletins section.

Microsoft IIS Security

In March of 2000, Microsoft released information about the Virtualized UNC Share vulnerability, a potential security issue for users of Microsoft Internet Information Server and products that are based under it. One of the statements was: "Under certain fairly unusual conditions, the vulnerability could cause a Web server to send the source code of .ASP and other files to a visiting user." A security patch was released that eliminated this security risk; however, the patch has not been fully regression tested and should be applied only to systems that are sure to be at risk concerning the issue. Microsoft adds in the statement that if recommended security practices are followed, these files will not be subject to compromise.

Proper LAT Configuration

The LAT is a very important feature of Proxy Server 2.0 as we have seen previously. Failing to configure this table correctly can result in multiple problems as well as opening up security risks. One such risk is IP spoofing. IP spoofing is a method used by hackers in which the attacker assumes the identity of a computer already in the internal network. The attacking computer imitates the IP address of an internal computer and sends data as if it were on the local network. By properly configuring the LAT and Web Proxy Service, the attacks can be prevented by not allowing these addresses to enter the internal network. Another problem may occur when users on the local network can bypass the proxy server and access internal resources. This happens when external addresses are included in the LAT, causing security features such as packet filtering not to be applied.

Microsoft Security Bulletins

Microsoft regularly issues security bulletins that can be used to help clients of Microsoft products stay aware of potential security risks associated with its products. Any user can obtain these security bulletins through e-mails from Microsoft simply by sending an e-mail containing the name of the product on which to receive bulletins to the following address: microsoft_security-subscribe-request@announce.microsoft.com, or, if the user is a member of or can access TechNet, by visiting the site www.microsoft.com/technet/security/default.asp. Microsoft also offers an archived site containing all previous security bulletins at www.microsoft.com/TechNet/security/archive.asp. See Figure 7.22.

Figure 7.22 Microsoft TechNet Archived Security Bulletins.

Configuration Lab

If possible, install Proxy Server 2.0 from scratch on a Windows NT or 2000 server. Make sure the requirements for installation are met, including hardware requirements, operating system requirements, and service packs. Construct the LAT, and install a client. Once Proxy Server 2.0 is successfully installed and configured, consider the following dilemma.

Problem

A medium-sized network needs to configure routing and fault tolerance for the clients on its network that access a proxy server to get out of the internal structure and onto the Internet. You would like to configure the proxy server on your network to provide this fault tolerance as well as an alternate route. How would you go about configuring an array to provide fault tolerance to upstream paths or downstream servers? Which service would you use?

Solution

Use the Web Proxy service since it is the only service that supports routing. Use the Internet Services Manager to access the Web Proxy properties page, and click on array in the shared services section. Choose to join an array, and type a name for the array. Next, open the Web Proxy Service Properties page and choose routing. You will see the screen shown in Figure 7.23.

Figure 7.23 The Routing tab.

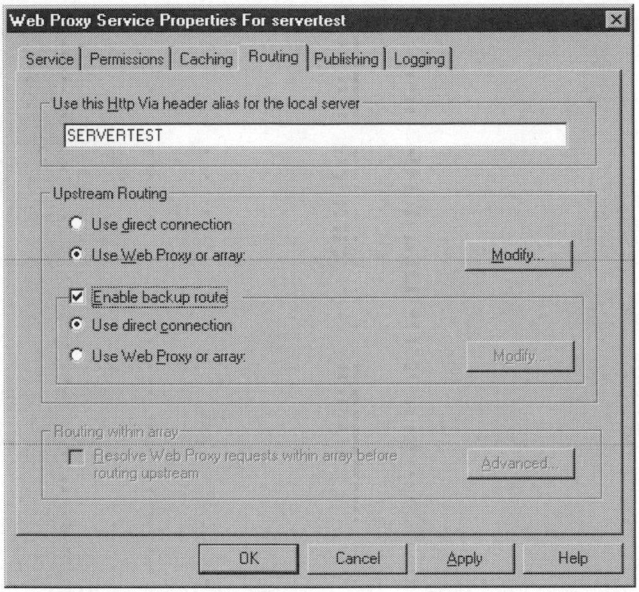

For upstream routing, select either User Direct Connection or Use Web Proxy or Array. Choose Use Web Proxy or Array and configure the remaining options. You can then choose to enable a back-up route; name the proxy server you'd like to use as the back-up route.

Real-World Problems and Work-Arounds

Oftentimes, after installing a new application like a new operating system, a proxy server, or new hardware, you realize that it doesn't always work exactly the way it should. In the real world, problems arise that are not always covered in the documentation and may have even been an unexpected bug in the system. Aside from potential bugs in the system, problems may occur with the configuration of your clients and servers. Listed below are some common real-life problems you may encounter, and Microsoft's suggested "work-arounds".

One problem that has surfaced with Proxy Server 2.0 is its compatibility with Macintosh Outlook Express and the SOCKS proxy service. The problem occurs when the e-mail client fails to connect to the Internet mail servers when using the SOCKS service offered in Proxy Server 2.0. Rather than going into the technical end of the cause of this problem, understanding the solution may prove useful someday.

First you'll need to make sure that Outlook Express is configured properly on the client's machine. Under Edit | Preferences and E-mail, set the SMTP Server address to the IP address of the SMTP server, not the DNS name. The receiving mail section should be configured for the POP server's IP address and not the DNS name. Verify that proxies are enabled, and that SOCKS is the protocol being used. Next, type the address of the proxy server's internal network interface card in the address section under Method, and set the port number to 1080. Save your changes. Make sure you check the proxy server too, and make sure that port 1080 is open and configured properly.

Another problem that may occur is if you need your DNS server and your proxy server to be configured on the same computer while packet filtering is enabled. To make this configuration work, several steps will need to be taken. By default, Proxy Server 2.0 has a predefined packet filter for DNS lookup that works for outbound requests only. To use DNS and Proxy Server on the same computer and to allow hosts to access the DNS server, it will have to be configured to accept incoming requests. To do this, perform the following steps:

1. Open the Winsock Proxy Server properties page.

2. Click the Security button and choose to add a new filter.

3. Choose Custom from the Packet Filter Properties dialog box.

4. Set the protocol ID to UDP and set direction to Both.

5. Specify the local port to be fixed at port 53.

6. Set remote port to Any and set local host to Default Proxy external address.

7. Set Remote host to allow Any host.

8. Choose OK to back out of all of the dialog boxes and restart the computer.

And finally, sometimes, even if you think you've configured the proxy server correctly, problems still arise when requests to the proxy server timeout or otherwise cannot reach the server. This could be happening because there is more than one gateway configured on the proxy server's network interface cards. Only the external adapter card should have the address of the gateway. Of course, the way around this is to remove the extraneous gateway addresses and make the other necessary configuration changes. These changes include defining static routes to the internal network segments, and adding these static routes using the route command at the command prompt. The route command has many switches available including Making These New Routes Persistent, as well as Clearing The Routing Tables Of All Gateway Entries. See Figure 7.24.

Figure 7.24 The Route command.

Another command line utility that can be used to check routes is TRACERT. Tracert can be used to trace a route that a packet takes on its way from one destination to another. Here's an example of requests timing out and a failed attempt to reach www.microsoft.com. See Figure 7.25. You could use this utility to check for failure to and from a proxy server on your network from another client computer on that network.

Figure 7.25 Timeout failures.

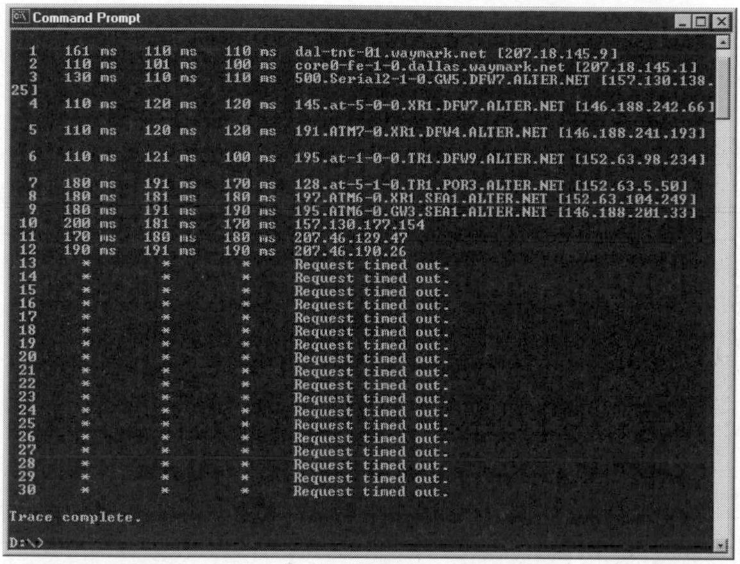

Summary

This chapter provides a general overview of the security features of Proxy Server 2.0. Proxy Server 2.0 is a valuable asset to any network and is provided with the means of protecting an internal network from unwanted attacks and requests from the outside world. Proxy Server can also be used to limit employees' access to the Internet. Both internal and external access controls can be set including access denial or acceptance of protocol use, port numbers, source addresses, and destination addresses.

The core components of Proxy Server 2.0 are the Web Proxy Service, the WinSock Proxy Service, the SOCKS Proxy Services, Reverse Hosting, and Reverse Proxy. The proxy services offer support for different platforms and Web browsers, and each has advantages and disadvantages. The Web Proxy Service is the only service offered that employs caching and routing of data, and the WinSock Proxy service is the only one that offers support for IPX clients. There are of course many other differences, and knowing which service to choose for a specific network infrastructure is an important step in utilizing proxy server successfully. Reverse Proxy and Reverse Hosting allow businesses to publish to the Web, and keep their Web servers hidden. The proxy server sits "in front" of the internal servers, accepting requests and responding to them on behalf of the servers in the network.

We also discussed the installation and configuration of the proxy server, and went into detail covering the configuration screens for the different services. The six configuration screens in the Web Proxy Service Properties page are Service, Permissions, Caching, Routing, Publishing, and Logging. The WinSock Proxy and SOCKS Proxy Properties pages do not offer as many options for configuration since they do not support caching or routing. Configuration issues can also involve making sure that you yourself are not putting the network at risk by incorrectly configuring the server to use IP forwarding or adding external addresses to the Local Address Table.

We also offered some application configurations and briefly discussed load balancing, multiple proxy servers, chaining, and distributed caching. Load balancing and configuring multiple servers is an important task when using Proxy Server 2.0 since usually more than one proxy server is needed on a network.

As with any security application, loopholes and security openings will appear, especially with the onslaught of so many e-businesses and Internet hackers coming together through public connections. Microsoft offers security bulletins when it finds such a hole, or if there is a security flaw found in the product. Keeping up with these security updates is also a large part of an administrator's duties.

In conclusion, Proxy Server can be an effective way to protect your network from unwanted attacks from hackers, and to keep your network secure by protecting it from its own users. Access controls by protocols and addresses can be used to keep the right clients in and the wrong ones out.

FAQs

Q: What client platforms does Proxy Server 2.0 support?

A: Web Proxy supports any client operating system that uses HTTP like Windows, Macintosh, or UNIX. WinSock Proxy supports Winsock 1.1 or above like Windows for Workgroups, Windows 9x, Windows NT, or Windows 2000. SOCKS supports any application on any platform that is SOCKS-compliant like Windows, Macintosh, or UNIX.

Q: Can Routing and Remote Access be used on the same computer as Proxy Server 2.0?

A: Yes, but only if you install the "hotfix" from Microsoft. This hotfix can be downloaded from Microsoft's Web site and resolves issues associated with reliable, secure integration between Routing, RAS, and Proxy Server 2.0.

Q: What does Microsoft recommend its customers do when using Proxy Server concerning connecting to the Internet, firewall protection and dynamic packet filtering, and assigning permissions?

A: Concerning Internet connections, Microsoft recommends that only protected networks be connected. Concerning firewall protection and dynamic packet filtering, Microsoft recommends that dynamic packet filtering remain enabled to limit communications outside the network. Finally, Microsoft recommends that user-level access controls be put in place and appropriately enforced for all required protocols.

Q: Does Proxy Server 2.0 improve network performance, and if so, how?

A: Proxy Server's caching abilities do indeed improve network performance. This is achieved since obtaining information from cache is must faster that obtaining it from a wide area network (WAN) or local area network (LAN) connection.

Q: On a Windows NT 4.0 Server computer, in what order should I install the latest Service Pack, Option Pack, Proxy Server, Remote Access Service (RAS), and Internet Explorer?

A: Install the latest Service Pack first, followed by Windows Routing and Remote Access, Internet Explorer, the Option Pack, Proxy Server 2.0, and then reinstall the Service Pack.

Q: How does SOCKS Proxy differ from WinSock Proxy?

A: With SOCKS, application must be built with SOCKS support in mind, and SOCKS does not support UDP-based applications like Net Show and VDO live. WinSock, on the other hand, provides support for both TCP and UDP, and supports applications like Real Audio, Net Show, and AOL. WinSock also supports IPX.

Traffic Filtering on Cisco IOS

Solutions in this chapter:

- Access Lists

- Lock and Key Access Lists

- Reflexive Access Lists

- Context-Based Access Control (CBAC)

Introduction

Traffic filtering consists of controlling the type of traffic that can be forwarded to and from a network. This function is used to enforce security policies at a specific point on a network, often between networks with different levels of security.

This chapter will cover the different traffic filtering mechanisms available in Cisco Internetwork Operating System (IOS) and Cisco Secure Integrated Software. In the simplest case, IP filtering can consist of an access list that permits or denies traffic based on the source or destination IP address. Very often, basic traffic filtering does not provide sufficiently adequate security in a network. Today, modern security products provide more control over the network traffic entering and exiting the network. To achieve that, the traffic must be inspected and the state of the connection must be kept. These advanced features require the router or firewall to understand the internal workings of the protocol it is trying to secure.

There are several types of access lists available with the Cisco IOS: Standard, Extended, Lock and Key, and Named. Standard access lists allow for a very basic set of parameters. This includes things such as permit, deny, source-address, and wildcard mask. Extended access lists expand upon the standard list by adding support for protocol, operator port, and precedence, among others.

Lock and Key access lists (first seen in IOS version 11.1) are also referred to as Dynamic access lists. The basic operating premise is to dynamically allow traffic from authenticated sources. This type of access list can be used in conjunction with both Standard and Extended access lists.

Named access lists, unlike numbered lists, will allow you to edit and change a portion of the access list without the need for deleting the whole access list and regenerating it.

Access Lists

An essential security function is the capability to control the flow of data within a network. A way to achieve this function is to utilize one of the features of the Cisco IOS known as an access list. The role of an access list will depend of the context in which it is used. For instance, access lists can:

- Control access to networks attached to a router or define a particular type of traffic that is allowed to pass to and from a network.

- Limit the contents of routing updates that are advertised by various routing protocols.

- Secure the router itself by limiting access to services such as Simple Network Management Protocol (SNMP) and Telnet.

- Define *interesting traffic* for dial-on-demand routing (DDR). Interesting traffic defines which packets allow the dial connection to occur.

- Define queuing features by determining what packets are given priority over others.

An access list is composed of a sequential series of filters defined globally on the router. Think of each filter as a statement that you enter into the router. Each of these filters performs a comparison or match, and permits or denies a packet across an interface. The decision to permit or deny is determined by the information contained inside the packets. This process is commonly referred to as *packet filtering*. The criteria that must be met for action to be taken can be based on only a source address, or a source and destination address, a protocol type, a specific port or service type, or other type of information. This information typically is contained within the Layer 3 and Layer 4 headers. Once an access list is defined, it will need to be applied on the interface where access control is required. As we just stated, we define access lists globally on the router. The key here is to remember that after defining the access list it must be applied on the interface, or your access list will have no effect. Traffic moves both in and out of the interface of the router—so access lists can be applied either in the inbound or in the outbound direction on a specific interface. One method commonly used to avoid confusion is to assume you are inside the router; simply ask yourself if you want to apply the access list statements as traffic comes in (inbound) or as traffic moves out (outbound). You can have one access list, per protocol, per interface, per direction. So, for example, it is possible to have one access list for outbound IP traffic and one access list for inbound IP traffic applied to the same interface. See Figure 8.1.

Figure 8.1 Managing traffic entering and exiting the router interface.

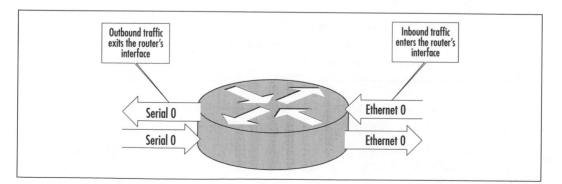

Access List Operation

When a packet enters a router, a route is looked up for the packet's destination, and an interface is determined for the packet to exit the router. When using access lists, before the packet can enter or exit the router there is a "stack" of filters that are applied to the interface through which the packet must pass. This stack would consist of the commands you entered on your router with the **access-list** global configuration command. Think of each line of your access list as a filter. The following example represents a user-defined access list with three filters. (A complete description on the access list syntax is given in a later section.)

```
access-list 3 permit 192.168.10.15 0.0.0.0
access-list 3 permit 192.168.10.16 0.0.0.0
access-list 3 deny 192.168.10.17 0.0.0.0
```

The packet exiting the router will be tested against each condition until a match occurs. If no match occurs on the first line, the packet moves to the second and the matching process happens again. When a match is established, a permit or deny action, which is specified on each filter statement, will be executed. What happens if the packet ends up at the end of the stack, or the last line of our access list, and a match never occurred? There is an implicit *deny all* at the end of every access list. So any packet that passes through an access list with no match is automatically dropped. You will not see this line on any access list that you build; just think of it as a default line that exists at the end of your access list. In some cases you may want to enter the last line of the access list as **permit any**.

With this line in place, all packets that pass through the access list with no match will be permitted and will never reach the implicit deny all. In Figure 8.2 we can see the direction of a packet as it flows through the access list.

Table 8.1 describes the **ip-access-group** command.

Table 8.1 IP Access Group Command

Command	Description
ip	Defines the protocol used.
access-group	Applies the access list to the interface.
list number	Identifies the access list.
in/out	Keyword **in** or **out** defines the direction in which the access list will be applied. This indicates whether packets are examined as they leave or as they enter the router.

Table 8.3 Continued

Access List Type	Range of Numbers
Extended IPX	900–900
IPX SAP	1000–1099
Extended transparent bridging	1100–1199
NLSP route summary	1200–1299

Notice that some of the number ranges are the same for different protocols. For example, Ethernet type code and Source-route bridging have the same number but are different protocols. In this case, the router will distinguish between the access list types by the format of the access list instead of the number. You can choose any number in the range of the access you are creating and do not have to follow any order. For example, when using a Standard IP access list, you can choose a number in the range of 1 through 99. So, the first Standard IP access list on the router does not have to be access list 1; however, each list must be uniquely numbered on the router.

Access lists may also be identified by name instead of a number. Named access lists are beneficial to the administrator when dealing with a large number of access lists for ease of identification, and also if more than 99 Standard access lists are required. Named access lists are also helpful if using Extended access lists.

Another advantage of named access lists over numbered access lists is in modifying the access list. With numbered access lists, the entire access list and all its statements are considered one entity. To delete or change a statement you will have to delete the entire numbered access list and reenter the statements you want to keep. Named access lists allow you to delete one statement within the access list.

Standard IP Access Lists

In the following example, any field represented by { } is mandatory for the access list. Any field represented by [ ] is optional. The syntax of a Standard IP access list is:

```
access-list list-number {permit | deny} source-address [wildcard-mask][log]
```

Table 8.4 lists the configuration for a Standard IP access list.

Table 8.4 Standard IP Access List Configuration

Command	Description
access-list list number	Defines the number of the access list. The Standard access list numbers range from 1-99.
permit	If conditions are met, traffic will be allowed.
deny	If conditions are met, traffic will be denied.
source-address	Identifies the host or network from which the packet is being sent. The source can be specified by an IP address or by using the keyword **any**.
wildcard-mask	By default, this field will be 0.0.0.0. This defines the number of wildcard bits assigned to the source address. The wildcard-mask can be specified by using the keyword **any**.
log	This keyword results in the logging of packets that match the permit or deny statement.

Note first that a hyphen is required between the words **access** and **list**. Next is the list number. Since we are referencing a Standard IP access list, the numbers would range from 1–99. The access list number actually serves a dual purpose here. Typically, you will find several access lists on one router; therefore, the router must have a way to distinguish one access list from another. The number performs this purpose along with merging the lines of an access list. The number also tells the router the access list's type.

The keyword **permit** or **deny** indicates the action to be performed if a match occurs. For example the keyword **permit** would allow the packet to be forwarded by the interface. The keyword **deny** will drop the packet if a match is found. If a packet is dropped an Internet Control Message Protocol (ICMP) error message of destination unreachable will be sent back to the source. Table 8.5 describes the following access list commands:

```
access-list 3 permit 192.168.10.15 0.0.0.0
access-list 3 permit 192.168.10.16 0.0.0.0
access-list 3 permit 192.168.10.17 0.0.0.0
access-list 3 deny 192.168.10.0 0.0.0.0.255
access-list 3 permit 0.0.0.0 255.255.255.255
```

Table 8.5 Description of Access List Commands

Command	Description
access-list 3 permit 192.168.10.15 0.0.0.0 access-list 3 permit 192.168.10.16 0.0.0.0 access-list 3 permit 192.168.10.17 0.0.0.0	Allow hosts 192.168.10.15, 192.168.10.16, and 192.168.10.17.
access-list 3 deny 192.168.10.0 0.0.0.0.255	Deny any host from network 192.168.10.0.
access-list 3 permit 0.0.0.0 255.255.255.255	Allow any host.

Source Address and Wildcard Mask

When using a standard IP access list, the source address must always be specified. The source address can refer to the address of a host, a group of hosts, or possibly an entire subnet. The scope of the source address is specified by the wildcard-mask field.

The wildcard mask is typically one of the most misunderstood topics when dealing with access lists. When using the wildcard mask, think of the reverse manner in which a subnet mask works. The job of a subnet mask is to specify how many bits of an IP address refer to the subnet portion. Remember, a binary 1 in the subnet mask indicates the corresponding bit is part of the subnet range, and a binary 0 in the subnet mask indicates the corresponding bit is part of the host portion. For example, take the following IP address and subnet mask:

```
Source address=172.16.130.77-10101100.00010000.10000010.01001101

Subnet Mask=255.255.255.0-11111111.11111111.11111111.00000000

Subnet          =172.16.130.0    -10101100.00010000.10000010.00000000
```

In the first three octets of the subnet mask, we have set all the bits to one (decimal 255 = 11111111 in binary). This tells us that all of the bits in the first three octets are now part of the subnet field. This is accomplished by using what is known as a Boolean AND operation. A Boolean AND is performed on the host address and the subnet mask, giving us a subnet or network number. When comparing two bits in the previous example, the result will be one only if both of the bits are set to one.

Now let's move from the subnet mask to the wildcard mask. When using a wildcard mask, a zero is used for each bit that should be matched, and a one is used when the bit position doesn't need to be matched. Take the following IP address and wildcard mask (our wildcard mask here is 0.0.0.255):

```
Source address   =172.16.130.77-    10101100.00010000.10000010. 01001101

Wildcard Mask    =0.0.0.255   -      00000000.00000000.00000000.11111111

Subnet           =172.16.130.255-10101100.00010000.10000010.11111111
```

Here, a Boolean OR is performed. When comparing these two bits, the result will be zero only if both of the bits are set to zero. The meaning of both bits are the 32 bits in the source address and the 32 bits in the wildcard mask. So, in the previous example, the router will perform the Boolean OR starting with the leading bit in the first octet of the source address and the leading bit in the first octet of the wildcard mask. Then continue with the Boolean OR through all 32 bits of the source address and wildcard mask. Therefore, in the previous example, all of the host addresses on subnet 172.16.130.0 will be permitted or denied depending on what is specified in the access list. The first three octets (172.16.130) must match and the last octet (.255) is not concerned with matching any bits. The default wildcard mask for a standard IP access list is 0.0.0.0. The 0.0.0.0 indicates that all bits in the source address must match. In the following access list, the IP address in each line must be matched exactly (all 32 bits). Table 8.6 describes the following access list commands:

```
access-list 17 deny 172.16.130.88 0.0.0.0

access-list 17 deny 172.16.130.89 0.0.0.0

access-list 17 deny 172.16.130.90 0.0.0.0

access-list 17 permit 0.0.0.0 255.255.255.255
```

Table 8.6 Description of Access List Commands

Command	Description
access-list 17 deny 172.16.130.88 0.0.0.0	Deny host 172.16.130.88
access-list 17 deny 172.16.130.89 0.0.0.0	Deny host 172.16.130.89
access-list 17 deny 172.16.130.90 0.0.0.0	Deny host 172.16.130.90
access-list 17 permit 0.0.0.0 255.255.255.255	Allow any host

Now let's look at the last line in the preceding access list. Remember, we are performing an OR on the bits here, so using the wildcard mask of 0.0.0.0 255.255.255.255 tells us that all bits will be permitted. (The 255.255.255.255 means any source address will be permitted.) Remember that there is an implicit deny all at the end of every access list. To change that behavior to a permit by default, you must enter a permit statement at the end of your access list as shown in the example. Since the default wildcard mask for a standard IP address is 0.0.0.0, we could write the access list as follows with the same effect:

```
access-list 17 deny 172.16.130.88
access-list 17 deny 172.16.130.89
access-list 17 deny 172.16.130.90
access-list 17 permit any
```

Table 8.7 describes these access list commands.

Table 8.7 Description of Access List Commands

Command	Description
access-list 17 deny 172.16.130.88	Deny host 172.16.130.88
access-list 17 deny 172.16.130.89	Deny host 172.16.130.89
access-list 17 deny 172.16.130.90	Deny host 172.16.130.90
access-list 17 permit any	Allow any host

Notice that we have removed the wildcard mask for the access list because the value of 0.0.0.0 is the default. This mask will try to match on all 32 bits of the IP address, so if you choose not to enter a wildcard mask, an exact match is assumed. We also changed the last line of our access list by using **permit any**. This has the same effect as using a source address of 0.0.0.0 with a wildcard mask of 255.255.255.255.

What would happen if the lines in the access list were reversed? Let's rewrite our access list as follows:

```
access-list 17 permit any
access-list 17 deny 172.16.130.88
access-list 17 deny 172.16.130.89
access-list 17 deny 172.16.130.90
```

Table 8.8 describes these access list commands.

Table 8.8 Description of Access List Commands

Command	Description
access-list 17 permit any	Allow any host
access-list 17 deny 172.16.130.88	Deny host 172.16.130.88
access-list 17 deny 172.16.130.89	Deny host 172.16.130.89
access-list 17 deny 172.16.130.90	Deny host 172.16.130.90

Access lists operate in sequential order. They test packets one statement at a time from top to bottom. So in the preceding example, all traffic would be permitted when it is tested on the first statement. No packet would ever have the chance to be denied.

> **NOTE**
>
> Access lists operate in sequential order, from top to bottom. It is easy to inadvertently make a mistake that can interrupt services or have other serious effects. Access lists should be double-checked to make sure that the logic is correct (having someone else check them is a good idea).

Keywords *any* and *host*

Keywords are typically used in Extended access list statements; however, some are applicable in Standard access lists. In the previous example, we used the keyword **any** to specify that we will permit any IP address as a source. The keyword **host** can be used in our access to indicate a wildcard mask of 0.0.0.0, or more specifically, an exact match. This would be written as follows:

```
access-list 17 deny host 172.16.130.88

access-list 17 deny host 172.16.130.89

access-list 17 deny host 172.16.130.90

access-list 17 permit any
```

Keyword *log*

When including the keyword **log** in an access list statement, a match of that statement will be logged. That is, any packet that matches the access list will cause a message to be sent to the console, memory, or to a syslog server. Using the global **logging console** command controls this. This feature has been available with Standard access lists since IOS 11.3. Previously, this capability was available in extended IP access lists only. When using the **log** keyword, the first packet that matches the access list causes a logging message immediately. Following matching packets are gathered over a five-minute interval before they are displayed or logged. Let's look at how this would work in the following example:

```
access-list 17 deny 172.16.130.88 log

access-list 17 deny 172.16.130.89 log
```

```
access-list 17 deny 172.16.130.90 log

access-list 17 permit any
```

Suppose the interface receives 10 packets from host 172.16.130.88, 15 packets from host 172.16.130.89, and 20 packets from host 172.16.130.90 over a five-minute period. The first log will look as follows:

```
list 17 deny 172.16.130.88 1 packet

list 17 deny 172.16.130.89 1 packet

list 17 deny 172.16.130.90 1 packet
```

After five minutes, the log would display as follows:

```
list 17 deny 172.16.130.88 9 packets

list 17 deny 172.16.130.89 14 packets

list 17 deny 172.16.130.90 19 packets
```

When using the keyword **log,** we are provided with an observant capability. Here you are able to analyze not only who has tried to access your network but also the number of attempts. The log message will indicate the number of packets, whether the packet was permitted or denied, the source address, and the access list number. There will be a message generated for the first packet that matches the test, and then at five-minute intervals you will receive a message stating the number of packets matched during the previous five minutes. Table 8.9 lists the keywords available for use with Standard access lists.

Table 8.9 Keywords Available with Standard Access Lists

Keyword	Description
any	Available as an abbreviation for an address or the wildcard-mask value of 0.0.0.0 255.255.255.255. Can be used in the source address field.
host	Available as an abbreviation for a wildcard mask of 0.0.0.0. Can be used in the source address field.
log	Used for logging of packets that match **permit** and **deny** statements.

Access Lists

When applying an access list to an interface, there are three steps. The first step is to create the access list. You can create your access list on the router when attached through the console, or with a word processor or text editor. If you want to load this file from the PC to the router, you will need to install a Trivial File Transfer Protocol (TFTP) program on the PC. When using TFTP software, the file is stored on the TFTP server in ASCII text and the router will act as a client to retrieve the file that you created. Next, you must specify the interface where you plan to apply the access list. For example, to apply the access list to the Ethernet interface 0, you must first define the interface. This is accomplished with the following command:

```
interface ethernet 0
```

You have the option to abbreviate keywords in a command. The preceding command could be used as follows:

```
interface e0
int e0
```

If you plan to apply the access list to a serial port on your router, the command would look as follows:

```
interface serial 0
```

The next step is to actually apply the access list to the interface and define the direction of the access list with the **ip access-group** command. The **ip access-group** command allows you to select a specific group of hostnames to use for the access list. The format of the command is as follows:

```
ip access-group {list number}[in|out]
```

Extended IP Access Lists

An option for more precise traffic-filtering control would be an Extended IP access list. Here both the source and destination address are checked. In addition, you have the ability to specify the protocol and optional Transmission Control Protocol (TCP) or User Datagram Protocol (UDP) port number to filter more precisely. In the following example, any field represented by { } is mandatory for the access list. Any field represented by [ ] is optional. The format of an Extended IP access list is:

access-list access-list-number {**permit** | **deny**} protocol source source-wildcard [operator port] destination destination-wildcard [**precedence** precedence number] [operator port] [**tos** tos] [**established**] [**log**]

Bold items represent keywords that are part of the access list syntax. Table 8.10 lists the configuration for an Extended IP access list.

Table 8.10 Extended IP Access List Configuration

Command	Description
access-list list number	Defines the number of the access list. The Extended access list numbers range from 100–199.
permit	If conditions are met, traffic will be allowed.
deny	If conditions are met, traffic will be denied.
protocol	Defines the protocol for filtering. Available options here are keywords such as **TCP** or **UDP**.
source-address	Identifies the host or network from which the packet is being sent. The source can be specified by an IP address or by using the keyword **any**.
source wildcard-mask	This defines the number of wildcard bits assigned to the source address. The source wildcard-mask can be specified by an IP address or by using the keyword **any**.
operator port	Defines the name or decimal number of a TCP or UDP port.
destination-address	Identifies the host or network to which the packet is being sent. The destination can be specified by an IP address or by using the keyword **any**.
destination wildcard-mask	This defines the number of wildcard bits assigned to the destination address. The destination wildcard-mask can be specified by an IP address or by using the keyword **any**.
precedence / precedence number	Used for filtering by the precedence level name or number.
Type of Service (TOS)	Defines filtering by service level specified by a name or number (01–5).
Established	Reset (RST) or Acknowledgement (ACK) bits are set.
Log	Log the event when a packet matches the access list statement.

In Figure 8.3 we would apply this access list on the serial 0 interface in the outbound direction as follows:

```
Router(config)# interface serial 0
Router(config-if)# ip access-group 141 out
```

Figure 8.3 The access list applied to interface serial 0 outbound.

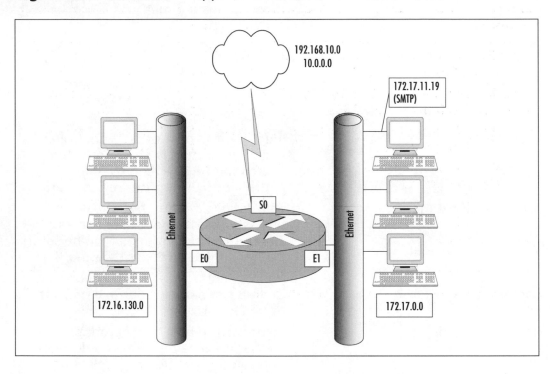

An example of an Extended access list is as follows:

```
access-list 141 permit ip 172.16.130.88 0.0.0.0 10.0.0.0 0.255.255.255
access-list 141 permit ip 172.16.130.89 0.0.0.0 10.0.0.0 0.255.255.255
access-list 141 permit ip 172.16.130.90 0.0.0.0 10.0.0.0 0.255.255.255
access-list 141 deny ip 172.16.130.0 0.0.0.255 192.168.10.118 0.0.0.0
access-list 141 permit ip 0.0.0.0 255.255.255.255 0.0.0.0
255.255.255.255
```

Table 8.11 describes the Extended access list commands.

Just as in our Standard access list, the Extended access list will require a hyphen between the words **access** and **list**. Next is the list number. Since we are referencing an extended IP access list, the numbers would range from 100–199. The access list number serves the same dual purpose here as we looked at earlier with the Standard access list. The router must have a way to distinguish between access lists. The number performs this purpose along with merging the lines of an access list together and designates in which access list the filter is part. The number also tells the router the type of the access list.

Table 8.11 Description of Access List Commands

Command	Description
access-list 141 permit ip 172.16.130.88 0.0.0.0 10.0.0.0 0.255.255.255	Allows host 172.16.130.88 to any host on network 10.0.0.0.
access-list 141 permit ip 172.16.130.89 0.0.0.0 10.0.0.0 0.255.255.255	Allows host 172.16.130.89 to any host on network 10.0.0.0.
access-list 141 permit ip 172.16.130.90 0.0.0.0 10.0.0.0 0.255.255.255	Allows host 172.16.130.90 to any host on network 10.0.0.0.
access-list 141 deny ip 172.16.130.0 0.0.0.255 192.168.10.118 0.0.0.0	Denies any host on network 172.16.130.0 to host 192.168.10.118.
access-list 141 permit ip 0.0.0.0 255.255.255.255 0.0.0.0 255.255.255.255	Allows all hosts from any network to any network.

The last line of our Extended access list example could have read as follows:

```
access-list 141 permit ip any any
```

Protocol

You have the option of filtering several different protocols using the Extended access list. The protocol field defines what protocol to filter, such as TCP, UDP, ICMP, and IP, to name a few. It is important to remember here that an IP header is used to transport TCP and UDP; therefore if you choose to filter the IP protocol, you will permit or deny all the protocols transported over IP, such as an ICMP message, TCP, or UDP. If you plan to filter a specific protocol, you must specify that protocol. You must use a systematic approach when designing your access list. For example, if your first line in the access list permits IP for a specific address, and the second line denies UDP for the same address, the second statement would have no effect. The first line would permit IP, including all the above layers. An option here may be to reverse the order of the statements. With the statements reversed, UDP would be denied from that address, and all other protocols would be permitted.

Source Address and Wildcard Mask

The source address and wildcard mask perform the same function here as in a standard IP access list. So in the preceding example, we could have used the keyword **host** followed by the IP address. The access list would look as follows:

```
access-list 141 permit ip host 172.16.130.88 10.0.0.0 0.255.255.255

access-list 141 permit ip host 172.16.130.89 10.0.0.0 0.255.255.255

access-list 141 permit ip host 172.16.130.90 10.0.0.0 0.255.255.255

access-list 141 permit ip 172.16.130.0 0.0.0.255 192.168.10.118 0.0.0.0

access-list 141 permit ip 172.17.0.0 0.0.31.255 192.168.10.0 0.0.0.255
```

In the first three lines, we are permitting or allowing packets from individual hosts on subnet 172.16.130.0 to any host on network 10.0.0.0. In line 4, we are permitting packets with the source address that belongs to subnet 172.16.130.0 to the destination of host 192.168.10.118. Line 5 tells us that we are permitting packets with a source address between 172.17.0.0 and 172.17.31.255 with a destination of network 192.168.10.0. The implicit **deny all** will deny all other traffic that passes through the interface to which we have applied the access list. Remember that Standard IP access lists have a default mask of 0.0.0.0. This does not apply to Extended access lists, so we must specify one. Shortcuts are available, such as the keyword **host** (as used in the preceding example) and the keyword **any**.

Destination Address and Wildcard Mask

The destination address and wildcard mask have the same effect and structure as the source address and wildcard mask. So here, the keyword **host** and **any** are also available. You can utilize these keywords to specify any destination address as well as a specific destination without using the wildcard mask. Remember that Extended access lists try a match on both source and destination. A common mistake is trying to build an Extended access list with the idea of filtering only the source address, and forgetting to specify the destination address. Figure 8.3 shows an example of our network with the access list applied to interface serial 0 outbound.

Source and Destination Port Number

Both the source and destination ports may be specified. We must apply the access list to the interface. The access list will be applied to the serial interface, inbound. Let's look at the following example:

```
Router(config)# interface Serial 0
```

```
Router(config-if)# ip access-group 111 in
```

```
access-list 111 permit tcp any host 172.17.11.19 eq 25
access-list 111 permit tcp any host 172.17.11.19 eq 23
```

Table 8.12 describes these access list commands.

Table 8.12 Router Commands and Description

Router Command	Description
access-list 111 permit tcp any host 172.17.11.19 eq 25	Permit Simple Mail Transfer Protocol (SMTP) to host 172.17.11.19
access-list 111 permit tcp any host 172.17.11.19 eq 23	Permit Telnet to host 172.17.11.19
interface Serial 0	Enter interface submode
ip access-group 111 in	Apply access list inbound on interface

In line 1, we are permitting TCP packets from any source to the destination of host 172.22.11.19 if the destination port is 25 (SMTP). In line 2, we are permitting TCP packets from any source to the destination of host 172.22.11.19 if the destination port is 23 (Telnet). Let's take a look at filtering with TCP and UDP. When using TCP, for example, the access list will examine the source and destination port numbers inside the TCP segment header. So when using an Extended access list, you have the capability to filter to and from a network address, and also to and from a particular port number. You have several options when using the operator port, such as:

- **eq** equal to
- **neq** not equal to
- **gt** greater than
- **lt** less than
- **range** an inclusive range or ports (two port numbers are specified)

The port specifies the application layer port to be permitted or denied.

The Established Option

One of the options available for use with an Extended access list is the *established option*. This option is available only with the TCP protocol. The idea is to restrict traffic in one direction as a response to sessions initiated in the opposite direction.

Let's look at the following access list:

```
Router(config)# interface Serial 0


Router(config-if)# ip access-group 111 in

access-list 111 permit tcp any host 172.17.0.0 0.0.255.255 established

access-list 111 permit tcp any host 172.17.11.19 eq 25

access-list 111 permit tcp 12.0.0.0 0.255.255.255 172.22.114.0
0.0.0.255 eq 23
```

Figure 8.4 shows an example of our network with the access list applied inbound on interface serial 0 (S0). The first line of the access list permits TCP packets from any source to the network 172.17.0.0 with the TCP flag ACK or RST bit set. This would be beneficial if you need to prevent TCP sessions from being established into your network. It would also ensure that incoming traffic from TCP sessions initiated from network 172.17.0.0 would be allowed. The second line tells the router to permit TCP packets from any source, if the destination is 172.17.11.19 and the destination port is 25 (SMTP). Line 3 is allowing a TCP segment with a source address from network 12.0.0.0 to port 23 (Telnet), to any address on subnet 172.22.114.0. What will happen to all other packets? Once again the implicit **deny all** will drop all other packets.

Figure 8.4 The access list applied to serial 0 inbound.

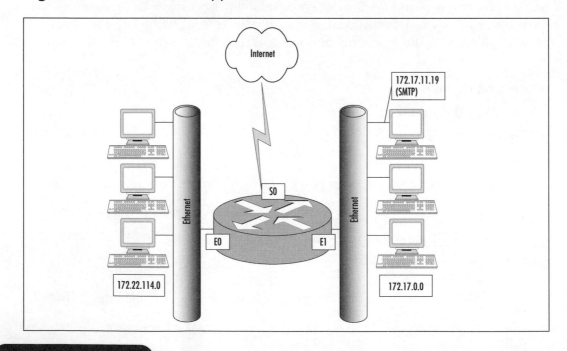

In the TCP segment, there are six flag bits, two of which are the ACK and RST. If one of these bits is set, then a match will occur. The SYN bit indicates that a connection is being established. A packet with a SYN bit without an ACK bit is the very first packet sent to establish a connection. Figure 8.5 shows the TCP setup handshake.

Figure 8.5 A TCP session being established.

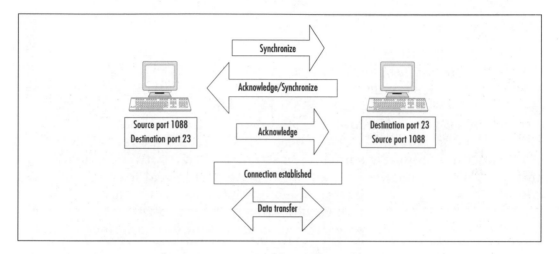

Another issue to consider here is that, as the administrator, you may not be certain what protocols the host may be using; however, we do know ports are chosen by workstations randomly between the port ranges of 1024 through 65535. Keeping that in mind, we could modify the first line of the access list as follows:

```
access-list 111 permit tcp any host 172.17.0.0 0.0.255.255 gt 1023
established
```

This would ensure that no packets would be accepted inbound to our network unless the destination port is higher than 1023. The hacker could spoof the ACK or RST bit in the packet but the destination port would still have to be higher that 1023. Typically, our servers running services such as Domain Name System (DNS) run below port 1024. However, it is not a good idea to let through all ports over 1023.You become vulnerable to network scans and Denial of Service attacks.

Now let's look at what happens when we decide to allow restricted TFTP access to host 172.17.11.19, DNS access to host 172.17.11.20, and unrestricted Simple Network Management Protocol (SNMP) access. TFTP, DNS, and SNMP are UDP-based protocols. We have added to our Extended access list again in the following example:

```
access-list 111 permit tcp any host 172.17.0.0 0.0.255.255 established
access-list 111 permit tcp any host 172.17.11.19 eq 25
access-list 111 permit tcp 12.0.0.0 0.255.255.255 172.22.114.0
0.0.0.255 eq 23
access-list 111 permit udp 192.168.10.0 0.0.0.255 host 172.17.11.19 eq
69
access-list 111 permit udp any host 172.17.11.20 eq 53
access-list 111 permit udp any any eq 161
```

You will notice there is no keyword established here. Remember that UDP is a connectionless protocol, therefore no connections will be established between hosts, and there is no SYN-ACK negotiation. Since we have not changed the first three lines of our access list, we will begin by discussing line 4. Line 4 is allowing UDP datagrams from subnet 192.168.10.0 to port 69 (TFTP) on host 172.17.11.19. Line 5 is allowing UDP datagrams from any source to host 172.17.11.20 with a destination port of 53 (DNS). Line 6 allows all SNMP (port 161) to and from any destination. Remember, any packets not matching the list will be dropped by the implicit **deny all**. Figure 8.6 shows the addition of a DNS server in our network. Here we would apply the access list inbound on interface serial 0.

Figure 8.6 The access list applied to serial 0 inbound.

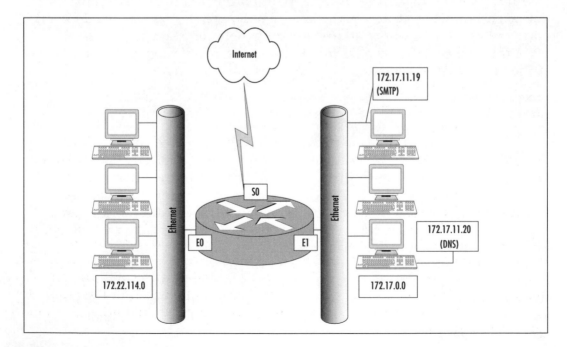

Named Access Lists

Each access list type has a range of acceptable numbers that can be used. For example, there are 99 standard (1–99; IOS 12.1 adds 1300–1399) and 100 extended (100–199; IOS 12.1 adds 2000–2699) access lists available in the Cisco IOS. This seems to be more than enough; however, maybe on your enterprise router you need to create more than 100 extended IP access lists. Named access lists provide an alternative to allow this. Also, named access lists provide a description that is typically more manageable than a large group of numbers.

Named access lists are, just as the title implies, an access list that is referenced by name instead of a number. They also allow you to delete a specific entry in your access list. When using numbered access lists, this is not an option. When using a numbered access list, you must recreate the entire access list to remove an unwanted entry. When adding to an access list, both the named and numbered lists will place the new line at the bottom of the access list.

When creating a named access list, it must begin with a standard alphabetic ASCII character. Names are case-sensitive, so the access list SYDNEY and Sydney will be looked at as two unique names or two different access lists. With the exception of the number, the named access list will look identical to a numbered access list. The following is an example of a named access list:

```
ip access-list extended filter_tx


permit tcp any 172.17.0.0 0.0.255.255 established

permit tcp any host 172.17.11.19 eq smtp

permit tcp 12.0.0.0 0.255.255.255 172.22.114.0 0.0.0.255 eq 23

permit udp 192.168.10.0 0.0.0.255 host 172.17.11.19 eq 69

permit udp any host 172.17.11.20 eq 53

permit udp any any eq 161
```

Editing Access Lists

When applying access lists, there are several factors to consider. One of the most important things to remember is that access lists are evaluated from the top down, so packets will always be tested starting with the top line of the access list. Careful consideration should be taken in the order of your access list statements. The most frequent match should always be at the beginning of the access list.

Another thing to consider is the placement of the access list. When looking at your network, a Standard access list should be placed closest to the destination of where you are trying to block the packets. Remember that a Standard IP access list filters on the source IP address. If the IP address is blocked, then the entire protocol suite (IP) would typically be denied. So, if you denied an IP address close to the source, the user would be denied access anywhere on the network. When applying an Extended access list, the access list should be placed closest to the source. When using an Extended access list, both the source and destination addresses are checked along with a protocol, therefore the access list will be most effective if applied to the source. For example, if denying Telnet from one network to another, the access list would have very little effect if applied near the destination. The user could Telnet to another router on the network and then establish a new Telnet session with a different IP address.

TIP

Packets generated by the router are not affected by an outbound access list. To filter routing table updates or any traffic generated by the router, you should consider inbound access lists.

When using a named access list, we can delete a specific entry; however, with a numbered access list, we do not have this option. We have learned that when you need to add an entry into the access list in a specific position (such as the fifth line) the entire access list must be deleted and then recreated with new entries. This applies to both numbered and named access lists. Does this mean that if I have just created a 35-line access list and need to make a change, the only option is to start over? Not really. There are several ways to avoid recreating your entire access list. One option to explore here may be the use of the TFTP protocol. When utilizing TFTP, we have the ability to copy our configuration to a server as a text file. Remember when you copy from anywhere to the running configuration, a merge will occur. So if your intention is to change line 14, make your changes to the configuration file while on the TFTP server. Then when you copy the file to the running configuration, the merge will replace line 14 with your new changes. Once on the server, we can use a text editor to modify and then reload the configuration to our router. Another option may be to have a template of an access list on your TFTP server. Having the template will help to ensure you enter the command correctly. Remember the commands you use here will be the exact commands you would enter at the command line of the router. When copying this file to your running configuration, it will merge the new access list with your current configuration; if the syntax is incorrect, the operation will fail. Following is an example of how a session would look when loading an access list from a TFTP server. We will merge the access list with the running configuration.

```
Router# copy tftp running-config

Address or name of remote host []? 172.16.1.1

Source filename []? accesslist.txt

Destination filename [running-config]?

Accessing TFTP://172.16.1.1/accesslist.txt… OK - 1684/3072 bytes]

Loading accesslist.txt from 172.16.1.1 (via Ethernet 0): !! [OK -
1388/3072 bytes]

1388 bytes copied in 3 secs (462 bytes/sec)
```

Problems with Access Lists

Some issues you may encounter with access lists are their limited capability to test information above the IP layer. Extended access lists have the capability to check on Layer 4, but not in the detailed sense.

Another issue to consider is that the access list will examine each packet individually, and does not have the capability of detecting if a packet is part of an upper-layer conversation. The keyword **established** can be used to match TCP packets that are part of an established TCP session. You need to be cautious when relying on the keyword **established**. Remember that it is applicable only when using TCP, for the presence of an RST and ACK flag in the packet automatically makes this packet part of an established TCP session. Although this filtering technique is suitable in many cases, it does not protect against forged TCP packets (commonly used to probe networks), nor does it offer any facility to filter UDP sessions. Reflexive access list and Context-Based Access Control (CBAC), introduced later in this chapter, offer better control and more facilities to do session filtering.

Last but not least, we must take into consideration human error. You must remember the basics—be sure to apply the access list to an interface after you create it. The access list must be created in the correct order, and when changes are made the new entries must be placed in the correct order.

Lock and Key Access Lists

Lock and Key is a traffic filtering security feature that can automatically create access lists on the router to allow incoming traffic from an authenticated source. These access lists are also referred to as Dynamic access lists. Lock and Key can be used in conjunction with other Standard and Extended access lists. Traditional Standard and Extended access lists cannot create Lock and Key access list entries. Once an entry is added to a traditional access list, it remains there until it is removed manually. With Lock and Key you can create a temporary opening in an access list by utilizing a response to a user authentication procedure. The idea here is to give temporary access, after proper authentication, to designated users who normally have their IP traffic blocked at the router. Lock and Key reconfigures the interface's existing IP access list to permit designated users to reach their destination.

When the connection is terminated, the interface is configured back to its original state. Let's say, for example, that a user in Figure 8.7 is working at a branch office and needs to log into the corporate office. The user will attempt to log in from a PC that is connected to a router (typically via a local area network, or LAN). A Telnet session will be opened to the router to provide authentication. The router at the corporate site (which is configured for Lock and Key) receives the Telnet packet and opens a Telnet session. Next the router will prompt for a password and then perform authentication by using a test that is configured by the administrator, such as a name and password. The authentication process can be done locally by the router using local username/password configuration, or through an external Authentication, Authorization, and Accounting (AAA) server such as Terminal Access Controller Access Control System Plus (TACACS+) or Remote Authentication Dial-In User Service (RADIUS). When the user successfully authenticates, the Telnet session closes and a temporary entry is created in the Dynamic access list. This Dynamic access list typically will permit traffic from the user's source IP address to some predetermined destination. This Dynamic access list will be deleted when a timeout is reached, or can be cleared by the administrator. A timeout can be configured as an idle-timeout or maximum-timeout period expires.

A user may not have a static IP address in a situation where a Dynamic Host Configuration Protocol (DHCP) is in use in a LAN environment or when a user is connected through a dial up to an Internet service provider (ISP). In both cases, users may typically get a different IP address. Lock and Key access lists can be used to implement a higher level of security without creating large holes in your network. The format of a Lock and Key access list is as follows:

```
access-list access-list-number [dynamic dynamic-name[timeout minutes]]
{deny | permit} protocol source source-wildcard destination
destination-wildcard[precedence precedence] [tos tos] [established]
[log]
```

Figure 8.7 Using Lock and Key.

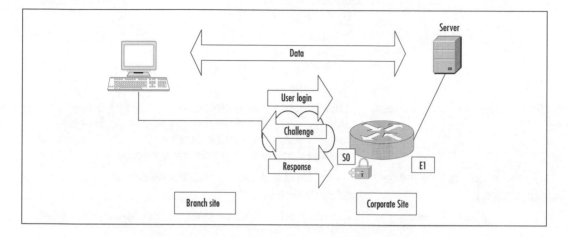

Table 8.13 describes Lock and Key access lists.

Table 8.13 Lock and Key Access List Configuration

Command	Description
access-list list number	Defines the number of the access list. The Extended access list numbers range from 100–199.
dynamic dynamic-name	Designates the name of the Dynamic access list.
timeout minutes	The timeout is optional and designates and absolute timeout for dynamic entries.
permit	If conditions are met, traffic will be allowed.
deny	If conditions are met, traffic will be denied.
protocol	Defines the protocol for filtering. Available options here are keywords such as **TCP** or **UDP**.
source-address	Identifies the host or network from which the packet is being sent. The source can be specified by an IP address or by using the keyword **any**.

Continued

Table 8.13 Continued

Command	Description
source wildcard-mask	This defines the number of wildcard bits assigned to the source address. The source wild-card-mask can be specified by an IP address or by using the keyword **any**.
destination-address	Identifies the host or network to which the packet is being sent. The destination can be specified by an IP address or by using the keyword **any**.
destination wildcard-mask	This defines the number of wildcard bits assigned to the destination address. The destination wildcard-mask can be specified by an IP address or by using the keyword **any**.
precedence / precedence number	Used for filtering by the precedence level name or number.
TOS	Defines filtering by service level specified by a name or number (01–5).
Established	When using TCP filtering will occur if RST or ACK bits are set.
Log	Results in the logging of packets that match the **permit** or **deny** statement.

- The access-list number has the same format as an Extended access list using the number 100–199.

- The dynamic-name parameter is used to name your access list.

- The timeout parameter is optional. This is where a maximum timeout for your Dynamic access list is configured. If no timeout is specified the temporary access list entry will remain configured indefinitely on the interface. The entry would have to be removed manually.

- The permit or deny field tells the router the action to perform.

- The protocol field can be any TCP/IP protocol field; TCP will be used in most cases. When using UDP, remember it is a connectionless protocol and contains no SYN-ACK bits for negotiation. UDP also contains no bits in the header for us to determine if it is part of an existing conversation.

- The source IP address is always replaced with the IP address of the authenticating host so the keyword **any** is typically used here.

- The destination address and destination wildcard mask will specify the destination that will be allowed by the Dynamic access list.

Previously when defining standard and Extended access lists, we had two steps—build the access list and then apply it to an interface. When using Lock and Key access lists, there are a few more steps we must follow. After creating the access list and applying the access list to an interface, we must configure our virtual terminal (VTY) ports.

By default the router has five VTY ports available for Telnet sessions, numbered 0–4. When a user connects to a router, the connection will reserve a VTY port for the duration of that session; five different Telnet sessions can be established on the router simultaneously. If you specify multiple VTY ports, they must all be configured identically because the software hunts for available VTY ports on a round-robin basis. If you do not want to configure all your VTY ports for Lock and Key access, you can specify a group of VTY ports for Lock and Key support only.

We have chosen to use three VTY ports in the following configuration:

```
Line vty 0 2
login local
autocommand access-enable host timeout 10
```

You must use the autocommand; when using the autocommand, the host parameter is an important player also. Without the host parameter, the dynamic entries would not replace the source IP address of the authenticating host—therefore any host would be allowed. The timeout parameter is optional and specifies the idle-timeout. If no maximum-timeout or idle-timeout is specified, the entry will not be removed until the router is rebooted. If you use both timers, the idle-timeout should be set to a lower number than the maximum-timeout.

Another issue to consider when using Lock and Key access lists is that if no additional steps are taken, every Telnet session incoming to the router will be treated as an attempt to open a dynamic entry. Remember that after authentication, the Telnet session is closed! So we would never be able to Telnet to our router for management purposes. We have to specify another command in our router to alleviate this problem. Beneath our remaining VTY ports, the **rotary 1** command is needed. The **rotary 1** command will enable normal Telnet access to our router on port 3001. You will need to specify the use of port 3001 when attempting to access the router via a Telnet session by specifying the port number immediately after the destination IP address. The following is an example:

```
telnet 172.16.1.1 3001
Line vty 3 4
login local
rotary 1
```

IP Spoofing

One security breach to be on the alert for is an attacker using IP spoofing. IP spoofing occurs when a hacker changes the source IP address of the packets that are sent to an IP address believed trusted by the network.

When packets arrive at your router, it is nearly impossible to determine if the packets are from a real host. Lock and Key access lists play a big role in assisting here, due to the fact that the openings are only temporary. This lowers the chance of the hacker determining the trusted source IP address.

It doesn't lower the chance of determining the source IP, but it does reduce the window of opportunity to exploit the temporary opening.

Consider this drawback, however. When a client who is behind Network Address Translation (NAT) and Network Port Address Translation (NPAT) (PAT in Cisco nomenclature) uses Lock and Key to a remote site to get access to some private resource, the Dynamic access list on the remote router will use the external or public address of the NPAT device. That address potentially is used by a number of users, and they will automatically be allowed access without any authentication. This is a serious security consideration.

We must ensure that our configuration looks like this before we save. There is no autocommand associated with lines 3 and 4. If our VTY ports are not configured properly, we could disable all Telnet capability to the router. When establishing a Telnet session to the router you must specify the port number after the destination IP address. The command would look as follows:

```
telnet 192.168.200.1 3001
```

Let's look at how this would be configured on our router. In the following example, only relevant potions of the configuration are shown:

```
Username cisco password san-jose
!
interface serial 1
ip address 192.168.200.1 255.255.255.0
ip access-group 114 in
!
access-list 114 permit tcp any host 172.16.4.1 eq telnet
access-list 114 dynamic cisco timeout 10 permit ip any any
!
line vty 0 2
login local
autocommand access-enable host timeout 10
line vty 3 4
login local
rotary 1
```

In this example, our username is *cisco*, and it is referenced in the second line of our access list. You have the option to specify only the password here, but that is not recommended. In the case of specifying one generic password for all users, it is far easier for a hacker to create an opening to the router. Also, if using a password only, it is impossible to track the individual user actions. When using both the ID and password, the hacker must guess both before access is gained. When using Telnet (using conventional username and password) everything is sent in clear text, allowing anyone to capture your authentication data.

NOTE

It should be reiterated that using clear-text passwords over an untrusted network such as the Internet could be detrimental to the security of your network. This configuration would not be recommended due to the fact that the passwords are in clear text.

The first line of the access list enables users to establish a Telnet session for authentication. In the next line we see the words *dynamic* and *timeout*. Dynamic signals the use of a Dynamic access list and the timeout is the maximum timeout period. We are allowing all IP packets in this statement also. The dynamic entry created will allow all IP packets from authenticated hosts to any IP address. This could be changed to permit only certain protocols or destinations. Only the source IP address is replaced, so all users will have the same access.

NOTE

Lock and Key will install only one Dynamic access list in any given access list. Although the router will allow you to specify more than one entry in a Dynamic access list, these will not have any effect. After entering multiple entries in your access list, enter the **show access-list** command and you will only see the results of the original entry. It is meaningless to specify multiple entries.

Reflexive Access Lists

The Reflexive access list alleviates some of the limitations of the basic and Extended access lists. Reflexive access lists allow IP packets to be filtered based on upper-layer session information, as in Extended access lists; however, the Reflexive access list can do session filtering by creating dynamic openings for IP traffic that is part of the allowed session. By so doing, Reflexive access lists provide a way to maintain information about existing connections. You have the option to permit IP traffic for sessions originating from within your network, but to deny IP traffic for sessions originating from outside your network. This sounds the same as an Extended access list. Reflexive access lists are referred to as a separate type of access list; however it is important to note that a Reflexive access list is a feature added to an Extended access list. It is important to point out that Reflexive access lists can only be defined using Extended Named IP access lists.

One instance where a Reflexive access list could be used is when an IP upper-layer session (such as TCP or UDP) is initiated from inside the network, with an outgoing packet traveling to the external network. In this case, a new, temporary entry will be created. Here, the ingoing traffic would be permitted only if it was part of the session, and all other traffic would be denied. For example, a temporary access list will be created inside the Reflexive access list when an outbound TCP packet is forwarded outside of your network. This temporary access list will permit ingoing traffic corresponding to the outbound connection.

Reflexive access lists are similar to other access lists in several ways. As with other access lists, Reflexive access lists contain entries that define criteria for permitting IP packets. These entries are evaluated in a top-down process in form until a match occurs. Reflexive access lists have significant differences. For example, they contain only temporary entries. The idea is that we create a Reflexive access list, and that access list will contain temporary entries. As stated earlier, these temporary entries are created automatically when a new IP session begins and matches a reflexive permit entry (for example, with an outbound packet), and the entries will be removed when the session ends. Reflexive access lists are not applied directly to an interface. They are placed within an Extended Named IP access list that is applied to the interface. Reflexive access lists do not have the implicit **deny all** at the end of the list. Remember they are nested in another access list.

The idea with a Reflexive access list basically is to create a mirror image of the reflected entry. For example, in Figure 8.8, Host0 on network 172.22.114.0 initiates a Telnet session to Host1 on network 172.17.0.0. Telnet uses the TCP protocol, therefore Host0 will pick a random source port number—let's use port 1028. Also here we will have a source IP address, destination IP address, and destination TCP port number. Since we are using Telnet, the destination port number will be 23. So far we have the following information:

```
Source TCP port-1028
Destination TCP port-23
Source IP address-172.22.114.1
Destination IP address-172.17.0.1
```

Figure 8.8 Utilizing a Reflexive access list with the Cisco IOS.

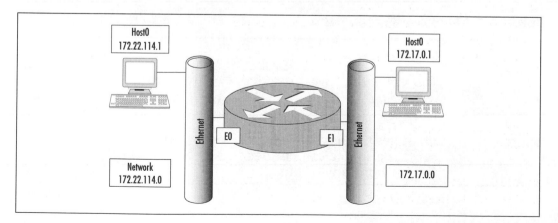

In our configuration we will have a Reflexive access-list statement that will trigger a reflected access list entry. This will allow inbound return traffic and would look as follows:

```
Router(config)#permit tcp host 172.17.0.1 eq 23 host 172.22.114.1 eq
1028
```

The following shows our information as a reflected access list entry:

```
Source TCP port-23

Destination TCP port-1028

Source IP address-172.17.0.1

Destination IP address-172.22.114.1
```

In this example of a reflected entry, the source and destination addresses have been swapped, along with the source and destination port numbers, giving the "mirror image."

Building Reflexive Access Lists

When building a Reflexive access list, we must first design an Extended named access list. You must use an Extended named access list when defining your Reflexive access list and there is no implicit **deny all** at the end. We enter a **permit** statement to allow all protocols in which you want a reflected entry created. So what must we do to indicate a reflexive opening? You need to use the keyword **reflect** in each of your permit statements. This tells us that a reflexive opening will occur. The following example shows the format of a Reflexive access list.

permit `protocol source destination` **reflect** `name` [**timeout** `seconds`]

Table 8.14 describes Reflexive access lists.

Table 8.14 Reflexive Access Lists

Command	Description
Permit	This entry will always use the keyword **permit**.
Protocol	Any TCP/IP protocol that is supported by an extended named IP access list.
Source	Identifies the host or network from which the packet is being sent. The source can be specified by an IP address or by using the keyword **any** or **host**.

Continued

Table 8.14 Continued

Command	Description
Destination	Identifies the host or network to which the packet is being sent. The destination can be specified by an IP address or by using the keyword **any** or **host**.
Reflect	Allows the permit statement to create a temporary opening.
Name	The name must be included so a reflexive entry can be used.
Timeout	Timeout is optional and has a default value of 300 seconds.

The format here is very comprehensible:

- This entry will always use the keyword **permit**. The keywords **permit** and **reflect** work hand-in-hand. To allow the **permit** statement to create a temporary opening you must have the reflect statement.

- The protocol field can depict any UDP, TCP, IP, and ICMP protocol that is supported by an extended named IP access list.

- The source field represents the source IP address. Keywords such as **any** and **host** are applicable here.

- The destination field represents the destination IP address. Keywords such as **any** and **host** are applicable here.

- You must include the name of the access list. A reflexive entry can be used only with an extended IP named access list.

- The timeout field is optional. If no value is specified, a default of 300 seconds will be used. The timeout is necessary when using connectionless protocols such as UDP. UDP offers nothing in the header to determine when the entry should be deleted. When using TCP, the timeout is not used. Instead, the Reflexive access list is deleted after receiving a packet with the RST flag set, or when the TCP session closes (i.e., both ends have sent FIN packets), the Reflexive access list is deleted within five seconds of detecting the bits.

To nest our Reflexive access list within an access list we use the **evaluate** command. This is done with the keyword **evaluate**. By default the Reflexive access list does not evaluate. This command is used as an entry in the access list and points to the Reflexive access list to be evaluated, therefore traffic entering your network will be evaluated against the Reflexive access list.

The following example shows that we are using a Named IP access list named Sydney. The entry would look as follows:

```
evaluate Sydney
```

Let's refer back to Figure 8.7. In our network, we need to allow from network 172.17.0.0, dynamic openings in response to any host that Telnets to network 172.22.114.0. Our named extended IP access list is represented by the name Sydney. The entry would look as follows:

```
permit tcp any any eq 23 reflect Sydney
```

Even though Reflexive access lists give more control in our networks, they do have a major shortcoming. Reflexive access lists are capable of handling only single channel applications such as Telnet. An application such as Telnet uses a single static port that stays the same throughout the conversation. Reflexive access lists do not offer the ability to support applications that change port numbers in a session. So how do we handle File Transfer Protocol (FTP)? Normal mode FTP is a multichannel operation that uses one channel for control and the second channel for data transmission and is not supported by Reflexive access lists, because the data port is chosen by the server, not the client. If using the passive mode FTP we can generally have a more favorable result. With passive mode, the server does not perform an active open to the client. What happens is that the client uses the command channel to exchange port information. The client then performs an open to the server on an agreed port. Both of the sessions we just discussed are outbound from the client; therefore, the Reflexive access list would create an additional entry. Here we would have success! FTP is not the only protocol that might be a potential problem. Many other protocols with similar behavior such as Remote Procedure Call (RPC), SQL*Net, Java, StreamWorks, and multimedia such as H.232 (e.g., NetMeeting, ProShare) will have problems.

When applying a Reflexive access list, there are a few things to consider. Do you need to apply this on an internal interface or external interface? Just as it sounds, an internal interface refers to the internal network (for example, your Ethernet port on the router) and the external interface refers to the external network (for example, your serial port on the router), typically your connection to the Internet. In most cases, the reflex statements will be defined in an outbound Extended named access list. Here a temporary opening in the inbound direction will be created. This opening would be created only if it were part of a session already established from within the internal network. This prevents unwanted IP traffic from entering the router, therefore protecting the internal network.

Applying Reflexive Access Lists

The first step in applying a Reflexive access list is to define the access list in an inbound or outbound Extended named access list. Refer to the following example to determine if your access list needs to be applied inbound or outbound. Next we have to nest the access list in an inbound or outbound Extended named access list. Then we have the option of setting a global timeout value. When using an entry in an Extended Named IP access list the entry must contain the **reflect** keyword in each permit statement.

You can use the keyword **timeout** to specify a timeout period for individual entries. If the timeout field is not used, a default value of 300 seconds is used. Remember, this will not apply when using TCP. When using TCP, the access list will close immediately after receiving the RST bit or within five seconds after both ends have closed the TCP session. To set the timeout, the following format is used:

```
ip reflexive-list timeout seconds
```

The following command is used to define an Extended named access list (see the section, "Named Access Lists" for more details):

```
ip access-list extended name
```

Normally, when a packet is tested against entries in an access list, the entries are tested in sequential order, and when a match occurs, no more entries are tested. When using a Reflexive access list nested in an Extended access list, the Extended access list entries are tested sequentially up to the nested (reflexive) entry, then the Reflexive access list entries are tested sequentially, and then the remaining entries in the Extended access list are tested sequentially. After a packet matches *any* of these entries, no more entries will be tested. As we stated earlier, you must use the **evaluate** command to nest a Reflexive access list.

Reflexive Access List Example

If our serial port provides Internet access and our internal network is connected to the Ethernet 0 port, we want to allow users on network 172.22.114.0 to access the Internet and DNS information along with providing Telnet capability. First let's create our Extended named access lists. Here we will put a permit statement for all the protocols that we want a reflexive entry created. We must use a named IP Extended access list. Our access list could look as follows:

```
ip access-list extended protection-out
permit tcp 172.22.114.0 0.0.0.255 any eq 23 reflect Sydney
```

```
permit tcp 172.22.114.0 0.0.0.255 any eq 80 reflect Sydney
permit udp 172.22.114.0.0.0.0.255 any eq 53 reflect Sydney


ip access-list extended protection-in
evaluate Sydney
```

Now we need to apply our access list to the appropriate interface. Here we will apply the extended IP named access list of protection-out, in the outbound direction on the serial port. This will allow for dynamic openings in the inbound direction. These openings will be created only in response to network 172.22.114.0, initiating the three sessions that we defined. It is important to remember the default **deny all** at the end of both access lists. In Figure 8.9 we would apply the access lists to the interface as follows:

```
Interface serial 0
Ip access-group protection-in in
Ip access-group protection-out out
```

Figure 8.9 Applying a Reflexive access list to an interface.

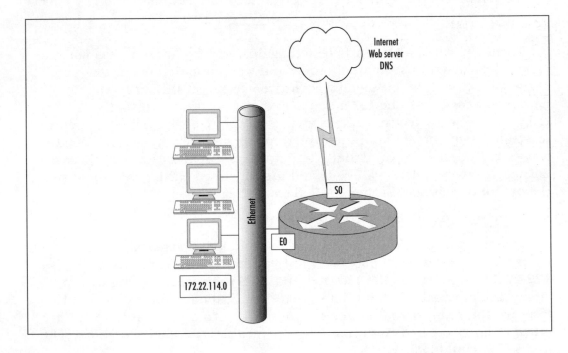

Context-Based Access Control (CBAC)

As discussed earlier, the Reflexive access list can handle only single channel applications. This could prove to be detrimental in your enterprise network. Now we will discus how CBAC overcomes some of these issues. Provided in Cisco Secure Integrated Software, Context-Based Access Control (CBAC) includes an extensive set of security features. The idea of Context-Based Access Control is to inspect outgoing sessions and create temporary openings to enable the return traffic. Sound familiar? We just described a Reflexive access list; the difference here is that CBAC can examine and securely handle various application-based upper-layer information. For example, when the traffic that you specify leaves the internal network through an interface, an opening is created that allows returning traffic based on the traffic being part of a data session that was initiated from an internal network. These openings are created when specified traffic exits your internal network through the router and allows returning traffic that would normally be blocked, similar to a Reflexive access list. The openings also allow additional data channels to enter your internal network back through the router if it is part of the same session as the originating traffic.

With other types of access lists, such as Reflexive or Extended access lists, traffic filtering is limited to filtering packets at the network layer or transport layer. CBAC examines the network layer and transport layer along with application-layer protocol information to learn about the state of the TCP or UDP session. Some protocols create multiple channels as a result of negotiations used in the control channel and it is not possible to filter those protocols using only the information available in the IP and transport layers. By examining the information at the application layer, CBAC provides support for some of these protocols.

As previously stated, CBAC inspects outgoing sessions and creates temporary openings to enable the return traffic just as a Reflexive access list does. However, unlike Reflexive access lists, CBAC has the ability to make decisions based on the behavior of the application. With a Reflexive access list, the information inside the packet can be examined up to the transport layer, or Layer 4, only. When using CBAC, the packets are examined when leaving or entering an interface on the router, and the information will be placed in a packet state information table. The information may be an IP address and port numbers from Layer 4. This state table is used by CBAC to create a temporary opening in the access list for return traffic. CBAC also inspects application-layer information to ensure that the traffic being allowed back through the router is applicable. Recall the issue we had with FTP; a Reflexive access list could support passive mode only where a single channel is used. Now we can use normal mode where multiple channels are used. CBAC would observe the outgoing session, then permit the data connection that will be established from the server to the client by creating an opening in the inbound access list. Another difference with CBAC is that a CBAC access list can be created separately from Extended or Standard access lists and are applied to the interface. Table 8.15 indicates the protocols where CBAC performs the equivalent function.

Table 8.15 Applications CBAC Securely Handles

Protocols and Applications
Single-channel TCP
Single-channel UDP
CU-SeeME
FTP
H.323
Java (applets embedded in HTTP)
Microsoft Netshow
UNIX r commands
RealAudio
RPC
SMTP
SQL*Net
StreamWorks
TFTP
VDOLive

There are a few limitations when using CBAC:

- Any packets with the router as the source address or destination address will not be inspected. Only TCP and UDP packets are inspected, so traffic originating or in destination for the router itself cannot be controlled with CBAC.

- CBAC cannot inspect IP Security (IPSec) traffic. If the traffic needs to be inspected, the router must be configured as the IPSec tunnel endpoint.

- IP traffic such as ICMP must be filtered with an Extended or named access list.

The Control-Based Access Control Process

This section describes a sample process of the events that occur when we configure CBAC on an external interface.

1. The outgoing packet reaches the router and is evaluated against the outgoing access list (inspected by CBAC) and is permitted.

2. Information is recorded including the source and destination IP address and port numbers. The information is recorded in a state table entry created for the new connection.

3. A temporary access list entry is created based on this state information. This access list entry is placed at the beginning of the Extended access list on the routers external interface.

4. This temporary opening is designed to permit inbound packets that are part of the same connection as the outbound packet that was inspected previously. The outbound packet now leaves the interface.

5. The return packet is tested against the inbound access list and permitted because of the temporary access list previously created. Here CBAC will modify the state table and inbound access list if necessary.

6. All inbound and outbound traffic in the future will be tested; therefore the state table access list will be modified as required.

7. When the connection is closed, the state table entry is deleted along with the temporary access list.

Configuring Control-Based Access Control

There are several steps to follow here. We must specify which protocols you want to be inspected. We must also specify an interface and direction where the inspection originates. Context-Based Access Control will inspect only the protocols we specify here. For the specified protocols, packets entering or exiting the router are inspected. They must flow through the interface where inspection is configured. Refer to Figure 8.10. The packets must pass the inbound access list applied on the interface to be inspected by Context-Based Access Control. If a packet is denied by the access list, the packet is dropped and Context-Based Access Control will have no effect.

Figure 8.10 Configuring Control-Based Access Control.

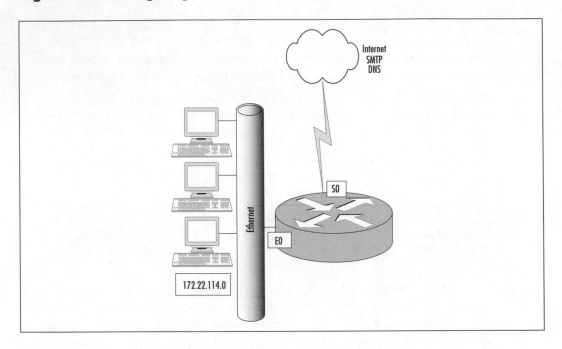

1. **Choose the interface** Here the decision is to configure CBAC on an internal or external interface such as Ethernet 0 or Serial 0. The internal interface is where the client sessions originate. The external interface is where the client sessions exit the router. In most cases, CBAC will be configured on the external interface, inspecting any traffic entering the network.

2. **Configure Access Lists** When using CBAC, the access list must be configured for both inbound and outbound traffic to operate properly. The traffic to be inspected by CBAC is specified in the outbound or inbound access list. The outbound access list may be a standard or extended IP access list. The temporary openings are created and managed by CBAC with the inbound access list. This must be an extended IP access list. It is important to note that an access list filtering inbound traffic could be applied either inbound (on the untrusted interface) or outbound (on the trusted interface).

3. **Configuring Global Timeouts and Thresholds** CBAC uses timeouts and thresholds to determine the duration of an inactive session before it is deleted. CBAC helps prevent Denial of Service (DoS) attacks. This is accomplished by monitoring the number and frequency of half-open connections. For example, when using TCP,

an example of a half-opened session is one that has not completed the three-way handshake, or if using UDP, a session in which the firewall has not detected return traffic. CBAC counts both TCP and UDP when determining the number of half-open sessions. Half-open sessions are monitored only for connections configured for inspection by CBAC. These timeouts and thresholds apply globally to all sessions. You can use the default timeout and threshold values, or you can change to values more suitable to your security requirements. You should make any changes to the timeout and threshold values before you continue configuring CBAC. Table 8.16 lists available CBAC commands used to configure timeouts and thresholds.

4. **Inspection Rules** After configuring global timeouts and thresholds, you must define an inspection rule. This specifies which application-layer protocols will be tested by CBAC at an interface. Typically you define only one inspection rule. One exception might be if you want to enable CBAC in two directions—in this case, you should define two rules, one in each direction. The inspection rule should specify each desired application-layer protocol as well as TCP or UDP if desired. The inspection rule consists of a series of statements each listing a protocol and specifying the same inspection rule name. Included here are rules for controlling alert and audit trail messages and for checking IP packet fragmentation.

Table 8.16 Available Timeout Commands and Thresholds

Command	Description	Default Values
IP inspect tcp synwait-time *seconds*	Length of time of wait for TCP session to establish	30 seconds
IP inspect tcp finwait time *seconds*	Length of time TCP is managed after FIN-exchange	5 seconds
IP inspect tcp idle-time *seconds*	TCP idle timeout	3600 seconds
IP inspect udp idle-time *seconds*	UDP idle timeout	30 seconds
IP inspect dns-timeout *seconds*	DNS lookup idle timer	5 seconds
IP inspect max-incomplete high *number*	Max number of half-open connections before CBAC begins closing connections	500 sessions

Continued

Table 8.16 Continued

Command	Description	Default Values
IP inspect max-incomplete low *number*	Max number of half-open connections causing CBAC to stop closing connections	400 sessions
IP inspect one-minute high *number*	Rate of half-open sessions per minute before CBAC begins closing connections	500 sessions
IP inspect one-minute low *number*	Rate of half-open sessions per minute causing CBAC to stop deleting connections.	400 sessions
IP inspect tcp max-incomplete host *number* block-time *seconds*	Number of existing half-open sessions with the same destination address before CBAC begins closing sessions	50 sessions

Inspection Rules

The following is the format for defining inspection rules:

```
ip inspect name inspection-name protocol [alert {on|off} [audit-
trail{on|off}][timeout seconds]
```

The keyword **alert** allows CBAC to send messages to a syslog server when a violation occurs in a monitored application. Each application will have an individual alert the router will send to the server for illegal conditions. The keyword **audit trail** permits the tracking of connections used for a protected application. Here the router logs information about each connection including ports used, number of bytes transferred, and source and destination IP address. A key issue here is if a large amount of traffic is being monitored, the logging produced will be significant!

Applying the Inspection Rule

Now that we have defined the inspection rule, the final step is to apply it to an interface. Apply the inspection rule the same way we apply access lists on the interface. You must also specify inbound for traffic entering the interface, or outbound for traffic exiting the interface. The command is as follows:

```
ip inspect inspection-name {in | out}
```

The following is an example of performing Java blocking. A list of permitted IP addresses must be created using a standard IP access list.

access-list list-number {permit | deny} source-address [wildcard-mask][log]

ip inspect name inspection-name **http** [**java**-list access-list] [alert {on | off}] [audit-trail {on | off}] [**timeout** seconds}

By default an undefined access list in the java-list definition will deny all Java applets. CBAC can block only Java applets, not ActiveX.

There are several commands that are useful in gathering information about CBAC. The **sh ip inspect config** will be discussed first. This command allows all specific portions of a configuration. An example would be as follows:

Router# sh ip inspect config

Session alert is enabled

One-minute (sampling period) thresholds are [400:500] connections

max-incomplete sessions thresholds are [400:500]

max- incomplete tcp connections per host is 50.

Block-time 0 minute.

tcp synwait-time is 30 sec - tcp finwait - time is 5 sec

tcp idle - time is 3600 sec - udp idle - time is 30 sec

dns - timeout is 5 seconds

The **show ip inspect interfaces** command shows the interfaces that CBAC inspection is configured. An example would be as follows:

Router# sh ip inspect interfaces

Interface FastEthernet 3/0

Inbound inspection rule is Protector

tcp alert is on audit-trail is off timeout 3600

udp alert is on audit-trail is CBAC off timeout 30

fragment Maximum 50 In Use 0 alert is on audit-trail is off timeout 1

Inbound access list is 114

Outbound access list is not set

Refer to the section, "Protecting Public Servers Connected to the Internet" for the required configuration for CBAC.

Configuring Port to Application Mapping

A limitation of CBAC is the fact that only services running on standard ports can be controlled. For example, traffic going to a Web server running on a port other than the standard Hypertext Transfer Protocol (HTTP) port (80) cannot be inspected and protected using CBAC. Port to Application Mapping (PAM) can be used to override this limitation. Port to Application Mapping gives you the capability to customize TCP or UDP port numbers for network services or applications. Upon startup, PAM will build a table of ports associated with their default applications, known as a PAM table or database. Kept in this table are all of the services supported by CBAC. Here is where the link with CBAC comes into play. The information built in the PAM table will give CBAC the ability to function on a nonstandard port. If you are running applications on nonstandard ports, PAM and CBAC have the ability to work together to identify the ports associated with their applications. Without the use of PAM, CBAC is limited to well-known ports and their applications.

PAM comes standard with the Cisco Secure Integrated Software Feature Set. Network services or applications that use nonstandard ports will require you to place entries in the PAM table manually. You can also specify a range of ports used by an application by establishing a separate entry in the PAM table for each port number in the range. All manual entries are saved with the default mapping information when you save the router configuration, so upon startup, the mapping will be in the PAM table. If you use an application that requires a nonstandard port, you will need to enter this manually in the PAM table (for example, if you use the Telnet application with port 8000 instead of port 23).

Configuring PAM

When configuring PAM the following format is used:

```
ip port-map application_name port port number m
```

Next, we map well-known port 23 (Telnet) to port 8000:

```
ip port-map telnet port 8000
```

Let's take this example a step further, and define a range of nonstandard ports for well-known port 23. An example looks as follows:

```
Ip port-map telnet port 8001
Ip port-map telnet port 8002
```

```
Ip port-map telnet port 8003
Ip port-map telnet port 8004
```

We also have the option of mapping an application to a port for a specific host or subnet. Mapping an application to a host would look as follows:

```
Access-list 1 permit 172.16.144.1
Ip port-map Telnet port 8000 list 1
```

When mapping to a specific subnet the list looks like:

```
Access-list 1 permit 172.16.144.0
Ip port-map Telnet port 8000 list 1
```

Protecting a Private Network

Typically, when protecting a private network, a standard or Extended access list is all that is necessary. You can create an access list that allows traffic from only three subnets, for example. The access list may look as follows:

```
access-list 7 permit 172.17.0.0
access-list 7 permit 192.168.200.0
access-list 7 permit 10.0.0.0
```

Protecting a Network Connected to the Internet

We are not concerned with restricting packets going *out* to the Internet; we are only interested in restricting what comes *in*. Let's say we want to allow external users to establish TCP connections to a server for HTTP access to our Web page, and Telnet and SMTP sessions for mail. We also need to allow UDP packets to pass for DNS traffic. Remember, we are concerned with TCP ports 80 (HTTP), 23 (Telnet), and 25 (SMTP). Our access list needs to permit connections using ports 80, 23, and 25 to the IP address of the server only, and apply that access list to packets inbound. Our access list looks as follows:

```
access-list 111 permit tcp any host 201.12.12.1 eq 80
access-list 111 permit tcp any host 201.12.12.1 eq 23
access-list 111 permit tcp any host 210.12.12.1 eq 25
access-list 111 permit udp any host 210.12.12.1 eq 53
Router(config)# interface so
Router (config-if)# ip access-group 111 in
```

Protecting Server Access Using Lock and Key

Here our organization has a router with two Ethernet segments. One is attached to interface E0 (172.16.4.0) and the other attached to E1 (215.31.12.0). We also have an Internet connection on serial interface 0 (11.1.2.34). We need to restrict when we allow external users to connect to the server using the IP address 172.16.4.1. Also, we want our internal users on the 215.31.12.0 network access to the Internet other than WWW and FTP sites, so here we will use FTP passive mode. We also need to block access from E0 to E1. Our access list may look as follows:

```
access-list 118 permit tcp any host 11.1.2.34 eq telnet
access-list 118 permit udp any eq 53 215.31.12.0 0.0.0.255 gt 1023
access-list 118 permit tcp any 215.31.12.0 0.0.0.255 gt 1023
established
access-list 118 dynamic test timeout 90 permit ip any host 172.16.4.1
time-range my-time log
access-list 118 deny ip any 215.31.12.0 0.0.0.255
access-list 118 permit tcp any any established
time-range my-time
periodic weekdays 8:00 to 18:00
line vty 0 2
login local
autocommand  access-enable host timeout 10
line vty 3 4
login local
rotary 1
```

Protecting Public Servers Connected to the Internet

Here we have serial interface 0 on our router connected to the Internet, and Ethernet interface 0 connected to our internal network. Refer back to Figure 8.10. We need to permit our internal users to access the Internet for Web browsing, e-mail, and FTP. We also want to know how much FTP traffic is in use. The internal users need to be able to ping and traceroute to hosts on the Internet for troubleshooting purposes. We have no internal servers, so all services are provided by the ISP. Our access list looks as follows:

```
ip inspect alert-off

ip inspect name protector ftp audit-trail on

ip inspect name protector smtp

ip inspect name protector udp

ip inspect name protector tcp

interface Ethernet 0

ip address 172..22.14.1 255.255.255.0

ip access-group 111 in

interface serial 0

ip address 12.1.1.1 255.255.255.252

ip inspect protector out

ip access-group 112 in

ip access-list 1 permit 209.12.12.0 0.0.0.255

ip access-list 111 permit ip any any

ip access-list 112 permit icmp any any echo-reply

ip access-list 112 permit icmp any any time-exceeded

ip access-list 112 permit icmp any any unreachable
```

Summary

A Standard IP access list filters on source IP address only. With Extended access lists we have the capability of filtering on source and destination address along with specific protocols, source and destination port. Named access lists are beneficial to the administrator when dealing with a large number of access lists for ease of identification, and are also helpful if using Extended access lists. Another advantage of named access lists is that, unlike numbered access lists, they allow you to delete one statement within the access list to modify it. Lock and Key access lists offer our first look at enhanced access-list capability. Lock and Key are also known as Dynamic access lists that create dynamic entries. Traditional access lists do not offer this capability; with a traditional access list, the entry remains until you delete it manually. Dynamic access lists create a temporary, specific opening in an access list after a user is authenticated.

Reflexive access lists create dynamic openings for IP traffic on one side of a router, based on sessions originating from a different side of the router.

CBAC can be used with multiple applications and provides a higher level of security than a traditional access list. Here we create dynamic openings in an inbound access-list in response to an outbound data connection. Traffic is permitted from untrusted networks to our internal network only when traffic is part of a session that was initiated from the internal network.

FAQs

Q: I have created my access list and there seems to be no effect on traffic entering or exiting the router. What could be the problem?

A: After creating the access list globally on the router, you must remember to apply the access list to an interface and give a direction (inbound or outbound). The default direction for access lists is outbound.

Q: After applying an access list on our enterprise router, there has been a drastic decrease in throughput. What could be a potential problem here?

A: First recall how an access list works. An access list utilizes top-down processing when testing traffic. Typically on an enterprise router an access list can get quite lengthy. One problem could be that the majority of your traffic is permitted or denied near the end of the access list. When creating an access list it is important to test the majority of your traffic first.

Q: A customer wants us to configure an access list that has an opening only when a user establishes an outbound Telnet session. What type of access list could apply here?

A: A Reflexive access list would be a good choice. When using Reflexive access lists, an entry is created, enabling inbound return traffic.

Chapter 9

Configuring and Securing the Cisco PIX Firewall

Solutions in this chapter:

- Overview of the Security Features

- Performing the Initial Configuration

- Configuring NAT and NAPT

- Configuring your Security Policy

- PIX Configuration Examples

- Securing and Maintaining the PIX

Introduction

A firewall is a security mechanism located on a network that protects resources from other networks and individuals. A firewall controls access to a network and enforces a security policy that can be tailored to suit the needs of a company.

There is some confusion on the difference between a Cisco PIX firewall and a router. Both devices are capable of filtering traffic with access control lists, and both devices are capable of providing Network Address Translation (NAT). PIX, however, goes above and beyond simply filtering packets, based on source/destination IP addresses, as well as source/destination Transmission Control Protocol/User Datagram Protocol (TCP/UDP) port numbers. PIX is a dedicated hardware device built to provide security. Although a router can also provide some of the functions of a PIX by implementing access control lists, it also has to deal with routing packets from one network to another. Depending on what model of router is being used, access lists tend to burden the CPU, especially if numerous access lists must be referenced for every packet that travels through the router. This can impact the performance of the router, causing other problems such as network convergence time. A router is also unable to provide security features such as URL, ActiveX, and Java filtering; Flood Defender, Flood Guard, and IP Frag Guard; and DNS Guard, Mail Guard, Failover, and FTP and URL logging.

Cisco Systems offers a number of security solutions for networks. Included in those solutions are the Cisco Secure PIX Firewall series. The PIX firewall is a dedicated hardware-based firewall that utilizes a version of the Cisco IOS for configuration and operation. This chapter will introduce and discuss security features, Network Address Translation (NAT), Network Address Port Translation (NAPT, or referred to as PAT on the PIX firewall IOS), developing a security policy for your network, applying the security policy on the PIX, and finally, maintaining your PIX and securing it from unauthorized individuals.

The PIX Firewall series offers several models to meet today's networks' needs, from the Enterprise-class Secure PIX 520 Firewall to the newly introduced Small Office/Home Office (SOHO) class Secure PIX 506 Firewall model.

- **520 and 520 DC** The largest of the PIX Firewall series, it is meant for Enterprise and Internet Service Provider (ISP) use. It has a throughput of 385 Mbps and will handle up to 250,000 simultaneous sessions. The hardware specifications include two Fast Ethernet ports, 128MB of RAM, a floppy disk drive for upgrading

the IOS image, and support for up to six additional network interface cards in the chassis. Additionally, other available interfaces
are 10/100 Ethernet cards, Token Ring cards, and dual-attached
multimode FDDI cards.

- **515R and 515UR** This particular model is intended for small- to
  medium-sized businesses and remote offices. The 515R and
  515UR have a throughput of 120 Mbps with the capacity to handle
  up to 125,000 simultaneous connections. The hardware specifications include two Fast Ethernet 10/100 ports, 32MB of RAM for
  the 515R and 64MB of RAM for the 515UR model, and will support
  up to two additional network interface cards in the chassis.
  Additionally, 10/100 Ethernet cards are available, but Token Ring
  cards are not supported on the 515 model.

- **506** The most recent addition to the Secure PIX Firewall series is
  the 506, intended for high-end small office/home office use, with a
  throughput measured at 10 Mbps. The 506 offers two Fast
  Ethernet 10/100 ports, and does not support any additional network interface cards in the chassis. The 506 comes with 32MB of
  RAM and does not support additional RAM upgrades.

Overview of the Security Features

With the enormous growth of the Internet, companies are beginning to
depend on having an online presence on the Internet. With that presence
come security risks that allow outside individuals to gain access to critical
information and resources.

Companies are now faced with the task of implementing security measures to protect their data and resources. These resources can be very
diversified, such as Web servers, mail servers, FTP servers, databases, or
any type of networked devices. Figure 9.1 displays a typical company network with access to the Internet via a leased line without a firewall in
place.

As you can see in Figure 9.1, company XYZ has a direct connection to
the Internet. They are also using a class C public IP address space for
their network, therefore making it publicly available to anyone who wishes
to access it. Without any security measures, individuals are able to access
each of the devices on the network with a public IP. Private information
can be compromised, and other malicious attacks such as Denial of
Service (DoS) can occur. If a firewall was placed between company XYZ's
network and the Internet, security measures can then be taken to filter
and block unwanted traffic. Without any access control at the network

perimeter, a company's security relies on proper configuration and security on each individual host and server. This can be an administrative night-mare if hundreds of devices need to be configured for this purpose.

Figure 9.1 Typical LAN with no firewall.

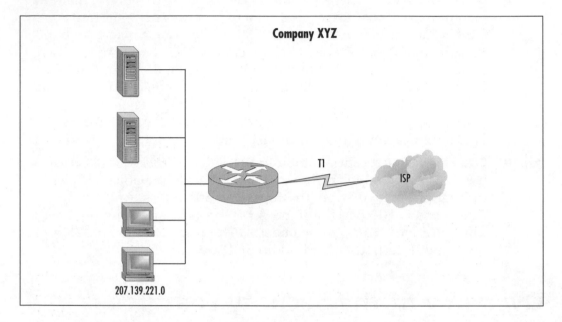

Routers have the ability to filter traffic based on source address, desti-nation address, and TCP/UDP ports. Using that ability as well as a firewall can provide a more complete security solution for a network.

Another example of how a PIX firewall can secure a network is in a company's intranet. Figure 9.2 illustrates a network in which departments are separated by two different subnets. What is stopping an individual from the Human Resources network from accessing resources on the Finance network? A firewall can be put in place between the two subnets to secure the Finance network from any unauthorized access or to restrict access to certain hosts.

Since the PIX is designed as a security appliance, it provides a wealth of features to secure a network, including:

- **Packet filtering**, a method for limiting inbound information from the Internet. Packet filters use access control lists (ACLs) similar to those used in routers to accept or deny access based on packet source address, destination address, and TCP/UDP source and destination port.

Figure 9.2 LAN segmented by a department with no firewall.

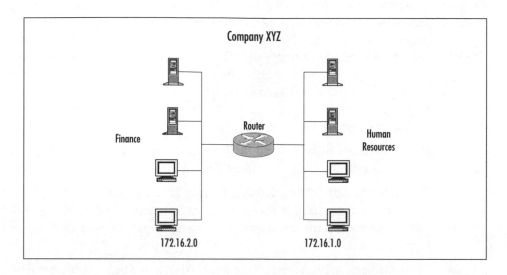

- **Proxy server**, a device that examines higher layers of the Open
  Systems Interconnection (OSI) model. This will act as an interme-
  diary between the source and destination by creating a separate
  connection to each. Optionally, authentication can be achieved by
  requiring users to authenticate with a secure system by means of
  a proxy such as a Cisco IOS Firewall Authentication Proxy Server.
  Some of the drawbacks for this method of security are that it provides authentication at the cost of performance, and that a proxy
  supports only a limited number of protocols.

- **Stateful filtering**, a secure method of analyzing packets and
  placing extensive information about that packet in a table. Each
  time a TCP connection is established from an inside host accessing
  an outside host through the PIX firewall, the information about the
  connection automatically is logged in a stateful session flow table.
  The table contains the source and destination addresses, port
  numbers, TCP sequencing information, and additional flags for
  each TCP connection associated with that particular host. Inbound
  packets are compared against the session flows in the table and
  are permitted through the PIX only if an appropriate connection
  exists to validate their passage. Without stateful filtering, access
  lists would have to be configured to allow traffic originating from
  the inside network to return from the outside network.

- **Network Address Translation and Network Address Port Translation.** Using NAT is often mistaken as a security measure. Translating private IP addresses into global IP addresses was implemented to assist in the problem of rapidly depleting public IP addresses. Even though private IP addresses are used for an inside network, an ISP is still directly connected. It is not unheard of that a sloppy routing configuration on behalf of the ISP will leak a route to your network, to other clients. NAT will hide your network, but it should not be relied upon as a security measure.

- **IPSec**, which provides VPN (Virtual Private Network) access via digital certificates or preshared keys.

- **Flood Defender, Flood Guard, and IP Frag Guard**, which protect a network from TCP SYN flood attacks, controlling the AAA service's tolerance for unanswered login attempts and IP fragmentation attacks.

- **DNS Guard**, which identifies an outbound DNS resolve request, and allows only a single DNS response.

- **FTP and URL logging**, which allow you to view inbound and outbound FTP commands entered by users, as well as the URLs they use to access other sites.

- **Mail Guard**, which provides safe access for SMTP (Simple Mail Transfer Protocol) connections from the outside to an inside e-mail server.

- **ActiveX Blocking**, which blocks HTML *object* commands and comments them out of the HTML Web page.

- **Java Filtering**, which allows an administrator to prevent Java applets from being downloaded by a host on the inside network.

- **URL Filtering.** When used with NetPartners WebSENSE product, PIX checks outgoing URL requests with policy defined on the WebSENSE server, which runs on either Windows NT/2000 or UNIX.

- **AAA**, which provides authentication, authorization, and accounting with the aid of an AAA server such as a RADIUS or TACACS+ server.

Differences between IOS 4.x and 5.x

The following new features are available in the recent release of the PIX IOS:

- Cisco IOS access lists
- IPSec
- Stateful fail-over
- Voice-over IP support

Cisco IOS access lists can now be specified in support of the IPSec feature. In addition, access lists can now be used to specify the type of traffic permitted through the PIX in conjunction with the **access-group** command. IOS 4.x used **conduit** and **outbound** statements to limit the type of traffic permitted through the interface. For example, the following command set can be rewritten using **access-list** and **access-group** statements.

```
pixfirewall(config)#write terminal
static (inside,outside) 207.139.221.10 192.168.0.10 netmask
>255.255.255.255
```

Create a static translation for private 192.168.0.10 to globally unique IP 207.139.221.10.

```
conduit permit tcp any host 207.139.221.10 eq www
```

Specify that only HTTP traffic will be permitted to reach host 207.139.221.10.

```
outbound 10 permit any any 80 tcp
outbound 10 permit any any 23 tcp
outbound 10 deny any any any tcp
outbound 10 deny any any any udp
```

Specify that HTTP and Telnet traffic will be permitted from a higher level security interface to a lower level security interface (inside, outside), followed by an explicit **deny all** statement.

```
apply (inside) 10 outgoing_src
```

Apply outbound list 10 to inside interface. This configuration can be rewritten using **access-list** and **access-group** commands available in 5.x IOS.

```
pixfirewall(config)#write terminal
static (inside,outside) 207.139.221.10 192.168.0.10 netmask
>255.255.255.255
```

Create a static translation for private 192.168.0.10 to globally unique IP 207.139.221.10.

```
access-list acl_out permit tcp any any eq www
access-list acl_out permit tcp any any eq telnet
access-list acl_out deny tcp any any
access-list acl_out deny udp any any
```

Specify that HTTP and Telnet traffic will be permitted, followed by an explicit **deny all** statement.

```
access-list acl_in permit tcp any host 207.139.221.10 eq www
access-list acl_in permit tcp any host 207.139.221.10 eq ftp
```

Specify that HTTP and FTP traffic will be permitted from any source to host 207.139.221.10.

```
access-group acl_out in interface inside
```

Apply access list acl_out to the inside interface.

```
access-group acl_in in interface outside
```

Apply access list acl_in to the outside interface.

Using the **access-list** and **access-group** commands instead of the **outbound** and **conduit** statements provides a common operating environment across various platforms. If an individual is able to implement access lists on a router, then implementing access lists on a PIX should be no different.

The IPSec feature is based on the Cisco IOS IPSec implementation and provides functionality with those IPSec-compliant devices. IPSec provides a mechanism for secure data transmission by providing confidentiality, integrity, and authenticity of data across a public IP network. Refer to Chapter 3 for more information on IPSec and VPNs.

The stateful fail-over feature provides a mechanism for hardware and software redundancy by allowing two identical PIX units to serve the same functionality in case one fails in an unattended environment. One PIX is considered an active unit and the other is in standby mode. In the event that the active unit fails, the standby unit becomes active, therefore providing redundancy.

PIX provides support for Voice-over IP in its H.323 RAS feature; however, Cisco CallManager is not supported. For more information on Voice-over IP, please refer to Cisco's Web site (www.cisco.com).

Other new commands that were introduced in the 5.x IOS are as follows:

- **ca**, which provides access to the IPSec certification authority feature.

- **Clear flashfs**, which clears Flash memory. Use before downgrading to any version 4.x release.

- **Crypto-map**, which provides IPSec cryptography mapping.

- **Debug crypto ca**, which debugs certification authority (CA) processing.

- **Debug crypto ipsec**, which debugs IPSec processing.

- **Debug crypto isakmp**, which debugs ISAKMP processing.

- **Domain-name**, which changes the domain name.

- **Failover link**, which enables stateful fail-over support.

- **Ipsec**, which is shortened for the **cyrpto ipsec** command.

- **Isakmp**, which lets you create an IKE security association.

- **Sysopt connection permit-ipsec**, which specifies that the PIX implicitly permit IPSec traffic and bypass the checking of the **conduit** or **access-group** commands that are associated with IPSec connections.

Initial Configuration

The initial configuration of the Secure PIX Firewall greatly resembles that of a router. A console cable kit consisting of a rollover cable and DB9/DB25 serial adapter is needed to configure the device out of the box. It is recommended that the initial configuration not take place on a live network until the initial set up has been completed and tested. Initial configuration should take place in a test bed environment, which is isolated from any production network. If initial configuration takes place on a production network and an incorrect IP address is assigned to an interface on the PIX, and is already in use on the network, IP address conflicts will occur. It is generally a bad idea to set up a firewall or other security device on a nonisolated network. The default configuration is often not secure and can be compromised between the set-up stage and the security-policy stage. Installing the PIX consists of removing the unit from the packaging, installing any optional hardware such as an additional NIC, mounting the PIX in a rack (optional), and connecting all the necessary cables such as power and network cables. Once the hardware portion of the PIX setup has been completed the software portion of the setup can begin.

Before configuring the software, be sure to have a design plan already in place. Items such as IP addresses, security policies, and placement of the PIX should already be mapped out. With a proper design strategy the basic configuration will have to be done only once to make the PIX functional.

Installing the PIX Software

In this section we will discuss the initial software configuration of the PIX to allow traffic to pass through it. Other features such as configuring NAT, NAPT, and Security Policies will be covered later in this chapter.

When the PIX is first powered on, the software configuration stored in Flash memory permits the PIX to start up, but will not allow any traffic to pass through it until configured to do so. Newer versions of the IOS may be available from Cisco depending on what version shipped with the PIX, so it may be a good idea to complete the basic configuration to establish connectivity and then upgrade the version of the IOS.

Basic Configuration

We will now detail the basic configuration of the PIX on how to connect to it as well as how to identify each interface.

Connect to the PIX

To upgrade the IOS or to begin allowing traffic to pass through the PIX, some basic configuration is needed to make the PIX operational.

1. Connect the serial port of your PC to the console port on the PIX firewall with the serial cable supplied with the PIX.

2. Using a Terminal Emulation program such as HyperTerminal, connect to the COM port on the PC.

NOTE

Make sure the COM port properties in the terminal emulation program match the following values:

- 9600 baud
- 8 data bits
- No parity
- 1 stop bit
- Hardware flow control

3. Turn on the PIX.

4. Once the PIX has finished booting up, you will be prompted as follows:

   ```
   pixfirewall>
   ```

5. Type **enable** and press the Enter key. The follow prompt appears:

   ```
   Password:
   ```

6. Press the Enter key again and you will now be in privileged mode, which is represented by the following prompt:

   ```
   pixfirewall#
   ```

7. Set an enable password by going into configuration mode. A good, nonguessable password should be chosen. The example uses <password> to designate where your password should be typed.

   ```
   pixfirewall#configure terminal
   pixfirewall(config)#enable password <password>
   ```

8. Permit Telnet access to the console from the inside network:

   ```
   pixfirewall(config)#telnet 0.0.0.0 0.0.0.0 inside
   ```

9. Set the Telnet console password. This password should be different from the enable password chosen in step 7.

   ```
   pixfirewall(config)#passwd  <password>
   ```

10. Save your changes to NVRAM with the **write** command:

    ```
    pixfirewall(config)#write memory
    ```

NOTE

The configuration used in the following examples is based on IOS version 5.1(1).

Identify Each Interface

On new installations with only two interfaces, PIX will provide names for each interface by default. These can be viewed with the **show nameif** command. The **show nameif** command output will resemble the following:

```
pixfirewall# show nameif
nameif ethernet0 outside security0
nameif ethernet1 inside security100
```

If additional NICs are going to be used, you must assign a unique name and security value to each additional interface.

The default behavior of the PIX includes blocking traffic originating from the *outside* interface destined for the *inside* interface. Traffic originating from the *inside* interface destined to the *outside* interface will be permitted until access lists are implemented to restrict traffic. The inside interface will be assigned a security value of 100 and the outside interface will be assigned a value of 0. These values are important when creating security policies in which traffic will flow from a lower security interface to higher security level interface. If additional interfaces are added to the PIX, it is important to properly plan which interfaces will be used for what purposes. For example, in a situation where three interfaces are used to separate an inside network, outside network, and DMZ (discussed later in this chapter), assign the DMZ interface a security value between the inside and outside interfaces, such as 50. This configuration will reflect the purpose of the DMZ, which is a network separated from the inside and outside networks, yet security can still be controlled with the PIX.

To assign a name to an interface use:

Nameif hardware_id name security_level

where:

- *Hardware_id* is either **ethernet***n* for Ethernet or **token***x* for Token Ring interfaces, where *n* and *x* are the interface numbers.

- *Name* is the name to be assigned to the interface.

- *Security_level* is a value such as **security40** or **security60**. You can use any security value between 1 and 99.

```
pixfirewall#configure terminal
pixfirewall(config)#nameif ethernet2 dmz1 security40
pixfurewall(config)#show nameif
pixfirewall(config)#nameif ethernet0 outside security0
```

```
pixfirewall(config)#nameif ethernet1 inside security100
pixfurewall(config)#nameif ethernet2 dmz1 security40
```

Be sure to use a naming convention that will easily describe the function of each interface. The dmz1 interface represents a *demilitarized zone*, which is intended to be an area between the inside and outside networks. This is a common implementation for companies that host Web servers, mail servers, and other resources.

By default each interface is in a shutdown state and must be made active. Use the **interface** command to activate the interfaces:

```
Interface hardware_id hardware_speed [shutdown]
```

where:

- *Hardware_id* is either **ethernet**n for Ethernet or **token**x for Token Ring interfaces.

- *Hardware_speed* is either **4mpbs** or **16mpbs** for Token Ring, depending on the line speed of the Token Ring card, or, if the interface is Ethernet, use **auto**.

- **Auto** activates auto-negotiation for the Ethernet 10/100 interface.

- **Shutdown** disables the interface. When the PIX is configured for the first time, all interfaces will be shutdown by default.

The following examples will enable the **ethernet0** interface into auto negotiation mode, and the Token Ring interface token into 16 Mbps mode.

```
pixfirewall(config)#interface ethernet0 auto
pixfirewall(config)#interface token0 16mpbs
```

Installing the IOS over TFTP

The follow steps will guide you through upgrading the PIX IOS.

1. Download the latest version of the IOS from Cisco's Web site (www.cisco.com).

2. Download and install the TFTP server application, which can also be found on Cisco's Web site. The TFTP server is an application

that is installed on a host computer to provide a TFTP service. This service is used by the PIX firewall to download or upload software images and configuration parameters.

NOTE

You need to download the TFTP server software if you are using a Windows NT/2000 machine as a server. A UNIX server has a TFTP server by default.

3. Make sure the TFTP software is running on a server. Also confirm that the server is on the same subnet as one of the interfaces.

4. Once the connection to the PIX console port has been established, power on the PIX.

5. Immediately send a BREAK character by pressing the Escape (ESC) key. The monitor prompt will appear.

6. Use the **address** command to specify an IP address on the interface in the same network where the TFTP resides.

7. Use the **server** command to specify the IP address of the TFTP server.

8. Use the **file** command to specify the name of the file to download from the TFTP server.

9. If the TFTP server resides on a different subnet than that of the PIX interface, use the **gateway** command to specify the IP address of the default gateway in order to reach the TFTP server.

10. To test connectivity, use the **ping** command to ping the TFTP server.

11. Finally, use the **TFTP** command to start the TFTP download of the IOS.

For example, assume that the TFTP server has been configured with the IP address 172.16.0.39, and that a new software image file *pix512.bin* is stored on that server. We can download this new image on the PIX as follows:

```
monitor>
monitor>address 172.16.0.1
monitor>server 172.16.0.39
```

```
monitor>file pix512.bin

monitor>ping 172.16.0.39

Sending 5, 100-byte 0x5b8d ICMP Echoes to 172.16.0.39, timeout is 4
seconds:

!!!!!

Success rate is 100 percent (5/5)

monitor>tftp

tftp pix512.bin@172.16.0.39.............................

Received 626688 bytes


PIX admin loader (3.0) #0: Mon July 10 10:43:02 PDT 2000

Flash=AT29C040A @ 0x300

Flash version 4.9.9.1, Install version 5.1.2


Installing to flash
```

The following commands are available in monitor mode:

- **Address** Set IP address.
- **File** Specify boot file name.
- **Gateway** Set gateway IP address.
- **Help** List available help commands and syntax.
- **Interface** Specify type of interface (Ethernet, Token Ring).
- **Ping** Test connectivity by issuing echo-requests to a specified IP address.
- **Reload** Halt and reload system.
- **Server** Specify server by the IP address in which the TFTP application is running.
- **Tftp** Initiate the TFTP download.
- **Trace** Toggle packet tracing.

Command Line Interface

The Command Line Interface (CLI) used on the PIX is very similar to the one used on routers. Three modes exist in order to perform configuration and troubleshooting steps: unprivileged, privileged, and configuration. When you first initiate a console or Telnet session to the PIX, you will be in unprivileged mode. Virtually no commands will be available in unprivileged mode; only the **enable, pager,** and **quit** commands are permitted. Once in privileged mode, commands such as **show, debug,** and **reload** are available. From privileged mode, configuration tasks may take place by entering the **configure** command followed by the location from which the PIX will accept configuration commands. For example, when you first connect to the PIX either through a Telnet or console session, you will be in unprivileged mode (unprivileged mode password must be entered when accessing the PIX by Telnet). Unprivileged mode is represented by the following prompt:

```
Pixfirewall>
```

To access privileged mode, you must type **enable** at the prompt. After providing the required authentication you will be in privileged mode. Privileged mode is represented by the following prompt:

```
Pixfirewall>enable
Password: ********
Pixfirewall#
```

If the system did not request a password after typing **enable**, it means that no enable password has been configured as described earlier in the section, "Basic Configuration." It is very important that an enable password be configured.

Finally, to perform configuration tasks, you must be in configuration mode. This mode is represented by the following prompt:

```
Pixfirewall#configure terminal
Pixfirewall(config)#
```

Table 9.1 lists some of the shortcut key combinations that are available on the PIX CLI.

Table 9.1 Key Combination Shortcuts

Command	Result
TAB	Completes a command entry
Ctrl + A	Takes cursor to beginning of the line
Ctrl + E	Takes cursor to end of the line
Ctrl + R	Redisplays a line (useful if command gets interrupted by console output)

Continued

Table 9.1 Continued

Command	Result
Arrow up or Ctrl + P	Displays previous line
Arrow up or Ctrl + N	Displays next line
Help or ?	Displays help

IP Configuration

Once the interfaces on the PIX have been named and assigned a security value (additional interfaces only), IP must be configured on the interfaces in order to allow traffic to pass through the PIX.

IP Address

Once the interfaces have been named and are activated, an IP address needs to be assigned to them. To assign an IP address to an interface, use the command:

ip address interface-name netmask

where:

- *Interface-name* is the name assigned to the interface using the **nameif** command.

- *Netmask* is the network mask that will be assigned to the interface.

```
pixfirewall(config)#interface ethernet0 auto
pixfirewall(config)#interface ethernet1 auto
pixfirewall(config)#ip address inside 172.16.0.1 255.255.255.0
pixfirewall(config)#ip address outside 207.139.221.1 255.255.255.0
pixfirewall(config)#show interface ethernet1
interface ethernet1 "inside" is up, line protocol is up
   Hardware is i82559 ethernet, address is 0050.54ff.2aa9
   IP address 172.16.0.1, subnet mask 255.255.255.0
   MTU 1500 bytes, BW 100000 Kbit full duplex
         147022319 packets input, 3391299957 bytes, 0 no buffer
         Received 12580140 broadcasts, 0 runts, 0 giants
         0 input errors, 0 CRC, 0 frame, 0 overrun, 0 ignored, 0 abort
```

```
166995559 packets output, 1686643683 bytes, 0 underruns

0 output errors, 0 collisions, 0 interface resets

0 babbles, 0 late collisions, 0 deferred

0 lost carrier, 0 no carrier
```

Once the interfaces have been configured, test them to make sure they have been configured properly. A simple connectivity test is to ping another interface on your network or test lab environment. To do this:

Ping interface ip_address

where:

- *Interface* is the interface from which you want the ping to originate (similar to an extended ping on a router).

- *Ip_address* is the target IP address to ping.

```
pixfirewall#ping inside 172.16.0.2

        172.16.0.2 response received — 0ms

        172.16.0.2 response received — 0ms

        172.16.0.2 response received — 0ms
```

If no response is received, confirm that the network cables are connected to the interfaces and that the interfaces have been configured correctly.

```
pixfirewall#ping inside 172.16.0.4

        172.16.0.4 NO response received — 940ms

        172.16.0.4 NO response received — 900ms

        172.16.0.4 NO response received — 920ms
```

Default Route

Now that all the interfaces have been configured, a default gateway must be assigned. A typical implementation will have a PIX firewall positioned between the ISP and the company's network (see Figure 9.3).

A default gateway must be assigned to the outside interface to allow traffic to reach the ISP. To do this use the command:

route interface_name ip_address netmask gateway_ip [metric]

where:

- *Interface_name* is the internal or external network interface name.

Figure 9.3 Default route.

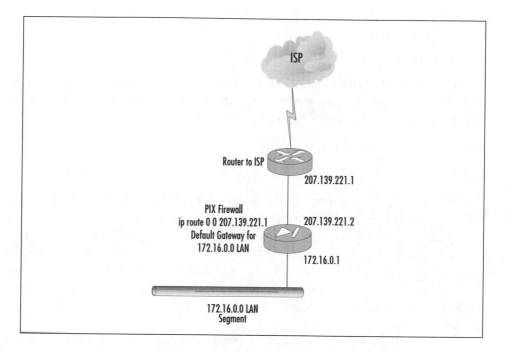

- *Ip_address* is the internal or external IP address. Use **0.0.0.0** to specify a default route. The **0.0.0.0** can be abbreviated as **0**.

- *Netmask* specifies a network mask to apply to *ip_address*. Use **0.0.0.0** to specify a default route. The **0.0.0.0** can be abbreviated as **0**.

- *Gateway_ip* is the IP address of the gateway router (next hop address for this route).

- *Metric* specifies the number of hops to *gateway_ip*.

```
pixfirewall>enable
pixfirewall#configure terminal
pixfirewall(config)#route outside 0 0 207.139.221.1
```

If different networks are present on the inside or outside interface, the PIX will need information about how to reach those networks. Since the PIX is not a router, it does not support the different routing protocols that a router does. Currently the PIX supports only RIP as its routing protocol. Since PIX is not a router, it is not recommended to use RIP; instead, add static routes to the PIX to make other networks reachable.

To add a static route:

```
pixfirewall>enable
pixfirewall#configure terminal
pixfirewall(config)#route inside 192.168.1.0 255.255.255.0 172.16.0.2 1
```

Configuring NAT and NAPT

Now that the interfaces have been named and security values have been assigned, and network connectivity has been established by configuring and testing the IP settings, NAT and PAT can be configured to allow traffic to pass through.

Permit Traffic Through

When an outbound packet arrives at a higher security level interface (inside), the PIX checks the validity of the packet based on the adaptive security algorithm, and then checks whether or not a previous packet has come from that host. If no packet has originated from that host, then the packet is for a new connection, and PIX will create a translation in its table for the connection.

The information that PIX stores in the translation table includes the inside IP address and a globally unique IP address assigned by the Network Address Translation or Network Address Port Translation. The PIX then changes the packet's source IP address to the global address, modifies the checksum and other fields as required, and then forwards the packet to the lower security interface (outside, or DMZ).

When an inbound packet arrives at a lower security level interface (outside, or DMZ), it must first pass the PIX Adaptive Security criteria. If the packet passes the security tests (static and Access Control Lists), the PIX removes the destination IP address, and the internal IP address is inserted in its place. The packet then is forwarded to the higher security level interface (inside). Figure 9.4 illustrates the NAT process on the PIX.

In the example, Host A initiates a session with Host Z. Since Host A is not on the same subnet as host Z, the packet must be routed. When the packet arrives at the inside interface of the PIX, it examines the source address. NAT has been enabled on the PIX, and a global pool of IP addresses has been allocated for translations. The PIX then modifies the IP header and alters the source address of the IP header to an IP address from the global pool of IP addresses. Once the translation occurs, the packet is then routed to Host Z. When Host Z replies to Host A, the PIX examines the packet that arrives on the outside interface. Since there is an active translation for Host A, the PIX knows that packets destined for IP address 207.139.221.2 must be translated back to 192.168.1.2. Once the PIX alters the IP header, it then routes the packet back to Host A. This process occurs until no more traffic needs to be translated between the two devices and the translation times out.

Figure 9.4 NAT example.

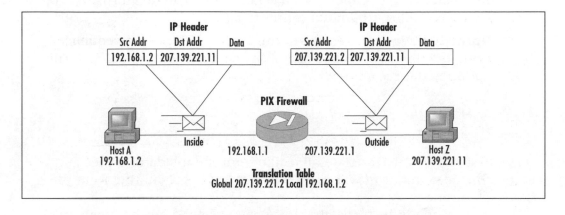

To allow traffic to flow from a higher level security interface to a lower level security interface (inside, outside), you must use the **nat** and **global** commands. To permit traffic from a lower level security interface to flow through a higher level security interface, you must use the **access-list** and **access-group** command.

Network Address Translation (NAT) is a feature that dynamically maps IP addresses originating from the higher security level interface into IP addresses on the same subnet as the lower level security interface.

To enable NAT on an interface use the command:

nat [(*interface_name*)] nat_id local_ip [*netmask* [*max_conns* [*em_limit*]]] [**norandomseq**]

where:

- *Interface_name* is the internal network interface name.

- *Nat_id* is used in the **global** command statement. All **nat** commands with the same *nat_id* are in the same **nat** group.

- *Local_ip* is the internal network IP address to be translated. You can use **0.0.0.0** to allow all hosts to start an outbound connection originating from the inside interface. The **0.0.0.0** IP can be abbreviated as **0**.

- *Netmask* is the network mask for *local_ip*. You can also use the **0.0.0.0** to allow all outbound connections originating from the inside interface.

- *Max_cons* is the maximum TCP connections limit. The default is 0, which will allow unlimited connections.

- *Em_limit* is the embryonic connection limit. The default is also 0, which will allow unlimited connections.

- **Norandomseq** specifies not to randomize TCP packet sequence numbers. Because this is one of the security features of PIX, this option is not recommended.

```
pixfirewall(config)#nat (inside) 1 0.0.0.0 0.0.0.0
pixfirewall(config)#nat (inside) 2 172.16.0.0 255.255.0.0
```

The first *nat_id* will translate all traffic from the inside interface, whereas the second *nat_id* will translate only traffic originating from the 172.16.0.0 subnet.

Once the traffic to be translated has been specified on the inside interface, it is time to specify the IP address pool to which the inside traffic will be translated. To do this the **global** command will be used:

global [(interface_name)] nat_id global_ip[-global_ip] [**netmask** global_mask]

where:

- *Interface_name* is the external network interface that these global addresses will use.

- *Nat_id* is the number shared with the **nat** command that will group the **nat** and **global** statements together.

- *Global_ip* is one or more global IP address to which the PIX will translate the inside interface traffic. If the external network interface is connected to the Internet, each global IP must be registered with the Network Information Center (NIC). You can either specify a single IP address or a range of IP addresses by separating the addresses with a dash (-).You can create a Port Address Translation (PAT) by specifying a single IP address in the **global** statement.

- *Global_mask* is the network mask for the *global_ip* statement.

```
pixfirewall(config)#global (outside) 1 207.139.221.1-207.139.221.254
netmask >255.255.255.0
    Global 207.139.221.1-207.139.221.254 will be Network Address
        Translated
    pixfirewall(config)#global (outside) 1 207.139.221.1 255.255.255.255
Global 207.139.221.128 will be Port Address Translated
```

WARNING

If PAT is used, the IP address must be different from the IP address assigned to any of the interfaces on the PIX.

In the first statement, inside IP addresses will be translated to an IP address in the range of 207.139.221.1 to 207.139.221.254. In the second statement, inside IP addresses will be Port Address Translated in a single IP address, 207.139.221.128.

NOTE

When PAT is used, the PIX will keep track of each translation by adding a unique source port number to the source IP address for each translation. This feature is valuable when only limited IP address space is available from the Service Provider. To display the active translations, use the command **show xlate** from the enable prompt.

TIP

When NAT is used, the PIX has a specified range of global IP addresses with which to perform translations. Once the last available global IP is used, no other traffic from the inside interface will be permitted through until one of the translations times out. It is a good idea to use a NAT statement followed by a PAT statement. This way when all IP addresses are used in NAT, the PAT will then be used until a NAT address has timed out.

Security Policy Configuration

Security Policy Configuration is probably one of the most important factors in establishing a secure network. To follow are some security strategies and "best practice" policies you can implement to ensure the best possible security.

Security Strategies

In order for the PIX to protect a network, managers and administrators must figure out what type of security strategy to employ. Do we deny everything that is not explicitly permitted, or do we allow everything and deny only certain things? The security policy is the most important element when designing a secure network. Without a policy, the necessary devices and configurations cannot be implemented properly. The security policy should aim for a balance between security and cost/productivity. It is impossible for a network to be totally secure; the security policy should reflect the risks of a potential security incident that the company is willing to take. For example, by allowing users the ability to browse Web sites to perform research on the Internet, a company opens itself up to numerous security risks that can be exploited. Weigh this against restricting access to browsing Web sites in a company that relies heavily on that information to function. If the security policy is designed and implemented properly, these risks will be minimal. Once a security policy has been established, a firewall can then be used as a tool to implement that security policy. It will not function properly at protecting your network if the security policy is not carefully defined beforehand.

Avoiding Reactive Security Measures

A security policy is the most important aspect in network security. As a manager, you must take many things into careful consideration when planning your policy. Tasks such as identifying the resources to protect, balancing security risks with cost/productivity, and the ability to log items are very important. Creating regular reports on usage will assist in identifying possible weaknesses in your security policy. If weaknesses have been overlooked they can then be remedied quickly. PIX allows you to utilize a feature called a syslog. With the addition of third-party software such as Open Systems Privatel, detailed analysis on the contents of a syslog can be achieved. The ability to generate reports on the types of

Continued

traffic that are being permitted or denied by the PIX is crucial to a security policy. If you suspect that your network is being attacked, the ability to look at logs over certain time periods is invaluable in proving your suspicion.

As a manager, proactive measures are always better than reactive measures. Instead of generating reports and looking for weaknesses after the fact, it may be beneficial to create a strict policy and then remove elements of that policy as necessary. For example, if a company has set up a Web server on the inside network and has used PIX to translate that inside address to a globally unique address on the outside, the server has now become fully exposed. To reduce the risk of the server being compromised, access lists can be used to limit the type of TCP/UDP traffic that will be permitted to reach the server through the PIX. By allowing only HTTP traffic to reach the Web server from the outside network and explicitly denying all other traffic, the risk of it being compromised has been greatly reduced. If the server becomes an FTP server as well as a Web server, the security policy can be modified to permit FTP as well as HTTP traffic to the server from the outside interface by adding another access list that permits FTP traffic. A security policy can take many forms, depending on the needs of an organization. Careful planning is a necessity prior to implementing the PIX firewall.

Deny Everything That Is Not Explicitly Permitted

One of the most common strategies used for security policies is to permit only certain IP traffic and to deny the rest. For example, Company XYZ wishes to permit HTTP, FTP, and Telnet traffic for users. Managers and administrators agreed that as a company policy, only these three types of traffic are to be permitted. All other traffic, such as Real Audio, ICQ, MSN Messenger, etc., will be blocked. Using Access Control Lists (ACLs) similar to those used on routers, the PIX will allow an administrator to specify which type of IP traffic to permit or deny based on destination address/network, source address/network, TCP port number, and UDP port number. This implementation makes configuring the security policy for the administrator very simple. The administrator has to worry only about entering statements to permit HTTP, FTP, and Telnet traffic, and then at the end of the ACL he/she will add an explicit Deny All statement.

Allow Everything That Is Not Explicitly Denied

On a network where many different types of IP traffic will be permitted, it may be easier for an administrator to use a different approach for a security policy. This strategy is to allow all types of traffic and deny specific IP traffic. For example, suppose Company XYZ is not concerned about the types of traffic users are going to access, but managers and administrators agreed that since they only have a T1 connection to their Internet Service Provider that services 1000 users, they do not wish their users to use Real Player because it is bandwidth intensive. To implement this strategy, only one Access Control List needs to be implemented on the PIX. This ACL will deny the TCP/UDP port that Real Audio uses, but will allow everything else.

WARNING

This is not a recommended strategy. Be sure to plan carefully in advance what types of traffic will be permitted through the firewall. This example was shown as an alternative to the "Deny Everything That Is Not Explicitly Permitted" strategy, and in some network scenarios may be useful. By using this type of implementation in a situation where the ISP charges by the byte may cause quite a shock when the first bill from the ISP arrives.

Identify the Resources to Protect

In the context of a security policy, a resource can be defined as any network device that is susceptible to attack, which will then cost a company either financially or otherwise. Examples of resources can be Web servers, mail servers, database servers, servers that contain sensitive information such as employee records, or even just a stand-alone server that does not provide any services to clients. If any of these servers are attacked, functionality can be affected, which then costs a company money.

It is important to evaluate carefully the assets a company wishes to protect. Are some resources more important than others, therefore requiring a higher security? Is a mail server more important to the operation of the company than a print server?

Areas of weaknesses must also be identified prior to implementing the security policy. If a company uses an ISP for Internet access, a pool of modems for dial-in access, and remote users tunneling into the LAN via the Internet through VPN, each of these points of entry must be looked at as a weakness. Once weaknesses have been identified, a security policy can be shaped to protect a company's LAN from those various weaknesses. For example, using the previous scenario of an ISP, dial-in access, and remote VPN access, placement of the PIX will be critical to the overall security of the LAN. If the PIX is placed between the LAN and the ISP, how does this protect the LAN from unauthorized dial-in users? By adding an additional NIC to the PIX, a DMZ (covered later) can be used to isolate the dial-in and VPN users from the rest of the LAN.

An example of protecting resources is in a situation where a public Web site is hosted internally by the company. The Web server is definitely considered an asset and must be protected. Some decisions will need to be made as to how the PIX will secure the Web server. Since the company hosts only one Web site, which uses a private IP address space, a static translation in which the Web server is assigned an internal IP address is then translated by the PIX firewall with a Global IP address allowing outside users to gain access to it.

Depending on the security policy, having servers on an internal network—which are then translated to global IP addresses—may be too risky. An alternative is to implement a demilitarized zone in which the public resources will reside.

Demilitarized Zone (DMZ)

A DMZ is a zone that is logically and physically separated from both the inside network and outside networks. A DMZ can be created by installing additional NICs to the PIX. By creating a DMZ, administrators can remove devices that need to be accessed publicly from the inside and outside zones, and can place them into their own zone. By implementing this type of configuration, it helps an administrator establish boundaries on the various zones of his/her network.

NOTE

Remember that only the PIX 515 and 520 models will allow additional interfaces to be added. The PIX 506 is a SOHO class firewall and currently does not support additional interfaces.

Figure 9.5 illustrates how a DMZ zone is used to secure public resources.

In this scenario, a DMZ has been used to separate the public servers from the inside and outside zones. This will allow administrators to control the flow of traffic destined for the DMZ zone. Since all traffic must pass through the outside interface in order to reach the DMZ zone, Access Control Lists can be applied to the outside interface specifying the type of traffic permitted to reach the DMZ zone. For example, since the public servers are Web, e-mail, and DNS servers, HTTP, DNS, and SMTP traffic will be permitted to reach the DMZ zone—everything else will be denied.

Figure 9.5 DMZ.

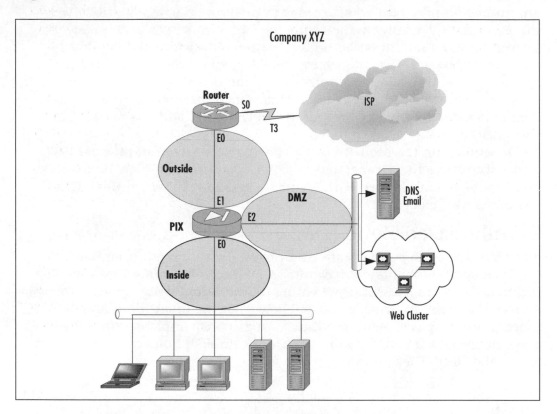

It is very difficult to secure a server. The operating system and software applications can contain bugs and security flaws and need to be updated continuously. As soon as you install a server that offers a public service, there is always a risk that the server can be compromised. Creating a new perimeter (DMZ) where the public servers are located allows more control over the traffic that will be permitted towards the internal network. For example, once a DMZ has been set up and the public servers have been removed from the inside network, a rule can be created that denies all traffic destined for the inside network, therefore increasing the security.

No matter what type of network a company has, careful planning will be needed well in advance to implement a successful security policy. Planning in advance will help to avoid making unnecessary changes in the way the PIX operates while in production. If a company continuously alters how resources are to be protected, availability of those resources will fluctuate. In a situation where a company relies heavily on that availability, careless planning may cost the company money.

Identify the Security Services to Implement

Depending on how your security policy is designed will reflect on how you design and implement your network. Various factors such as resources to protect, user authentication, traffic filtering, and confidentiality all come into play when designing the security policy.

Authentication and Authorization

Authentication is a mechanism that verifies that users are who they say they are. Authorization is a mechanism that will determine what services a user can use to access a host. An administrator must design a security policy that will specify the resources that need to be protected, what type of user will be able to access those resources, and which services a user can use to access those resources. Once a security policy that requires authentication has been outlined, an authentication server such as a RADIUS or TACACS+ server must be put in place in order to implement the security policy.

Once authentication and authorization have been enabled on the PIX, it will provide credential prompts on inbound and outbound connections for FTP, Telnet, and HTTP access. The authentication and authorization server will make the actual decision about which users are permitted or denied, and which services are used.

Access Control

In a network of any size, various administrators have control over different areas of the network. How does one administrator know where his or her responsibility stops and another administrator's responsibility begins? It is important to lay out the perimeters either inside a network or surrounding a network. For example, if a network is connected to the Internet via a T1 leased line, does the administrator maintain the network on the other side of the T1? Probably not—that is where the ISP will take over responsibility. Perimeters must be established in order to help with designing a security policy. By defining perimeters, an administrator can secure resources under their control, and this will also aid in the decision of where traffic should be filtered. Access control lists (ACL) are used to permit or deny traffic based on various criteria. These ACLs are used to assist in securing various resources by filtering the traffic that will get to them.

Confidentiality

Confidentiality is achieved by encrypting the information that travels along the network. If an individual used a network-monitoring tool, there is a good chance they would be able to look at the data in the packets. An example of this is PAP (Password Authentication Protocol). When using PPP (Point-to-Point) with PAP, information is sent in clear text during the authentication phase. If a network monitor is used to capture these packets, the password used to authenticate the two parties would be readily available. To remedy this problem CHAP (Challenge Handshake Authentication Protocol) encrypts the negotiation phase. IPSec was developed to provide confidentiality, access control, authentication, and integrity for data traversing a network. IPSec is a suite of protocols to assist in the encryption of data across a network. Commonly found in VPN tunnels, IPSec uses various encryption algorithms, keys, and certificates to validate information passed throughout a network.

URL, ActiveX, and Java Filtering

Access control lists are limited to certain criteria; destination address, source address, and ports are all taken into consideration for ACLs. ActiveX blocking occurs by the PIX commenting out HTML <object> commands on Web pages. As a technology, ActiveX creates many potential problems for clients including causing workstations to fail, introducing network security problems, or causing servers to fail.

Java filtering is accomplished by denying applets that are downloaded to a client once they access a URL.

URLs themselves can also be filtered. Typically a company will introduce an AUP (Acceptable Usage Policy) that dictates the usage of the Internet for the employees. This can be enforced somewhat by the PIX as well as third-party applications. The PIX can redirect URL requests to a server running a third-party application. This application will decide whether to permit or deny access to that URL and then pass response back to the PIX.

NOTE

URL filtering can be accomplished with the addition of a server running WebSENSE (www.websense.com). The configuration on the PIX will allow URLs to be forwarded to the WebSENSE server, which will then permit or deny the destination URL.

Implementing the Network Security Policy

Once a security policy has been created, it is time to implement that security policy on the PIX. To completely implement a policy, other devices (such as AAA server or IPSec) must be used.

Authentication Configuration in PIX

To configure authentication on the PIX, it must first be enabled. To enable AAA authentication, use **aaa-server** and **aaa** commands:

`aaa-server` group_tag if_name `host` server_ip key `timeout` seconds

where:

- *Group_tag* is an alphanumeric string that is the name of the server group. Use the *group_tag* in the **aaa** command to associate **aaa authentication** and **aaa accounting** command statements to an AAA server.

- *If_name* is the interface name on which the server resides.

- **Host** *server_ip* is the IP address of the TACACS_ or RADIUS server.

- *Key* is a case-sensitive, alphanumeric keyword of up to 127 characters. The key must be the same one that is used on the TACACS+ server.

- **Timeout** *seconds* is a retransmit timer that specifies the duration that the PIX retries access four times to the AAA server before choosing the next AAA server.

- **Protocol** *auth_protocol* is the type of AAA server, either **tacacs+** or **radius**.

`aaa authentication include | exclude` authen_service `inbound | outbound | if_name local_ip local_mask foreign_ip foreign_mask group_tag`

where:

- **Accounting** enables or disables accounting services with the authentication server.

- **Include** creates a new rule with the specified service to include.

- **Exclude** creates an exception to a previously stated rule by excluding the specified service from authentication, authorization, or accounting to the specified host.

- *Acctg_service* is the account service. Accounting is provided for all services, or you can limit it to one or more services. Possible values are **any, ftp, http, telnet**, or *protocolport*.

- **Authentication** enables or disables user authentication, prompts user for username and password, and verifies information with the authentication server.

- *Authen_service* is the application with which a user is accessing a network. Use **an, ftp, http,** or **telnet**.

- **Authorization** enables or disables TACACS+ user authorization for services (PIX does not support RADIUS authorization).

- *Author_service* are the services that require authorization. Use **any, ftp, http, telnet,** or *protocolport*.

- **Inbound** authenticates or authorizes inbound connections.

- **Outbound** authenticates or authorizes outbound connections.

- *If_name* is the interface name from which users require authentication. Use *if_name* in combination with the *local_ip* address and the *foreign_ip* address to determine where and from whom access is sought.

- *Local_ip* is the IP address of the host or network of hosts that you want to be authenticated or authorized. Set this to **0** for all hosts.

- *Local_mask* is the network mask of *local_ip*. If IP is 0, use **0**. Use **255.255.255.255** for a host.

- *Foreign_ip* is the IP address of the hosts you want to access the *local_ip* address. Use **0** for all hosts, and **255.255.255.255** for a single host.

- *Foreign_mask* is the network mask of *foreign_ip*. Always specify a specific mask value. Use **0** if the IP address is 0, use **255.255.255.255** for a single host

- *Group_tag* is the group tag set with the **aaa-server** command.

```
pixfirewall>enable
pixfirewall#configure terminal
    pixfirewall(config)#aaa-server AuthOutbound protocol tacacs+
    pixfirewall(config)#aaa-server tacacs+ (inside) host 172.16.0.10 cisco
        >timeout 20
```

```
pixfirewall(config)#aaa authentication include any outbound 0 0 0 0
   >AuthOutbound
```

```
pixfirewall(config)#aaa authorization include any outbound 0 0 0 0
```

The first **aaa-server** statement specifies TACACS+ as the authentication protocol to use, and the second **aaa-server** statement specifies the server that is performing the authentication. The last two statements indicate that all traffic outbound will need to be authenticated and authorized.

Access Control Configuration in PIX

Access control can be achieved through the use of access control lists (ACLs). Similar to those used on routers, ACLs can limit the traffic able to traverse the PIX based on several criteria including source address, destination address, source TCP/UDP ports, and destination TCP/UDP ports.

To implement access control lists on a PIX, the **access-list** and **access-group** commands are used:

```
access-list acl_name deny | permit protocol src_addr src_mask operator
port dest_addr dest_mask operator port
```

where:

- *Acl_name* is the name of an access list.

- **Deny** does not allow a packet to traverse the PIX. By default PIX denies all inbound packets unless explicitly permitted.

- **Permit** allows a packet to traverse the PIX.

- *Protocol* is the name or number of an IP protocol. It can be one of the keywords **icmp, ip, tcp**, or **udp**.

- *Src_addr* is the address of the network or host from which the packet originated. To specify all networks or hosts, use the keyword **any**, which is equivalent to a source network and mask of 0.0.0.0 0.0.0.0. Use the **host** keyword to specify a single host.

- *Src_mask* are netmask bits to be applied to the *src_addr*, if the source address is for a network mask. Do not apply if the source address is a host.

- *Dst_addr* is the IP address of the network or host to which the packet is being sent. Like the *src_addr*, the keyword **any** can be applied for a destination and netmask of 0.0.0.0 0.0.0.0, as well as the **host** abbreviation for a single host.

- *Dst_mask* are netmask bits to be applied to the *dst_addr*, if the destination address is for a network mask. Do not apply if the destination address is a host.

- *Operator* is a comparison that lets you specify a port or port range. Use without the operator and port to indicate all ports. Use **eq** and a port to permit or deny access to just that single port. Use **lt** to permit or deny access to all ports less than the port specified. Use **gt** and a port to permit or deny access to all ports greater than the port you specify. Use **neq** and a port to permit or deny access to every port except the ports you specify. Finally, use **range** and a port range to permit or deny access to only those ports named in the range.

- *Port* is a service or services you allow while accessing *src_addr* or *dest_addr*. Specify services by port number or use the literal name.

- *Icmp_type* permits or denies access to ICMP message types.

access-group acl_name **in interface** interface-name

where:

- *Acl_name* is the name associated with an access list.

- **In interface** filters on inbound packets at the given interface.

- *Interface_name* is the name of the network interface.

```
pixfirewall>enable
pixfirewall#configure terminal
pixfirewall(config)#access-list acl_out permit tcp any any eq http
pixfirewall(config)#access-list acl_out permit tcp any any eq ftp
pixfirewall(config)#access-list acl_out permit tcp any any eq ftp-data
pixfirewall(config)#access-list acl_out permit tcp any any eq telnet
pixfirewall(config)#access-list acl_out permit tcp any any eq smtp
pixfirewall(config)#access-list acl_out deny tcp any any
pixfirewall(config)#access-list acl_out deny udp any any
pixfirewall(config)#access-group acl_out in interface inside
```

- The **access-list** statements for ACL *acl_out* will permit http, ftp, ftp-data, telnet, and smtp traffic. The last two statements of the **access-list** will explicitly deny all traffic.

- The **access-group** statement will apply ACL *acl_out* to the inside interface.

Securing Resources

An example of securing resources would arise if Company XYZ has numerous consultants that need access to a resource on the internal LAN. Previously the consultants have been using a RAS connection to dial in but have complained several times that the link to their work is too slow. To remedy this, administrators have decided to permit terminal access to the server via the Internet. The internal server is a Windows NT 4.0 Terminal Server and the consultants have been provided with the Terminal Server client. For security reasons, administrators have also requested the IP and subnet from which the consultants are going to be connecting.

This configuration example will explain the commands necessary to protect a server with a private IP address that is translated to a global IP address.

To create a translation for an internal IP address to a public IP address, use the **static** command:

static (internal_if_name, external_if_name) global_ip local_ip **netmask** *network_mask* max_conns em_limit **norandomseq**

where:

- *Internal_if_name* is the internal network interface name (the higher security level interface you are accessing).

- *External_if_name* is the external network interface name (the lower security level interface you are accessing).

- *Global_ip* is a global IP address. This address cannot be a Port Address Translation IP address.

- *Local_ip* is the local IP address from the inside network.

- **Netmask** specifies the network mask

- *Network_mask* pertains to both *global_ip* and *local_ip*. For host addresses, always use the 255.255.255.255. For networks, use the appropriate class mask or subnet mask.

- *Max_cons* is the maximum number of connections permitted through the static at the same time.

- *Em_limit* is the embryonic connection limit. An embryonic connection is one that has started but not yet completed. Set this limit to prevent attack by a flood of embryonic connections.

- **Norandomseq** specifies not to randomize the TCP/IP packet's sequence number. Use this option only if another inline firewall is also randomizing sequence numbers. Using this feature opens a security hole in the PIX.

Once a translation for an internal IP to an external IP has been made, you must specify the type of traffic that will be permitted to access it. To do this, use the **access-list** command:

```
access-list acl_name deny | permit protocol src_addr src_mask operator
port dest_addr dest_mask operator port
```

where:

- *Acl_name* is the name of an access list.

- **Deny** does not allow a packet to traverse the PIX. By default PIX denies all inbound packets unless explicitly permitted.

- **Permit** allows a packet to traverse the PIX.

- *Protocol* is the name or number of an IP protocol. It can be one of the keywords **icmp, ip, tcp**, or **udp**.

- *Src_addr* is the address of the network or host from which the packet originated. To specify all networks or hosts, use the keyword **any**, which is equivalent to a source network and mask of 0.0.0.0 0.0.0.0. Use the **host** keyword to specify a single host.

- *Src_mask* are netmask bits to be applied to the *src_addr*, if the source address is for a network mask. Do not apply if the source address is a host.

- *Dst_addr* is the IP address of the network or host to which the packet is being sent. Like the *src_addr*, the keyword **any** can be applied for a destination and netmask of 0.0.0.0 0.0.0.0, as well as the **host** abbreviation for a single host.

- *Dst_mask* are netmask bits to be applied to the dst_*addr*, if the destination address is for a network mask. Do not apply if the destination address is a host.

- *Operator* is a comparison that lets you specify a port or port range. Use without the operator and port to indicate all ports. Use **eq** and a port to permit or deny access to just that single port. Use **lt** to permit or deny access to all ports less than the port specified. Use **gt** and a port to permit or deny access to all ports greater than the port you specify. Use **neq** and a port to permit or deny access to every port except the ports you specify. Finally, use **range** and a port range to permit or deny access to only those ports named in the range.

- *Port* is a service or services you allow while accessing *src_addr* or *dest_addr*. Specify services by port number or use the literal name.

■ *Icmp_type* permits or denies access to ICMP message types.

```
pixfirewall>enable
pixfirewall#configure terminal
    pixfirewall(config)#static (inside,outside) 207.139.221.10 172.16.0.32
        >netmask 255.255.255.255
    pixfirewall(config)#access-list acl_consult permit tcp 198.142.65.0
        >255.255.255.0 host 207.139.221.10 eq 3389
    pixfirewall(config)#access-list acl_consult permit tcp 64.182.95.0
        >255.255.255.0 host 307.139.221.10 eq 3389
pixfirewall(config)#access-group acl_consult in interface outside
```

TIP

TCP port 3389 is the corresponding port for Microsoft Terminal Server client. For a listing of valid TCP and UDP port numbers, refer to www.isi.edu/in-notes/iana/assignments/port-numbers.

The first **static** statement will provided a translation for the inside server with an IP address of 172.16.0.32 to a global IP address of 207.139.221.10.

The **access-list** statements specify that ACL *acl_consult* will permit only Microsoft Terminal Server client traffic originating from 198.142.65.0 and 64.182.95.0.

Finally, the **access-group** statement will apply the *acl_consult* access control list to the outside interface.

It is also important to note that implementing a security policy does not revolve around configuration of the PIX. In the previous example, a PIX will not assist as a security measure if the information passed from terminal server to terminal server client is not encrypted. If information is passed as clear text, a network monitoring tool could be used to capture packets, which can then be analyzed by other individuals. Once a consultant has connected to the terminal server, how is the authentication handled? What permissions does that account have? Have various Windows NT security flaws been addressed with the latest service packs?

URL, ActiveX, and Java Filtering

To implement URL, ActiveX, and Java filtering, use the **filter** command:

```
filter activex port local_ip mask foreign_ip mask
```

where:

- **Activex** blocks outbound ActiveX tags from outbound packets.

- *Port* (**filter activex** only) is the port at which Web traffic is received on the PIX firewall.

- *Local_ip* is the IP address of the highest security level interface from which access is sought. You can set this address to **0** to specify all hosts.

- *Mask* is the network mask of *local_ip*. You can use **0** to specify all hosts.

- *Foreign_ip* is the IP address of the lowest security level interface to which access is sought. You can use **0** to specify all hosts.

- *Foreign_mask* is the network mask of *foreign_ip*. Always specify a mask value. You can use **0** to specify all hosts.

filter java port[-port] *local_ip mask foreign_ip mask*

where:

- **Java** blocks Java applets returning to the PIX firewall as a result of an outbound connection.

- *Port[-port]* (**filter java** only) is one or more ports on which Java applets may be received.

- *Local_ip* is the IP address of the highest security level interface from which access is sought. You can set this address to **0** to specify all hosts.

- *Mask* is the network mask of *local_ip*. You can use **0** to specify all hosts.

- *Foreign_ip* is the IP address of the lowest security level interface to which access is sought. You can use **0** to specify all hosts.

- *Foreign_mask* is the network mask of *foreign_ip*. Always specify a mask value. You can use **0** to specify all hosts.

filter url http|except *local_ip local_mask foreign_ip foreign_mask* [**allow**]

where:

- **url** filters URLs from data moving through the PIX firewall.

- **http** (**filter url** only) filters HTTP URLs.

- **except** (**filter url** only) creates an exception to a previous **filter** condition.

- *Local_ip* is the IP address of the highest security level interface from which access is sought. You can set this address to **0** to specify all hosts.

- *Mask* is the network mask of *local_ip*. You can use **0** to specify all hosts.

- *Foreign_ip* is the IP address of the lowest security level interface to which access is sought. You can use **0** to specify all hosts.

- *Foreign_mask* is the network mask of *foreign_ip*. Always specify a mask value. You can use **0** to specify all hosts.

- **Allow** (**filter url** only) lets outbound connections pass through PIX firewall without filtering when the server is unavailable. If you omit this option and if the WebSENSE server goes offline, the PIX firewall stops outbound port 80 traffic until the WebSENSE server is back online.

Once filtering has been enabled on the PIX, to successfully filter URLs, you must designate a WebSENSE server with the **url-server** command.

url-server (*if_name*) **host** *ip_address* **timeout** *seconds*

where:

- *If_name* is the network interface where the authentication server resides. Default is inside.

- **Host** *ip_address* is the server that runs the WebSENSE URL filtering application.

- **Timeout** *seconds* is the maximum idle time permitted before PIX switches to the next server you specify. Default is 5 seconds.

```
pixfirewall>enable
pixfirewall#configure terminal
pixfirewall(config)#filter url http 0 0 0 0
pixfirewall(config)#filter activex 80 0 0 0 0
pixfirewall(config)#filter java 80 0 0 0 0
pixfirewall(config)#url-server (inside) host 172.16.0.38 timeout 5
```

The **filter url** statement specifies that all http traffic passing through the PIX will be filtered. In addition, the **url-server** statement will specify which server is running WebSENSE to provide the actual filtering.

The **filter activex** and **filter java** statements specify that all http traffic will be filtered for ActiveX controls and Java applets.

PIX Configuration Examples

The following examples will illustrate how a PIX firewall can be used in various real world scenarios, as well as the configuration needed on the PIX.

Protecting a Private Network

Due to security reasons, Company XYZ management has decided to restrict access to the Finance servers. Management has assigned the task of securing the Finance network from unauthorized access. Only individuals who are in the Finance departments network will have access to any of the Finance resources, any traffic originating from the Finance LAN will be permitted to any destination, and all other departments will not be permitted to access the Finance LAN. Figure 9.6 illustrates how the LAN will be set up.

```
pixfirewall(config)#write terminal
nameif ethernet0 public security0
nameif ethernet1 finance security100
```

Figure 9.6 Secure department to department.

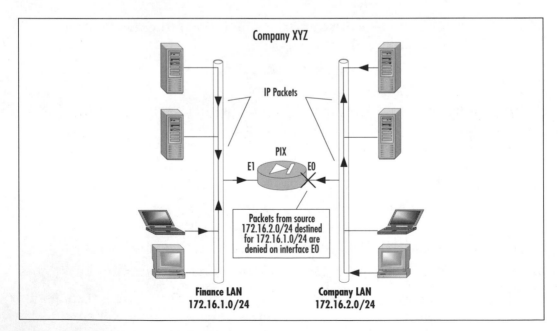

Assign names and security values to each of the interfaces.

```
interface ethernet0 inside auto
interface ethernet1 outside auto
```

Set each Ethernet interface to 10/100 auto negotiation.

```
ip address public 172.16.2.1 255.255.255.0
ip address finance 172.16.1.1 255.255.255.0
```

Assign unique RFC1918 IP addresses to each of the interfaces.

```
access-list deny tcp any 172.16.1.0 255.255.255.0
    >eq any
access-list deny udp any 172.16.1.0 255.255.255.0
>eq any
```

Specify that traffic originating from the 172.16.1.0/24 subnet will be denied.

```
access-group acl_out in interface public
```

Apply access-list acl_out to public interface.

```
telnet 172.16.1.0 255.255.255.0 public
telnet 172.16.2.0 255.255.255.0 finance
```

Specify that only clients from the 172.16.1.0/25 and 172.16.2.0/24 subnets will be able to Telnet to the PIX.

NOTE

This configuration—where two departments are separated for security reasons—can easily be achieved by using a router with access control lists. The PIX is a very versatile device and can also be used to protect internal networks as shown in this example.

Protecting a Network Connected to the Internet

Company XYZ management has decided that in order to keep up with the rapidly evolving world of technology, Internet access is a necessity. Managers and administrators have decided that a T1 leased line will be sufficient for their users to access the Internet, and an ISP has already been chosen. Since the LAN uses an IP address scheme using the private 172.16.0.0 network, Network Address Translation or Network Address Port Translation will be needed in order to translate internal IP addresses to Global IP addresses. The ISP has also provided the company with eight public addresses, which consist of 207.139.221.1 to 207.139.221.8. A Cisco Secure PIX 515 Firewall has been chosen to provide security for Company XYZ.

Management and administrators have established a security policy in which users will be permitted to access only HTTP, FTP, Telnet, Email, DNS, and News. Web site filtering will be performed by a third-party application called WebSENSE web filtering software (www.websense.com). ActiveX controls will be also filtered due to the security problems associated with them. The ability to Telnet to the inside interface will be restricted to the administrator's workstation. Figure 9.7 shows how the network will be set up.

Figure 9.7 Two interfaces.

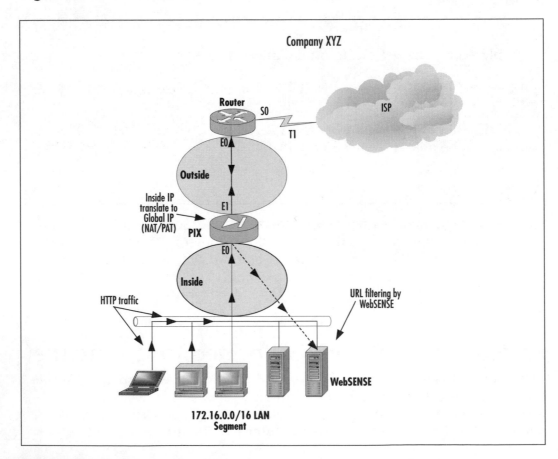

```
pixfirewall(config)#write terminal
interface ethernet0 inside auto
interface ethernet1 outside auto
```

Set each Ethernet interface to 10/100 auto negotiation.

```
ip address inside 172.16.0.1 255.255.0.0
ip address outside 207.139.221.2 255.255.255.248
```

Assign unique IP addresses to each of the interfaces.

```
route outside 0.0.0.0 0.0.0.0 207.139.221.1
```

Add a static route for the outside interface.

```
nat (inside) 1 0.0.0.0 0.0.0.0
```

Allow any address on the inside interface to be NAT'ed.

```
global (inside) 1 207.139.221.3
```

Set up a global pool using the unique IP address 207.139.221.3 for NAPT.

```
filter url http 0 0 0 0
```

Filter any HTTP URL requests to any destination address.

```
filter activex 0 0 0 0
```

Filter any ActiveX controls in HTML pages to any destination address.

```
url-server (inside) host 172.16.0.10 timeout 5
```

Specify the server in which WebSENSE is running for URL filtering.

```
access-list acl_out permit tcp any any eq http
access-list acl_out permit tcp any any eq ftp
access-list acl_out permit tcp any any eq ftp-data
access-list acl_out permit tcp any any eq smtp
access-list acl_out permit tcp any any eq telnet
access-list acl_out permit tcp any any eq nntp
access-list acl_out permit tcp any any eq domain
access-list acl_out permit udp any any eq domain
access-list acl_out deny tcp any any
access-list acl_out deny udp any any
```

Specify types of traffic that will be permitted through the PIX (inside, outside) with an explicit **deny all** statement to block any other traffic.

```
access-group acl_out in interface inside
```

Apply access-list acl_out to the inside interface.

```
telnet 172.16.0.50 255.255.255.255. inside
```

Only permit host 172.16.0.50 for Telnet sessions on the inside interface.

Protecting Server Access Using Authentication

The Finance department in Company XYZ is concerned about users in other departments accessing their Finance Web server. To alleviate this concern, IT has decided to limit access to the Finance server using the PIX firewall. A new server has been provided, which will serve as the AAA server that runs Cisco Secure ACS. Figure 9.8 illustrates this scenario.

```
pixfirewall(config)#write terminal
interface ethernet0 inside auto
interface ethernet1 outside auto
```

Figure 9.8 Protecting a server using AAA.

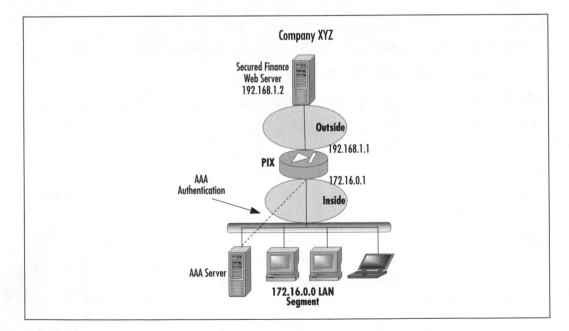

Set each Ethernet interface to 10/100 auto negotiation.

```
ip address outside 192.168.1.1 255.255.255.0
ip address inside 172.16.0.1 255.255.255.0
```

Assign unique IP addresses to each of the interfaces.

```
nat (inside) 1 0 0
```

Allow any address on the inside interface to be NAT'ed.

```
global (outside) 1 192.168.10-192.168.20 netmask >255.255.255.0
```

Set up a global pool using address 192.168.10-192.168.20 for NAT.

```
global (outside) 1 192.168.10.21 netmask >255.255.255.255
```

Set up a global pool using 192.168.10.21 for NAPT. This is used when addresses from the NAT pool have been exhausted.

```
aaa-server AuthOutbound protocol tacacs+
```

Specify TACACS+ for AAA protocol.

```
aaa-server AuthOutbound (inside) host 172.16.0.10 >cisco timeout 20
```

Specify host 172.16.0.10 as AAA server.

```
aaa authentication include any outbound host >192.168.1.2 0 0
```

Authorize any traffic with a destination address of 192.168.1.2.

Protecting Public Servers Connected to the Internet

Company XYZ management has discussed the possibility of hosting their public servers internally. Currently the Web servers are hosted elsewhere by another company in which connectivity, security, and maintenance is provided for them. The security policy dictates that the risks of having public servers on the internal network are unacceptable. A new perimeter (DMZ) will need to be defined to secure the public servers. Three web servers, one e-mail server, and one DNS server will be placed in the DMZ.

The company's ISP assigns a class C subnet. To allow the company to utilize as many of the class C public addresses as possible, Network Address Port Translation will be used instead of NAT.

Management would like to restrict the amount of traffic that traverses the PIX from their local LAN to the Internet. Administrators have decided that the only traffic permitted from the LAN will be HTTP, FTP, Telnet, and

DNS requests to their DNS server. Figure 9.9 illustrates how the LAN will be set up.

```
pixfirewall(config)#write terminal
nameif ethernet2 dmz security 50
```

Figure 9.9 Three interfaces without NAT.

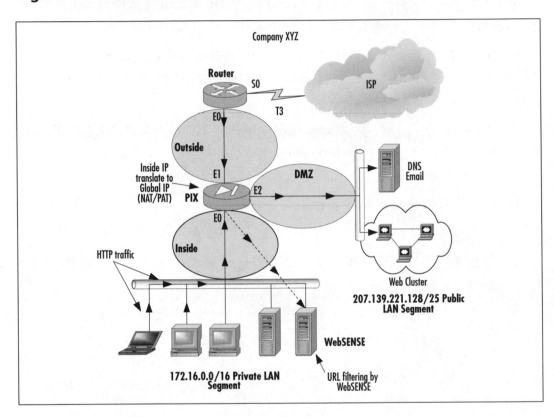

Name and assign security value to ethernet2 interface.

```
interface ethernet0 inside auto
interface ethernet1 outside auto
interface ethernet2 dmz1 auto
```

Set each Ethernet interface to 10/100 auto negotiation.

```
ip address inside 172.16.0.1 255.255.0.0
ip address outside 207.139.221.2 255.255.255.128
ip address dmz 207.139.221.129 255.255.255.128
```

Assign unique IP addresses to each interface.

```
route (outside) 0.0.0.0 0.0.0.0 207.139.221.1
```

Set static route for the outside interface.

```
nat (inside) 1 0.0.0.0 0.0.0.0
```

Enable NAT for all traffic originating from the inside interface.

```
Nat (dmz) 0 0.0.0.0 0.0.0.0
```

Disable NAT feature on DMZ interface. Since hosts on DMZ interface will be using global IP addresses; NAT translations are not necessary.

```
global (inside) 1 207.139.221.3
```

Set up a global pool using global IP address 207.139.221.3 for NAPT.

```
static (dmz,outside) 207.139.221.129 207.139.221.129 >netmask
255.255.255.128
```

Create a static translation for:

```
static (dmz,outside) 207.139.221.130 207.139.221.130 >netmask
255.255.255.128
    static (dmz,outside) 207.139.221.131 207.139.221.131 >netmask
        255.255.255.128
filter url http 0 0 0 0
```

Filter any HTTP URL requests with any destination address.

```
filter activex 0 0 0 0
```

Filter any ActiveX controls in HTML pages to any destination address.

```
url-server (inside) host 172.16.0.10 timeout 5
```

Specify the server in which WebSENSE is running for URL filtering.

```
access-list acl_out permit tcp any any eq http
access-list acl_out permit tcp any any eq ftp
access-list acl_out permit tcp any any eq ftp-data
access-list acl_out permit tcp any any eq smtp
access-list acl_out permit tcp any any eq telnet
access-list acl_out permit tcp any any eq domain
access-list acl_out permit udp any any eq domain
access-list acl_out deny tcp any any
```

```
access-list acl_out deny udp any any
```

Specify types of traffic that will be permitted through the PIX (inside, outside) with an explicit **deny all** statement to block any other traffic.

```
access-list dmz_in    permit tcp any 207.139.221.128
>255.255.255.128 eq http
access-list dmz_in permit tcp any 207.139.221.128
   >255.255.255.128 eq domain
access-list dmz_in permit udp any 207.139.221.128
   >255.255.255.128 eq domain
access-list dmz_in permit tcp any 207.139.221.128
   >255.255.255.128 eq smtp
access-list dmz_in permit tcp any 207.139.221.128
>255.255.255.128 eq pop3
```

Specify types of traffic that will be permitted through the PIX (outside, dmz). All traffic not explicitly permitted will be denied.

```
access-group acl_out in interface inside
```

Apply access-list acl_out to the inside interface.

```
access-group dmz_in in interface outside
```

Apply access-list acl_in to the DMZ interface.

```
telnet 172.16.0.0 255.255.0.0 inside
```

Permit Telnet access on the inside interface from any host on 172.16.0.0/16 network.

Figure 9.10 illustrates an example of a DMZ that uses private IP addresses, therefore requiring NAT.

```
pixfirewall(config)#write terminal
nameif ethernet2 dmz security 50
```

Name and assign security value to ethernet2 interface.

```
interface ethernet0 inside auto
interface ethernet1 outside auto
interface ethernet2 dmz1 auto
```

Figure 9.10 Three interfaces with NAT.

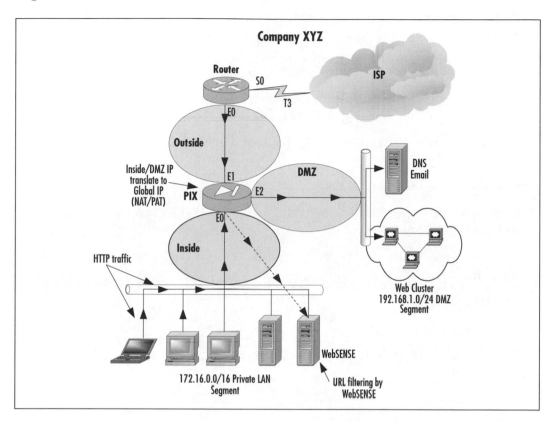

Set each Ethernet interface to 10/100 auto negotiation.

```
ip address inside 172.16.0.1 255.255.0.0
ip address outside 207.139.221.2 255.255.255.0
ip address dmz 192.168.1.1 255.255.255.0
```

Assign unique IP addresses to each interface.

```
route 0.0.0.0 0.0.0.0 207.139.221.1
```

Set static route for outside interface.

```
nat (inside) 1 172.16.0.0 255.255.0.0
```

Enable NAT for all traffic originating from the inside interface.

```
nat (dmz) 1 0.0.0.0 0.0.0.0
```

Enable NAT for all traffic originating from the DMZ interface.

```
global (inside) 1 207.139.221.3
```

Set up a global pool using global IP address 207.139.221.3 for NAPT.

```
global (dmz) 1 192.168.1.10-192.168.1.30
```

Set up a global pool using IP addresses 192.168.1.10-192.168.1.30 for DMZ.

```
static (dmz,outside) 207.139.221.129 192.168.1.2 >netmask 255.255.255.0
```

Create a static translation for DMZ host 192.168.1.2 to Global unique IP 207.139.221.129.

```
static (dmz,outside) 207.139.221.130 192.168.1.3 >netmask 255.255.255.0
```

Create a static translation for DMZ host 192.168.1.3 to Global unique IP 207.139.221.130.

```
static (dmz,outside) 207.139.221.131 192.168.1.4 >netmask 255.255.255.0
```

Create a static translation for DMZ host 192.168.1.4 to Global unique IP 207.139.221.131.

```
filter url http 0 0 0 0
```

Filter any HTTP URL requests with any destination address.

```
filter activex 0 0 0 0
```

Filter any ActiveX controls in HTML pages to any destination address.

```
url-server (inside) host 172.16.0.10 timeout 5
```

Specify the server in which WebSENSE is running for URL filtering.

```
access-list acl_out permit tcp any any eq http
access-list acl_out permit tcp any any eq ftp
access-list acl_out permit tcp any any eq ftp-data
access-list acl_out permit tcp any any eq smtp
access-list acl_out permit tcp any any eq telnet
access-list acl_out permit tcp any any eq domain
access-list acl_out permit udp any any eq domain
access-list acl_out deny tcp any any
access-list acl_out deny udp any any
```

Specify types of traffic that will be permitted through the PIX (inside, outside) with an explicit **deny all** statement to block any other traffic.

```
access-list dmz_in   permit tcp any 207.139.221.129
>255.255.255.255 eq http
```

```
access-list dmz_in permit tcp any 207.139.221.130
   >255.255.255.255 eq domain
```

```
access-list dmz_in permit udp any 207.139.221.130
   >255.255.255.128 eq domain
```

```
access-list dmz_in permit tcp any 207.139.221.131
>255.255.255.131 eq smtp
```

Specify types of traffic that will be permitted through the PIX (outside, dmz). All traffic not explicitly permitted will be denied.

```
access-group acl_out in interface inside
```

Apply access-list acl_out to the inside interface.

```
access-group dmz_in in interface outside
```

Apply access-list acl_dmz to the outside interface.

```
telnet 172.16.0.0 255.255.0.0 inside
```

Securing and Maintaining the PIX

Part of creating a security policy is not only to protect network resources but also to protect the PIX itself. PIX provides several mechanisms in assisting an administrator in limiting access to the PIX and reporting various items such as security violations.

System Journaling

As with most Cisco products, the system message logging feature can save messages in a buffer or redirect the messages to other devices such as a system logging server to be analyzed or archived. This feature allows administrators to reference these logs in case of security violations.

System journaling is often an overlooked security mechanism. Logging is essential to the security of the network. It can be used to detect security violations, and to help determine the type of attack. If logging is done in real time, it can be used to detect an ongoing intrusion.

PIX also has the added feature that if for any reason the syslog server is no longer available, the PIX will stop all traffic.

UNIX servers by default provide a syslog server; on Windows NT/2000 servers, a syslog server must be downloaded. Cisco provides a syslog server on their Web site (www.cisco.com).

By default, system log messages are sent to the console and Telnet sessions. To redirect logging messages to a syslog server use the **logging** command. Some of the variables used with the **logging** command are as follows:

- **On** starts sending syslog messages to all output locations. Stop all logging with the **no logging on** command.

- **Buffered** sends syslog messages to an internal buffer that can be viewed with the **show logging** command. To clear the buffer, use the **clear logging** command.

- **Console** specifies that syslog messages appear on the console. You can limit which type of messages appear by using the *level* option.

- **Host** specifies a syslog server that will receive the messages sent from the PIX. You may use multiple **logging host** commands to specify multiple syslog servers.

- *In_if_name* is the interface in which the syslog server resides.

- *Ip_address* is the IP address of syslog server.

- *Protocol* is the protocol in which the syslog message is sent, either **tcp** or **udp**. PIX sends only **TCP** messages to the PIX syslog server unless otherwise specified. You cannot send both protocols to the same syslog server. Use multiple syslog servers in order to log both UDP and TCP traffic.

- *Level* specifies the syslog message level as a number or string. See Table 9.2 for the different syslog levels.

- *Port* is the port in which the PIX sends either UDP or TCP syslog messages. Default for UDP is port 514 and port 1470 for TCP.

- **Timestamp** specifies that the syslog messages sent to the syslog server should have a time stamp value on each message.

Table 9.2 lists the different SNMP trap levels.

Table 9.2 SNMP Trap Levels

Level	Type	Description
0	Emergencies	System unusable messages
1	Alerts	Take immediate action
2	Critical	Critical condition
3	Errors	Error messages

Continued

Table 9.2 Continued

Level	Type	Description
4	Warnings	Warning message
5	Notifications	Normal but significant condition
6	Informational	Information message
7	Debugging	Debug messages and log FTP commands and WWW URLs

An example of sending warnings to a syslog server is:

```
pixfirewall>enable
pixfirewall#configure terminal
pixfirewall(config)#logging trap 4
pixfurewall(config)#logging host inside 172.16.0.38 tcp
```

> **NOTE**
>
> Syslog is *not* a secure protocol. The syslog server should be secured and network access to the syslog server should be restricted.

Securing the PIX

Since the PIX is a security device, limiting access to the PIX to only those who need it is extremely important. What would happen if individuals where able to Telnet freely to the PIX from the inside network? Limiting access to the PIX can be achieved by using the **telnet** command. Telnet is an insecure protocol. Everything that is typed on a Telnet session, including passwords, is sent in clear text. Individuals using a network-monitoring tool can then capture the packets and discover the password to login and enable a password if issued. If remote management of the PIX is necessary, the network communication should be secured.

It is also a good idea to limit the idle-time of a Telnet session and log any connections to the PIX through Telnet. When possible, use a RADIUS, Kerberos, or TACACS+ server to authenticate connections on the console or vty (Telnet) ports:

```
telnet ip_address netmask interface_name
```

where:

- *Ip_address* is an IP address of a host or network that can access the PIX Telnet console. If an interface name is not specified, the address is assumed to be on the internal interface. PIX automatically verifies the IP address against the IP addresses specified by the **ip address** commands to ensure that the address you specify is on an internal interface.

- *Netmask* is the bit mask of *ip_address*. To limit access to a single IP address, use 255.255.255.255 for the subnet mask.

- *Interface_name* is the name of the interface in which to apply the security.

- **Timeout** is the number of minutes that a Telnet session can be idle before being disconnected by the PIX. Default is 5 minutes.

TIP

When permitting Telnet access to an interface, be as specific as possible. If an administrative terminal uses a static IP address, permit only that IP address for Telnet access.

The following is an example of limiting Telnet access to the PIX to one host on the inside network.

```
pixfirewall>enable
pixfirewall#configure terminal
pixfirewall(config)#telnet 172.16.0.50 255.255.255.255 inside
pixfirewall(config)#telnet timeout 5
```

If features are not used on the PIX they should then be disabled. If SNMP is not used, deactivate it. If it is used, changed the default communities and limit access to the management station only.

Finally, a security measure that is often forgotten is to keep the PIX a secure area. By locking it away in a server room or wiring closet, only limited individuals will be able to physically reach the PIX. How would your security policy be enforced if an individual were able to walk up to the PIX and pull out the power cable?

Take the extra time to secure the PIX according to the security policy. The PIX is typically the device that enforces the majority of a company's security policy. If the PIX itself is not secured, and an unauthorized individual gains access to it, the security of the network will be compromised.

Summary

The Cisco PIX Firewall is a very versatile security device. From the PIX 506 SOHO model to the Enterprise class PIX 520 model, the PIX can fulfill the security needs of any size network.

In this chapter we covered numerous topics including the design of a security policy and then implementing that security policy on the PIX. It is extremely important to design a policy thoroughly before implementing it. Identifying the resources to protect, the services you wish to allow (HTTP, FTP etc), and requiring users to authenticate in order to access a resource ahead of time will permit an organization to implement the security policy in a quick and efficient manner. By creating a security policy on the fly, your resources can be compromised and data can be corrupted. Instead of being reactive to attacks and other security holes, creating a detailed security policy is a proactive measure in protecting your network.

Remember the key security features of the PIX: URL, ActiveX, and Java filtering; access control lists; DMZs; AAA authentication and authorization; DNSGuard, IP FragGuard, MailGuard, Flood Defender, and Flood Guard; IPSec; stateful filtering; securing access to the PIX; and syslog. These features will aid you in creating and implementing your security policy. NAT and NAPT should not be relied on as a security measure. Using a syslog server will allow you to archive all of the traffic that passes through your firewall. By using syslog, you will always have a record of anyone attempting to attack your firewall from the inside or outside.

FAQs

Q: I have two inside networks. I would like only one of them to be able to access the Internet (outside network). How would I accomplish this?

A: Instead of using the NAT (inside) 1 0 0 statement, which specifies all inside traffic, use the NAT (inside) 1 xxx.xxx.xxx.xx yyy.yyy.yyy.yyy statement where x is the source network you wish to translate, and y is the source network subnet mask.

Q: I am setting up my outbound access control lists to specify which traffic I will permit users to use. How do I know which TCP or UDP port a particular application uses?

A: Usually the application vendor will have the TCP or UDP port(s) listed in the documentation, or available on their Web site. For a comprehensive list of Well Known Ports, Registered Ports, and Dynamic/Private ports, visit www.isi.edu/in-notes/iana/assignments/port-numbers.

Q: A user has informed me that he believes that his application is not running due to firewall restrictions. After researching the application, I am unable to figure out which TCP or UDP port the application uses. How can I find this information?

A: If you are using a syslog server or third-party application to analyze the syslog on the PIX, you can query the syslog for instances of the IP address being denied. From that output, you should be able to determine the port in question. The following is one line of output from the syslog:

```
106019: IP packet from 172.16.0.39 to 212.214.136.27, protocol 17
received from interface "inside" deny by access-group "acl_out"
```

From this output you can clearly see that host 172.16.0.39 is trying to access a foreign IP address on port 17. After checking to which service port 17 corresponds, you find that the user is trying use an application that gives "Quote of the day" messages.

Q: My organization uses Microsoft Exchange server for our mail. How would I allow our Exchange server to receive external mail if the server is located on the inside network and a PIX firewall is in place?

A: Since the server is physically located on the inside network, a static translation will need to be created to assign the Exchange server a global IP address. Once the translation has been created, use ACLs to limit to the type of traffic able to reach the server; that is, SMTP. For example, the Exchange server's internal IP address is 172.16.0.16, and the globally assigned IP address will be 207.139.221.40:

```
pixfirewall(config)#static (inside,outside) 207.139.221.40 172.16.0.16
>netmask 255.255.255.255
    pixfirewall(config)#access-list acl_mailin permit tcp any host
       207.139.221.40 eq smtp
pixfirewall(config)#access-group acl_mailin in interface outside
```

Chapter 10

Axent Technologies Raptor Firewall 6.5

Solutions in this chapter:

- Configuring Axent Raptor Firewall

- Applying the Firewall to Your Security Model

- Avoiding Known Security Issues

Introduction

Axent's Raptor Firewall is a full-featured security package that will allow you to protect your network from outside threats. One of the nicest things about this package is that it is available on many platforms including Windows NT, Sun Solaris, HP-UX, and soon Windows 2000.

The Raptor Firewall package is easy to install and configure. It includes many security measures like content filtering, Out Of Band Authentication (OOBA), Windows NT Domain Authentication, and Axent Defender, which can be used with SecureID or CRYPTOCard.

This chapter will give you an overview of the firewall's capabilities and discuss some common applications used; then it will discuss some of the security issues associated with it and help you diagnose common problems.

Configuring Axent Raptor Firewall 6.5

Before you get into the installation and configuration of Raptor, you need to make sure that you have met the software requirements. The current minimum requirements for Raptor 6.5 to run on Windows NT are listed in Table 10.1.

Table 10.1 Raptor 6.5 Minimum System Requirements for Windows NT

Component	System Requirements
CPU	Pentium II 233 MHz
Memory	If the site will have less than 200 users: 64MB RAM with a 300MB paging file.
	If the site will have more than 200 users: 128MB RAM with a 500MB paging file.
	Note that these are the minimum requirements, and more memory is recommended for more efficient operation.
Disk Space	If the site will have less than 200 users: 2GB HD with at least 200MB free for Raptor installation files.
	If the site will have more than 200 users: 4GB HD.
Web Browser	Internet Explorer 5.0 or later
Operating System	Windows NT 4
Service Pack	5 or 6a
Network Interface Card (NIC) support	See Axent's Web site for a list of supported NICs.

Notes on Installation

There are a few important items to note regarding a Raptor 6.5 install.

- If you are installing Raptor 6.5 on Windows NT4 Server, it must be a Member Server. The current software package does not support an install to a Domain Controller.

- If you have Service Pack 6a installed on your Windows NT 4 machine, there is a known issue that could curtail functionality. It involves TCP sessions held in an infinite wait state even after a termination has been requested. Microsoft has released a patch to correct this issue, and a work-around is included with the Raptor 6.5 installation kit. You can find more information on this problem at http://support.microsoft.com/support/kb/articles/q254/9/30.asp.

- Raptor Firewall 6.5 currently does not support software redundant array of disks (RAID) or Disk Mirroring. Installation will have to take place on a system that does not have this implemented.

- You can install the firewall package with only one NIC, but dual NICs on separate subnets are recommended for installation.

If you find that your current setup does not meet all of these minimum requirements, those issues will need to be corrected before you begin with the software installation.

Installing Raptor Firewall 6.5

To begin the installation process, go to the Axent software directory; we will be concerning ourselves with the International folder for the time being. Go to International | Gateway | NT and you will see a Windows NT Command Script (Setup.cmd). Double-click on the command script to begin the installation process. If you have downloaded the firewall package from Axent's Web site, the executable zip file will extract to the root of your drive. For more information on the discussed paths, please refer to Table 10.2.

Table 10.2 Default Directory Structure of the Axent Installation Software

Folder	Path
International	\\%System Root%\AxentSW\International
ADDITIONAL SOFTWARE	\\%System Root%\AxentSW\International\ ADDITIONAL SOFTWARE
Gateway	\\%System Root%\AxentSW\International\Gateway
Nt	\\%System Root%\AxentSW\International\Gateway\Nt
Setup.cmd	\\%System Root%\AxentSW\International\Gateway\Setup.cmd

1. After you have launched the Setup.cmd file, you will see a screen similar to the one found in Figure 10.1. Click Next to advance into the software setup.

Figure 10.1 Raptor Firewall initial setup screen.

2. Click Yes for the software license agreement to continue. Read the agreement thoroughly and make sure that you understand what you are agreeing to.

3. The next screen is the setup for the Raptor License Key and Product Serial Number. As stated in Figure 10.2, if you leave this field blank you will have a 30-day evaluation period for the Raptor firewall software.

4. After you have entered your serial number, you are ready to select the package you would like to install. For the purposes of this chapter, we will be concerned with the Raptor Firewall selection as seen in Figure 10.3. Make sure that the management console box is checked so that it will also be installed.

Figure 10.2 License Key setup dialog box.

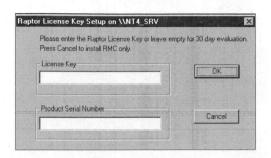

Figure 10.3 Product selection dialog box.

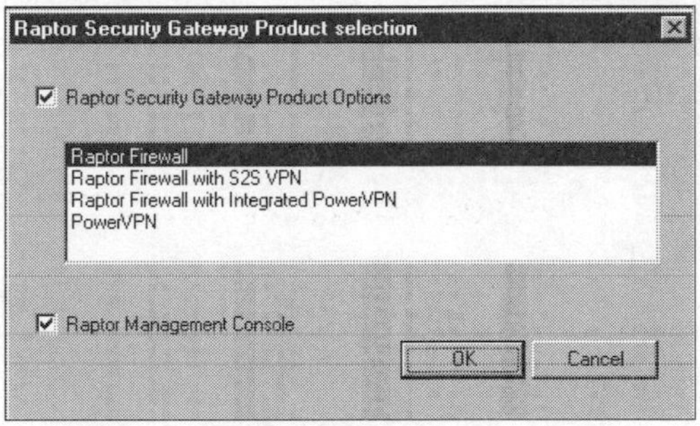

5. Once you have selected the software package, you must select the desired installation location, as shown in Figure 10.4.

Figure 10.4 Installation directory dialog box.

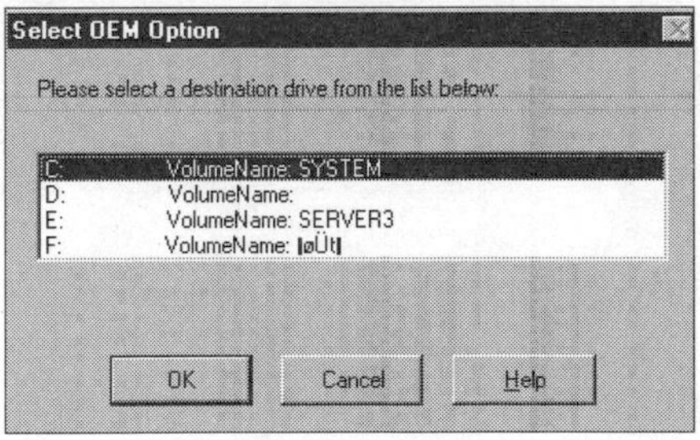

6. After you have selected your destination directory, the Raptor Firewall 6.5 package will be installed. Once the installation has finished, you will need to select which of your installed NIC(s) should be set up for the external network and which NIC(s) should be set up for the internal network (see Figure 10.5). Note that the NIC(s) on the internal and external networks must be configured on different subnets for proper operation.

Figure 10.5 Network selection for NICs.

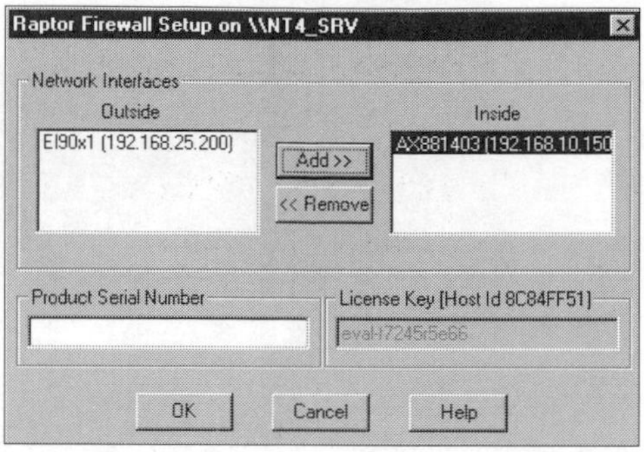

7. After your NICs have been set up on the network, you will need to configure a local administration password for the Raptor Management Console (RMC), as shown in Figure 10.6.

Figure 10.6 Set the local administration password for the Raptor Firewall.

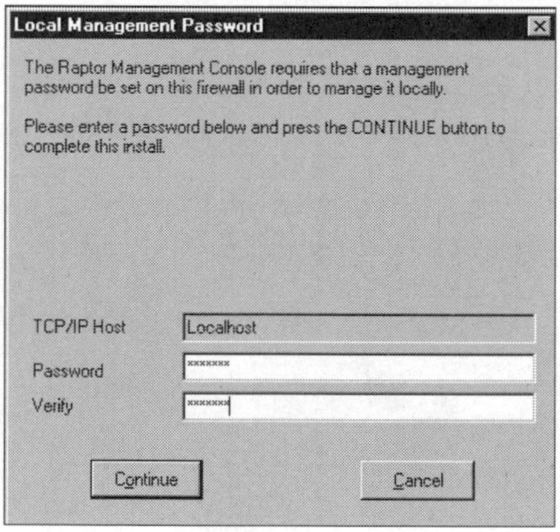

8. After you have completed this step, the software installation will go through some final stages before you need to restart your computer. Upon restart you will be ready to configure the Raptor Firewall.

9. Once you have restarted your system, you can verify proper installation in two ways. You can double-click on the Raptor Firewall Setup, and verify the proper location for your NICs. Alternatively, you may check your network settings. On the desktop, right-click on Network Neighborhood and then select Properties. Once the Properties screen is opened, go to the Adapters tab (see Figure 10.7). For each adapter you have loaded in your system, you should see a virtual NIC provided by the Raptor Firewall software.

Figure 10.7 Checking Network Properties for installation verification.

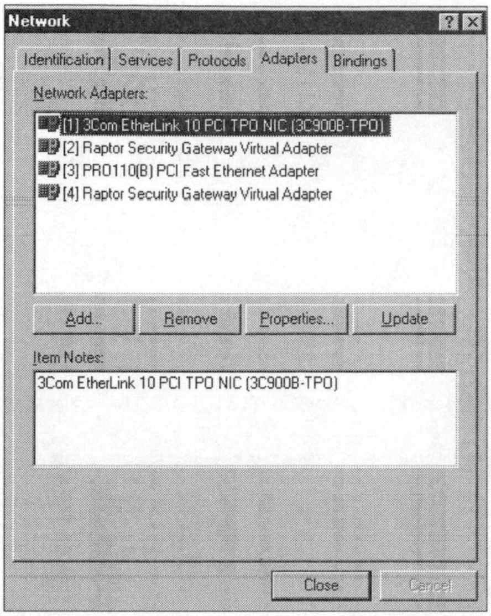

Configuring Raptor Firewall 6.5

Once the Raptor Firewall has been installed, you are ready to configure the rest of the settings to allow you to secure your network. You will access and modify the configuration options from the Raptor Management Console. During the installation, a shortcut was placed on the desktop for the RMC.

1. Locate the RMC shortcut on your desktop, and double-click it to launch the RMC application. When you open your first session, you will not have any connections to Raptor Firewalls configured. Expand AXENT Technologies, and you will find an icon for the Raptor Management Console. Your first screen should look like Figure 10.8.

2. You will need to click on the New Connection button to bring up the connection dialog box for the firewall. Once you have done that, you should see a dialog box like the one in Figure 10.9. If you are managing a local firewall (located on this system), you will need to make sure that you enter **localhost** in the Name field of the dialog box. You will also be required to provide the password that you used during the setup phase of the firewall.

Figure 10.8 Getting connected to the Raptor Firewall for the first time.

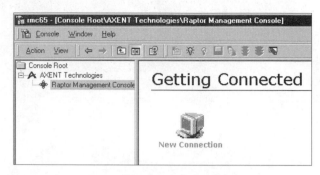

Figure 10.9 Creating a connection for a local firewall.

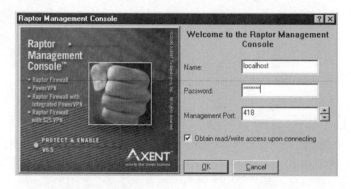

3. After you have successfully logged into the Raptor Firewall, your screen should look like Figure 10.10. First of all, notice the "nt4_srv(Connected)" icon to the left side of the screen. This shows you that you have successfully logged into the Raptor Firewall. To the right, you will see several icons for QuickStart and SMTP Wizard, wizards to help you set up some initial configuration parameters. The last icon, Disconnect from nt4_srv, will allow you to close a session while still keeping the RMC open.

QuickStart Configuration Wizard

After you have logged in, it is recommended, but not required, that you go through the wizards to help you set up your firewall. The QuickStart Wizard will help you configure Web and File Transfer Protocol (FTP) access, as well as assist you with setting up e-mail services.

Figure 10.10 The initial configuration wizards available upon login.

1. After you click on the QuickStart button, your first screen should look like Figure 10.11. Click Next to continue to the first configuration screen.

Figure 10.11 Welcome screen for the QuickStart Configuration Wizard.

2. The next screen (see Figure 10.12) will allow you to select which services you would like to configure. You may or may not need to configure either of these options, depending on your setup.

3. The next screen will ask for the server's Internet Protocol (IP) or Domain Name System (DNS) address for e-mail redirection (see Figure 10.13).

Figure 10.12 Select the services you would like to set up using the wizard.

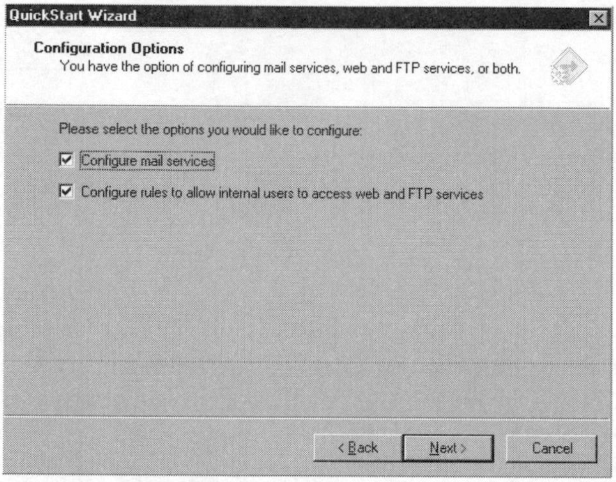

Figure 10.13 Enter the IP or DNS address of the server.

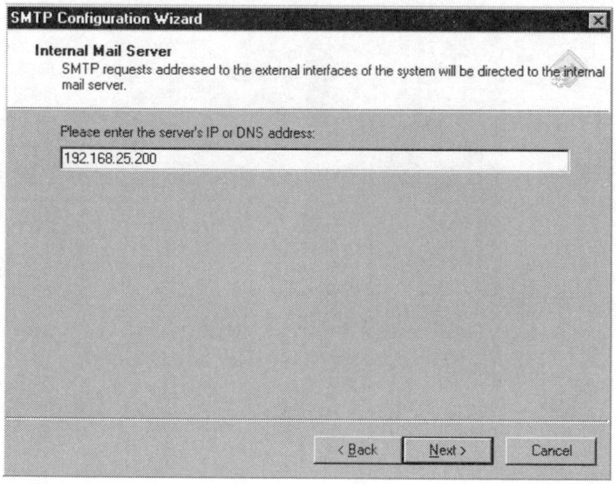

4. Next, select whether to allow internal users to send e-mail to external locations (see Figure 10.14). As the wizard states, if this is not selected, any rules that allow mail to be sent to all systems will be deleted.

Figure 10.14 Select whether or not internal users will be able to send e-mail outside the internal network.

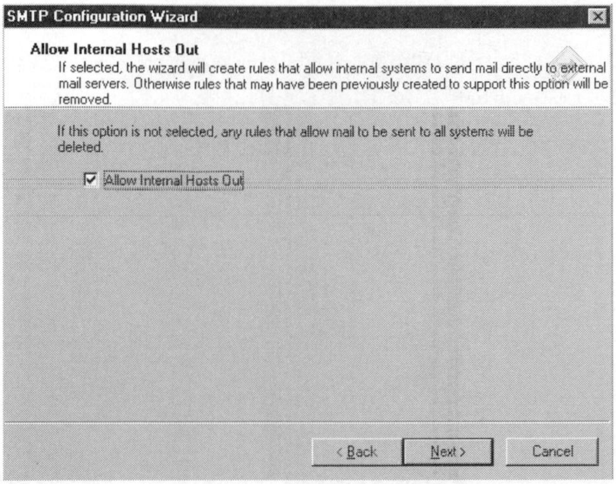

5. After you have configured these settings, the wizard will configure the proper rules for the firewall, and will restart the affected firewall services (see Figure 10.15). You have now completed this wizard, and you may go on to the next one if desired.

Figure 10.15 The QuickStart Wizard completes the desired settings.

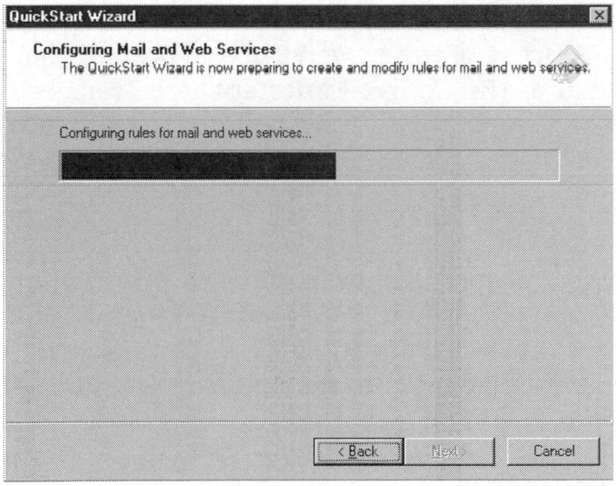

SMTP Configuration Wizard

Although the QuickStart Wizard did have some steps for e-mail, the SMTP Configuration Wizard provides more control over e-mail configuration.

1. When you click on the SMTP Configuration Wizard, your first screen will look like Figure 10.16.

    Figure 10.16 SMTP Configuration Wizard.

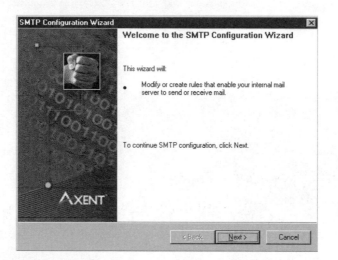

2. You will recognize the next two screens from the QuickStart Wizard (Figures 10.13 and 10.14), which ask you to enter the IP or DNS address of the server. The purpose of this is to allow e-mail directed at the external interface to be redirected to the internal mail server. After you have entered the IP address of the server, you will be asked whether to allow internal hosts to send e-mail outside of the internal network.

3. The next screen will allow you to set up anti-spam features for the firewall; you can add or modify current Realtime Blackhole List (RBL) servers, which allows you to block mail from specific sites that are known to be spam sites. Upon receipt of a message from an included spam site, the message will not be relayed beyond the firewall. See Figure 10.17.

4. The next screen, shown in Figure 10.18, will allow you to set up anti-relay settings for your e-mail rules. This works in hand with the anti-spam settings that you just set, but you may also add specific domains at this time if you wish.

Figure 10.17 Set up RBL servers to be included in your e-mail rules.

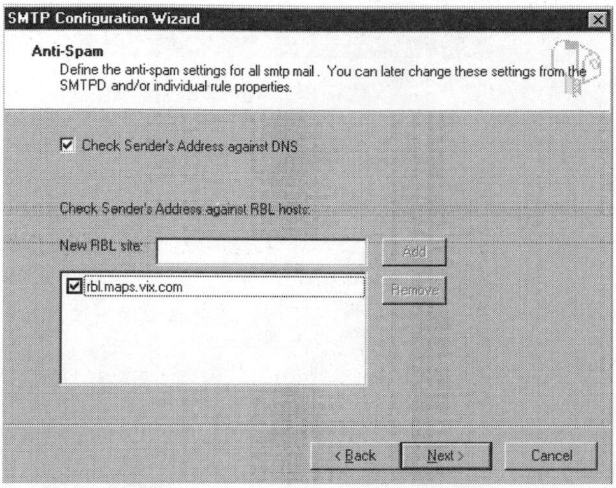

Figure 10.18 Set up anti-relay settings for e-mail.

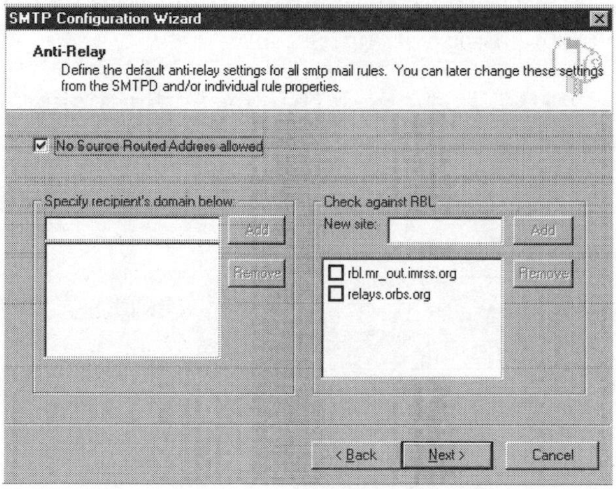

5. The next screen allows you to set your system to check a Dial-up User List (DUL). Utilizing a DUL is another way of keeping spam from riddling your network. You may select from one of the included sites or add your own, as shown in Figure 10.19. For more information on spam prevention, RBL, or DUL, check www.mail-abuse.org.

Figure 10.19 Set up DUL services with provided servers or add your own.

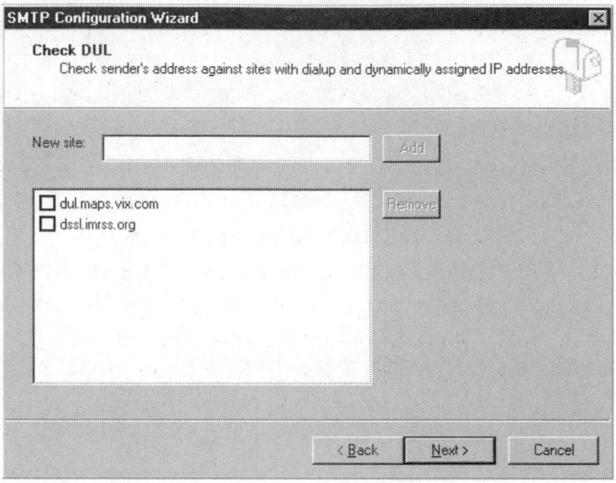

6. You have now completed the SMTP Configuration Wizard (Figure 10.20). Save and reconfigure now, as some of the settings will not take effect until you do.

Figure 10.20 Save your changes and reconfigure the Raptor Firewall.

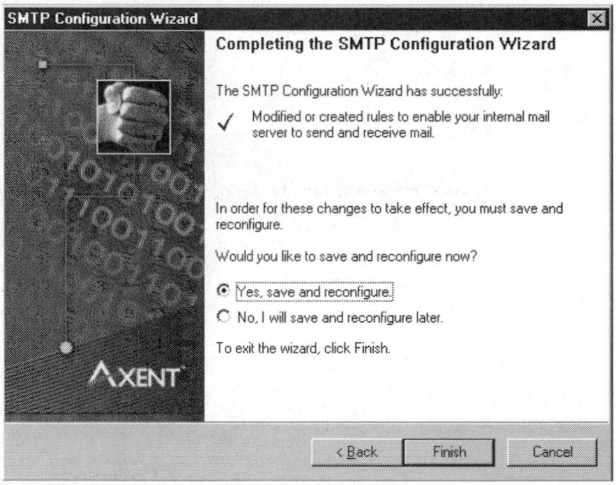

False Protection Against Spoofing and SYN Attacks

Note that in the anti-relay screen of the SMTP Configuration Wizard (see Figure 10.18) there is a checkbox for No Source Routed Address allowed. This box will cause the firewall to drop any of these packets that it receives. Source route addressing is where an incoming packet has a source address that is on the local subnet.

Although this is a good security practice to have, it does not protect you from SYN flooding or IP spoofing. To protect yourself from these threats, you should incorporate ingress filters on your routers. Cisco has a considerable amount of information on these topics on their Web site, as do other network solution providers such as 3Com, Sun, and Nortel Networks.

DNS Configuration

Raptor Firewall includes the capability to proxy DNS information for your internal network for IP to hostname translation.

1. To verify that you are using DNS Proxy, go to Access Controls and then go to Proxy Services. On the right-hand side of the screen you will see what proxy services are available. To check on the status of the DNS Proxy Daemon (DNSD), right-click on it and select Properties, as shown in Figure 10.21.

Figure 10.21 Select DNSD and go to properties for current settings.

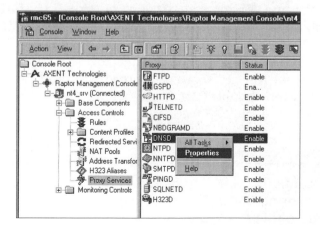

2. The Status tab in the Properties menu will allow you to turn DNSD on or off (see Figure 10.22).

Figure 10.22 Use this screen to select whether or not you will use DNSD.

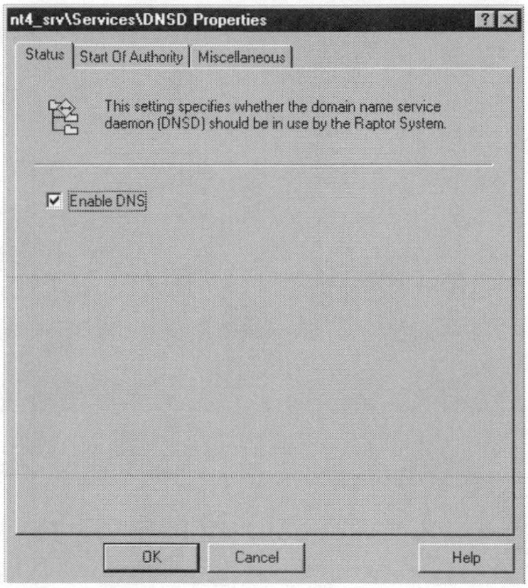

3. The Start of Authority (SOA) tab allows you to set the DNS timers such as refresh, retry, and expiration, as well as the Time-to-Live (TTL).

4. The Miscellaneous tab, shown in Figure 10.23, will allow you to specify a location for a Hosts file of your choice or use the default (which is the Windows NT 4 Host file). This tab will also allow you to log any DNS requests or deny outside RFC1597 addresses. RFC1597 is the allocation of address spaces for internal network use. These ranges include 10.0.0.0–10.255.255.255, 172.16.0.0–172.31.255.255, and 192.168.0.0–192.168.255.255. (Note that RFC 1597 was superceded by RFC 1918 in February of 1996, even though Raptor still shows 1597 in their dialog windows.)

WARNING

Do *not* configure a DNS server on the same server as the Raptor Firewall if you are using DNSD. This combination is not supported and will cause problems within the Raptor Firewall.

Figure 10.23 Set the location of the Hosts file.

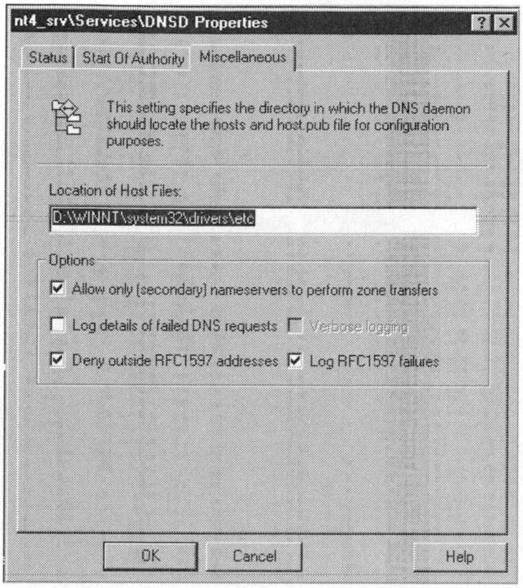

Creating DNS Host Entries

To create DNS entries for servers or other devices, perform the following steps.

1. Go to DNS Records and right-click in the right-hand section of the screen. Select New and then Host, as shown in Figure 10.24.

Figure 10.24 Select Host from the New menu to create a new DNS Host entry.

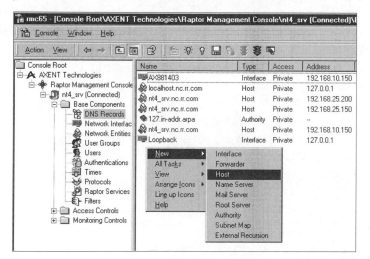

2. Next, select what type of entry this is to be. If you select Private, only users on the internal network will have access to this entry and it will be added to the Hosts file. If you select Public, this entry will be added to the Hosts.pub file and it will be accessible to everyone. See Figure 10.25.

Figure 10.25 Select the desired options for the new Host entry.

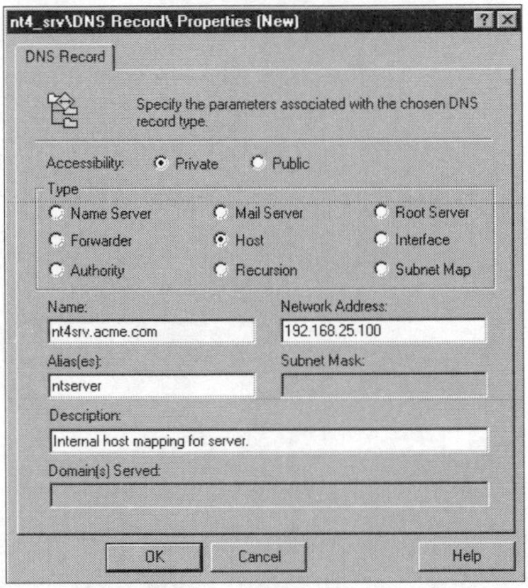

Network Interface Configuration

There are several options that you can configure on your installed NICs, including filters, IP addresses, and card names.

1. To access the configuration options, select Network Interfaces under Base Components (Figure 10.26).

2. Right-click on the desired NIC and go to Properties (we are beginning with the internal network NIC). Under Properties, you will see several tabs (Figure 10.27). The first tab is for general information. The NIC was given a name by Raptor, so you may want to change it if it will help you remember it better. You may also enter a Description or change the IP address.

3. Under the Options tab (shown in Figure 10.28), you will be able to select whether this NIC is part of the internal network or external network. You may also allow Multicast Traffic, which is traffic destined to a group of nodes. Two things to be sure you are aware of are SYN Flood Protection and the Port Scan Detection. See

Chapter 5 for more information on SYN flooding. Port Scan detection will allow the firewall to detect if someone is scanning this interface for open ports. Since we are configuring an internal network NIC, we will not enable Port Scan Detection or SYN Flood Protection. This, of course, is up to you and how you will set up your network.

Figure 10.26 Locate the Network Interfaces section of the Raptor configuration.

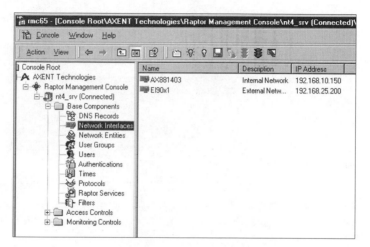

Figure 10.27 General options menu of a selected NIC.

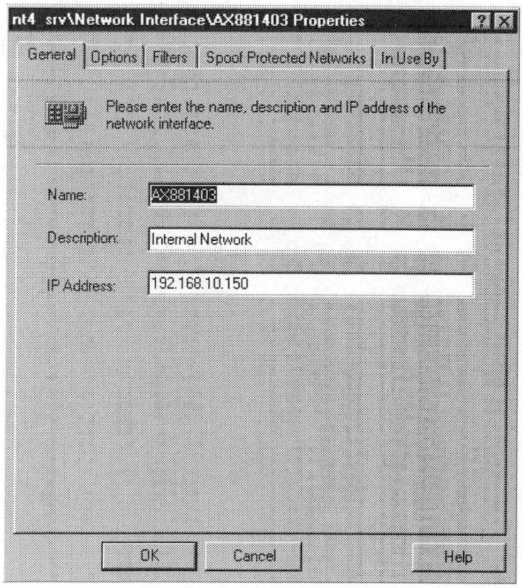

Figure 10.28 Select options for your NIC.

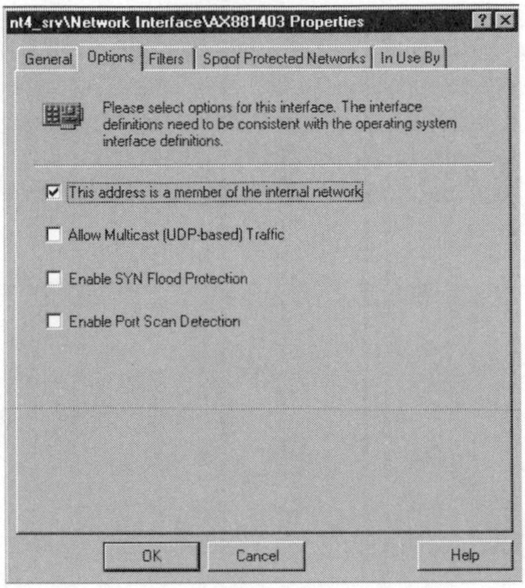

4. The Filters tab, shown in Figure 10.29, will allow you to set any filters you have created as input or output filters on this interface. Note that Raptor Firewall ships with a sample Denial of Service (DoS) filter.

Figure 10.29 Select any filters that are to be applied to this interface.

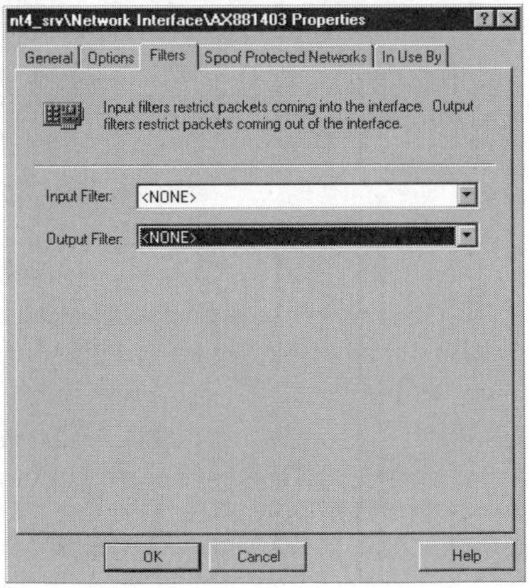

5. Under the Spoof Protected Networks tab (see Figure 10.30), you select any network entities that should be spoof protected. Universe* is the default network entity and is not protected by default. If you have specific areas that should be protected, you should create a network entity for that area and enable protection here. Network entities will be covered later in this chapter.

Figure 10.30 Select any network entities that should be spoof protected.

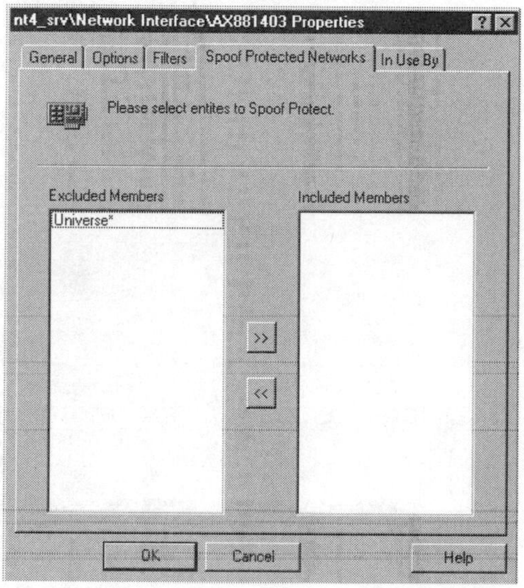

6. The In Use By tab lists the services and rules that are utilizing the selected NIC (see Figure 10.31).

External NIC Configuration

In this section, we will be configuring the external NIC that will interface with networks outside of your own.

1. Select your NIC that is being used by the external network. Right-click on it and select Properties. Once you are in the Properties screen, there are several changes you can make that are different from the default setup.

2. Under the Options tab (see Figure 10.32), you could also set up SYN Flood Protection and Port Scan Detection. You should make sure that the This Address Is A Member Of The Internal Network checkbox is not checked because obviously this NIC is not. If this box is checked, Raptor will treat this NIC as if it were on the trusted internal network.

Figure 10.31 This tab details the services and rules that are using this NIC.

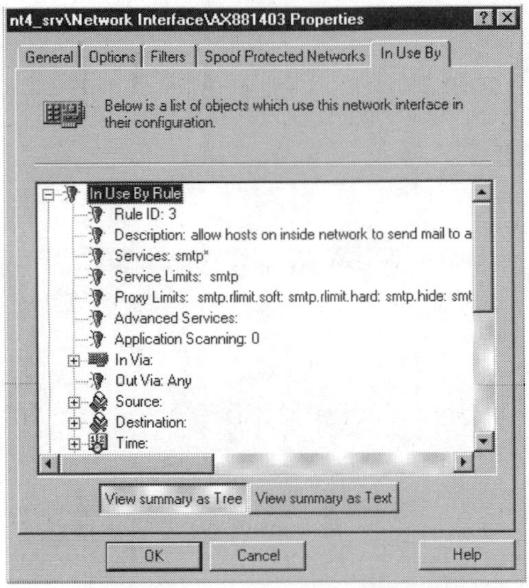

Figure 10.32 Interface options for setting up your external network NIC.

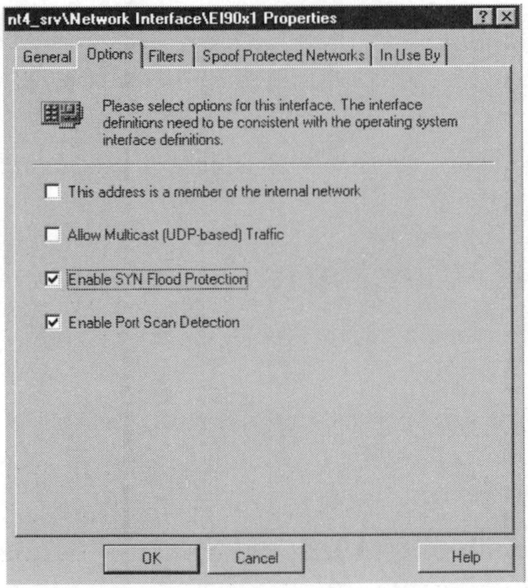

> ## WARNING
>
> You should enable SYN Flood Protection only *during* an attack. Otherwise you could cause services or daemons to fail. This should never be enabled for more than a couple of hours at a time.

3. You should also go to the Filters tab and select any input or output filters you desire for this NIC (see Figure 10.33). In this case, I have selected the sample DoS filter that is included with the Raptor package.

    Figure 10.33 Select any input or output filters that you would like to associate with this NIC.

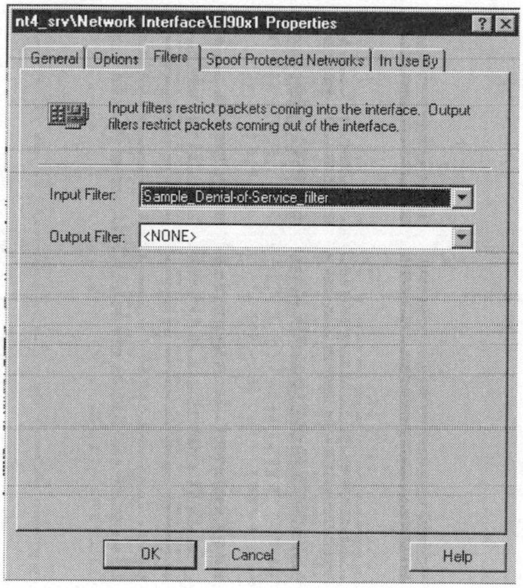

Creating Network Entities

Network entities must be created for the Raptor Firewall for any user, group, subnet, or domain (not NT domain) that will be passing data through the firewall. The first steps are for a subnet entity, and they are followed by settings for a domain entity.

1. To add a new network entity, go to Base Components | Network Entities. Once you have clicked on the Network Entities section (see Figure 10.34), you will see the default network entity Universe*.

Figure 10.34 Select network entities under the Base Components folder.

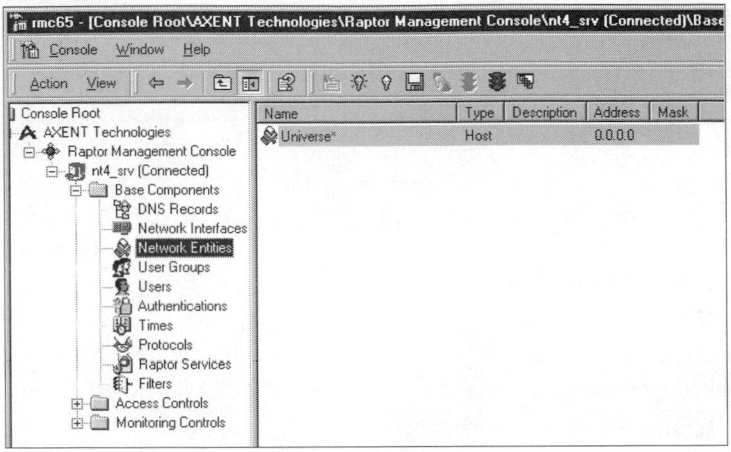

2. First, you will create a network entity for your subnet. Right-click on the right-hand pane, and then select New | Subnet, as shown in Figure 10.35. This will create a new subnet network entity file.

Figure 10.35 Creating a new subnet network entity.

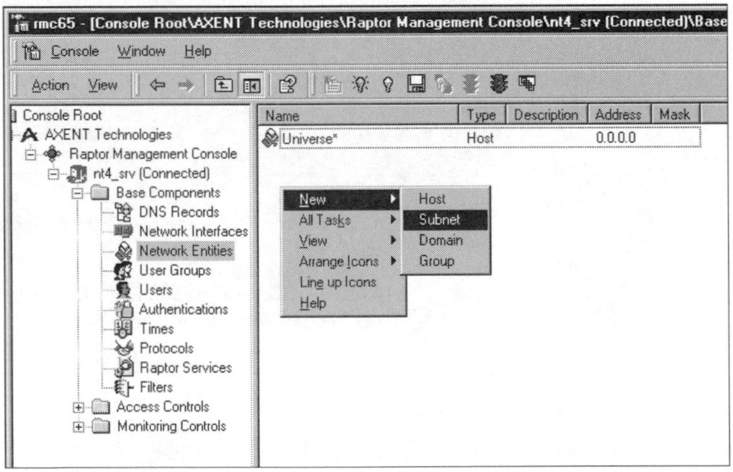

3. You are given a Properties dialog box for the configuration for the new network entity. The Name field (under the General tab, as seen in Figure 10.36) can be populated only by contiguous alphanumeric characters, without any spaces. Make sure that the type is *Subnet* before proceeding.

Figure 10.36 General information screen in a new subnet network entity.

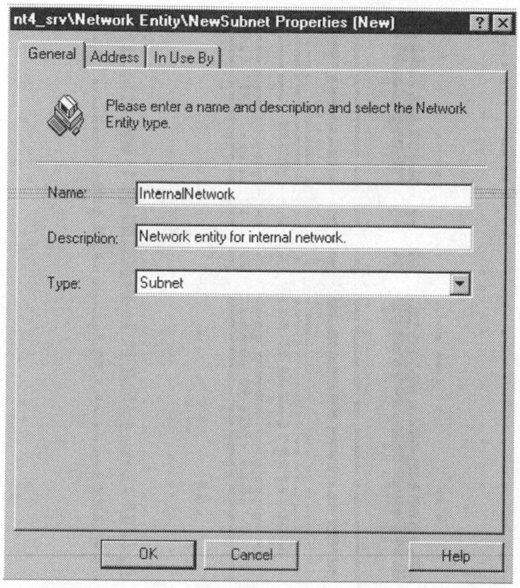

4. In the Address tab, select the proper IP address subnet or individual address. If you wanted to enter 10.16.1.1 by itself, you would enter 10.16.1.1 with a mask of 255.255.255.255. In this case, we are going to enter the network 192.168.10.0 with a mask of 255.255.255.0 (see Figure 10.37).

Figure 10.37 Indicate the desired subnet or individual address for this network entity.

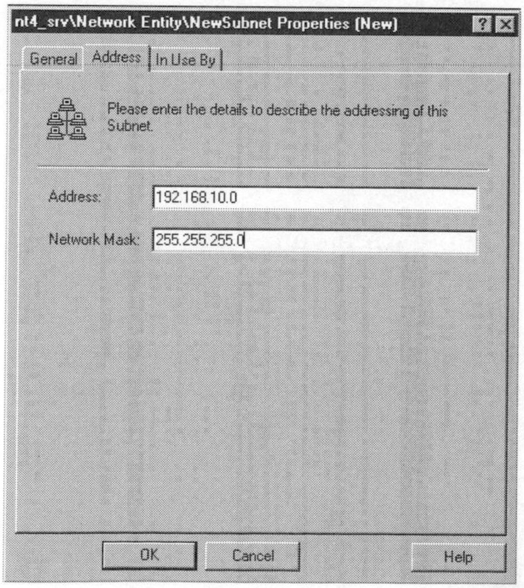

5. If you would like to view what this entity is used by, you can look at the In Use By tab. Since this has not been saved or activated yet, it will not have anything listed (see Figure 10.38). At this point, you may click OK, and you should find your new network entity in the list.

Figure 10.38 Services and rules utilizing this network entity.

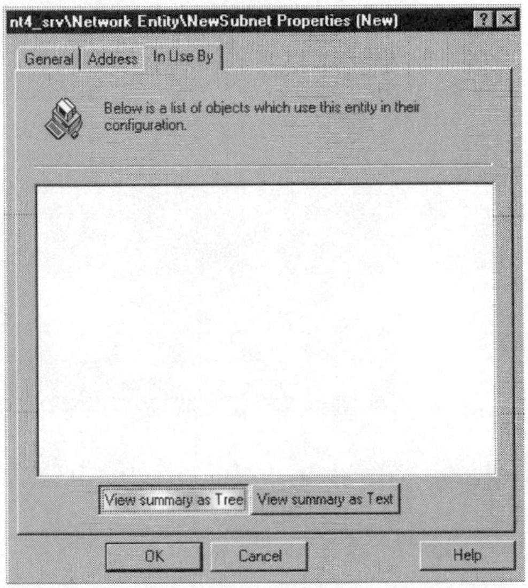

Now that we have completed the configuration of a subnet network entity, we will go through the configuration of a domain network entity.

1. Right-click on the right-hand pane and select New | Domain. You should see the New Domain Properties screen as shown in Figure 10.39.

2. You will need to list the domain that you would like to be accepted. After you have listed the domain (shown in Figure 10.40), you have completed the setup of the network entity.

You have now configured your Raptor Firewall to be functional. You still need to make sure that you can access necessary resources like Web, e-mail, and FTP. You may create specific rules to allow other network services or proprietary applications. More information about the installation and configuration of Axent's Raptor Firewall may be found on their Web site at www.axent.com.

Figure 10.39 Name your domain network entity and give it a description.

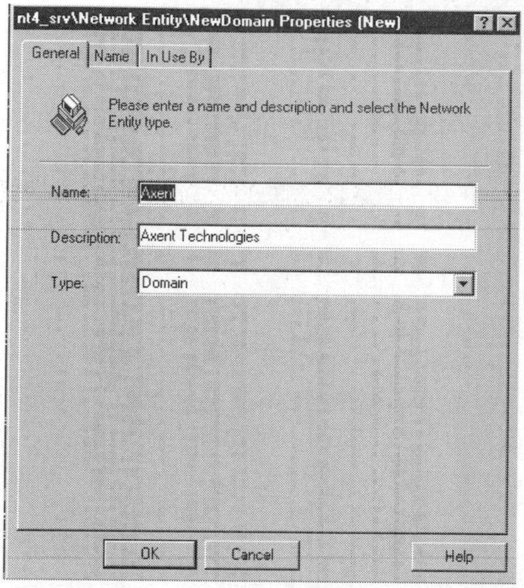

Figure 10.40 Add the name of the domain that you would like to have access through the Raptor system.

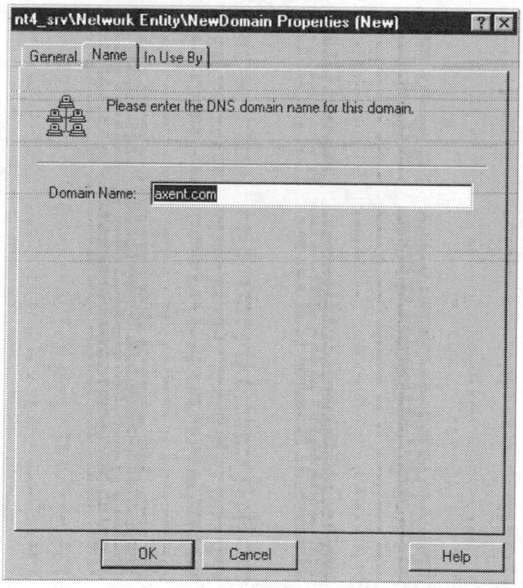

Applying the Firewall to Your Security Model

Like any other firewall application there are many different ways that you can deploy it. We will look at some of the more common ways to deploy the Raptor Firewall in a network security model. We will look at a basic setup, a deployment of the firewall with a DMZ, and a setup that will utilize multiple Raptor Firewall systems.

Basic Deployment

In a very basic deployment, we can utilize the Raptor Firewall as the direct communication device to the network services (see Figure 10.41). Using a router as a filtering mechanism (for spoofing attacks), we can also protect against SYN Flooding and DoS attacks. Some drawbacks to this design are that there is a single point of failure, and there isn't a Demilitarized Zone (DMZ) deployed for network services such as Web servers or mail servers.

Figure 10.41 Basic Raptor deployment.

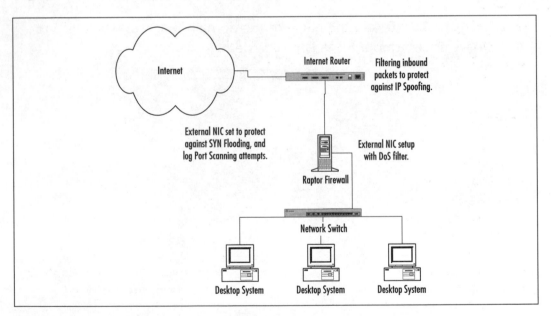

Deployment with a DMZ

It is also possible to deploy the Raptor Firewall in conjunction with some of the networking concepts described in Chapter 2. For instance, a lot of corporate environments set up a DMZ to separate their mail and Web servers from the rest of the network.

The basic premise behind this is to limit traffic where it isn't needed. Since there is a need for a lot of traffic to pass through the Web and mail servers, having them on the network where the internal users are just adds to the likelihood of intrusion. Deploying a DMZ with protocol switching will also limit the effectiveness of TCP/IP-based attacks (see Figure 10.42).

Figure 10.42 Deployment with protocol switching and a DMZ.

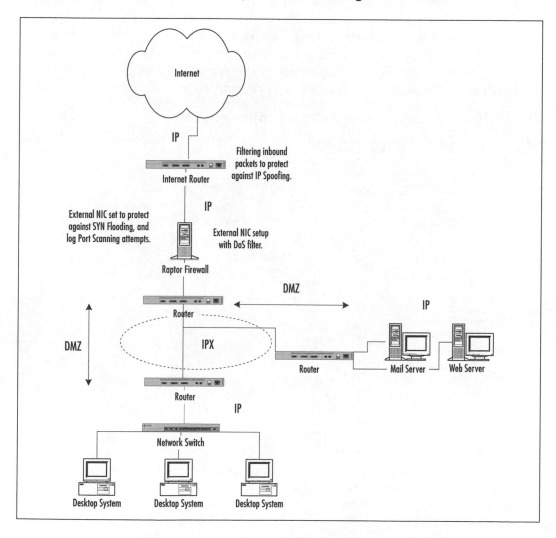

Deployment of Multiple Raptor Firewall Systems

One thing to remember about your configuration and deployment of the Raptor system is that you are not limited to the number of firewalls that you may deploy. As long as you paid for the proper licensing, you may deploy a firewall wherever you perceive there to be a weakness in your network (see Figure 10.43). Keep in mind that as you add more firewalls, you will also be adding to the administrative effort required to get and keep everything operational. In areas that require very high throughput, make sure that your proposed network server can handle the demand. In other words, it may not be a good idea to put a Raptor system in place with 10 Mbps NICs if it is protecting a busy Web or mail server.

Figure 10.43 Deployment of multiple Raptor firewalls.

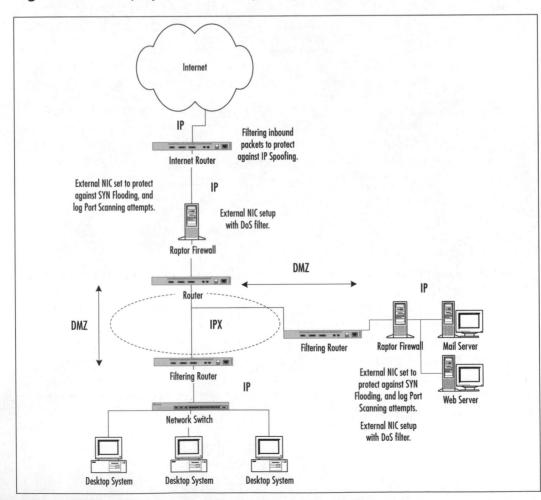

Avoiding Known Security Issues

There are some security issues associated with the Raptor Firewall and with firewalls in general, that we will cover in this section. It is important that you understand them, and understand how to protect yourself from them. Some of the other things we will cover in this section are some specific ways to protect your network from Distributed Denial of Service (DDoS) attacks.

Connectivity

Axent's Raptor Firewall is susceptible to the same design rules that you would apply to any other firewall. Since this package is based on a server, you have to be aware of software configuration rules as well as hardware connectivity. To review a couple of warnings covered in Chapter 2:

- Never connect both of your installed NICs (or more if you have them installed) to the same switch. That will most assuredly defeat the purpose of the firewall.

- Do not place high traffic systems such as mail or Web servers on the same segment as your internal local area network (LAN).

A note from Axent's Web page reminds you to make sure that if you ever uninstall or disable the Raptor Firewall, you also disconnect the external network from the machine until you can ensure proper security. If you were to uninstall it and leave all of the connections up, that machine would be susceptible to attack.

Setting Up a DDoS Filter

DDoS attacks have become quite a nuisance in the corporate sector lately, so it is a good idea to prepare your network for an encounter with one. Raptor Firewall can be set up to protect you from most DDoS attacks, and this could help alleviate some of your management worries. However, it doesn't protect your network from everything associated with DDoS, so you may have to take further action.

More detail on the following steps can be found in the support documentation for the Raptor software package. Please note that several of these steps will affect network bandwidth. If the amount of bandwidth used is too great, you may need to turn some of these off and use another device to provide this function.

1. You may utilize the sample DoS filter that was included with the firewall. If you recall, earlier in the chapter we applied it to the external network NIC to filter inbound packets. This filter will block everything but DNS and TCP. Axent makes it a point to let you know that if you need other network services, you will need to modify this filter to include them.

2. Turn on the Connection Rate Limit, which can be located in the **\%root%\Raptor\Firewall\sg** directory. The file you are looking for is **config.cf.** This function is disabled by default (with a value of −1), but it can be used to limit the number of connections allowed to a client. To enable it, use the following settings:

   - **connection_rate.limit=X**, where X equals the number of connections desired per client. Axent recommends a number of 1000. This means that anything over 1000 will be discarded.

   - **connection_rate.interval=30**, as the way to gauge the time buckets for counting connections. Axent recommends leaving this at 30 seconds when under attack.

   - **connection_rate.blocktime**=3600. This has to do with the amount of time Raptor will block traffic from a client that has exceeded one or more of the other settings. This timer is measured in seconds, and is set to 3600 by default (1 hour). This default value is also recommended when under attack.

   - **connection_rate.limit=x.x.x.x**, where x.x.x.x is equal to the desired IP address. This command allows you to specify IP addresses to associate with the connection rate limit. You may use this to increase a connection limit to a client, but you should not use this to decrease a client's limit. This can cause problems with the firewall.

3. In that same file you may also set the maximum allowed size for a Packet Internet Groper (PING) packet. PING utilizes Internet Control Message Protocol (ICMP) echoes to verify connectivity, and the following command will allow you to limit the PING packet size: **Ping.maxlength=xxxx,** where **xxxx** is the desired size of the packet.

4. Remember to enable the SYN Flood protection on the necessary interfaces only during an attack. Doing so will allow the NIC to keep bandwidth available for true TCP connections.

5. Turn *off* Port Scan Detection on the necessary interfaces. If your network is deluged with port scans, logging it would create an

entry for each time the attacker scans a port. If there is a lot of this kind of activity, the generation of such packets could severely impact performance.

6. Disable Interface Input Packet Filter Logging. Disabling this logging service keeps Raptor from trying to track all of the open connections. In times of an attack, there can be several thousand connections. This causes the system to track individual, bogus connections. You should have an Intrusion Detection System (IDS) in place to assist with this operation. To complete this task, follow these steps:

- Stop the firewall service in the RMC.

- Locate the rstartgw.cmd file in the **\%root%\Raptor\Firewall\bin** directory. Open this file with a text editor (don't launch it).

- Locate the following string of text:

```
- vpn set "/interfaces/1.1.1.1/Suppress Input FilterLog"
true
```

You will need to put your firewall's interface IP address in place of the 1.1.1.1, and then uncomment the line to disable this logging.

7. Disable all packet logging. This is recommended by Axent *only* as a last resort. Disabling all logging will allow you to free up even more resources to help combat the DDoS attack. The steps for this are as follows:

- Stop the firewall service from the RMC.

- Locate the rstartgw.cmd file in the **\%root%\Raptor\Firewall\bin** directory. Open this file with a text editor (don't launch it).

- Locate the string of text:

```
vpn set "/global/Don't_Log_Packets" true
```

and uncomment this line. That will enable this feature for your use.

For more information on this setup guide for DDoS attacks, please go to www.axent.com.

Summary

This chapter shows how to install and configure the Raptor Firewall package. We have covered a lot of the basics required to get you up and running with this firewall suite, but be sure to visit Axent's Web site for more information and helpful hints.

Remember that Raptor 6.5 currently supports Member Server configurations and that Primary Domain Controllers (PDCs) and Backup Domain Controllers (BDCs) are currently not supported. Also, Raptor does not support NT's implementation of software RAID, so plan accordingly.

After you have successfully installed the firewall, you will need to log in locally to the Raptor Firewall using the password you created during installation and the localhost name. Once you have connected, you may run the QuickStart and SMTP wizards to assist you in the initial configuration of the firewall. After you have run these wizards you should have Web, mail, and FTP connectivity.

There are steps that can be taken to provide decent protection from DDoS attacks, but remember that some of them will affect firewall performance. Enabling SYN Flood protection on the desired interface, applying the sample DoS filter to the input of the external network NIC, setting the connection rate limits, and disabling several types of logging will help alleviate some of the problems encountered with DoS attacks.

FAQs

Q: How can I use more network services on my system?

A: Raptor Firewall uses a program called Vulture to kill any programs or services not being used by or not needed by the firewall. The default activation timer is set to every 60 seconds, and this timer may be modified on a per-user basis. To set this on a per-user basis, enter a username below the 60-second value.

The location of Vulture is **\%root%\Raptor\Firewall\sg\ vulture.runtime**. If you change the default value of 60 to –1, you will disable Vulture. Of course, this is not recommended for proper firewall operation.

Q: I have installed the Raptor Firewall, so why has my network still received some of the recent viruses?

A: First and foremost, one of the pitfalls of a firewall is that it doesn't protect your network from viruses, worms, and Trojan horses. Standard firewalls don't have any method of scanning e-mail to verify whether malicious code is attached. The solution for this problem is to add a virus software package like Norton AntiVirus Corporate Edition 7.5 from Symantec, to allow scanning of your e-mail content. Another good way to help defend against this problem is to block specific file types. For more information on this, please refer to Chapter 5.

Q: After I installed Raptor Firewall, I could no longer access Web sites outside of my internal network. What could be the problem?

A: There are a couple of things that you can look at regarding your firewall:

- First of all, make sure that you have applied all of the latest patches and upgrades for the Raptor Firewall. Any number of the known issues may be causing your system to experience problems.

- Make sure that you don't have SYN Flood protection turned on for any of your interfaces. SYN Flood protection should be turned on only *during* an attack, and should never be left on for more than a couple of hours. Doing so could cause the HTTP Daemon (HTTPD) to fail.

- Make sure that you have enough disk space available on your system and make sure that your page file has enough room on the hard drive. Lack of space can cause a number of problems, not just with the firewall but with Windows NT 4 as well.

Chapter 11

Check Point Software's Check Point FireWall-1

Solutions in this chapter:

- FireWall-1 Features
- Requirements and Installation
- Configuring FireWall-1
- Troubleshooting
- Avoiding Possible Security Issues

Introduction

This chapter will focus on another software solution for network security. Check Point Software's FireWall-1 is a product that offers an intuitive configuration interface and strong security measures. FireWall-1 provides good security for your network without complex configuration tasks.

FireWall-1 Features

The functionality and security provided by the features of a particular software package are what determines whether you will choose that software on your network. The features in FireWall-1 address a number of elements of enterprise security, which are integrated and managed through the components that make up the firewall product.

FireWall-1 offers a modular, scalable architecture, allowing you to add additional modules to the firewall and thereby add more features. For example, FireWall-1 provides the ability to add Virtual Private Network (VPN) services through a separate, optional module. This module must be purchased separately from FireWall-1, as must several others, which we'll discuss in the sections that follow. The primary components that come with FireWall-1 include:

- Graphical User Interface (GUI) Console
- Management Server
- Firewall Module

These components allow you to design and implement security policies that can be centrally managed through a single console.

The Graphical User Interface is used to design and manage your security policy, and serves as a Policy Editor. As shown in Figure 11.1, the GUI Console allows you to create rules for various network objects. These objects include such network elements as gateways, hosts, and users, so that you can create security policies for them at a granular level. As we'll see later in this chapter, the security policy is created by modifying the properties of these objects through the Policy Editor.

The security policy you create with the GUI Console is stored on the Management Server, which maintains the databases in FireWall-1. These databases store information regarding user definitions, network object definitions, log files, and of course, the security policy. It also downloads the security policy you create with the GUI to the Firewall Module. This module can be deployed to the same computer as the Graphical User Interface.

Figure 11.1 Rules for your network are displayed, created, and set in FireWall-1's Graphical User Interface.

No.	Source	Destination	Service	Action	Track	Install On	Time
1	external_net	MAIL_Server	smtp	accept	Long	PDTarget	Any
2	external_net	DMZserver	http ftp	accept	Short	PDTarget	Any
3	local_net	Any	Any	accept	Long	PDTarget	Any

The Firewall Module consists of the Inspection Module and the Security Servers. The Inspection Module inspects packets to ensure they adhere to the security policy, and the Security Server provides authentication and content security. We will discuss each of these in the sections that follow. The Firewall Module is deployed on network access points, such as Internet gateways.

Although FireWall-1 is made up of different server components that can be installed on different server machines, you don't necessarily need to install them on more than one. For example, you might decide to have one server provide anti-virus checking, and have files passing through FireWall-1 diverted to this server. You could just as easily set up anti-virus checking to be performed on a single server running FireWall-1. In designing your firewall structure, you will need to decide whether you will use one or more servers.

Is Check Point FireWall-1 Right for You?

A good method of deciding whether a firewall meets the functionality requirements and level of security needed by your company is to look at what other organizations have found. Word of mouth speaks volumes, and you will be able to discover success stories and pitfalls. By contacting the IT Management of enterprises similar to your own, you may learn from their experiences and make a better decision in choosing a firewall product.

I know numerous success stories from the experiences of law enforcement agencies that have chosen FireWall-1 to protect information on their internal networks. Obviously, it is important that hackers aren't able to access internal law enforcement networks. In choosing FireWall-1, this speaks to the security provided by this firewall software.

Continued

It is also important to note that Check Point is integral as a member of the Open Platform for Security (OPSEC) Alliance. OPSEC was founded with the mandate to provide users with integrated security solutions, and provides integrated security related applications for the Check Point platform. OPSEC has over 200 members, which makes it the leading platform alliance in this area.

Access Control

Of all the features provided by FireWall-1, access control is one of the most basic, and most important. Access control is the method by which you keep out the people who shouldn't have access to your network, and allow through the firewall those who should have access. It also determines who on your network has the ability to pass through the firewall to go onto the Internet.

FireWall-1's access control abilities can grow as your company grows, making it a suitable choice for small businesses and large enterprises alike. FireWall-1 has access control for more than 150 predefined applications, services, and protocols, and allows you to define custom services. It also allows you to set multiple levels of user access, so that you can assign different rights to users and administrators. These access levels are set through a Graphical User Interface, and the rules you create are saved to the rule base. When a user is authenticated, they inherit access rights that are stored in the security policy.

FireWall-1's Inspection module is used to examine packets passing through Internet gateways, routers, switches, servers, and workstations on your network. These packets don't enter the network unless they adhere to the security policy you've implemented. As shown in Figure 11.2, the Inspection module resides at the lowest possible software level, below the network layer. This module is in the operating system kernel, and analyzes all packets before higher protocol layers process them.

Stateful Inspection

Check Point FireWall-1 uses a patented method of inspection technology called *stateful inspection*. This provides the highest possible level of security and performance, as every packet that passes through key locations of your network (such as Internet gateways, servers, workstations, routers, and switches) is inspected. If unwanted communication is attempted, based on rules you create for FireWall-1 security policy, then the stateful inspection method will intercept the communication and block it.

Figure 11.2 Placement of FireWall-1 Inspection Module in the Open Systems Interconnection (OSI) Reference Model.

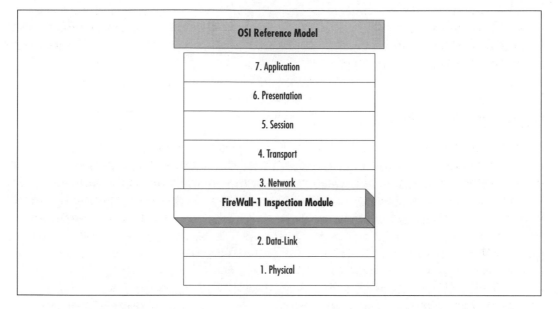

This inspection is performed by the Inspection Module that was mentioned in the previous section. Communications from the IP protocol, or any application using IP, are inspected. This includes stateless protocols like User Datagram Protocol (UDP) and Remote Procedure Call (RPC). As shown by Figure 11.2, this resides in the lowest level of software, so that packets won't be passed to higher levels unless they meet the policy you set. Data stored within the packet is extracted, so that state and context information can be stored in dynamic connection tables. The dynamic connection tables are updated regularly, which is then used to check any subsequent packets that FireWall-1 receives.

FireWall-1 also uses a special language called INSECT. This language is used to create scripts that allow you to integrate application, state, and communication information as well as security rules that you specify. It is an object-orientated language that is used to provide FireWall-1's Inspection Module with rules. While you create a policy using FireWall-1's GUI interface, the rules are stored within an Inspection Script. The script is an ASCII file, which is generated automatically from your settings, and compiled and loaded in the Inspection Module. In cases where you need special security rules, or want to perform certain tasks, you can edit the script using the INSPECT language. This can be done using any text editor.

Content Security: Anti-Virus, URL, and Java/ActiveX Screening

Content security determines what Web content can get through the firewall. When visiting Web pages or downloading e-mail with file attachments, these files may contain elements that are dangerous to your network. Some may contain viruses, others may have programs embedded in them that can cause damage. Content security allows you to protect your network from viruses and malicious programs in the form of ActiveX or Java applets. This allows you to control what is passed onto your network from Web pages, e-mail, and so forth.

In FireWall-1, you are able to choose the virus scanner that you want to use with the firewall. This allows you to purchase the anti-virus program you want to use separately, and integrate it with FireWall-1. You can install this anti-virus software on the same server as FireWall-1 or different servers on your network. Once this software is installed, rules dealing with how virus scanning will be used are created using the Security Policy Editor, which is the GUI Console used to set security rules.

In terms of anti-virus scans, rules allow you to specify how elements going onto your network will be dealt with. For example, you could create a rule that requires e-mail to be checked for viruses before it is passed through the firewall. When FireWall-1 finds communications that meet this rule, the e-mail is diverted used the Content Vectoring Protocol (CVP). The e-mail attachment goes to the server running the anti-virus software, and is checked. If it passes the scan, it is passed back to FireWall-1, which allows it to continue to its destination. The user for whom the e-mail is destined is unaware of this, but can remain confident that any attachments he or she receives are safe to open and use.

You can also create rules that will filter Java and ActiveX applets and scripts, so that these can't get through the firewall and damage your network. Because rules can be set at a granular level, you are able to create rules based on user authentication, host, or URL. This allows you to filter Java and ActiveX applets from all URLs except certain ones (such as Check Point's or Microsoft's Web sites).

FireWall-1's URL Filtering Protocol allows you to control what users of your network are able to access on the Internet. This should be used in conjunction with log files generated by FireWall-1, which show what URLs users are visiting. URL filtering can then be used to block users from visiting sites that aren't work related, or sites that may contain files that shouldn't be downloaded by users. This preserves bandwidth, so the network doesn't become bogged down by content that users shouldn't be viewing.

FireWall-1 also provides protection from the Simple Mail Transfer Protocol (SMTP). Despite the benefits of SMTP, it also poses problems for administrators. These problems include such things as unsolicited e-mail (spam), the release of internal information in the e-mail header, and so on. FireWall-1 deals with these problems through a variety of methods. Of great benefit, spam can be blocked by FireWall-1, so that users aren't bombarded with garbage e-mail. You can also redirect mail, so that it is sent to a specific e-mail account. This stops e-mail sent to the root address or to users who are no longer with the company. If you don't want such e-mail being redirected, it can also be dropped, so that it never gets past the firewall. In terms of security, FireWall-1 can hide the "From" address, and remove the address from the "Received" information in outgoing mail. Instead, a generic address is used, which hides the internal network structure and usernames from the outside world. Attachments included with incoming e-mail can be stripped from a message, or virus scanned (mentioned earlier). If you are concerned about particularly large files being sent to network users through e-mail, you can also configure FireWall-1 to drop messages that are larger than a specific size.

TIP

Once Internet access is given to users of a network, there is always a segment of your user population that will try to use the network to access Web sites that have nothing to do with their work. Some will go to text-based sites (such as those offering recipes), but there are always those who will decide to check out graphic-intensive sites (such as those offering pornographic images). In addition to wasting company time and money, the graphics that they may download can bog down your network. Graphic files can be quite large either by themselves or in groups, so this can become a major consideration when implementing a firewall. In addition, sites offering pirated software can create legal problems for your company, and may contain viruses. You should monitor logs of what sites users are visiting regularly, and visit them to view their content. If they aren't work related, then take advantage of URL filtering and block users from visiting them.

User Authentication

As mentioned previously, FireWall-1's Security Servers provide user authentication. If your security policy specifies authentication for File

Transfer Protocol (FTP), Hypertext Transfer Protocol (HTTP), Telnet, and RLOGIN, then the Inspection Module will redirect the connection to the appropriate Security Server. Once the connection is redirected, then the Security Server performs authentication based on the settings in the security policy.

FireWall-1 allows you to authenticate users of any IP application or service on a granular level. User authentication is transparent, and allows you to set access levels on a user-by-user basis. This is regardless of the IP address of the computer from which the user is working. You can define how individual users are authenticated, and what applications and services will be available to them. You can even specify the times that users will be able to access the network.

FireWall-1 supports a number of different authentication schemes. These schemes include:

- FireWall-1 password, which is a password set up through FireWall-1.

- OS password, which is an operating system password.

- S/Key, in which the user is challenged to enter the value of requested S/Key iteration.

- RSA SecureID tokens, which requires the user to enter a number displayed on a Security Dynamics SecureID token card. This is explained in greater detail in paragraphs that follow.

- Axent Pathways Defender, in which the user is challenged to enter a password defined by an Axent Defender server.

- Terminal Access Controller Access Control System/TACACS Plus (TACACS/TACACS+), which challenges the user for a response that's defined by the TACACS/TACACS+ server.

- Digital Certificates, which are used to establish your credentials electronically using information from a certificate authority.

- Remote Access Dial-in User Service (RADIUS), which allows users to dial into the network from a remote location. When users dial into the network, they are authenticated, so that unwanted users are kept from gaining access.

- X.509, which has the user authenticated through the presentation of a digital certificate that's issued by a Certificate Authority.

In addition to user authentication, FireWall-1 can authenticate based on sessions and clients. Client authentication allows access from a computer with a specific IP address. In this authentication method, access is based on the client and not the user. Session authentication is performed using a Session Authentication Agent, which FireWall-1 uses to open a connection to the computer. This allows any service to connect to a server on a per-session basis.

Client authentication is used for authenticating users of applications. This can be any of the 150+ predefined applications supported by FireWall-1, or custom applications that you specify. A number of the applications and services supported by FireWall-1 are shown in Table 11.1. With client authentication, authentication isn't transparent. The user first connects to FireWall-1 to be authenticated, and then client authentication takes place using Telnet or the Web browser used to connect to the firewall.

Session authentication is used to authenticate users of services on a session-by-session basis. Unlike client authentication, session authentication is transparent. When a user attempts to connect to a specific server, FireWall-1 interrupts and initiates the connection using the Session Authentication Agent. This agent performs the authentication, and allows the connection to continue (assuming the security policy allows it). If the security policy prohibits the user to access a particular service, then the user is denied connecting to it.

Table 11.1 Predefined Applications Supported by Check Point FireWall-1

Service or Application	Vendor
AOL Network Connection	America Online (AOL)
QuickTime	Apple Computer
BackWeb	BackWeb Technologies
H 323 VoIP	Clarent Corp.
Internet Phone	Intel Corp.
CreativePartner	eMotion, Inc.
Archie	FTP Search Service
Orbix	IONA Technologies
Notes	Lotus Development Corp.
Castanet	Marimba, Inc.
Channels	Microsoft
Conferencing	Microsoft
DCOM	Microsoft
Exchange	Microsoft
NetMeeting	Microsoft

Continued

Table 11.1 Continued

Service or Application	Vendor
SQL Server	Microsoft
Windows Media Services	Microsoft
Gopher	NCSA/Mosaic
CoolTalk	Netscape
NetCaster	Netscape
CORBA	Oracle Corp.
IIOP Application Server	Oracle Corp.
SQLnet	Oracle Corp.
PointCast Network	PointCast
RealAudio	RealNetworks, Inc.
RealVideo	RealNetworks, Inc.
RTSP RealPlayer G2	RealNetworks, Inc.
NFS	Sun Microsystems
Open Client	Sybase, Inc.
SQL Server	Sybase, Inc.
PCAnywhere	Symantec Corp.
PCTelecommute	Symantec Corp.
VDOLive	VDOnet Corp.
Vosaic Media Suite	Vosaic
Web Theatre	VXtreme
CU-SeeMe	White Pine
Streamworks	Xing

RSA Security

FireWall-1 integrates RSA Keon encryption, which encrypts your data so that others (who shouldn't access the data) will be unable to view it. Keon was developed by RSA Security, who invented Public Key Cryptography, and allows you to encrypt data that is transmitted through e-commerce applications, or applications and clients that need safe and secure data transmission. You can set certificates to be used when managing security for Internet access, VPNs, and e-commerce. It provides you with the ability to have secure business transactions over the Internet, and issue certificates to remote VPN clients.

Keon supports certificates through IPSec authentication using RSA Keon Certificate Server. This server software allows you to create and manage certificates used on your network. The software acts as a key management engine, certificate engine, and database, and LDAP certificate repository. Using it, you can set security procedures, trust relationships, and certificate formats and lifecycles.

Network Address Translation (NAT)

Network Address Translation (NAT) conceals IP addresses from being revealed as public information on the Internet. Each computer on your internal TCP/IP network has its own IP address assigned to it, and releasing this address on the Internet will reveal information that can be used by hackers. NAT provides an added level of security, as Web sites and individuals won't be able to view the IP addresses of users visiting those sites. By hiding this information, these individuals will be unable to determine the network addressing schemes used on your network.

There are two modes of Network Address Translation that can be used with FireWall-1, static mode and dynamic mode. Whether you use one or both of these modes will depend on the needs of your organization.

When NAT is used in dynamic mode, FireWall-1 uses a single IP address for users who are connecting to the Internet. Rather than seeing the actual IP address of the user, only the IP address used by dynamic mode is revealed. There is no limit to the number of internal IP addresses that can be mapped to the single corporate IP address. Because this single IP address is used only for outbound communication, and isn't used by internal servers or users, hackers cannot use the information to gain access to internal network resources.

An added bonus of dynamic mode is that you can use unregistered IP addresses on your internal network, while allowing these hosts access to the Internet. You'll remember that no two hosts on a network can have the same IP address, which is why IP addresses used on the Internet need to be registered. Since dynamic NAT doesn't reveal your company's internal IP addresses on the Internet, you don't need to register these IP addresses for corporate use. Only the IP address that these are mapped to through dynamic NAT needs to be registered.

When NAT is used in static mode, a registered IP address is mapped to an internal IP address. This is a one-to-one assignment, so only one published IP address is associated with one internal IP address. Static mode is commonly used when an enterprise has FTP servers, Web servers, or other servers that the public will access. This protects internal IP addresses from being exposed to the Internet, but doesn't associate the public IP with any other internal IP addresses.

Virtual Private Networks (VPNs)

In the late 1990s, virtual private networks became the big advancement for networks and the Internet. It seemed that everyone had one, wanted one, or was looking into the benefits of implementing a virtual private network (VPN). A VPN is a private network that makes use of public resources like secure telephone lines and the Internet for transmitting data. FireWall-1 offers optional VPN support to encrypt data so that transmission of the data is private and secure. VPN-1 provides VPN services, and integrates with FireWall-1 to protect communications through a VPN-1 Gateway. Through this integration, any installation of FireWall-1 can be upgraded to VPN-1 Gateway. The VPN-1 Gateway supports industry standard protocols and algorithms like Data Encryption Standard (DES), Triple DES, IP Security/Internet Key Exchange (IPSec/IKE), and digital certificates. This allows remote users to access the network, without worrying about others being able to access it.

Auditing, Reporting, and Logs

FireWall-1 provides auditing and reporting features, which allow you to monitor firewall activity. Of particular importance, these features allow you to monitor suspicious activity. You can generate reports detailing rejected connections, blocked traffic, failed authentication, and alerts. Using this, you can identify attempts to hack your network. The reporting features also allow you to monitor network traffic patterns, and see what resources are being used the most. These reports provide details, such as which users and departments in your organization are using particular resources. This is a valuable tool in seeing how Internet access is being used, but is also important when troubleshooting problems and monitoring perfor-mance.

Auditing and reporting of firewall traffic is offered through the Fire-Wall-1's Reporting Module. This module is broken into two components: the Reporting Client and the Reporting Server. These components can either be installed on the same machine or with the Reporting Server on the same server that FireWall-1 resides on, and the Reporting Client on a network workstation. This gives you the freedom of either monitoring the Firewall remotely, or using it on the firewall server.

The Reporting Server consists of several components: the Report Server, Log Consolidator Engine, and the database. The FireWall-1 module sends logs and alerts to FireWall-1 Server, which the Log Consolidation Engine then collects. This information is stored in the database.

The Reporting Module allows you to generate reports in ASCII or HTML. You can configure these reports to be sent to specific network objects. This allows you to distribute the reports by sending them to an e-mail address as an attachment, or to a Web Server as an HTML document. There are almost 20 predefined reports that can be generated, and customized reports can be created to suit your needs. This allows reports to be created for administrators and decision makers, so that your network can be analyzed properly as to its use and abuse.

To protect yourself from yourself, actions performed by administrators are logged to a file on the server running your firewall. This allows you to see what actions you've performed so that you can review your work, and also to see if you've made a mistake that led to a particular problem. The log is a text file, which can be viewed through any text viewer. This file logs failed and successful logon attempts, logoffs, saved actions, and actions dealing with installations of databases and policies. In FireWall-1 4.1 this file is called cpmgmt.aud; previous versions have a file called fwui.log. Regardless of the file, these log files are stored in the $FWDIR/log directory.

LDAP-based User Management

FireWall-1 supports the Lightweight Directory Access Protocol (LDAP). LDAP is a protocol that also allows user information to be stored in LDAP databases. The user information stored in these databases may be stored on one or more servers, and is accessible to FireWall-1 through the Account Management module. By accessing information in an LDAP database, it can be applied to the security policies used by FireWall-1.

Information stored in the LDAP database covers a variety of elements, including identification and group membership information. Identification information provides such data as the full username, login name, e-mail address, directory branch, and associated template. Group membership provides information on the groups to which the user belongs. Access control information in the database shows what each user has permissions to, and time restrictions indicate the times of day the user is able to log in and access resources. Finally, authentication information provides data regarding the authentication scheme, server, and password, and encryption information details the key negotiation scheme, encryption algorithm, and data integrity method to be used. As mentioned, this information can be available to LDAP clients such as FireWall-1 with the Account Management module installed.

The benefit of LDAP is that it eliminates the need for multiple data stores containing duplicate information on users. When the Account Management module is installed, security information can be stored on an LDAP server. FireWall-1 and other LDAP-compliant software can then use security information on users, which are stored in the LDAP database.

Malicious Activity and Intrusion Detection

FireWall-1 has the ability to detect malicious activity and possible intrusions. Such activity may indicate a hacker attempting to gain access to your network. The Malicious Activity Detection feature analyzes log files, and looks for known attacks and suspicious activity at the Internet gateway. When these are found, the security manager is then notified, allowing you to take action on attempted security policy violations.

One type of attack that FireWall-1 effectively deals with is known as flooding, or a SYN Flood. With this, a request is made to a server. In the header of the packet, the SYN flag is set, so that the server sends back a SYN/ACK packet. Basically, the client sends a TCP/IP packet called a SYN packet to make a connection. The server replies to this with another packet. This packet is called a SYN/ACK packet, and acknowledges receipt of the SYN packet. If the IP address in the header is not legitimate, then the server can't complete the connection, but it reserves resources because it expects a connection to be made. The hacker sends out hundreds or thousands of these requests, thereby tying up the server. Because resources are tied up from these requests, legitimate users are unable to connect to the server, and services are denied to them. To deal with these attacks, FireWall-1 uses a program called SYNDefender.

SYNDefender ensures that the connection is valid. If the handshake isn't completed, then resources are released. The SYNDefender Gateway enhances this protection, by moving requests of this sort out of a backlog queue and setting up a connection. If the connection isn't completed by the client's response to the SYN/ACK packet, then the connection is dropped.

Another type of attack that FireWall-1 can detect is IP spoofing. This involves a hacker using a fake IP address, so that he or she appears to be working on a host with higher access. When a packet is sent from this host, it may appear to be originating from a host on the internal network. FireWall-1 works against IP spoofing by limiting network access based on the gateway from which data is received.

Requirements and Installation

In this section we'll discuss the system requirements and installation procedures for Check Point FireWall-1. As with any software, minimal requirements must be met if the software is to function as expected. It is important that you compare these requirements to the server and network on which FireWall-1 is to be installed before installation actually takes place.

We will also discuss considerations for updating FireWall-1, installing Service Packs, and adding modules. As we've seen, FireWall-1 features are added through the installation of modules. As such, we will also discuss installing the Reporting module, which is important for monitoring and troubleshooting FireWall-1.

NOTE

In reading the following sections, it is important to realize that how you configure FireWall-1 will depend on the features you want to implement, and how your network is designed. Although system requirements are cut-and-dry, and must be met for the firewall to function properly, other information provided here is subjective. The information here should not be taken verbatim, but should be viewed as an outline that can be applied to your firewall design.

System Requirements

One of the most important parts of installing any software is ensuring that the computer meets the minimal requirements. This not only means that your server has enough RAM, hard disk space, and other necessary hardware, but also that it uses an operating system on which FireWall-1 can run. Before attempting to install FireWall-1 on a server, you should check the existing hardware and operating system to make certain that the firewall can be installed and will function properly. (See Table 11.2.)

The hardware requirements vary, depending on whether you are installing FireWall-1's Management Server & Enforcement Module or the GUI Client. The Management Server & Enforcement Module requires a minimum of 64MB of memory, but 128MB of RAM is recommended. You will also need 40MB of free hard disk space. To run FireWall-1's GUI Client on a workstation, you will also need to ensure that minimal hardware requirements are met. The GUI Client needs a minimum of 32MB of RAM, and 40MB of hard disk space. A network interface that is supported by FireWall-1 is also needed, so that the software can communicate over the network. The network interface can be Asynchronous Transfer Mode (ATM), Ethernet, Fast Ethernet, Fiber Distributed Data Interface (FDDI), or Token Ring. Finally, you will need a CD-ROM so that you can install the firewall software.

FireWall-1's Management Server & Enforcement Module can run on a number of different operating systems (OSs). As a majority of software is designed for Microsoft operating systems, it should come as no surprise that FireWall-1 supports Windows NT 4.0 Server and Windows 2000 Server. However, if Windows NT is used, you will need to ensure that the server has the proper Service Pack (SP) installed, as Service Pack 4 or higher (SP4 through SP6a) must be installed. Sun Solaris 2.6, 7, and 8 are also supported by FireWall-1, but these OSs must be running in 32-bit mode. Additionally, 32-bit mode must also be used if your server is running HP-UX 10.20 or 11.0. Red Hat Linux 6.1 is supported, but you will need to check that it is using kernel 2.2x. Finally, IBM AIX 4.2.1, 4.3.2, or 4.3.3 can also be used on the server on which FireWall-1 is being installed.

FireWall-1's GUI client also has a number of requirements. It can run on Microsoft Windows 9x, Windows NT/2000, Sun Solaris SPARC, HP-UX 10.20, or IBM AIX. Since this covers most of the popular operating systems, you probably have a workstation on your network running one or more of these OSs

The Reporting Module also has specific requirements, which are small in comparison to these other modules. The Reporting Server is installed on the Windows NT/2000 or UNIX server running FireWall-1. For Windows servers, this machine will need a minimum of an Intel Pentium II (233 Mhz or higher) processor with 3GB of free disk space and 128MB of RAM. UNIX machines will need a Sun Ultra sparc 5 (360 Mhz), Solaris 2.5.1 or higher, 3GB of free disk space, and 128MB or RAM. The Reporting Client can run on a machine running Windows 9x or NT that has 6MB of free disk space, 32MB of RAM, and an Intel x86 or Pentium processor.

Table 11.2 FireWall-1 System Requirements

Component	Requirement	Details
Management Server & Enforcement Module	Operating System	Windows NT 4.0 Server with Service Pace 4 or higher installed. Windows 2000 Server. Sun Solaris 2.6, 7, and 8 running in 32-bit mode. HP-UX 10.20 or 11.0 running in 32-bit mode. Red Hat Linux 6.1 with Kernel 2.2x. IBM AIX 4.2.1, 4.3.2, or 4.3.3.
	RAM	64MB.
	Hard Disk Space	40MB.
	Network Interface	Asynchronous Transfer Mode (ATM), Ethernet, Fast Ethernet, Fiber Distributed Data Interface (FDDI), or Token Ring.

Continued

Table 11.2 Continued

Component	Requirement	Details
GUI Client	Operating System	Microsoft Windows 9x, Windows NT/2000, Sun Solaris SPARC, HP-UX 10.20, or IBM AIX.
	RAM	32MB.
	Hard Disk Space	40MB.
	Network Interface	Asynchronous Transfer Mode (ATM), Ethernet, Fast Ethernet, Fiber Distributed Data Interface (FDDI) or Token Ring
Reporting Module	Operating System	Windows NT/2000 Server, Sun Solaris 2.5.1 or higher
	RAM	128MB
	Hard Disk Space	3GB
Reporting Client	Operating System	Windows 9x or NT/2000
	RAM	32MB
	Hard Disk Space	6MB

Installing Check Point FireWall-1

In this section we will discuss the procedures involved when installing Check Point FireWall-1. Because FireWall-1 can be installed on so many operating systems, it would be impossible to detail the installation on each and every one. As such, this section will focus on installation on a Windows NT Server. If your company uses a different server operating system, then you will find installation on that OS virtually identical. As such, you can use the information provided here as a guideline, and adapt it to the server operating system being used by your company.

After inserting your installation CD into your CD-ROM drive, open the Windows Start menu and click on the Run command. This will display the Run dialog box. Click the Browse button, and navigate to the Windows directory on the CD-ROM. Once you have gone to this directory, double-click on SETUP.EXE to start the installation.

The first screen that will appear is an introduction to the installation wizard. By clicking the Next button, the Select Components screen will appear. As shown in Figure 11.3, clicking on the checkboxes that are on this screen will select the components to install. You will need to select

FireWall-1 to install the server components of the firewall, and FireWall-1 User Interface to install the GUI Interface that is used to set your security policy.

Figure 11.3 Select Components Screen of the FireWall-1 Installation.

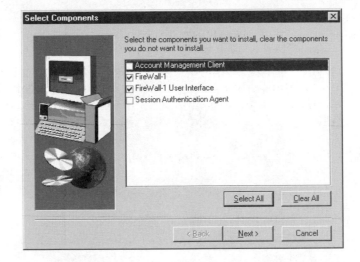

After you click Next, the Software License screen is displayed. This screen provides information on the agreement to use the firewall software. Click Yes to agree to the agreement and continue to the next screen. If you click No, then you will not be allowed to continue with the installation, and will be forced to exit the wizard.

After clicking Yes, the FireWall-1 Welcome screen will appear. Aside from the greeting, there is nothing to configure on this screen. Clicking Next will allow you to continue to the next screen.

The screen that follows is the Chose Destination Location screen. This screen allows you to specify the directory into which FireWall-1 will be installed. A default location is provided on this screen. If you decide to install FireWall-1 to a different location, then you will need to set the FWDIR environment variable to point to the directory in which the firewall has been installed. If the FWDIR variable isn't set, then the fwinfo debugging tool that comes with FireWall-1 won't be able to function properly. Upon accepting the default directory or choosing a new directory on the Chose Destination Location screen, click Next to continue.

The next screen is the Selecting Product Type window. On this screen, you will see different types of products available for installation. This allows you to decide whether to install VPN-1 products, FireWall-1 products, or both. Select the product(s) being installed and click Next.

FireWall-1 will be installed to the specified location, and the FireWall-1 service will be started. After this occurs, a Welcome window will appear for the GUI Console. Click Next to go to the next screen.

As seen in the FireWall-1 installation, the GUI installation will display a Choose Destination Location window. This allows you to specify where the User Interface, which will be used to manage FireWall-1, will be installed. Accept the default location, or enter the path of a new directory that will be used to install the GUI Console. Click Next to continue.

As shown in Figure 11.4, the Select Components Screen will appear next. This screen allows you to specify which components will be installed to the destination location you specified. Click on the Security Policy, Log Viewer, and System Status to select these components, then click the Next button to continue.

Figure 11.4 Select Components Screen of the FireWall-1 Installation.

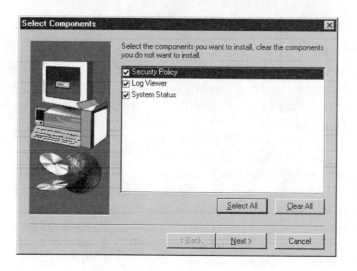

Once the software has been installed in the specified location, the Licenses screen is displayed as shown in Figure 11.5. Because this is a new installation, each of the fields on this screen will appear blank. To add a new license for FireWall-1, click the Add button. This will display the Add License dialog box. This is where you add licensing information that you received from Check Point. You must add information to three fields on this screen:

- Host
- Features
- Key

Figure 11.5 Licenses screen of the FireWall-1 installation.

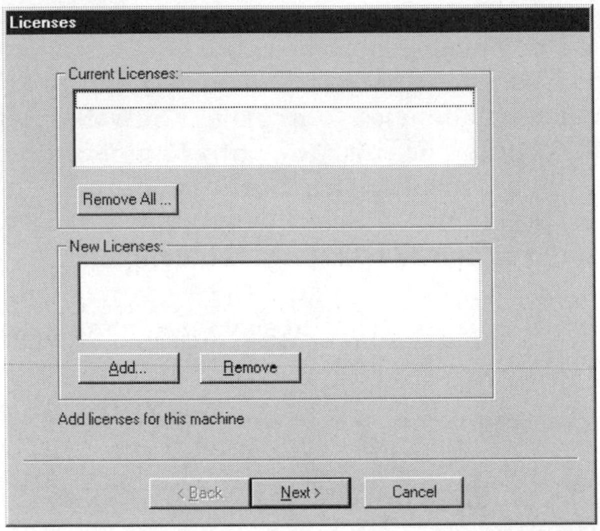

The Host field is where you enter the IP address of Windows NT Servers. If you are evaluating FireWall-1, then you would enter the word *eval*. The Features field is used to enter a string that lists the features of your license. Each of the features entered in this field should be separated by a space. Finally, the Key field is where you enter the registration key of your license. Upon entering this information, click the OK button to return to the Licenses screen, then click Next to continue.

The screen that follows is the Administrators screen, where you'll enter the usernames of those who will administer the firewall. As with the Licenses screen, if this is a new installation, there will be no administrators. To add a new username to this listing, click on the Add button to display the Add Administrators dialog box. This screen has several fields:

- Administrator's Name
- Password
- Confirm Password
- Permissions

Enter the name of the user you want to be an administrator in the Administrator's Name field. Type the password in the Password and Confirm Password fields. This will ensure that any password you enter will be spelled correctly. Finally, click on the Permissions drop-down box and select the permissions you want the administrator to have. To have full access, select Read/Write. After performing these steps, click OK to save the settings. To add additional administrators, click the Add button on the Administrators screen and repeat these steps.

When you have completed the wizard, you will then be ready to configure it. However, as the following sections will discuss, there may be other modules you want to install. Upon installing the modules you want to use with FireWall-1, you will then need to configure it, as we'll see later in this chapter.

Installing the Reporting Module

The Reporting Module is available on the Enterprise CD. To install this module, simply insert the installation CD into the CD-ROM of the server running FireWall-1. The installation wizard starts and the Welcome screen appears.

Click Next; the next screen lets you select the Server/Gateway components you'd like to install. On this screen, click on the checkbox labeled Reporting Module, and then click the Next button to install the module. Now you are ready to install the license.

Licenses for Check Point products are available from the Check Point Web site (http://license.checkpoint.com.). Once the license is installed, you can configure Reporting for your FireWall-1 server. We will discuss configuration later in this chapter.

Upgrade Issues

Before performing an upgrade you should perform a number of preliminary steps. If you are upgrading from version 3.0b to version 4.1, you should first upgrade to FireWall-1 4.0 Service Pack 3 before upgrading to the latest version. This will provide a cleaner installation, and will help you avoid problems during the upgrade. Regardless of the version you are upgrading from, you should always perform a backup of the server on which FireWall-1 resides. If a problem occurs during the upgrade, this will ensure that data isn't lost, and will keep you from needing to perform a full install and configuration if the upgrade fails badly.

After Installation

Once installation is complete, you should ensure that no service packs have been released for FireWall-1. Service packs fix known problems or issues with software, and are available from the manufacturer's Web site. Once you've installed FireWall-1, go to Check Point's Web site at www.checkpoint.com to see if any service packs are available, and occasionally visit the site so that you're sure the latest service pack has been applied to the firewall.

FireWall-1 Configuration

Configuration and management is done through FireWall-1's Graphical User Interface. This interface provides a representation of common objects to which rules will be applied. These resource objects allow you to define rules for users, hosts, servers, services, and other elements of a TCP/IP network. This centralized management is incredibly simple and easy to use.

Using the Graphical User Interface, shown previously in Figure 11.1 and later in Figure 11.6, you are able to select the object for which you want to design a rule. Upon selecting the object, you then bring up the properties for the object. As we will see in the sections that follow, the specific properties will vary depending on the object selected. By modifying these properties, a rule based on your specifications will be stored in the security policy for the firewall.

In this section, we will highlight what can be configured on Check Point FireWall-1, and then discuss how this is done. As we will see, there is considerable control over the FireWall-1 features through the GUI Console.

Configuring FireWall-1

To configure FireWall-1, you must start by opening the GUI console that's used to build your security policy. In Windows, start the user interface by clicking on the Start menu, selecting the FireWall-1 folder in Programs, and then clicking on the item called Security Policy. A logon screen appears; enter the username and password of an administrator (which you created during installation) and the name of the server you want to administer. After you click OK, the GUI Console appears.

As shown in Figure 11.6, menus and toolbars are used to create and manage policy; the main area of the window provides a display of existing rules. When you first open the console, no rules will be displayed. As shown in the figure, the Manage menu offers several areas of management:

- Network objects
- Services
- Resources
- Servers
- Users
- Time
- Keys

By selecting any of these elements that can be managed, a graphical management dialog box is then displayed.

Figure 11.6 Graphical User Interface used to configure FireWall-1.

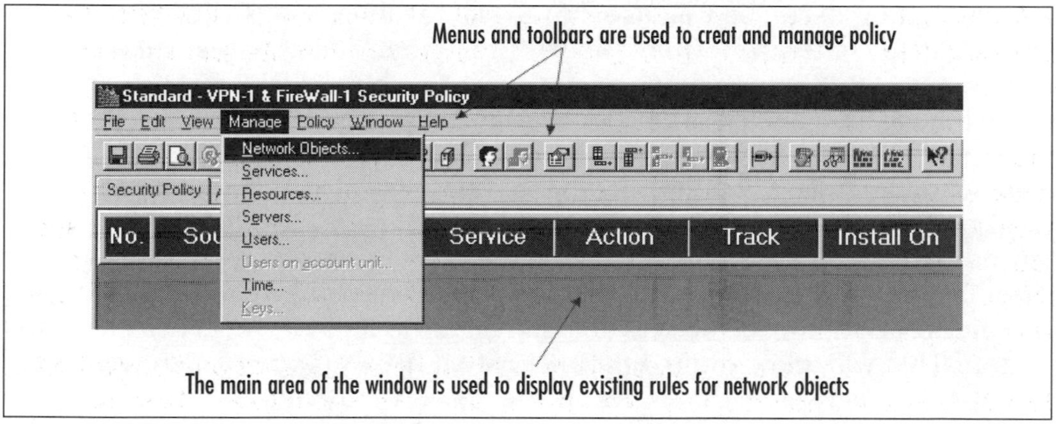

By selecting Network Objects from the Manage menu, the Network Objects Manager dialog box appears. A listing on the dialog shows existing objects that have already been added. To add a new network object, click on the New button on this screen. This will display a listing of objects. These objects include workstations, networks, domains, subnets, routers, switches, groups, logical servers, and address ranges. Once you select one of these objects, you can then enter information about that object. To edit the properties of objects you add, you would select the object from the listing, then click the Edit button. This displays a similar dialog box that can be used to modify an object's properties. To remove an existing object from your security policy, select the object from the listing, and then click the Remove button.

The Services item on the Manage menu displays the Services Manager dialog. This allows you to manage applications, services, and protocols. As mentioned, there are almost 150 predefined ones that can be managed. You can also use this dialog box to add custom applications, services, and protocols. By clicking the New button, another dialog box will appear that will allow you to enter specific information about what is being added. To edit an existing entry, the Edit button can be used in the same way you used the Edit button on the Network Objects Manager. To remove an application, service, or protocol, select it from the listing and then click Remove.

By selecting Resources from the Manage menu, the Resources Manager will appear. This is another dialog box that allows you to add, edit, and remove resources that may be used. This allows you to specify rules dealing with anti-virus scanning, acceptable or unacceptable URLs that can be accessed through the firewall, and rules dealing with the screening of Java and ActiveX applets, and JavaScript.

The Servers Manager is accessed by clicking on the Servers item on the Manage menu. This allows you to specify what servers will be used for authenticating users, as well as what servers will be used for UFP, CVP, and RADIUS content screening. As with the other dialog boxes, this one also provides Edit and Remove buttons for respectively editing and removing existing servers from the listing.

The Manage menu also has an item called Users that brings up the User Manager dialog box. By clicking on this menu item, you will see another dialog box that has a listing of existing users. By clicking the New button on this screen, you can add network users manually, or download them from a database that contains a listing of usernames and passwords. To edit an existing user, select the user from the listing, then click the Edit button. This will allow you to edit an existing user's properties. To remove an existing user, select the user and then click the Remove button.

The Time Manager is also accessed through the Manage menu. This dialog box allows you to define time and date ranges that will be used to regulate when users can access the Internet, or access the network through the Internet using a VPN. To add a new rule, click the Add button, and then specify the time and date rules you want to apply to your network. This dialog also provides an Edit and Remove button for respectively editing and removing existing time related rules.

The Keys Manager is used for managing encryption keys. By clicking on the Keys item on the Manage menu, a dialog box appears, which allows you to set what keys will be used with FireWall-1. This dialog also provides an Edit and Remove button for respectively editing and removing existing time related rules.

Once these have been set, you are ready to set criteria that will be used to build the rules used for the security policy. The rules set through the Policy Editor are used to allow or block communications through the firewall. All communication is intercepted by FireWall-1, and compared to rules in the security policy. By default, if a particular connection doesn't meet the rules in the policy, then it will be dropped. For a communication to be forwarded onto the network, it must meet several sources of criteria:

- Source
- Destination
- Service
- Time

Objects that you define are used to specify each of these criterion. Once each of these is met, an action that you chose is executed and the communication is tracked.

You specify the Source of a connection in the main window of the GUI Console by clicking on the Source column of a particular rule. This displays the Add Object dialog box, which contains a listing of source types. This listing includes entries that you added earlier, when you added servers, networks, and other network objects. The object selected would depend on the rule being created. For example, if you were controlling content accessed on the Web by your local area network, then you would select a particular site or Any. If you were setting authentication rules, then you would set a particular user or group.

The Destination column is used to specify a rule for a particular destination of a connection. This may be a particular server or host, or any destination. The entries found here include those that you added through the Manage menu. You might use this to specify a Web server, your local area network, remote networks, and so forth. As was the case with the Source column, the choice would depend on the rule that is being created.

The Service column allows you to specify rules for particular network services. This includes protocols like HTTP or FTP, or applications or services on your network that you define. As mentioned, there are almost 150 predefined services, protocols, and applications that you can choose.

The Time column is used to specify time- and date-related criteria for rules. This allows you to set when users can access resources outside of their network (i.e., the Internet) or when users of a VPN would be allowed to access resources located on your internal network.

Content Security

Content security is configured through the Security Policy Editor using resource objects. With FireWall-1, a resource object defines groups of entities that are accessed by a specific protocol. The protocols can be HTTP, SMTP, and FTP. The rules created through this Graphical User Interface allow you to set how Web content and e-mail will be dealt with. For added security, FireWall-1 also provides the ability to check transferred files for viruses when these protocols are used.

A rule base is used for content security. In the GUI Console, you specify rules and actions that will apply to specific resources that are accessed through a particular protocol. When a connection matches a rule, it is diverted to a specific Security Server. The Security Server can then query a third-party server to perform anti-virus screening or URL filtering. FireWall-1 will then process the connection based on the reply from this server and the action specified in the rule.

Because of third-party software support, FireWall-1 integrates third-party anti-virus software through the Content Vectoring Protocol (CVP) Application Programming Interface (API). To give an example of how this works, let's say you configured an FTP Resource definition (for FTP sites and downloaded files) or an HTTP Resource definition (for Web pages that are accessed). These files are to be scanned for viruses before being passed through the firewall to a user's workstation. By configuring this rule, FireWall-1 will divert these files to a CVP server. The server will check it for viruses. Depending on the results of this scan, FireWall-1 will either prohibit it from passing onto the network, or allow it to be passed through the firewall.

URL filtering can also be configured using resource objects, so that you can control what Web sites users are able to access. This prevents your network users from accessing Web pages that you consider problematic or inappropriate. FireWall-1's URL Filtering Protocol (UFP) API is used for this. This API allows you to integrate third-party UFP servers so that you can create logs of URLs and categorize them. With URL filtering, you can create databases that contain unacceptable URLs. When users attempt to access a URL in this listing, they are denied access.

Using resource objects, FireWall-1 also allows you to screen Java and ActiveX applets and scripts. Applets are programs that can be inserted into Web pages. In some cases, these are designed to obtain information about a network or to attack it like a virus. Using the screening capabilities of FireWall-1, you can strip ActiveX tags, scripts, and Java applets from Web pages. By setting rules to deal with such content, you can have FireWall-1 perform any or all of the following:

- Remove Java applet, ActiveX applet, and JavaScript tags from HTML documents

- Remove Java applets from server-to-client replies

- Block attacks by blocking suspicious back connections

Although the user is able to view other content (i.e., text and graphics), programs won't be accessible.

To implement content security, you would again use the Security Policy tab of the GUI Console. In the Source column, select the source object that applies to this rule. For example, you may wish to implement virus scanning for e-mail, and to select the source of the e-mail by clicking on the Source column and selecting Add. When the Add Object dialog appears, select the source from which you want to protect yourself, either trusted or untrusted sites. In the Destination column, specify to whom the e-mail is going (such as your local network and remote networks). In the Service column specify that this e-mail be scanned for viruses. You can set any anti-virus software you like to use for this purpose, and specify the action to be taken (such as deleting or removing the virus).

Access Control

FireWall-1's GUI Console is also used to specify access control. This allows you to set what users are allowed to access on your network using various objects. The rules created using this tool define the security policy, and each rule is a combination of network objects, services, logging mechanisms, and actions. Network objects include such elements as users, hosts, servers, and so forth. By bringing up the Properties Set-up window, you can then modify the properties of these objects. The properties you set define the rules associated with these objects.

FireWall-1 allows you to set different levels of access for different network objects. For example, you can specify that certain users have one level of access, and users working on a specific host will have a different level of access. As mentioned earlier, the access rights are stored within the security policy, and inherited by the user when he or she is authenticated.

There are several access levels that can be applied to security administrators. These are shown in the Table 11.3, which shows each level of access.

Table 11.3 Access Levels for Administrators

Access Level	Description
Read/Write	Provides full access to FireWall-1's management tools.
User Edit	Provides the access to modify user information only. Any other functions are read only.
Read Only	Provides read only access to the Policy Editor.
Monitor Only	Allows read-only access to the Log View and System Status tools.

To Add access control rules to FireWall-1, you need to select the Source to be monitored. By clicking on the Source column of a rule, you would select Add from the menu that appears. This will make the Add Objects dialog box appear. For example, you could select an object like the Local Area Network from the listing or select Any to specify that communications from any source would apply to this rule. You would then select the Destination column to specify the target of the connection, such as your Web server (for incoming connections) or any external site (for users on your LAN who are surfing the Web). Next, you would select the Service column. This would allow you to specify any traffic using HTTP or another protocol, or any service attempting to be used. Next you would specify how the communication will be treated. This may include accepting or dropping such connections, as we discussed earlier. Finally, you would then specify how you want communications meeting this rule to be logged.

Network Address Translation Configuration

The Graphical User Interface is also used to configure Network Address Translation in FireWall-1. This allows you to hide the IP addresses of each user's machine behind a single IP address, or hide a single server's IP address behind a single public IP. This protects internal IP addressing schemes from being revealed on the Internet. This is also particularly useful when your network is using a network-addressing scheme that isn't registered, and therefore not valid for use on the Internet. Dynamic IP addresses allow multiple hosts to be hidden by the single IP address, whereas static IP addresses are single internal IP addresses that are mapped to a registered IP address for use on the Internet.

An Address Translation Rule Base is integrated in the GUI Console, allowing you to configure NAT with greater ease. This allows you to specify network objects by name rather than IP address. The rules are created automatically when you enter information during the object definition process, or you can specify address translation rules manually. Rules can then be applied to destination IP addresses, source IP addresses, and services. Once you choose the object to which you want to apply rules, you then configure its properties through a dialog box.

The Network Address Translation dialog boxes allow you to easily configure NAT rules. By changing the properties associated with a specific object, the Address Translation Rules are configured automatically.

To use network address translation, select the Address Translation tab in the main window of the GUI console. In the Network Properties dialog box, click on the Add Automatic Address Translation Rules checkbox, and then specify the method of NAT you want to be used. You have two methods available to you in the drop-down list on this screen, Static and Hide. Static provides a one-to-one method of translation, where you can specify the IP address to be used. Hide allows you to use dynamic translation, where all of the IP addresses of hosts and servers will be hidden behind a registered IP address.

LDAP Account Management

As mentioned earlier, FireWall-1 supports LDAP through the Account Management module. This module integrates user information in LDAP directories into FireWall-1, so that security information on users can be applied to your security policy. The security data on users can be retrieved from any LDAP-compliant server.

As with other network objects, LDAP servers and users are defined through a rule base. Once the properties on the network object is set, the rules in the security policy for this object are created automatically. When a user then connects to the network through the firewall, the LDAP server is queried to get information on this server.

The difference between LDAP users and servers and other network objects is that the Account Management module comes with a Java-based GUI client that is used to configure the properties of LDAP users. This console can be launched as a separate application or through the FireWall-1's GUI Console.

Configuring the Reporting Module

Earlier in this chapter, we saw that a component of the Reporting Module is the Log Consolidator. To configure this component, the Log Consolidator Policy Editor is used. This tool has a GUI interface that provides a visual, easy-to-use interface for configuring reporting. To use this tool, you will need to enter your username and password, and enter the IP address of the server on which the Reporting Server component is installed. Once this is done, click OK to continue.

Upon connecting with the Reporting Server, the interface that appears will allow you to create reporting policies in the same way that policies for FireWall-1 are created. To install a new policy, select Install from the Policy menu. By configuring the Log Consolidator Properties, you specify how logging will occur.

As we saw when we configured FireWall-1, there are a number of fields that have different purposes in the Policy Editor. The ORIGIN is used to specify the FireWall-1 server from which logs will be generated. This is important if multiple firewalls exist on your network and you want to specify different policies for each. Other fields similar to those we've discussed are the SOURCE, DESTINATION, and SERVICE columns. Unlike the ACTION field previously discussed, the policies for log consolidation have one of two actions: Ignore and Store. If Ignore is selected, then the policy will not be stored in the database; only those with the Store action will be saved.

Options for the Store action allow you to configure how often events will be consolidated, and what details will be logged. Events can be consolidated every minute, 10 minutes, 30 minutes, hour, or day. Details that can be retained include URLs, authenticated users, rule number, service, source, destination, and action.

Troubleshooting

In this section, we will discuss some troubleshooting issues, including common problems and tools that can be used to solve those problems. Even if FireWall-1 is installed and configured properly, you may experience some problems once FireWall-1 is running on your network. This in no way reflects upon the stability of this software, but is part-in-parcel of any software running on a network.

Troubleshooting and Hardening the Operating System and FireWall-1 by Applying the Latest Service Packs

Troubleshooting is a combination of knowledge and experience, and should always begin by looking at the simplest solution first. Some of these potential problems may be the result of failing to install certain modules. As such, if a function is unavailable, you should first check to

Continued

see that it is installed and configured properly. Other problems may be due to glitches in operating system, which might be resolved by installing the latest Service pack. The same applies to service packs available for FireWall-1. Service Packs address known issues that have been identified and resolved. In other cases, you may need to investigate the problem more thoroughly to find a solution.

In troubleshooting, it is important to deal with problems proactively. This will keep a small problem from becoming a major catastrophe. It can't be stressed enough that you should monitor FireWall-1 regularly. Make good use of the reporting and auditing features to find how resources are being used, and whether suspicious activity is occurring.

Reports, Auditing, and Malicious Activity Alerts

Earlier in this chapter, we discussed how the Reporting Module is used to generate reports and audit certain events. These reports should be your first point of reference when determining whether an intrusion has occurred, or what events may have brought on particular problems. As mentioned, the Reporting Module allows you to distribute reports in ASCII or HTML formats to specific network objects, making it easy for you to access this information on a regular basis.

These reports allow you to take a proactive approach to troubleshooting. Information generated by these reports document alerts, rejected connections, blocked traffic, and failed authentication. It also documents network traffic patterns so that you can view what resources particular users and departments are using, and how often they are being used.

Finally, the alerts sent by the Malicious Activity Detection provide information about suspicious activities. As mentioned earlier, this feature analyzes log files, and looks for known attacks and suspicious activity at the Internet gateway. Because notification is sent when such possible problems are found, you are then able to take action on attempted security policy violations.

Viruses

Virus attacks are a major issue for networks. FireWall-1 works with third-party anti-virus software. For anti-virus software to detect viruses, you will need to ensure that the latest virus signature files have been installed. These allow the anti-virus program to properly detect and deal with viruses.

User Interface License Error

An error message you may experience using FireWall-1 will state "No License for User Interface." When this message appears, it does not necessarily mean that you need to purchase additional licenses for FireWall-1. If you have purchased and installed licenses, then it can indicate that, on Windows NT/2000 servers, the firewall service needs to be stopped and restarted. On UNIX machines, the motif license is purchased separately, and needs to be installed with the FireWall-1 license. Finally, this error may occur if the Management Module license isn't installed, or the module can't be located. In this case, you will need to verify that the licenses have indeed been purchased and installed properly.

Performance Monitor and FireWall-1

Performance Monitor (Perfmon) is a tool that is used in Windows NT to view the performance of various network elements. In Windows 2000, an updated version of this software called System Monitor is available. System Monitor is run from the Performance Console, and like Perfmon, allows you to view how your system and network is running. It does this by monitoring objects that are revealed to Perfmon, which are called object metrics. In viewing object metrics, you may be able to identify performance problems, and reveal clues that can be used in troubleshooting problems with FireWall-1 running on a Windows NT/2000 Server.

Perfmon can be used to view the performance of FireWall-1. On occasion, you may find that the FireWall-1 object metrics don't appear in Performance Monitor. When this occurs, it means that registry entries for Perfmon weren't created.

To recreate Perfmon metrics for FireWall-1, you would go to the $FWDIR\lib directory and type lodctr fwctrs.ini. If the fwntperf.dll is missing from the $fwdir\lib directory, reinstall this library to the $fwdir\lib directory and reboot. Upon doing so, you should then be able to view FireWall-1 object metrics in Performance Monitor.

To ensure that the server running FireWall-1 is functioning properly, it is wise to create a baseline. A baseline records how your network runs when it is considered to be running properly. As such, you should log the performance of various metrics in Performance Monitor, so that you can compare it to metrics recorded when a problem is experienced.

Dedicated Firewall versus a Firewall Running on a Server Used for Other Purposes

Although FireWall-1 can run on a server that's also acting as a file server, mail server, etc., there are benefits to running FireWall-1 by itself on a server. As you have probably experienced with workstations and server software you've installed, problems with one program may have an effect on other programs. If a server application freezes badly enough, it can lock up the entire server, forcing you to reboot it. In addition, libraries and other files in one program may conflict with the libraries and services of another piece of software running on the server. As such, running FireWall-1 by itself may solve a number of problems.

It is also important to realize that by providing users access to directories and other services running on a server, a user (or a good hacker) may be able to improperly gain access to areas you don't want users accessing. Basically, this boils down to the following: If a door is closed, go through a window. By running FireWall-1 only on a particular server, you have greater control over the methods of accessing areas of this server. Users won't have permissions to directories, and will only be passed through or blocked at this point.

Possible Security Issues

It is important to recognize that security risks not only come from outside of an organization, but from within as well. FireWall-1 allows you to create policies that deal with users on a large scale and on an individual basis, so that you can control access to network resources. By controlling access, you are able to define policies that deal with the source or destination of connection requests, the time of day, or the type of network traffic.

FireWall-1 provides a number of features to protect your data. It provides the ability to encrypt sensitive data, so that it cannot be ready by improper parties attempting to access it in transit. It can detect known types of attacks, and respond to them accordingly. It also allows you to generate reports and audits, which you can use to deal with attempts to access information improperly.

In protecting your network, it is important to use the abilities of FireWall-1 with the existing security controls of the operating system on which FireWall-1 runs. For example, if FireWall-1 is running on a Windows NT Server, then the file system used should be NTFS, as this provides the greatest protection of data. Although FireWall-1 is the main barrier between your network and the Internet, it should be used with other security measures.

The strictest policies possible should be used for most users; liberal access will allow curious and malicious hackers to invade your network. As such, allow users to access only what they specifically need to access. The stronger you control access, the more secure the network will be.

Implement strong password policies so that passwords aren't easy to guess. If users are using easy-to-remember passwords (such as the word PASSWORD) then hackers will be able to use such accounts to infiltrate your network. By combining numbers, letters, and other characters, the passwords will be difficult to crack.

Ports can be used to gain access to a network. An example of this is during an outbound FTP connection. During an FTP session, a back connection is made to the client using a dynamically allocated port number on the client's machine. The port number isn't known in advance, and packet filters may open a range of high numbered ports (greater than 1023) for the incoming connection. This can expose a network to various attacks. To deal with this, FireWall-1 tracks FTP sessions at the application level, and records the information about the request. When the back connection is made, it is checked and allowed, and a dynamic list of connections is maintained so that only the FTP ports that are needed are left open. The connections are closed after the FTP session is completed.

Summary

In this chapter we have discussed the features included with Check Point FireWall-1. We saw that many of the features are added through separate modules. Many of these modules come with FireWall-1, whereas others such as VPN-1 for Virtual Private Network support must be purchased separately.

We also discussed the minimal requirements needed to install Fire-Wall-1, and the procedures and considerations necessary for installation. These requirements not only apply to hardware on the server on which FireWall-1 is being installed, but also the operating systems supported. Before installing FireWall-1, it is important to ensure that these requirements are met. It is also important that you properly plan out the firewall implementation before installation begins.

Once installation is complete, FireWall-1 will need to be configured before it can be used. As we saw, FireWall-1 uses rules that make up a rule base. These rules determine how access to the network through the firewall, and from the internal network to the Internet, will be enforced. The rules are established for numerous network objects, and are used to configure FireWall-1 in respect to how it will function.

We also discussed common troubleshooting issues and tools. Even though a firewall may be installed and configured properly, we saw that there are a number of issues that may arise. We also discussed a number of the tools available for troubleshooting, including reports, logs, and tools included with the operating system on which FireWall-1 is running.

Finally, the chapter gave you some insight into common security issues that may arise in using FireWall-1. You should be aware of such security issues when administering FireWall-1, because in having this knowledge, you will be able to take a proactive approach to security.

FAQs

Q: I have FireWall-1 installed, but I can't find any reporting and auditing. Why?

A: Check to see if the Reporting Module is installed. The Reporting Module provides features for generating reports and auditing. If this module isn't installed and configured, then reporting will be unavailable.

Q: The server on which FireWall-1 is installed is located a distance from my office. Can I manage the firewall remotely?

A: Yes. The GUI Client can run on workstations on your network, and manage the server remotely.

Q: Can I still use security features of Windows NT with FireWall-1?

A: Yes. FireWall-1 doesn't replace the operating system of a server, but works with it. You can, and should, use NTFS and other security features on the server to protect your network.

Q: Where can I obtain licenses for FireWall-1 and optional modules used with FireWall-1?

A: The Check Point Web site (http://license.checkpoint.com) allows you to obtain licenses online.

Q: Where can I get the latest upgrades and service packs for FireWall-1, and how often should I check for them?

A: The Check Point Web site (www.checkpoint.com) allows you to download the latest service packs. You can also order upgrades to FireWall-1. You can also join a mailing list to obtain information about Check Point products, such as the release of new service packs.

Q: Certain servers are getting bogged down on my network because of traffic being passed through the firewall. Is there anything I can do through FireWall-1 to resolve this problem?

A: Implement load balancing. You can create a server group that will share the load of servicing client requests.

Q: My company is worried about viruses. What can I do to ensure that any file attachments that users receive in e-mail are virus scanned?

A: FireWall-1 allows you to create rules that deal with how e-mail will be handled. You can specify that any e-mail received by all or certain sources is first diverted to a server that will scan the e-mail and its attachments for viruses. You can set whether virus-infected attachments will be deleted or cleaned before being forwarded onto the user.

Index

Q

R

The Global Knowledge Advantage

Global Knowledge has a global delivery system for its products and services. The company has 28 subsidiaries, and offers its programs through a total of 60+ locations. No other vendor can provide consistent services across a geographic area this large. Global Knowledge is the largest independent information technology education provider, offering programs on a variety of platforms. This enables our multi-platform and multi-national customers to obtain all of their programs from a single vendor. The company has developed the unique CompetusTM Framework software tool and methodology which can quickly reconfigure courseware to the proficiency level of a student on an interactive basis. Combined with self-paced and on-line programs, this technology can reduce the time required for training by prescribing content in only the deficient skills areas. The company has fully automated every aspect of the education process, from registration and follow-up, to "just-in-time" production of courseware. Global Knowledge through its Enterprise Services Consultancy, can customize programs and products to suit the needs of an individual customer.

Global Knowledge Classroom Education Programs

The backbone of our delivery options is classroom-based education. Our modern, well-equipped facilities staffed with the finest instructors offer programs in a wide variety of information technology topics, many of which lead to professional certifications.

Custom Learning Solutions

This delivery option has been created for companies and governments that value customized learning solutions. For them, our consultancy-based approach of developing targeted education solutions is most effective at helping them meet specific objectives.

Self-Paced and Multimedia Products

This delivery option offers self-paced program titles in interactive CD-ROM, videotape and audio tape programs. In addition, we offer custom development of interactive multimedia courseware to customers and partners. Call us at 1-888-427-4228.

Electronic Delivery of Training

Our network-based training service delivers efficient competency-based, interactive training via the World Wide Web and organizational intranets. This leading-edge delivery option provides a custom learning path and "just-in-time" training for maximum convenience to students.

Global Knowledge Courses Available

Microsoft
- Windows 2000 Deployment Strategies
- Introduction to Directory Services
- Windows 2000 Client Administration
- Windows 2000 Server
- Windows 2000 Update
- MCSE Bootcamp
- Microsoft Networking Essentials
- Windows NT 4.0 Workstation
- Windows NT 4.0 Server
- Windows NT Troubleshooting
- Windows NT 4.0 Security
- Windows 2000 Security
- Introduction to Microsoft Web Tools

Management Skills
- Project Management for IT Professionals
- Microsoft Project Workshop
- Management Skills for IT Professionals

Network Fundamentals
- Understanding Computer Networks
- Telecommunications Fundamentals I
- Telecommunications Fundamentals II
- Understanding Networking Fundamentals
- Upgrading and Repairing PCs
- DOS/Windows A+ Preparation
- Network Cabling Systems

WAN Networking and Telephony
- Building Broadband Networks
- Frame Relay Internetworking
- Converging Voice and Data Networks
- Introduction to Voice Over IP
- Understanding Digital Subscriber Line (xDSL)

Internetworking
- ATM Essentials
- ATM Internetworking
- ATM Troubleshooting
- Understanding Networking Protocols
- Internetworking Routers and Switches
- Network Troubleshooting
- Internetworking with TCP/IP
- Troubleshooting TCP/IP Networks
- Network Management
- Network Security Administration
- Virtual Private Networks
- Storage Area Networks
- Cisco OSPF Design and Configuration
- Cisco Border Gateway Protocol (BGP) Configuration

Web Site Management and Development
- Advanced Web Site Design
- Introduction to XML
- Building a Web Site
- Introduction to JavaScript
- Web Development Fundamentals
- Introduction to Web Databases

PERL, UNIX, and Linux
- PERL Scripting
- PERL with CGI for the Web
- UNIX Level I
- UNIX Level II
- Introduction to Linux for New Users
- Linux Installation, Configuration, and Maintenance

Authorized Vendor Training
Red Hat
- Introduction to Red Hat Linux
- Red Hat Linux Systems Administration
- Red Hat Linux Network and Security Administration
- RHCE Rapid Track Certification

Cisco Systems
- Interconnecting Cisco Network Devices
- Advanced Cisco Router Configuration
- Installation and Maintenance of Cisco Routers
- Cisco Internetwork Troubleshooting
- Designing Cisco Networks
- Cisco Internetwork Design
- Configuring Cisco Catalyst Switches
- Cisco Campus ATM Solutions
- Cisco Voice Over Frame Relay, ATM, and IP
- Configuring for Selsius IP Phones
- Building Cisco Remote Access Networks
- Managing Cisco Network Security
- Cisco Enterprise Management Solutions

Nortel Networks
- Nortel Networks Accelerated Router Configuration
- Nortel Networks Advanced IP Routing
- Nortel Networks WAN Protocols
- Nortel Networks Frame Switching
- Nortel Networks Accelar 1000
- Comprehensive Configuration
- Nortel Networks Centillion Switching
- Network Management with Optivity for Windows

Oracle Training
- Introduction to Oracle8 and PL/SQL
- Oracle8 Database Administration

Custom Corporate Network Training

Train on Cutting Edge Technology
We can bring the best in skill-based training to your facility to create a real-world hands-on training experience. Global Knowledge has invested millions of dollars in network hardware and software to train our students on the same equipment they will work with on the job. Our relationships with vendors allow us to incorporate the latest equipment and platforms into your on-site labs.

Maximize Your Training Budget
Global Knowledge provides experienced instructors, comprehensive course materials, and all the networking equipment needed to deliver high quality training. You provide the students; we provide the knowledge.

Avoid Travel Expenses
On-site courses allow you to schedule technical training at your convenience, saving time, expense, and the opportunity cost of travel away from the workplace.

Discuss Confidential Topics
Private on-site training permits the open discussion of sensitive issues such as security, access, and network design. We can work with your existing network's proprietary files while demonstrating the latest technologies.

Customize Course Content
Global Knowledge can tailor your courses to include the technologies and the topics which have the greatest impact on your business. We can complement your internal training efforts or provide a total solution to your training needs.

Corporate Pass
The Corporate Pass Discount Program rewards our best network training customers with preferred pricing on public courses, discounts on multimedia training packages, and an array of career planning services.

Global Knowledge Training Lifecycle
Supporting the Dynamic and Specialized Training Requirements of Information Technology Professionals

- Define Profile
- Assess Skills
- Design Training
- Deliver Training
- Test Knowledge
- Update Profile
- Use New Skills

Global Knowledge

Global Knowledge programs are developed and presented by industry professionals with "real-world" experience. Designed to help professionals meet today's interconnectivity and interoperability challenges, most of our programs feature hands-on labs that incorporate state-of-the-art communication components and equipment.

ON-SITE TEAM TRAINING

Bring Global Knowledge's powerful training programs to your company. At Global Knowledge, we will custom design courses to meet your specific network requirements. Call (919)-461-8686 for more information.

YOUR GUARANTEE

Global Knowledge believes its courses offer the best possible training in this field. If during the first day you are not satisfied and wish to withdraw from the course, simply notify the instructor, return all course materials and receive a 100% refund.

REGISTRATION INFORMATION

In the US:
call: (888) 762–4442
fax: (919) 469–7070
visit our website:
www.globalknowledge.com

SYNGRESS SOLUTIONS...

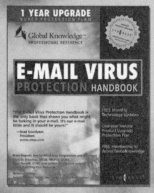